*Migrating to the Movies*

THE GEORGE GUND FOUNDATION
IMPRINT IN AFRICAN AMERICAN STUDIES

The George Gund Foundation has endowed
this imprint to advance understanding of
the history, culture, and current issues
of African Americans.

# Migrating to the Movies

*Cinema and Black Urban Modernity*

JACQUELINE NAJUMA STEWART

*University of California Press*

BERKELEY    LOS ANGELES    LONDON

*The publisher gratefully acknowledges the
generous contribution to this book provided by
the African American Studies Endowment Fund
of the University of California Press Associates,
which is supported by a major gift from the
George Gund Foundation.*

University of California Press
Berkeley and Los Angeles, California

University of California Press, Ltd.
London, England

Library of Congress Cataloging-in-Publication Data

Stewart, Jacqueline Najuma, 1970–.
    Migrating to the movies : cinema and Black urban modernity /
Jacqueline Najuma Stewart.
        p.      cm.
    Revision of the author's thesis (doctoral)—University of Chicago,
1999.
    Includes bibliographical references and index.
    ISBN 0-520-23350-6 (alk. paper) — ISBN 0-520-23349-2 (pbk. : alk.
paper)
    1. African Americans in the motion picture industry.    2. African
Americans in motion pictures.    3. Motion picture audiences—United
States.    4. African Americans—Migrations—History—20th
century.    I. Title.

PN1995.9.N4S74    2005
791.43'652996073—dc22                                    2004016541

Manufactured in the United States of America

14   13   12   11   10   09   08   07   06   05
10   9   8   7   6   5   4   3   2   1

*In loving memory of my aunts,*
*Constance Zenobia Lee,*
*Ardean Elizabeth Merrifield Brown,*
*and Frances Marie Koger*

*and for Maiya*

# Contents

# Illustrations

# Preface

This book might be read as an African American migration narrative, if a fragmented one. The chapters may seem to chart a progressive movement of Black people from cinematic objects (white-produced images) to interpreting readers (audiences, critics) to speaking subjects (filmmakers). By organizing my study in this way, I hope to convey some of the extraordinary ways in which African Americans staked their own claims in the cinema's development as an art and as a cultural institution. However, I realize that such a narrative also runs the risk of overstating the empowering consequences of African American migration and Black engagements with mass culture. One could just as easily read the material I gather here and, looking toward the dramatic social and psychological effects of the "Great Migration," maintain that racism has structured African American migrant and cinematic experiences in similarly demoralizing ways. The false promise of freedom and opportunity in the urban North is echoed in the persistently discriminatory practices of the cinema as the flagship medium of modernity: racist ideologies shape Black screen representations, determine the accessibility of theater spaces, and limit the opportunities available to Black filmmakers.

I explore the tensions between these positive and negative migration narrative trajectories by examining early Black relations to the cinema from multiple vantage points. Considered together, African American migrations onto the screen, into the audience, and behind the camera tell multiple, intersecting stories about how the cinema shaped the ways in which Black people were seen, and saw themselves, during a transformative period in American cultural life. That is, during the first decades of the twentieth century the cinema registered, from white and Black perspectives, both anxiety and optimism about the roles African Americans could play in a modern, multiracial society in which Black people had increasing legal rights, economic power, and access to political and commercially grounded public spheres. My investigation of the cinema's multilayered racial politics reveals that these expanded possibilities produced neither a monolithic set of racist responses in the dominant media nor radical breaks in African American representation and experience. Instead, the cinema provided a powerful new set of overlapping visual fields (representational, public, creative) in which the ongoing problems and possibilities presented by Black mobility, diversity, and insurgency were debated and staged.

The multiple modes of Black image-making in dominant cinema, spectatorship practices among diverse Black audiences, and production practices among African American filmmakers suggest the broad and widely varied set of performative strategies that were defining African American culture and identity in the transition to modern, urban life. My attempt to reconstruct these strategies seeks to synthesize the limited surviving evidence of early Black encounters with the cinema and owes much to recent revisionist scholarship and creative works that revisit scenes of African American migration, particularly those that highlight how Black movements into urban modernity were gradual, contradictory, and played out in highly visual terms.

For example, Julie Dash's 1992 film *Daughters of the Dust* narrates the Peazant family's last days together in their Gullah Island home before many of the family members migrate to city life on the mainland. Many viewers read *Daughters* as a nostalgic, lyrical homage to a Black southern rural past. Set in 1902, the film suggests qualitative differences between southern and northern life by rendering the southern landscape as a slow-paced, colorful world rich with natural beauty, family traditions (cooking, quilting, storytelling), and ancestral memory as juxtaposed with short black-and-white clips of New York City's crowded, chaotic streets teeming with streetcars and white immigrants. However, the film places potential Black migrants in an extended and meaningful dialogue with visual signifiers of modernity before they leave their island home. For instance, when one of the Peazant children (the Unborn Child) looks at city scenes through a stereoscopic viewer (a device that produces the illusion of a three-dimensional image), she sees no Black people but recites, perhaps ironically, the optimistic, democratic rhetoric of the day: "It was an age of beginnings, a time of promises. The newspaper said it was a time for everyone, the rich and the poor, the powerful and the powerless" (figs. 1 and 2).[1] Here the girl indicates how her family's migration is inspired, in part, by paradoxical relations to the "promises" circulating in dominant mass

FIGURE 1. The Unborn Child (Kai-Lynn Warren) looks through a stereoscope as her relatives prepare to migrate to the city. *Daughters of the Dust* (dir. Julie Dash, 1992).

FIGURE 2. Images of bustling urban life on the mainland. *Daughters of the Dust* (dir. Julie Dash, 1992).

culture, especially the new visual fields and technologies in which modern life was being represented and experienced. The absence of Blackness not-withstanding, the Unborn Child and her relatives have begun to develop reception strategies that anticipate and question the roles they might play in the urban landscape.[2]

Dash places numerous "modern" technologies of visual play and representation (stereoscopic viewer, kaleidoscope, still camera) and objects of consumption (a newspaper and a Sears and Roebuck catalogue) in the Peazants' remote, seemingly premodern world, thereby speaking to important revisions of migration historiography to the effect that "black people were becoming increasingly urbanized before they left for northern cities," via, for instance, the circulation of newspapers and letters from the North, exploratory visits to the North, and initial migrations to southern cities.[3] The Peazants' responses to these items—looks of both fascination and fear—reflect mixed Black reactions to the appeals of the city/North/mainland. And these objects, particularly a still camera capturing Peazant family portraits, call our attention to the presence of Dash's camera, her self-consciously cinematic intervention in reconstructing Black motivations for and anxieties about migration. Dash emphasizes the cinema's role in structuring Black relations to urban modernity when she presents the stereoscopic views of the city not as still images but as moving pictures. My own reconstructive project moves between looks at the screen and the audience, at early white and Black filmmaking practices, so that I can explore the profound connections and contradictions between methods of visualizing, through the cinema, the prospect, occurrence, and repercussions of increasing Black mobility.

While *Daughters of the Dust* posits that the introduction of modern modes of looking took place even before migrants physically made the journey, Zeinabu irene Davis's film *Compensation* (1999) more directly stages scenes of early Black film culture—spectatorship and film production—as they took place in the city.[4] More important for my purposes, Davis foregrounds the problem of compiling evidence, particularly visual evidence, of Black migrant and urban experience prior to the well-documented (and Harlem-centered) New Negro Renaissance of the 1920s. *Compensation* tells two love stories, set, respectively, at the dawn and at the end of the twentieth century, both set in Chicago and featuring the same actors. While courting, the couple in the early story (Arthur Jones and Malindy Brown) goes to a theater to see William Foster's Black-cast comedy *The Railroad Porter*, widely regarded as the first film made by an African American producer.[5] Davis shows Black viewers representing both recent Southern migrants (Arthur) and elite "Old Settlers" (Malindy) supporting and enjoying Foster's achievement. Echoing Dash, who evokes the fascinating but alienating nature of early cinema for Black viewers by inserting short clips of early film footage, Davis re-creates early Black moviegoing by presenting her own remake of Foster's long-"lost" film (figs. 3 and 4).

Generally speaking, Davis's reconstruction of Foster's film and its reception presents a positive view of early Black film culture, situating the movies as a space for African American pleasure and agency that has not necessarily survived into the present day. Arthur and Malindy enjoy a comfortable, all-Black environment free of racist white patrons or staff; the film they watch is a Black-cast comedy (made by a Chicago-based Black entrepreneur) that does not rely on minstrel-based stereotypes. This moviegoing experience is juxtaposed with a scene in the film's contemporary story, in which the couple goes to a multiplex to choose from a list of Hollywood films on a towering marquee (including *Sleepless in Seattle, The Last Action Hero,* and Disney's rereleased *Snow White*), none of which reflect Black experience or creative input. The style of *Compensation* is itself an homage to the silent film era, creating a consistency between Davis's filmmaking practice and Foster's pioneering efforts. While Julie Dash inserts brief clips of black-and-white archival footage in *Daughters of the Dust* to stand in stark contrast with the vibrant colors used in the body of the film, Davis shoots all of *Compensation* in black and white and uses title cards throughout to convey much of the story line and dialogue. Davis thus suggests that there are elements of silent film history, particularly early Black spectatorship and aesthetics, to be productively recovered.

*Compensation* may present a nostalgic, idealized version of early Black film culture. But throughout the film Davis illustrates, with the use of dozens of archival photographs, how the contours of Black life in the early twentieth century included not only exciting new commercial amusements and material gains but also segregation and poverty, foregrounding African American struggles of the past and anticipating those to come. Davis's skillful use of these images—of the Black working class and bourgeoisie, of families and laborers, in streets, stores, and schools—has the dual effect of historicizing the film's fictional events and animating the people captured in the still photographs. What is distinctive about the photographs Davis presents is that she uses images that do not appear repeatedly in historical studies of Black migration to Chicago and other northern destinations, suggesting that there are many facets of Black migration and urban life

FIGURE 3. Arthur and Malindy (John Earl Jelks and Michelle A. Banks, center) enjoy a moving picture in a Black Chicago neighborhood theater. *Compensation* (dir. Zeinabu irene Davis, 1999). Wimmin with a Mission Productions.

that remain to be discovered, shared, and explored.[6] While there are certainly many more facts and artifacts to be found and analyzed, the origins of African American film culture cannot be completely reconstructed from published materials and surviving films. Davis's restaging of *The Railroad Porter* and its reception suggests that some of our reconstructive work must be performed creatively, by imagining what might have been in order to fill the many gaps in the historical record and to recover lost episodes in the great African American migration narrative.

This book juxtaposes several archives of material in an attempt to balance the skepticism one might bring to evaluating early Black film images and African American urban migration with the hope and courage that so many thousands of African Americans displayed when they ventured to build modern, urban lives. African American film culture and Black urban migration emerged from a shared set of conditions and desires. For many migrants, the promise of "the North" and "the city" contained the dream of being liberated from the abuses and restrictions that characterized life in the South. The cinema held a related promise for Black migrants, offering a

FIGURE 4. Davis's re-creation of William Foster's comedy *The Railroad Porter* (1913). *Compensation* (dir. Zeinabu irene Davis, 1999). Wimmin with a Mission Productions.

space for expressing and experiencing a new sense of freedom and participation. This feeling is reflected in the range of Black responses (positive, negative, and ambivalent) that the cinema enabled. These included escape into screen fantasy (permitting, for example, cross-racial fandom and desire, and ways to pass the time); engagement with local, culturally specific aspects of exhibition (focusing more attention, sometimes, on live jazz accompaniment than on the images projected on screen); and challenges to racist films and segregationist seating policies (such as bringing suit against discriminatory theaters). In these ways, and others I describe in the chapters that follow, the cinema provided a constellation of new contexts for staging the continuing African American struggle for citizenship and cultural legitimacy.

# Acknowledgments

As the Chicago-born daughter and granddaughter of Black migrants from the South, I have always been fascinated by this extraordinary movement in African American history. This project was inspired by the stories family members have shared with me over the years and cultivated by a group of extraordinary scholars and friends.

This study began as my dissertation, and my committee members have sustained me and the project with constant, healthy doses of enthusiasm and critique. Miriam Hansen has nurtured this book from the very beginning. She consistently inspires me with her understanding of the complex relations between cinema, politics, and history, repeatedly going far above and beyond the call of duty as an adviser and friend. Kenneth Warren provided key conceptual contributions from the realms of African American literary and cultural criticism. Tom Gunning's close, rigorous reading of my work pushed me to ask questions about early film historiography and the contours of modern life that I never would have considered without his guidance.

The book's evolution has benefited from the contributions of a wide circle of readers and listeners. Matthew Bernstein, Lauren Rabinovitz, and Linda Williams read drafts of the entire manuscript, and their perceptive comments helped me to make crucial additions and clarifications. My colleagues at the University of Chicago have served as exacting critics and generous sounding boards. In particular, I wish to thank Danielle Allen, Lauren Berlant, Bill Brown, James Chandler, Janice Knight, James Lastra, David Levin, Deborah Nelson, Danilyn Rutherford, and Joshua Scodel. Members of the Mass Culture Workshop and the Workshop on Race and the Reproduction of Racial Ideologies at the University of Chicago, as well as the Chicago Film Seminar, provided feedback on drafts of several chapters as they took shape. Pearl Bowser, Mary Carbine, Susan Courtney, Corey Creekmur, Zeinabu irene Davis, Jane Gaines, James Grossman, J. A. Lindstrom, Anne Meis Knupfer, Charles Musser, Terry Parrish, Charlene Regester, Henry T. Sampson, Dan Streible, Michele Wallace, Chris Ware, and Yvonne Welbon shared many critical leads, insights, images, and suggestions. I owe special thanks to Elizabeth Alexander, Cathy Cohen, Gloria Gibson, and Jacqueline Goldsby for their wise counsel, stunning professional example, and unfailing personal encouragement at critical junctures in the development of this project and in my life as a scholar.

The assistance of staff at the following research institutions made the archival dimensions of this project possible: the Black Film Center/Archive at Indiana University; British Film Institute; Chicago Historical Society; Chicago Public Library, particularly the Department of Special Collections at the Harold Washington Branch and the Vivian Harsh Collection at the Carter G. Woodson Branch; George Eastman House; Margaret Herrick Library, Academy of Motion Picture Arts and Sciences; Film and Media Department of the Museum of Modern Art; Regenstein Library at the University of Chicago, particularly the Chicago Jazz Archive (Deborah Gillaspie, Curator); Theatre Historical Society of America; Department of Buildings, City of Chicago; Office of the Recorder of Deeds, Cook County, Illinois; Illinois Institute of Technology (especially Catherine Bruck, University Archivist); Motion Picture, Broadcasting and Recorded Sound Division of the Library of Congress (especially Madeline Matz); and the Department of Special Collections at the University of California at Los Angeles (especially Jeff Rankin for his cheerful and expert guidance through the George P. Johnson Negro Film Collection). Part Three of this book is informed by (and cites) interviews with George P. Johnson conducted in 1967 and 1968 by Elizabeth I. Dixon and Adelaide G. Tusler for the UCLA Oral History Program, Department of Special Collections, Charles E. Young Research Library, and published as *Collector of Negro Film History* (© 1970 The Regents of the University of California. All Rights Reserved. Used with Permission).

Grants and fellowships awarded by the University of Chicago, the Committee on Institutional Cooperation (CIC), and the Mellon Foundation enabled me to formulate this project and to conduct research. Final write-up was supported by the Andrew W. Mellon Foundation Career Enhancement Fellowship for Junior Faculty from Underrepresented Groups (administered by the Woodrow Wilson National Fellowship Foundation). Many thanks to my department chairs, Elizabeth Helsinger and Jay Schleusener, and to Deans Philip Gossett and Janel Mueller for supporting the research and writing of this book.

For their crucial help in getting the manuscript into print, I am grateful to Eric Smoodin for his early interest and advocacy, and to Mary Francis at the University of California Press for her patience. Tanji Gilliam expertly prepared the bibliography and collected images. An earlier version of chapter 3 was published in *Critical Inquiry* 29 (2003): 650–77; portions of chapters 1 and 2 appear in "What Happened in the Transition? Reading Race, Gender and Labor between the Shots," in *American Cinema's Transitional Era: Audiences, Institutions, Practices*, edited by Charlie Keil and Shelley Stamp, University of California Press (2004), 103–130.

Throughout the life of this project, I have been blessed with the encouragement of friends and relatives too numerous to mention here, but I would like to acknowledge just a few. Miriam Stewart-Early and James Early, Ariel Lang and Thomas Welk, Jennifer Kellogg and Tad Sennott, Terri Francis, and Jennifer Peterson opened their homes to me during research trips. The camaraderie of Jennifer Peterson, Elisabeth Ceppi and Colin Johnson, and members of the Department of English Association of Students of Color helped to make the treacherous road to the Ph.D. that much smoother. Ernestine, Ralph, Benjamin, and Danielle Austen, Leah Merrifield, Darlene Oliver, Olive Lucille Powell, and friends at Women in the Director's Chair and the Mellon Minority Fellowship Program provided a steady flow of kind words, inspirational e-mails, and cheerful diversions during the long process of getting this project over many hurdles and into this final form.

Finally, no words can adequately express how much I appreciate three people who have shown me unconditional love and support in this and every endeavor. My mother, Barbara Holt, teaches me to keep my eye on the ball and to know that all things are possible. My brilliant sister, Nikki Ayanna Stewart, has been a true friend and a shining star guiding me to the end of the tunnel. My husband and best friend, Jake Austen, always finds new ways to make me laugh, think, and appreciate the extraordinary world in which we live. I hope to be as supportive and animating a presence in his life, and in the life of our beautiful daughter, Maiya, as they are in mine.

# Introduction

## A Nigger in the Woodpile,
## or Black (In)Visibility in Film History

On the screen we see two white farmers talking to each other next to a pile of wooden logs. One of them places a stick of dynamite inside one of the logs, which he then slips back into the woodpile. When the white men exit, two Black men enter and surreptitiously steal several pieces of wood (figs. 5 and 6).

In the next shot, we see the interior of a cabin where a large Black woman is preparing food next to a wood-burning stove (fig. 7). The Black thieves enter, and one of them places log after log into the stove until the inevitable happens—the concealed dynamite is ignited and the stove explodes, blowing the cabin apart. The two white farmers then enter the smoke- and debris-filled cabin, looking and laughing at the Black thieves who, according to the film's catalogue description, have been "given a punishment they will not soon forget."[1]

This comedy, *A Nigger in the Woodpile* (American Mutoscope and Biograph, 1904), demonstrates many elements that are typical of Black representation in early cinema. The three Black characters are played by white actors in blackface, wearing costumes signifying their traditional racial "types": Mammy in apron and bandanna; an uppity "colored deacon," striking a Zip Coon figure in top hat and tails; and his partner in crime, a harmless, shabbily dressed, white-haired Uncle Remus. The film depicts African Americans as habitual thieves, this time stealing firewood instead of the usual chickens or watermelon. And the film's "punitive" ending (a commonplace in early film comedies) functions to bring about narrative closure at the expense of the Black transgressors.[2] Although *A Nigger in the Woodpile* contains elements, largely derived from the minstrel stage, that would seem to appeal to general (white) audiences, one wonders whether African Americans patronized such early films, and how they would have responded

FIGURE 5. White farmers set a concealed, explosive trap for thieves pilfering wood from their pile. *A Nigger in the Woodpile* (American Mutoscope & Biograph, 1904). Library of Congress, Motion Picture, Broadcasting and Recorded Sound Division.

to them. This question is particularly relevant because many potential Black moviegoers at the dawn of the twentieth century would have been recent migrants from the South who had fled from the kinds of poverty and violent repression that this film comically glosses over.

Few scholars have explored how the rise of the cinema as the predominant American entertainment during the first decades of the twentieth century coincided with the migration of hundreds of thousands of African Americans from their "traditional" homes in the South to increased social and economic opportunities in northern cities. Between 1890 and 1930, well over one million Blacks moved from the South to the urban North, making it "the largest movement of Black bodies since slavery" removed Africans to the New World.[3] Although this "Great Migration" coincided with the years in which the cinematic institution began to take shape, studies of both early American cinema and the African American migration have overlooked the significance of the entrance of Blacks onto moving picture screens and into film audiences.

FIGURE 6. Two unsuspecting Black thieves load up on wood. *A Nigger in the Woodpile* (American Mutoscope & Biograph, 1904). Library of Congress, Motion Picture, Broadcasting and Recorded Sound Division.

This book investigates how the urban and northern migrations of African Americans before, during, and immediately after World War I influenced, and were influenced by, the emergence and development of the cinema. I address two fundamental questions raised by the concurrence of the Black urban migration and the rise of the American film industry. First, how did the growing African American movement into urban centers influence the development of cinema as a major institution of American popular culture, including both its representational strategies and its practices as a social space? Second, what role did the cinema play in the process of modernization and urbanization of African Americans, in light of the fact that filmic representations of Blacks tended to be crudely stereotypical and retrogressive? Looking at some of the earliest relationships between African Americans and the cinema, from the medium's emergence in the mid-1890s to 1920, when both the dominant classical cinema and alternative Black "race film" production are firmly established, I argue that Black urban populations and the cinematic institution exercised greater influence

FIGURE 7. Inside the Black cabin, the head thief holds the booby-trapped log. *A Nigger in the Woodpile* (American Mutoscope & Biograph, 1904). Library of Congress, Motion Picture, Broadcasting and Recorded Sound Division.

over each other during these formative years than has been previously acknowledged. To be sure, the cinema's early racial politics prominently included racist portrayals on screen, segregation in theaters, and exclusion from the dominant sphere of production. In light and in spite of these conditions, the cinema functioned as a major site in which Black subjects could see and be seen in modern ways; it served as a contested discursive and physical space in which migrating Black public spheres were constructed and interpreted, empowered and suppressed.

I open with a description of *A Nigger in the Woodpile* not only because of its seeming typicality of Black representation in early films but also because it serves more broadly as a metaphor for the treatment of African Americans in the study of silent cinema. The film literalizes a common slang expression alluding to something suspicious, something uncertain, and, significantly, something concealed. Dating back to the mid–nineteenth century, (white) Americans have used the expression "a nigger in the woodpile" to indicate that something is amiss, that there is a "catch" or an unseen but important factor "affecting a situation in an adverse way."[4]

Thus, at a metaphoric level, this phrase serves as an apt description for the way in which early films frequently conceal and reveal Black figures, creating discomfort and disorder intended to amuse, fascinate, and/or alarm white viewers. In addition, I invoke this expression because I want to suggest that racial difference has functioned as something like the proverbial "nigger in the woodpile" of early film history and theories of film-viewer relations, including those developed by revisionist film scholarship.[5] That is, Blackness has been an ever-present but strangely inconspicuous, and therefore insufficiently theorized, element of the cinematic institution, concealed by emphasis on gender difference in film theory and obscured by readings of early Black film images as uniformly negative stereotypes in film history. In addition, though scholars have long recognized that early exhibitors were anxious about racial mixing in their theaters, few have explored how the segregation of the social space of the cinema (including theaters that seated Blacks and whites in different sections during the same screening, theaters that designated separate screenings for Black and for white viewers, and theaters that served only one racial clientele) affected how early audiences, particularly African American viewers, experienced this new "democratic" or "universal" medium. Therefore, I invoke the phrase "a nigger in the woodpile" as a problematic, to examine how it and similar racist expressions, film titles, and scenarios reflecting the pervasive racism of turn-of-the-century American culture have forestalled the kind of critical engagement that would expose how the "unsettled and unsettling" Black presence (to borrow a phrase from Toni Morrison) influenced the cinema's early social and aesthetic development.[6]

One significant way film historians have accounted for the vicious and casual racism exhibited in early cinema—from Edison's short comedies to D. W. Griffith's epic *The Birth of a Nation* (1915)—has been to relate it to the movies' large immigrant audiences. For decades, film scholars have noted and questioned the cinema's role in "Americanizing" European immigrants, debating the extent to which the movies actually functioned, for example, to teach Irish, Italian, Slavic, and Jewish newcomers how to speak American English and adopt the social customs, middle-class values, and racial ideologies necessary to assimilate into mainstream American life.[7] Similar to Eric Lott in his analysis of blackface minstrel performance, Michael Rogin has persuasively argued that cinematic constructions of Blackness allowed ethnically and culturally diverse immigrants whose racial status was in dispute to become American by identifying as "white." By appropriating Black identities, the most popular forms of American mass culture of the nineteenth and twentieth centuries—minstrel performance, followed by Hollywood filmmaking—functioned to, in Rogin's words, "move settlers and ethnics into the melting pot by keeping racial groups out."[8] Lott and Rogin offer crucial insights into how the systematic objectification of Blackness in the most popular forms of American mass culture of the last two centuries enabled the vast ideological task of homogenizing diverse white ethnic clienteles. But their accounts unwittingly replicate the marginalization of Blackness that characterizes minstrelsy and the dominant cinema by obscuring the roles African Americans have played as the *subjects* of their own history with mass culture, as individuals and communities who consistently challenged these racist and exclusionary representations.

Instead of providing an account of the cinema's social and representational development that revolves around the familiar paradigm of immigration, I propose an approach centered on the internal migration of Black people from southern and rural areas into northern and urban centers, and the unique pressures this movement brought to bear on Black representation, public circulation, and citizenship. During the first decades of the twentieth century, hundreds of thousands of African Americans moved away from the racial violence and repression of the South toward increased social, political, and economic freedoms in northern cities. Black urban migration increased from a trickle to a flood around 1916, when World War I sharply curtailed the supply of immigrant labor to northern industries, sending labor agents south to recruit Black workers. The lure of higher-paying work and freedom from social and political restrictions drew many southern Blacks away from sharecropping and tenant farming toward the northern "land of promise."[9]

This mass Black movement did more than transform America's racial demographics. It also inspired a major mode of twentieth-century African American cultural production—the migration narrative—that has been developed by numerous African American novelists, visual artists, musicians, and filmmakers. As Farah Jasmine Griffin has shown, the great diversity of Black artistic and intellectual work depicting the migration, its motivations, and its effects forces us to consider how this massive relocation profoundly changed African Americans' conceptions and representations of their roles in American modernity—including, I would add emphatically, mass culture.[10] The model of the migration narrative not only helps to situate the many Black-produced films that took up the theme of migration but also serves as a useful framework for understanding the history of a broader African American film culture, that is, the unique set of production, exhibition, and reception practices African Americans developed in order to participate in the racially exclusionary institution of the cinema. African Americans migrated to the movies—as producers and consumers—as part of their larger individual and collective efforts to challenge static, Old Negro stereotypes and to try on the roles of modern New Negroes entering urban modernity and seeking full American citizenship.[11]

The development, and contradictions, of several aspects of Black film culture can be better understood in relation to key themes in the African American migration narrative. This is certainly true for African American spectatorship and moviegoing, which lie at the heart of this study. For example, Griffin traces how migration narratives juxtapose the unsophisticated nature of power in the South (a power that is "immediate," "identifiable," and frequently violent) with the "more subtle and sophisticated" mechanisms of power at work in the northern city.[12] African American reception practices, along with other aspects of their daily lives in the urban North, were shaped by the more impersonal and unpredictable expressions of white power they encountered in the North. The extent to which Black people were restricted from public amusements because of northern de facto as opposed to southern de jure segregation raises serious questions about how they contextualized and enjoyed the new freedoms they sought by migrating northward. Urban migration did enable African Americans to enjoy a wide range of leisure activities that were unavailable or highly restricted in the South. Migrant interviews indicate that increases in leisure time, disposable income, and options for recreational activities represented significant improvements in the quality of life, alongside the higher-paying jobs, better educational opportunities, and greater political participation northern cities afforded. But the movies occupied an important space in the new cultural landscape Black migrants encountered up North not simply by offering an accessible and enjoyable leisure activity but by providing a public context, among many, in which to manage a new set of racist power relations.

In terms of Black filmmaking practice, directors like William Foster and Oscar Micheaux explored the numerous positive and negative implications of Black geographic movement for the moral, cultural, and political standing of the Race. Foster made short comedies that reflected the vibrant cultures African Americans were developing in cities but also poked fun at dishonest and vain Black urban types. Micheaux staged many migration narratives with different trajectories, frequently suggesting that African Americans should escape the violent, traditional forms of racism in the South *and* the subtle, modern forms of racism in northern cities by venturing out into the wide-open spaces of the West; he himself had attempted several homesteading ventures in South Dakota.

Black urban migration is one of the major themes addressed in the current wave of scholarship on Micheaux, his recently rediscovered early titles, and the cultural milieu in which he produced and exhibited his films. Recent publications include a cultural history of Micheaux's work by Pearl Bowser and Louise Spence, a study of Micheaux's aesthetics by J. Ronald Green, a biography by Betti Carol VanEpps-Taylor, and a diverse collection of essays accompanying a catalogue of films by Micheaux and other silent-era race filmmakers edited by Bowser, Jane Gaines, and Charles Musser.[13] These studies, along with Gaines's discussion of the "mixed-race" heritage of American cinema and Anna Everett's work on early African American film criticism (particularly the writings of *New York Age*'s prolific and influential critic Lester Walton), provide an extraordinary portrait of the creative cultural and political work performed by African American filmmakers and their audiences during the silent era.[14]

This book seeks to supplement those studies by focusing on the multiple relations between African Americans and the cinema (as subjects, spectators, and filmmakers) leading up to Micheaux's prolific career. Rather than placing individuals (like Micheaux or Walton) at the center of my account, I organize my discussion around the concepts of African American migration and urbanization, and the problems and possibilities of increased Black mobility and visibility that they represented. I explore the ways in which these social, geographic, and conceptual Black movements radically realigned African American individuals and communities in relation to each other, to the dominant American culture, and to white ethnic immigrants in order to situate the emergence of Black film culture within a broad constellation of historical and theoretical questions. I attempt to flesh out details about Black moviegoing and filmmaking as empirical, concrete, traceable practices, but I also attempt to reconstruct the unrecorded, ephemeral, and subtextual aspects of early Black spectatorship and representation. Thus my focus on Black migration is intended to illuminate the wide range of ways in which African Americans negotiated confrontations with the cinema as a major feature of modern American life.

Details about very early Black responses to the cinema, particularly before and during the nickelodeon era (pre-1907), have been difficult for scholars to trace. How can we know if African Americans went to see films like *A Nigger in the Woodpile* when there is so little documentation of Black reception in turn-of-the-century African American writing and in the trade press? What can we know about Black reactions to this and other early films with comic Black types? When African American filmmakers begin to produce Black-cast films in the mid-1910s, we begin to see more (and more detailed) Black commentary on the cinema. How effective were these initial Black efforts to respond to the much larger and more thoroughly organized dominant film industry? I attempt to bring such elusive issues into focus by bridging discussions of Black representation in white- and Black-produced films with a consideration of African American reception, focused on a particular northern urban locale: Chicago.

Chicago is the locus of a host of historical factors that productively illuminate the close relationships between race, modernity, and mass culture. As the country's fastest-growing turn-of-the-century metropolis, Chicago attracted large numbers of European immigrants and African American migrants who established distinct, separate neighborhood cultures as they competed for industrial jobs and municipal resources. As a prime destination for Black migrants from the South, Chicago's "Black Belt" quickly grew into a segregated "Black Metropolis" where African American entrepreneurship, entertainment culture, and political activity thrived in the face of hostile "native" and ethnic white resistance to Black insurgence and racial integration. Moving to Chicago signified a move into urban industrial modernity, and Black migrants discovered and contributed to a dynamic, confident Black urban community. Still, racial segregation profoundly shaped the housing, occupational, and recreational options available to Black people in Chicago, complicating the hopes and experiences of new arrivals.

As the film industry grew in scope and popularity during the first two decades of the twentieth century, Chicago's Black entertainment culture (including its film culture) came to national prominence. Compared with other major migration destinations, Chicago's South Side Black Belt boasted a very large number of theaters catering especially to African American audiences, mostly located along the "Stroll," Black Chicago's primary commercial and entertainment strip on South State Street. Moving pictures were exhibited in many of the same venues up and down the Stroll in which ragtime and jazz musicians were transforming American music. Amid music shops and poolrooms, pawn shops and restaurants, barbershops and saloons, theaters showing moving pictures participated in the lively social, business, and entertainment scene that was heavily promoted in the pages of the *Chicago Defender* (which also had its offices along the Stroll).

The *Defender* was widely regarded as the country's leading "race" newspaper. According to historian James Grossman, the *Defender* "grew into the largest-selling black newspaper in the United States by World War I, with two-thirds of its circulation outside Chicago."[15] As a strident campaigner for Black migration, as well as the first African American newspaper to feature a regular entertainment section, the *Defender* ran theatrical ads and reviews (as well as news articles, editorials, and letters from readers) that functioned as a guide to urban cultural life for Black readers in Chicago, and for potential migrants in the South. Black Pullman porters circulated the *Defender* on their southern routes, enabling Blacks outside of the city to learn about Chicago's attractive social, economic, and recreational opportunities.[16] At the same time that the *Defender* represented Black Belt activities to a national readership, Chicago-based Black filmmakers William Foster, Peter P. Jones, and Oscar Micheaux produced Black-cast films that relied on the performers and publicity networks that were centered in Chicago, but also circulated to African American audiences across the country. As one would expect, the *Defender* commented regularly on the efforts of these local pioneers, as well as other Black film companies springing up across the country. The *Defender*'s value as a record of early African American filmmaking, moviegoing, and film criticism, couched within discourses on migration, racial uplift, and political activism, cannot be overestimated, even if tracing the experiences of its largely working-class Black readership requires some reading between the lines. As the birthplace of African American filmmaking (with the production of Foster's *The Railroad Porter* in 1913), and a major center of Black entertainment and media culture (journalism, musical performance and publishing, sports, vaudeville), Chicago serves as an exceptional location for charting the development of African American relationships with the cinema as part of the expansion of Black urban communities.

The Stroll was not just a famous stretch of sidewalk; as Shane White and Graham White have documented, it was also a "form of expressive behavior" that had strong roots in southern displays of fashion, deportment, and cautiously constructed self-determination. In the growing Black districts of the "free" urban North (which for African Americans in the 1910s was exemplified by Chicago), the act of strolling "rapidly developed into one of the defining features of northern black city life," enabling African Americans to look and be looked at in ostensibly more liberal and glamorous contexts.[17] But while many African Americans enjoyed and celebrated the Stroll, a number of detractors pointed to its negative qualities as a stage for and method of modern Black public performance.

As tens of thousands of Black southerners arrived in Chicago during the Great Migration of the late 1910s, numerous white observers ridiculed

FIGURE 8. Caricatures of Black Belt types as they stroll in close proximity to the predominantly white Armour Institute campus. Armour Institute of Technology *Cycle* yearbook, 1916. IIT Archives, Paul V. Galvin Library, Illinois Institute of Technology, Chicago.

FIGURE 9. Armour Institute students combine racist cartoons and math humor in their characterization of the rapidly increasing numbers of neighborhood Blacks. Armour Institute of Technology *Cycle* yearbook, 1920. IIT Archives, Paul V. Galvin Library, Illinois Institute of Technology, Chicago.

Black attempts to enjoy rights and respect, partly by trying to look the part of urban sophisticates. For example, students at the predominantly white Armour Institute of Technology, which was located just west of the Stroll at Thirty-third Street and Armour Avenue (later Federal Street), featured insulting cartoons of neighborhood Blacks in their yearbooks (figs. 8 and 9). The institute watched, at close range, as the number of Black residents in its vicinity grew dramatically, heightening anxieties about controlling and sharing the public space surrounding its campus. The street scenes depicted in Armour Institute yearbooks—populated by African American male dandies and a would-be Black "lady"—render Black Belt residents as blackface caricatures (black skins, wide white lips, gaudy dress) that mock Black efforts to display class and refinement.[18] These illustrations of affected but shabby Black urban style seek to ridicule the public circulation and upward mobility that many Black Chicagoans associated with the specific act of promenading along the Stroll.

White racism was not the only challenge faced by Black Chicagoans seeking to take advantage of the city's public spaces and amusements. Although the cinema was one of the most attractive commercial entertainments available along the Stroll, not all members of Chicago's African American community were enthusiastic about the movies. Associations between cheap movie theaters and other "low" State Street entertainments led many race leaders to warn their followers away from such potentially degrading places. Still, Black moviegoing increased throughout the first decades of motion picture production, and by the late teens Black Chicagoans (like their counterparts in other urban locales) participated in the cinematic institution as audiences, theatrical reviewers, and filmmakers as well as screen performers, theater owners, managers and employees. My study describes how these individuals and groups interacted as constituent parts of larger cultural formations—Black urban public spheres—that coalesced around a variety of overlapping and competing institutions, from traditional, noncommercial venues such as churches to new, commercial entertainments such as the burgeoning film industry.

The notion of overlapping public spheres is central to my conception of Black film culture because it allows me to explore how Black interactions with the cinema were intimately related to other institutions, activities, and discourses that were prevalent in Black urban communities during the first two decades of the twentieth century. I seek to describe the ways in which the cinema provided spaces for the production of Black urban culture, while it also seemed to challenge and circumscribe this process. Drawing on the work of Oskar Negt and Alexander Kluge, who revised Habermas's notion of the bourgeois public sphere to include marginalized groups (e.g., women, the illiterate, the working classes) and spheres of production (e.g., mass media), I am interested in how a model of multiple public spheres can help us to understand how a diverse and migrating African American community attempted to engage in public life, political discourse, and the democratic process via engagements with mass culture.[19]

More specifically, Negt and Kluge's elaboration of public spheres as "horizons of experience" offers a useful lens through which to examine the development of Black film culture as a complex set of practices and responses performed by a group that has been systematically excluded from the dominant space of public life and opinion.[20] Their concept of "experience" as a mediating term between individual perception and larger social meaning enables us to read Black film culture as an alternative (but not always oppositional) formation that not only responds to the social dimensions of the cinema (such as efforts to gain access to the public space of movie theaters and to the means of producing films) but also involves an intersubjective field of individual psychic processes and collective energies.[21] How, for example, can we understand why Blacks would patronize an industry that repeatedly segregated them in exhibition venues and that figured Blackness in limiting, degrading stereotypes? What kinds of individual and collective, internalized and vocalized responses did these practices elicit? While I present and interpret historical evidence regarding the activities and responses of empirical African American viewers, the variability of a Black "public" and the unpredictability of Black "experience" can also be described as discursive constructions; issues of access, participation, and influence function together with those of perception, reflection, and interpretation to shape Black film culture. My aim is to think not just about how the movies affected Black society (even if understood to be diverse) but about how African Americans structured a multifaceted culture around the cinema as both a social (physical) and an imaginative (psychic, subjective) space, and how they exerted pressures on dominant film culture on both of these levels.

As a facet of public life, Black film culture must be read in relation to other cultures that structured Black urban experience during this period. In cities like Chicago, African Americans developed, among many others, vibrant Black religious cultures (from large, middle-class Protestant congregations to small, Pentecostal storefront churches); Black music cultures (including jazz and blues performance, elite classical musicales, and popular musical theater); Black political cultures (from the mounting of Black candidates for local offices to the advocacy work of women's clubs); Black sports cultures (such as Negro baseball leagues and boxing fandom); Black print cultures (such as literary salons and community-based journalism); and Black business cultures (including networks of entrepreneurs controlling major institutions like Black-owned banks and beauty product factories, smaller ventures like restaurants and retail stores, and disreputable "underworld" enterprises such as pool halls, policy shops, and houses of prostitution). These Black cultures intersected (across boundaries of class, gender, age) to structure Black work and leisure time in urban environments. They produced Black urban life as a matrix of experiences and sensations, including comfort and danger, familiarity and novelty, contemplation and action, proscription and empowerment.

As I will elaborate throughout this study, a variety of Black urban cultures intersected with and shaped Black film culture—as illustrated by the opposition of Black clergy to certain venues of film exhibition, the employment of jazz musicians in movie theaters, and the use of the Black press as a vehicle for expressing protest against and praise for particular theaters and films. Black film culture, among the many cultures African Americans developed in cities during the first decades of the twentieth century, addressed desires not only to participate equitably and meaningfully in American life but also to redefine and reconstitute African Americans individually and collectively. Just as it functioned for other communities, the cinema served as a public entertainment, an increasingly popular form of consumer culture, and as a field of fantasy, creativity, and interpretation for audiences, entrepreneurs, employees, and filmmakers. The cinema provided sites in which to flaunt and to manage increasing diversity, and to achieve a sense of control and coherence in a new and/or rapidly changing environment. For African Americans this was an extraordinary phenomenon, given the racist and exclusionary treatment of Black people by the dominant film industry. Local Black uses of the cinema suggest that from very early on African Americans approached the cinema as they approached so many other elements of public life—with a range of individual and collective strategies to incorporate, reject, and/or reconstruct the institutions and practices shaping their daily lives.

This book describes Black film culture not only in terms of the experiences and cultural practices of African Americans but also in relation to the ways in which Blackness was conceived and constructed by the mainstream film industry during this period. Foregrounding my discussion of the development of Black film culture are the persistent problems racial difference presents on the levels of representation and address, and the many devastating ways in which dominant cinema, from the very beginning, has reflected and reproduced America's repressive racial hierarchies. These issues surface not only in my efforts to determine what kinds of films early Black audiences were watching (e.g., films with Black stereotypes, films with no Blacks at all), but also, more significantly, in my attempt to trace the many different factors shaping American film culture at social and discursive levels.

Prompted by Toni Morrison's discussion of how an "Africanist presence" has structured the American literary imagination, I am interested in how this same "four-hundred-year-old" presence of Black people in the United States, "which shaped the body politic, the Constitution, and the entire history of the culture," has also shaped this country's dominant film culture.[22] Indeed, one of the most common colloquial uses of the expression "a nigger in the woodpile," which is not mentioned in most dictionaries (even dictionaries of American slang), is to imply a Black presence in a white family tree.[23] For example, white writer Anne Lamott recalls in her memoir that throughout her childhood her father's male friends would look at her and then joke "that there must have been a nigger in the wood-pile, I guess because of both the [wiry] hair and my big heavy-lidded eyes. . . . I knew it meant that a black man must have been my father."[24] The phrase has long functioned as a euphemism for the long history of interracial sexual relationships. It is a crude and knowing metaphor acknowledging that Blackness has long permeated "white" bloodlines. When considered alongside the meanings discussed earlier, it is clear that the notion of Black influence in "white" bodies—and by extension in "white" histories—raises connotations of illegitimacy, dubiousness, disruption, and, importantly, concealment. This usage of "a nigger in the woodpile," which has been less frequently acknowledged in official etymologies, points to the fundamental ways in which the consistent Black presence in American history and culture—in a "white" genealogy—is disavowed and obscured by dominant political and representational strategies.

By speaking to a "white" audience, mainstream preclassical cinema seems to negate Blackness. At the same time, though, early films feature countless Black images in a wide variety of contexts. I want to suggest that this dialectic of absence and presence can help us to understand how Black film culture operates not simply as an alternative to or protest against dominant cinematic practices but as a constitutive, if usually unacknowledged, part of the development of the dominant "white" film culture. Although major film companies may not seem to care much about Black moviegoers on Chicago's South Side, the ways in which Blackness emerges and is suppressed in their films, related discourses (advertising, criticism), and exhibition practices suggest how deeply the cinema was affected by the country's shifting racial relations. If we read the making of Black film culture as a migration narrative, an important part of the story is how migrations of Blackness into the dominant cinematic imagination reflected and affected larger Black efforts to move out of traditional, restricted roles associated with what one migrant called "the darkness of the south," and into the bright lights of modern American public life.[25]

*Migrating to the Movies* is elaborated in three parts, moving roughly chronologically from the first interactions between Blacks and the cinema—as recorded images—beginning in the mid-1890s, to some of the earliest documented instances of Black reception in the first decade of the twentieth century, to the beginnings of African American film production around 1913. I trace these relations through the increasing circulation of Black people in cities—particularly during the Great Migration out of the

South coinciding with World War I—to explore the ways in which growing Black urban populations and expressions of Black citizenship shaped dominant and African American filmmaking practices and Black spectatorship. My analysis concludes with the immediate aftermath of the "Red Summer" of 1919, when tensions stemming from the increased Black visibility and insurgency flared into interracial riots across the country, including several major migration destinations. These conflicts dramatically confirmed to Black migrants that the freedoms they sought in the urban North would have to be defended continually in multiple public spheres. My study seeks to understand the relations between migration-inspired racial violence in the streets and the treatment of Black cinematic subjects (e.g., punishments in films like *A Nigger in the Woodpile*) and spectators (segregation and exclusion). I trace how racial difference and Black mobility structured modern life during the years in which African Americans established conspicuous urban cultures, and the cinema developed from attractions to classical narrative, from novelty to cultural institution.

Part One, "Onto the Screen," considers how Black movement was registered in dominant cinema. I describe a wide variety of early films not so much to determine the kinds of films Black audiences might have patronized but to consider how African American migration affected the elaboration of cinematic racial codes in general, and the treatment of Blacks (as both spectators and images) in particular. Chapter 1, " 'To Misrepresent a Helpless Race': The Black Image Problem," explores the complexities of representing Blackness in early cinema. Moving beyond the "history of negative stereotypes" approach, I argue that Blackness constituted a representational problem in the cinema from the very beginning. I draw on postcolonial and feminist theoretical models to explore how racial performance and signification complicate the structures of cinematic vision and visual pleasure commonly associated with the seemingly literal cinematic "image," as well as the seemingly uncomplicated Black image.[26] Then, in chapter 2, "Mixed Colors: Riddles of Blackness in Preclassical Cinema," I survey particular films to illustrate how the problem of representing Blackness is organized around the power of the look and the visibility of Black people in a wide variety of cinematic contexts. Although D. W. Griffith's *The Birth of a Nation* (1915) is a watershed text in terms of how it mobilized Black stereotypes and African American outcry against cinematic racism, I analyze Black representation in films produced before *Birth*, focusing on those that foreground marking and seeing Blackness (e.g., plots in which white babies or female love interests are switched with Black ones). Speaking to a "white" viewership, preclassical cinema repeatedly staged scenarios of racial surveillance, misrecognition, and subversion, thereby registering (in many surprising ways) that African Americans were migrating—literally and figuratively—out of their prescribed social roles.

Part Two, "Into the Audience," describes African American spectatorship and moviegoing practices. Chapter 3, " 'Negroes Laughing at Themselves'? Black Spectatorship and the Performance of Urban Modernity," describes how Black urban spectators used the cinema as a public, collective arena in which to demonstrate their social progress. At a time when Black people sought to distance themselves from long-standing stereotypes, Black spectatorship involved not just responses to the screen but also the politics of representing "the Race" in one's public performance as an urban New Negro. Looking at critical and fictional accounts of Black spectatorship (that reach beyond the World War I era), I describe early Black viewing practices as a form of "reconstructive spectatorship," in which African Americans used the cinema as a literal and symbolic space in which to rebuild their individual and collective identities in a modern, urban environment. Then I explore how Black spectatorship was developed in relation to debates about Black urban public behavior in Chicago, and in response to the rise of the classical paradigm of narration and address, which encouraged absorption in the narrative on screen rather than in the social space of the theater. I argue that Black spectatorship was not an either/or proposition of passive acceptance versus oppositional criticism played out only between individual viewers and films. Rather, it was a varied, performative, and social element of Black film culture.

After establishing a new theoretical framework for considering the dynamics of early African American spectatorship, chapters 4 and 5 describe Black moviegoing in Chicago, a prime destination for southern migrants. Chapter 4, " 'Some Thing to See Up Here All the Time': Moviegoing and Black Urban Leisure in Chicago," describes Black patronage of movie theaters among a constellation of African American leisure activities from the turn of the century through the Great Migration (1916–19). I outline how factors like segregation and class stratification informed Black moviegoing within the context of debates about what constituted "appropriate" leisure activities for Chicago's diverse and rapidly growing Black population. I describe how the tenuous cultural legitimacy of the movies both mirrored and had unique implications for the similarly tenuous social standing of African Americans in the urban North, because both were commonly associated with "low," disreputable recreational activities (e.g., drinking, prostitution, gambling). Chapter 5, "Along the 'Stroll': Chicago's Black Belt Movie Theaters," locates and describes specific venues of film exhibition, detailing how owners and managers constructed their theaters—both architecturally and in promotional discourses—to attract African American patrons. Situated among businesses and institutions serving a wide variety of clienteles, Black Belt theaters, I argue, negotiated the cinema's contradictory cultural status by appealing to race pride and "high-class" pretensions, on the one hand, and flaunting elements of vice and sensationalism, on the other. In this way, Chicago's Black film culture grew out of a complex set of social pressures stemming from efforts to assert the Race's respectability and cultural autonomy, but also from the desires of many African Americans to participate in the popular and often "low" forms of American mass culture.

Finally, Part Three, "Behind the Camera," explores how African American filmmakers attempted to comment on dominant cinematic practices and to build and profit from developing Black consumer cultures. Chapter 6, "Reckless Rovers versus Ambitious Negroes: Migration, Patriotism, and the Politics of Genre in Early African American Filmmaking," analyzes the modes of audience address in some of the first Black-produced films, looking particularly at questions of place (settings of films and exhibition). Because these filmmakers attempted to speak to heterogeneous Black audiences dispersed (as a result of migration) throughout the rural and urban South, the industrial North, and western states, their films often stressed the "Americanness" of the Negro, employing popular themes of migration and patriotism in an effort to enlist the broad moral and financial support of a disparate African American market. But these filmmakers and their audiences also debated the appropriate genres for attracting and portraying African Americans. Most companies, like the Lincoln Motion Picture Company, focused on producing uplifting dramas. But Lincoln and others also circulated nonfiction films (e.g., documentary footage of African American soldiers), which were popular among Black audiences seeking realistic representations of the Race. A small number of companies, including the Ebony Film Corporation, risked offending African American audiences by producing comedies in which different Black types (e.g., Old Negroes and New Negroes) were juxtaposed for humorous effect. I argue that these debates and production practices highlighted rather than resolved the significant differences (in location, taste, approaches to uplift) among African American producers and publics.

As Black filmmakers debated the merits of various genres, they consistently struggled with the problems of producing Black-oriented films (not to mention developing a distinct Black cinematic aesthetic), such as securing funding, avoiding stereotypes, and competing with mainstream product. In chapter 7, " 'We Were Never Immigrants': Oscar Micheaux and the Reconstruction of Black American Identity," I describe how Micheaux mobilized themes used by other Black filmmakers to comment (usually didactically) on contemporary social and political issues such as migration, and to stake his unique cinematic claims on behalf of Black people for full American citizenship. For example, Micheaux concludes his migration tale, *Within Our Gates* (1920), by awkwardly combining a marriage proposal (adhering to classical cinematic conventions of closure) with a lofty proclamation of Black American patriotism in an effort to reconcile the racial violence haunting the southern past of the film's migrant heroine. Micheaux's films, more than those of his contemporaries, illustrate the range of modes available for rendering modern Black life and highlight the contradictions of defining and claiming Black American citizenship. In doing so, they also test the cinema's capacity to represent an increasingly mobile, diverse, and insurgent Black population.

My discussion of early Black film images and film culture seeks to demonstrate the centrality of questions of race in preclassical cinema and its reception. In addition, this project emphasizes the crucial role popular culture has played in the development of African American urban life in general, and the articulation of "modern" Black subjectivities in particular. As African Americans migrated, their engagements with mass culture produced new ways of seeing Black character and constituencies, as well as new ways of performing as Black viewing subjects. Blackness has been the metaphoric "nigger in the woodpile" of early film history. This book attempts to reconstruct the experiences and effects of those Black historical agents long shadowed by American mass culture's minstrel masks.

# PART ONE

# Onto the Screen

CHAPTER ONE

# "To Misrepresent a Helpless Race"

*The Black Image Problem*

Black people living in the North in the early twentieth century understood that they could not completely escape the kinds of racial insults and abuses that were regularly visited upon their counterparts living in the "unreconstructed" South. Lynchings, riots, and vicious media caricatures were recurring features of Black life in northern cities during this period, influencing local interracial relations, as well as the ways in which racial difference was understood by, represented to, and circulated for a national public. This period witnessed the emergence of cinema, and it comes as no surprise that its early methods of representing Blackness both entered into and reflected a long, complex tradition of Black "image" making in visual and nonvisual media, a tradition that had significant and often quite damaging personal and political ramifications for African American individuals and communities.

For example, in June 1915, Chicago-based journalist and activist Ida B. Wells faced two crises of Black media representation that demonstrate the gravity of the Black public image problem. Wells learned that a Black prisoner in the Joliet penitentiary, Joseph ("Chicken Joe") Campbell, had been accused of setting a fire that killed the warden's wife. Antipathy toward Campbell within the prison ran high, and Wells feared that he would be coerced into confessing that he murdered this white woman and would not receive a fair trial. "The evening papers told that he had been in solitary for forty hours on bread and water," Wells recalls. "As I sat down to my dinner, it seemed as if the food would choke me." Wells was particularly concerned about the treatment of the case in area newspapers and told her family: "When I think of that poor devil being persecuted down there in the penitentiary, the reports assuming that he was the guilty party without giving him a chance to defend himself, I can't eat." Excusing herself from the table, Wells resolved to approach the new editor of the *Chicago Record Herald* to see if he would publish an appeal to the citizens of Illinois "to suspend judgment until that Negro should have a chance to prove whether he was guilty or innocent of the horrible crime of which he was accused."[1]

As Wells strategized about how to intervene in the Campbell case, she was interrupted by news of another media attack on Black character, this time in motion pictures:

> Just at this moment my doorbell rang and two women friends came in to tell me that they had just been to see *The Birth of a Nation* and agreed with me that it was an outrage which ought never to have been perpetrated, nor allowed to be shown here.
>
> I said to them, "I am not worrying about that any more, so long as permission has been given and it is now being shown. I am worrying about that colored man down in Joliet, and have just decided to go down and see the editor of the *Record Herald*."[2]

Like other Black leaders of her era, Wells was called upon to defend the public Black image on a regular basis. In this instance, her decision to focus her attention on the Campbell case before addressing the "outrages" of *The Birth of a Nation* indicates important distinctions between Black protest against African American representation in traditional, print-based media versus the relatively new entertainment medium of film. Wells's experience and reputation as a journalist enabled her to take effective action via the press: she convinced the *Record Herald* to run a prominent item she penned on Campbell's behalf and eventually secured him an attorney (her husband, Ferdinand L. Barnett), who took the case to the Illinois Supreme Court, where Campbell's death sentence was commuted to life imprisonment at another facility. At the same time, though, Black Chicagoans were unable—or unprepared—to block screenings of *Birth*.[3] Wells describes with disgust the "farce of a trial" in which Griffith defended his film without substantial opposition from the Black community. "Not over a dozen colored persons showed up in the courtroom all day," Wells relates. "One could not blame Judge Cooper for refusing to grant an injunction against *The Birth of a Nation* . . . when so little interest had been shown by the colored people themselves."[4] Although Black Chicagoans surely recognized that moving pictures represented a new arena of potentially damaging Black representations, apparently most of them, like Wells, initially put *Birth* on the back burner.

This episode demonstrates a number of interrelated problems African Americans faced regarding Black image production and reception, particularly the mass circulation of "negative" Black images, at this historical moment. In the tradition of African American letters, Wells felt it her duty, in Henry Louis Gates's words, "to redefine—against already received racist stereotypes—who and what a black person was, and how unlike the racist stereotype the black original indeed actually could be."[5] But African Americans could not possibly respond to every public insult they suffered at the turn of the twentieth century, and long-standing stereotypes proliferated despite their constant attempts to discredit them. For instance, the persistent myth of the Black rapist was mobilized both in the Campbell case (a doctor testified that "Mrs. Allen had been assaulted before she was burned")[6] and in *Birth* (Gus, the "renegade" Union soldier, lustfully pursues Little Sister Cameron, forcing her to jump to her death). Both of these characterizations of Black men threatened to justify the continued segregation, disfranchisement, and violent repression of Black people. African Americans recognized that stereotypical media images worked hand in hand with other "images" of Black people in the white imagination (i.e., in legal discourse, political debates, public policy, social custom) to determine the treatment of Blacks in the real world. But where, exactly, did the cinema—in relation to other media—figure into the politics of producing Black images for mass, public consumption? And how did these images shape not only modern Black experience but also the emerging American film culture that was catering to a rapidly increasing (and increasingly diverse) white clientele?

This chapter considers some of the particular forms in which Black images were constructed and mobilized at the turn of the twentieth century, focusing on the relationship between African American efforts to "reconstruct" the image of the race and early white filmmakers' efforts to develop techniques to illustrate racial difference in this new visual and commercial medium. When creating Black images, preclassical filmmakers (at the Edison, American Mutoscope & Biograph, Vitagraph, Selig, Lubin, and other companies) adapted many of the widespread stereotypes about Black people that had long circulated in white American intellectual and popular thought and cultural production. At the same time, however, their films grappled with major changes that were taking place in interracial social, political, and economic relations during this period, motivated in part by African American northern and urban migration and its attendant transformation of American cultural life. As the cinema developed representational techniques from early attractions toward narrative coherence, Black images constituted a representational problem—not a foregone conclusion—reflecting a variety of conflicting and competing influences and desires structuring American race relations.

I use the term "preclassical cinema" to designate filmmaking practices that preceded the codification of "classical" norms of representation and address, as well as the rise of "Hollywood" as an institution. Preclassical cinema includes "early" cinema (practices dating from the beginnings of motion picture production to around 1907) and "transitional" cinema (practices dating from around 1907 to the midteens). Many film historians have outlined the dramatic changes in film form and style, as well as in methods of making, distributing, and exhibiting films, that took place during these years (e.g., shift of emphasis to narrative over spectacle, increased use of editing, longer film lengths, consolidation of production companies, standardization of local screening conditions).[7] I am interested in describing the extremely diverse and distinct ways in which Blackness is figured on film in these years before the film industry thoroughly organized and standardized modes of production, style, and reception.

Early Black film images have long been something of a stumbling block for critics. Michele Wallace captures the often demoralizing experience of studying these representations when she observes that "there is no topic more depressing than that of blacks in early American cinema."[8] Unfortunately, the way in which Black representations in early films seem to be limited to either glaringly racist caricatures or seemingly objective recordings of Black subjects has closed off many potentially fruitful areas of discussion. Noting the limits of traditional critical readings of early Black film images, including a reliance on the classical model, I offer a historical and theoretical framework that draws on postcolonial and feminist challenges to the seeming literality of the cinematic "image." Postcolonial interventions provide models for denaturalizing the "reality effect" of early Black film images by insisting that they are cultural constructs produced by multiple, contradictory, and historically specific racial discourses. Feminist approaches illuminate the ways in which these images function as ideological constructs produced by the cinematic apparatus (i.e., framing, editing, and other methods of positioning the spectator's "look"). However, my consideration complicates apparatus-based analyses because I explore how racial difference (as distinct from but related to gender difference) structures cinematic vision and visual pleasure. Through these lenses, it becomes easier to recognize the many different levels (e.g., social, discursive, ideological) on which early Black film images are constructed, and to understand how anxieties about Black mobility and visibility inform these constructions.

The Birth of a Problem:
Black Images in Preclassical Cinema and Their Critics

Most studies of African Americans and the cinema argue that Black people have always been victims of misrepresentation by white filmmakers, and very often *The Birth of a Nation* is cited as the defining moment of this negative relationship.[9] Stereotypical Black figures like the sexless, devoted mammy, the tragic mulatto, and the rapacious Black brute are said to have first and/or most significantly appeared in *Birth*, forcing Black people into a position of reactive protest.[10] However, Ida B. Wells's response to the film is illuminating because, although she deeply resented *Birth*'s attack on the "racial integrity" of her struggling people, she did not read the film as cause to dismiss the cinema entirely: "That [Griffith] should prostitute his talents in what would otherwise have been the finest picture presented, in an effort to misrepresent a helpless race, has always been a wonder to me."[11]

The phrasing of Wells's critique deliberately overstates Griffith's "talents" in order to highlight her displeasure with his use of Black stereotypes. Her dual gesture of complimenting and chastising Griffith wittingly outlines *Birth*'s contradictory place in American and African American film history. For obvious reasons, Wells's view that the film's racial politics destroys its aesthetic achievements stands diametrically opposed to the way the film has been canonized by decades of dominant film criticism that has insisted on the distinction between (or the paradox presented by) the film's politics and aesthetics. But Wells's response also stands in contrast to views expressed by more critical and revisionist readings of the film. Like Wells, many of these critics have refused to divorce *Birth*'s racist representations from its much celebrated cinematic innovations. This body of work tends to cast *Birth* as the film that coalesced and mythologized previous racist images, codifying racist representational practices for subsequent generations of classical Hollywood filmmaking. However, while this characterization of *Birth* is not entirely inaccurate, its preoccupation with the film's function as an originary text rarely leaves room for a sustained, detailed discussion of the relationship of *Birth* to the array of Black images that appear in films produced before it. Certainly the various contexts of Black representation in films released earlier than 1915—from travelogues to fight films, plantation dramas to slapstick comedies—construct "Blackness" in many ways, sometimes resembling (and informing) *Birth*, sometimes not. Wells's rhetorical style in her discussion of Griffith's technique and the artistic possibilities of cinema more broadly suggests that early Black responses to films, like the films themselves, were more complex and diverse than most film historians have presumed.

With *The Birth of a Nation* positioned as the watershed moment in African American film history, Black film scholarship tends to give superficial treatment to the representations of Blacks in earlier films, making broad generalizations based on brief plot descriptions and a catalogue of racist (sounding) film titles. Black film criticism has generally been preoccupied with the enumeration and analysis of Black images, usually reading Black representation throughout American cinema as a litany of false, negative stereotypes.[12] Although many of these important, image-based studies were published during the 1970s, marking the convergence of two recently institutionalized fields of academic inquiry—African American studies and cinema studies—James Snead has pointed out that they were primarily sociological in their approach to Black representation and did not engage with the considerable theoretical developments in film studies emerging during that period. According to Snead, "invaluable semiotic, poststructuralist, feminist, and psychoanalytic tools were neglected," while these scholars catalogued and assessed Black film images for their "positive" or "negative" qualities.[13] More recently, critics like Mark Reid, Karen Ross, and Valerie Smith have enumerated various shortcomings of the long-standing "history of Black stereotypes" approach, turning to important formal, stylistic, and ideological questions.[14] As Clyde Taylor concurs in his recent work on the racial implications of "aesthetic discourse" in *The Birth of a Nation*, the reactive "negative images" approach, which focuses on "isolated characterizations within a given work, tends to bypass considerations of narrative, formal devices, motifs, and, most important of all, meaning."[15] Such a shift of emphasis in recent Black film criticism is long overdue. However, these revisionist accounts continue to focus on Black representation in films produced after *Birth*, during the classical era.

Too often, all Black film images are understood in historical and theoretical terms defined almost entirely by classical Hollywood cinema. Contemporary Black film criticism continues to describe early films as if they represent mere baby steps toward the inevitable formal and stylistic systems that would come to characterize dominant American film practice during the classical era. Thus, a second generation of Black film scholarship has not taken full advantage of major developments in film history and theory, in this case the abundance of recent work on early cinema, which has radically revised previous assumptions about the development of film form and style, as well as the systems of meaning and relations between film and

FIGURE 10. The Black maid douses her rude white employer. *A Bucket of Cream Ale* (American Mutoscope & Biograph, 1904). Library of Congress, Motion Picture, Broadcasting and Recorded Sound Division.

spectator that distinguish early cinematic practices from later ones. In terms of its Black representations, preclassical cinema should be understood as much more than a field of racist seeds that would come to fruition in *Birth* and later classical films.

A closer look at the distinctive and diverse qualities of Black representation in preclassical cinema can complicate the "stereotypes" approach in Black film criticism in a number of ways. Preclassical cinema features numerous Black representations that seem to problematize racial hierarchies. For example, how do we read the Black maid in *A Bucket of Cream Ale* (American Mutoscope & Biograph, 1904), who dumps beer over the head of her unsuspecting white employer (fig. 10)? Also, the approach centering on stereotypes does not explore the range of ways in which "Blackness"— as a social or cultural construction and as an explicitly visual marker—is rendered on screen. For example, how can we account for the differences between appearances by both Black and white actors in blackface in "Black" roles in preclassical cinema, sometimes side by side within the same frame? In these and other ways, early films do not simply reiterate immutable

Black stereotypes; instead, they force us to reconsider previous, oversimplified accounts of what stereotypes are and how they function. Homi Bhabha has described the stereotype (in the context of colonial discourse) as "a complex, ambivalent, contradictory mode of representation, as anxious as it is assertive."[16] This formulation of the stereotype gets at the distinctive ways in which preclassical cinema assertively but anxiously puts Black figures into play in a variety of visual, generic, and performative modes that reproduce, combine, and reconfigure Black "images" circulating in other media and public discourses. But while all stereotypes are complex formations in themselves, preclassical cinema employs practices beyond "stereotyping," including a range of stylistic models and formal structures, in its efforts to represent and manage anxieties about racial difference.

## Reconsidering the Black Film Image: Voices and Looks

How, methodologically, can we overcome the limitations of the "history of Black stereotypes" approach when we look at what seem to be hopelessly offensive Black images? Postcolonial theorists Ella Shohat and Robert Stam suggest that we should move away from assessing the authenticity or falseness of racialized media representations by speaking "less of 'images' than of 'voices' and 'discourses' "—that is, use a discursive approach that would subvert the centrality of the visual as the primary register of racial representation, and search for the "cultural voices" that are "distorted or drowned out by the text." This approach, they argue, would "emphasize less a one-to-one mimetic adequacy to the sociological or historical truth than the interplay of voices, discourses, perspectives, including those operative within the image itself."[17]

At first glance, many Black images in silent cinema might appear merely to reflect prevailing racist beliefs whites held about African Americans. The common practices of rendering Black characters with white actors in blackface and Black speech as awkward dialect in intertitles would seem to suggest that these silent images "speak" only in voices created by and for whites invested in maintaining racist social and representational hierarchies.[18] Although heavy makeup, ethnic dialect, and other representational strategies drawn from the vaudeville stage were used to render a number of other "racialized" figures in early cinema (e.g., Latinos, Native Americans, Asians, as well as the Irish and Jews), in many critical accounts Black cinematic images are described as being somehow more stereotypical (i.e., less realistic, more malicious) than those of any other racial group. We must recognize that ethnic whites were part of the imagined audience of these films; therefore, the cinema's representational strategies were developed to speak directly *to* these groups, not simply speak *of* them, as was the case with Blacks and other people of color. Still, Black images in preclassical cinema, including recurring racist stereotypes, should be read as constructs produced by multiple "cultural voices," not only by the racist presumptions of their makers and primary (white) audiences.

The very labeling of many early Black film images (and the people who made and enjoyed them) as "racist" has been contested. For example, in her article on racial dynamics in silent slapstick comedy, Eileen Bowser warns that it is not "entirely accurate" to describe these films as "racist" because that word might not properly describe how these films were read by white audiences (or perhaps even Black ones) at the time. She argues that the humor in these films merely reflects the "state of racial relations" in America during this period, and that these "little film comedies" were not particularly significant or influential. This view might help to explain Ida B. Wells's seeming lack of concern about Black representation in a multitude of short films preceding *The Birth of a Nation* (including many directed by Griffith at Biograph). However, given the volume and popularity of these films, and the ways in which they clearly delineate racial hierarchies, I agree with Daniel Bernardi's general observation that "a discourse of race, one which was dominated by a white 'ideal,' significantly, even profoundly, informed the history of early cinema."[19] The prevalence of white supremacist ideals in early cinema's narrational and representational strategies leads me to argue that the Black images they contain are, in fact, racist because they reinforce and reproduce a social formation in which nonwhites are systematically disempowered. What we must consider, then, are the many layers and historical contexts of the racial discourses in play, as well as the other terms of the dialogue in which these films and images participate.

Early Black film images should be read as being polyphonic, "speaking of" and "speaking to" constructions of Blackness produced by both whites and African Americans at the turn of the twentieth century. As whites produced and consumed images of Black subservience, ignorance, and inferiority, Black people responded by refuting limiting stereotypes and by constructing new images for themselves and their white observers. In addition, the Black photographic images that constitute these films are influenced by other kinds of images, both visual (e.g., postcards, illustrations, artifacts, live performance) and nonvisual (e.g., literature, journalism, and other print media; political, legal, religious, and scientific discourses). In the various media and discourses in which "Black images" circulated during this period, Blackness is structured by notions of the progress of the Race, on the one hand, and the stasis, or even regression, of Black people, on the other. These competing discourses shaping Black depictions in both visual and nonvisual media produced numerous representational challenges and contradictions when long-standing and contested Black images were adapted and recontextualized by the cinema, revealing the complex and political/politicized nature of the very notion of the "Black image."

At the turn of the twentieth century, debates and discussions about the American race "problem" revolved around describing the nature and characteristics of African Americans, both in terms of their ostensibly inherent, biological qualities and in relation to various structural changes occasioned by, among other things, the failure of Reconstruction, industrialization, and Black migration. In different public and private discourses, white American thinkers and policy makers appealed to a variety of images of Black people, and created new ones, to rationalize America's current and projected racial arrangements. In his study *The Black Image in the White Mind*, George Fredrickson outlines the racial ideas "espoused and applied by race-conscious intellectuals, pseudointellectuals, publicists, and politicians" from the early nineteenth to the early twentieth century, emphasizing those "aspects of race thinking that were most readily communicated to a fairly large public" and examining "the broad policy implications of what were regarded at a given time as authoritative white opinions on black character and potentialities."[20] Tracing white "opinions" about African Americans as expressed by abolitionists and apologists, radicals and liberals, Fredrickson illustrates how white perceptions of Black people—in relation to issues such as the vote, education, and lynching—both produced and were based on carefully constructed images. For example, "militant racists" justified the widespread lynching of African American men by promulgating the image of the Negro as an uncontrollable, oversexed beast; in response, "new accommodationists" emphasized the Negro's helpless, childlike qualities, the more palatable but no less dehumanizing half of the "perennial racist dichotomy" that deemed African Americans unfit for full citizenship.[21] In these instances and many others, Fredrickson's intellectual history demonstrates how Black images were constructed and mobilized in print (i.e., in academic papers, pamphlets, articles in periodicals) in an effort to delimit the boundaries of African American capabilities in the collective public "white mind" to forestall Black claims to social and political equality.

American fiction produced at the turn of the century also participated in efforts to construct images of the American Negro that rearticulated his or her inability to assume the privileges and responsibilities of full American citizenship. Novels such as Thomas Dixon's *The Leopard's Spots* (1902) and *The Clansman* (1905, upon which *Birth* was based) presented the worst white fantasies of bestial Blackness, while works by Joel Chandler Harris and Thomas Nelson Page celebrated the docile, faithful Blacks of slavery days. According to Fredrickson, Page lamented the fact that the "good darkies" of his antebellum stories would disappear now that slavery could no longer impose white patriarchal control over Blacks' naturally savage tendencies. Thus Page "drew a sharp distinction between the 'old time darkies' who were passing away and the 'new issue,' whom he described as 'lazy, thriftless, intemperate, insolent, dishonest, and without the most rudimentary elements of morality.' "[22] This pernicious image of the postbellum "new issue" functioned alongside racial ideologies expressed by other writers who would seem, superficially, to have been less invested in maintaining racist hierarchies. For example, as Kenneth Warren argues in his study of American literary realism, realist novels "assisted in the creation of a climate of opinion that undermined the North's capacity to resist Southern arguments against political equality for African Americans during the 1880s and 1890s through its conflicted participation in discussions about the American social order."[23] Warren observes that by clinging to "genteel mores" such as discriminating taste, realists actually supported the segregationist notion that "social discrimination was unavoidable" along racial lines, even though realist fiction seemed to equate social and civil equality.[24] Thus, in different ways, both realist and romantic literature contributed to the notion that African Americans constituted social problems (and, I would add, representational problems) that would only get worse if they were allowed to pursue democracy unchecked.

Visual representations of Blackness echoed the themes and concerns circulating in the aforementioned nonvisual media. Whereas some postbellum visual representations (like political cartoons) illustrated the purported violent, bestial side of Black character, most Black visual images produced for popular consumption emphasized the nonthreatening quality of Black figures, marshaling an array of visible signifiers to render Blackness palatable, humorous, and therefore more commercially viable. As art historian Richard J. Powell has observed, "These grotesque, garishly dressed beings, with black skins, protruding red lips and bulging eyeballs, were usually shown in impoverished settings with yard fowl, watermelons, and so on."[25] These kinds of images appeared with great frequency in turn-of-the-century graphic arts, such as trade cards, cigar box labels, and posters. In addition, Black likenesses were used for a variety of household

items, from cookie jars and salt and pepper shakers to pipes and pencil/
letter opener sets and children's games. Patricia Turner notes that because
many of these mass-produced "contemptible collectibles" were made for
use in white homes, "the most popular icons are those that contain safe,
nonthreatening servile depictions of blacks or those that imply that inherent ineptness and imbecility will prevent the race from earning social parity."[26] By operating at the level of humor, satire, and caricature, these objects, along with the other images discussed here, support one fantasy of
Blackness in the white imagination—that it is fixed, is visually familiar,
and can be placed safely under white control.

While the proliferation of mass-produced Black caricatures in graphic
arts and everyday objects circulating in turn-of-the-century American life
attempted to freeze Blackness in a limited set of racist poses, Blackness was
also staged for a white public through live performance. Theatrical representations of Blackness, including most notably the tradition of blackface
minstrelsy, further demonstrate white efforts to disavow, via mass culture, Black agency and progress in the elaboration of a modern American
social order. For instance, the adaptation of Harriet Beecher Stowe's abolitionist novel, Uncle Tom's Cabin (1852), to various theatrical productions
throughout the second half of the nineteenth century, and then to numerous motion pictures after the turn of the twentieth century, offers one of
the most popular and critically examined examples of the evolution of particular Black images (Uncle Tom, Topsy the pickaninny) across time and
media in the service of different political and entertainment programs, not
to mention white psychological and epistemological needs.[27] As studies by
Eric Lott, Michael Rogin, and Linda Williams have shown, white appropriations and performances of Blackness in Cabin and later productions functioned to define the boundaries of and qualifications for U.S. citizenship, to
work through anxieties about class and gender hierarchies among diverse
white populations, and to decipher increasingly complex codes of morality,
conduct, and sympathy in a world in the throes of modernization.[28] In addition to the unprecedented popularity of the abolitionist minstrelsy tradition, blackface performance on the vaudeville stage developed and codified
numerous Black types and modes of behavior (Jim Crow and Zip Coon,
"coon" songs, breakdown dances, and stump speeches) that would persist,
in different forms, in popular media and entertainments for decades.

In response to this already-overdetermined landscape of racist Black
representations, African Americans raised their voices (literally and meta-
phorically) to challenge dominant Black images. Race leaders and artists
took up this challenge in various ways, often invoking the notion of a

Black voice or sound to complicate prevailing racist ideologies. For example, in *The Souls of Black Folk* (1903), W. E. B. Du Bois structures his discussion of the characterization of the Negro as a social and political "problem" with samples of African American "sorrow songs" (reproductions of bars of music from Negro spirituals) to illustrate the contributions that people of African descent have made to American (and world) culture. By citing examples of Black music in notation in each chapter heading and at the book's climax, Du Bois attempts to elevate Black folk culture to the level of fine art (with its connotations of timelessness and universality) while linking the processes of reading, hearing, speaking, and singing to the project of making visible the plight of the post-Reconstruction Black subject.[29] In another invocation of the Black "voice," the collection of essays *A Voice from the South* (1892), Anna Julia Cooper claims to speak on behalf of the "mute and voiceless" victims of racism and sexism—Black women—who have yet to be fully considered in discussions of the "race problem" or the women's movement.[30] Cooper extends her social and political arguments into the realm of American literature, where she singles out literary realists like William Dean Howells, who, in her view, cannot produce "realist" representations of African Americans given his scant and superficial personal knowledge about them.[31] Instead, Cooper calls upon African Americans to take up the pen to create more representative images from their own perspectives: "There is an old proverb 'The devil is always painted *black*—by white painters.' And what is needed, perhaps, to reverse the picture of the lordly man slaying the lion, is for the lion to turn painter."[32]

This call was being answered not only by Black writers (including Frances Ellen Watkins Harper, Charles Chesnutt, Paul Lawrence Dunbar, and Pauline Hopkins) but also by visual artists like painter Henry O. Tanner, who responded to negative Black representations in fine art with a realist aesthetic intended to challenge "the prevailing assumptions of black inferiority, shallowness, and bestiality."[33] In addition, black photographers were active in cities across the country during the late nineteenth and early twentieth century, offering evidence of Black success by taking portraits of leading and affluent members of the African American community.[34] Black newspapers regularly offered visual and textual race-centered accounts of local, national, and international events, highlighting Black social, uplift, and business activities. In these ways, African Americans (and a number of sympathetic whites) voiced alternative discourses that emphasized the Race's progress into modernity by offering evidence of Black social progress, business success, and educational attainment.[35]

These and other Black voices sought both to educate whites and to reha-
bilitate Black self-perception. Henry Louis Gates has shown that between
1895 and 1925, Black leaders responded to racist images by repeatedly mobilizing a "New Negro" rhetoric to "reconstruct their public, reproducible
images."[36] Gates graphically illustrates his point by reproducing portraits
that members of the Black elite circulated of and among themselves to
model the physical features of Black dignity, intelligence, and character as
redefined for the new century. Gates concludes his argument with a "visual
essay" consisting of reproductions of what he calls "Sambo" figures from
turn-of-the-century postcards, sheet music, and advertisements. Although
Gates's text emphasizes the assertion of an African American literary
"voice" during this period, his inclusion of so many Black images and
counterimages demonstrates why and how African Americans worked to
"reconstruct" their public image in visual terms as well. The multiple
forms of racist discourse required Black responses on many levels—including the verbal and the visual.[37]

I sketch out this large field of Black representation to suggest the active
interplay of multiple and conflicting "cultural voices" that informed the
production of turn-of-the-century Black images in general, and Black film
images in particular. Specifically, I am interested in how these images reflect concerns—Black and white—about the implications of Black mobility and visibility by embodying tensions between discourses on Black
movement or progress, on the one hand (signified by the New Negro),
and notions of Black stasis and/or retrogression, on the other (signified by
the "Sambo"). Gates argues that these are antithetical formations signifying a reconstructed Black presence in response to a racist sign of "truly
negated absence."[38] But by reading the Sambo/New Negro figures as a di-
alectical rather than an antithetical framework, we can analyze preclassical Black representations as complex "fictive-discursive constructs,"[39] in
which long-standing, negating stereotypes collide with the increasingly
vocal and visible threat of Black challenges to white, racist power structures, particularly in northern and urban sites of Black migration and
mass cultural production and consumption.

Shohat and Stam's shift to a discursive analysis of racialized film images
beyond their operations as "stereotypes" recalls strategies developed by
feminist film theorists who similarly recognized the limits of comparing
women's film images to women's lived realities. Critics like Mary Ann
Doane, Patricia Mellencamp, and Linda Williams responded by confronting
the literalness of the notion of the film "image" itself. They observed that
unlike the symbolic nature of the "image" in literature, in film there seems

to be a smaller gap between sign and referent, so that "even the most blatant stereotype is naturalized by a medium that presents a convincing illusion of a flesh and blood woman." Therefore, to denaturalize these stereotypical images, feminist film critics shifted away from "images of women" analyses toward "the axis of vision itself—to the modes of organizing vision and hearing" that produce the "images" in question.[40]

This feminist work considers the psychological determinations that produce the cinematic apparatus; or, as Philip Rosen puts it, how the literal "machinery" of the cinema ("the basic camera-projector mechanism") operates within "the context of a larger social and/or cultural and/or institutional 'machine.'"[41] Feminist film theorists have investigated how signifying practices specific to the cinema (camera placement, framing, editing) have been structured by a dominant patriarchal order to produce subject positions based on gender difference. Laura Mulvey's landmark essay, for example, graphically complicates the "images of" approach by identifying three "looks" in the cinema—the camera's look at the profilmic action; the spectator's look at the recorded image, and the look characters exchange within the film—as the components of the "voyeuristic-scopophilic look that is a crucial part of traditional [i.e., patriarchal] filmic pleasure."[42] Of course, Mulvey's account of the gendered gaze and the nature of cinematic pleasure has been radically revised and reformulated during the last thirty years.[43] Still, I return to Mulvey's elaboration of the three looks and how they arrange film-viewer relations because it still provides a useful model for recontextualizing early Black film images within a larger consideration of the cinematic apparatus—how these images circulate between the machines that record and project them and the social/cultural/institutional "machines" that determine their modes of address and reception.

In my consideration of Black representation in early cinema, I cannot simply insert "Black" in place of "woman" in Mulvey's model, as Manthia Diawara does in his provisional essay on Black spectatorship, because this would elide important differences between the kind of pleasure Black images ostensibly provide for white viewers with the pleasure female images in dominant cinema are said to produce for male spectators.[44] As I discuss in chapter 3 regarding theoretical approaches to African American spectatorship, collapsing differences between racial and gender oppression, and then equating the cinematic objectification of women and people of color, does not acknowledge the unique questions race raises regarding spectatorial identification and mastery. When I refer to the "viewer" here, I am talking about the hypothetical term of address constructed by the films in question. What we can take from Mulvey's model is a framework for understanding how Blackness is not only figured in social terms but also structured within the dominant cinema's developing looking relations. More specifically, we can explore ways in which Black migration and reconstructive processes influenced and problematized figurations of Blackness within a cinematic apparatus that codes its viewer as white.

I also realize that I cannot directly apply feminist critiques of dominant, classical cinematic practice to many early films, like those nonnarrative displays Tom Gunning has termed the "cinema of attractions," because the same looking relations between film and viewer do not necessarily obtain. Mulvey's formulation of the gendered roles in cinematic representation and spectatorship (the "active" masculinized viewer whose look is aligned with that of the male protagonist, positioning him in a role of mastery over a "passive" female image) is based on the patriarchal structures she identifies in the classical Hollywood cinema. As Miriam Hansen notes, however, even though it did not fully formalize strategies to predetermine its modes of reception, "early cinema is no less patriarchal than its classical successor."[45] I would add that early cinema is no less invested in maintaining racial hierarchies than its classical successor. Therefore, although preclassical cinema does not "position" its viewer's perceptions as consistently as do classical narratives (e.g., with the use of point-of-view shots, eyeline matches, and other components of continuity editing), it does use a variety of formal and stylistic strategies to position its viewers ideologically. Feminist film theory's elaboration of the complex structure of looks in the cinema offers useful tools for considering how the cinematic apparatus attempts to place the "ideal" viewer (coded as white) in relation to the Black image on screen, as well as the unstable social and perceptual structures underlying this looking relation. Close analysis of two preclassical films, *A Nigger in the Woodpile* (American Mutoscope & Biograph, 1904, discussed in the introduction) and *Laughing Gas* (Edison, 1907, dir. Edwin S. Porter), illustrates the usefulness of discursive and apparatus-based approaches for denaturalizing the relations between Black cinematic images and the sociohistorical Black subjects they seem to signify.

## Reading between the Gags:
## *A Nigger in the Woodpile* and *Laughing Gas*

I resume the discussion of *A Nigger in the Woodpile* begun in the introduction to suggest further the many formal and discursive layers that constitute Black images that seem to be one-dimensional in their construction and reception (see figs. 5 through 7). The comic plot of *A Nigger in the Woodpile* mobilizes multiple discourses on Black character. It also hinges upon the disguise and exposure of acts of Black transgression, as well as white retaliation, as seen by the camera, the viewer, and the characters in the film. When the film opens, two white farmers know that Blacks have been stealing their wood, even though they, and the viewer, have not yet witnessed this act; Black criminality is the already understood subtext of the action before a single Black figure has appeared. One could certainly argue that viewers would continue to expect the confirmation of the Black criminal stereotype throughout the history of American cinema. However, early cinema depended much more heavily on audience foreknowledge than classical narratives, presenting well-known stories and events derived from the theater, novels, newspapers, political cartoons, comic strips, folktales and fairy tales, and popular songs.[46] In this case, the film constructs a scenario around a common slang expression, "a nigger in the woodpile," and takes it beyond its colloquial usage. The saying, as discussed in the introduction, refers to a situation involving something suspicious and/or concealed. In the film bearing this title there are, literally, two niggers (Black men) sneaking into a woodpile; as such, there is no need to narratively motivate their criminal actions. The "niggers" presented in this film confirm the popular expression by embodying its literal and figurative meanings. These characters are not the only "niggers in the woodpile" operating in the film—there is also the stick of dynamite the white farmers have concealed inside one of the logs to expose the thieves. Thus, *A Nigger in the Woodpile* plays with the stereotype of Black criminality by multiplying the meaning of the title to signify the identity of the criminals, the scene of the crime, and the means of their exposure and punishment.

The film also enacts an interesting variation on the term's use as a sexual metaphor, indicating the presence of "Black blood" in a white person, typically suggesting that a Black man has had sexual relations with a white woman and produced a child from the encounter. In the film, the white men retaliate against Black men in a violent reversal of this dreaded phenomenon: the Black men come home with a dangerous, concealed surprise—a stick of dynamite inside a wooden log—in place of white men bringing home an impregnated white wife or daughter.

Another set of discourses about Blackness is evident in the way in which the film's blackfaced and stereotypically costumed characters—the uppity colored deacon, his accomplice, an old Uncle Remus, and the mammy—serve as stand-ins for the African American community in order to criticize notions of Black leadership. It is the deacon (described in the Biograph catalogue as "one of the shining lights in the African Church") who orchestrates the doomed heist, implicating the two otherwise harmless types in his criminal scheme.[47] This lazy, exploitative deacon makes sure the coast is clear after the whites leave the frame, calls in the nervous older man, and piles a large load of logs into the old man's shaky arms, while he himself carries off only one log. In this way, the film and its promotional materials not only mobilize long-standing stereotypes about the duplicity of Black religious leaders but also mark the distinction between Old and New Negroes. As the arrogant New Negro figure in the film encourages the more docile types to usurp and enjoy white property, we can see how familiar Black stereotypes interact with each other, as well as with the increasingly present threat of Black empowerment and collusion, and their eminent transgression of racist social, political, and economic structures.

*A Nigger in the Woodpile* also constructs its Black characters at the level of the gaze, within the exchange of looks and the power relationships these looks imply. The farmers' method of punishing the thieves involves a "mischief gag" in which they conceal a stick of dynamite and then wait for the explosion that will simultaneously expose and punish the thieves. In the interval between what Gunning has called the gag film's "preparatory phase" and its "result and effect," the white characters disappear, waiting off-screen for the culmination of their passive-aggressive plot, while the (presumed white) viewer watches the plot unfold.[48] By using a hidden and delayed means of exposing the thieves, the film illustrates that Black transgressors are subject to systems of white surveillance and retribution that only they cannot see. The Black characters bring home the booby-trapped wood and insert it into their stove, becoming the agents of their own undoing precisely because they are below whites in the racial hierarchy of vision and power.

To be sure, the majority of mischief gag films produced during the silent period involve many kinds of "victims" who are white (e.g., authority figures, unsuspecting lovers). But unique pleasures are implied when Black characters are tricked into exposing their own mischief because the film viewer is positioned to enjoy both the Black(face) crime and the white-inflicted punishment. This kind of spectatorial pleasure recalls Eric Lott's argument about the appeal of blackface minstrelsy for working-class white male audiences as consisting of a dialectic of love/theft, attraction/repulsion, desire/appropriation. Like blackface theatrical performance, *A Nigger in the Woodpile* invited viewers to vicariously enjoy the experience of stealing as performed by blacked-up white actors. What is different about the cinematic staging of such a scene is the voyeuristic manner in which the viewer is positioned to enjoy the stereotypical spectacle of Black(face) criminality and then, when the tables are turned on the would-be Black tricksters, how the viewer's pleasure is also structured to derive from the alignment of his perspective with that of the white men who catch the thieves. When we add the third term of the cinematic apparatus to Lott's love/theft dialectic—in this case framing and editing—we can see how preclassical films organize cinematic looks to provide a distinct sense of mastery by emphasizing the visual construction of the scene or narrative as it unfolds.

As I have outlined earlier, representations of African Americans as objects of desire/derision are staged in a variety of media, not unlike the representation of woman as castration threat, which Mulvey contends is not exclusive to cinema. "What makes cinema quite different in its voyeuristic potential from, say, striptease, theater, shows, etc.," Mulvey argues, is that cinema goes "far beyond highlighting a woman's to-be-looked-at-ness" to build "the way she is to be looked at into the spectacle itself."[49] While Mulvey believes that the cinema's voyeuristic potential derives from its ability to vary and expose "the place of the look" through techniques such as narrative, editing, and variations in camera distance as employed in the classical model, preclassical cinema achieves similar effects in its treatment of Blackness by linking cinematic methods of structuring looks with those of other visual media.

In preclassical films, modes of address are drawn from a variety of representational models, from fairground attractions to train rides to vaudeville and legitimate theater. In *Woodpile*, the looks of the camera and the viewer seem to be aligned in a way that replicates live theatrical modes of staging and viewing (e.g., distant framing, static camerawork, painted sets rather than location shooting). Of Mulvey's three cinematic "looks," the look of the camera can be difficult to distinguish from that of the viewer, though they are of distinctly different orders. The look of the camera is related to the authorial, designating what profilmic action the filmmakers choose to include within the frame. The look of the viewer, however, is tied to reception, determined by what the viewer chooses to watch within the frame (and when, and for how long). Both of these looks raise questions about the extent to which an ideal viewer can be constructed by cinematic modes of address, and how thoroughly spectatorial attention can be directed.

As in a theatrical production, the scenes in *Woodpile* contain a variety of actions the viewer might focus on, and we can imagine that live musical accompaniment and (interactive) audience behavior during a screening of such a film could be similar to that for a live (perhaps vaudeville) performance in which there is much room for variation and distraction in the viewer's relation to the "show." At the same time, certain actions occurring on screen (e.g., the placement of the dynamite in the log, the insertion of the logs into the stove) are staged in the center of the frame, directing the viewer's look in the elaboration of the film's narrative. The film's proscenium framing attempts to align the looks of camera and viewer in a vantage point like that from a seat a few rows back in a live performance venue. The actors gesture broadly, often toward the camera, as if to make their actions visible to spectators in the back of the house. But they do not look at the camera in the exhibitionist fashion displayed in much live comedy and musical performance, or in many early films characterized by Tom Gunning as the "cinema of attractions."[50] Thus the film attempts to subordinate both the camera's and the viewer's looks to the looks exchanged between characters, not only maintaining the illusion of the fourth wall employed in some theatrical traditions but also enabling the kind of voyeuristic-scopophilic gaze Mulvey identifies in the classical narrative cinema. But the film still emphasizes the presentation of Black (punishment as) spectacle, tying it to nonnarrative modes of Black theatrical representation and to the predominant attractions aesthetic of early cinema.

In addition to the various modes of staging by/for the camera based on theatrical models, *A Nigger in the Woodpile* uses editing to produce a sense of coherent space between two shots/settings (the outdoor woodpile and the Black home) and to enhance its comic conclusion. The film's second shot contains an edit in which the Uncle Remus figure is repositioned to fall from the ceiling to the floor, the cut obscured by the billows of smoke from the explosion. *Woodpile* thus uses the cinema's capacity to manipulate temporal and spatial relations to create a sense of a ubiquitous gaze across narrative spaces, while emphasizing the comic/violent visual gag of the thieves' punishment.

In these ways, the orchestration of looks in *Woodpile* does not suggest a radical alterity from or strict adherence to either theatrical precedent or immanent classical conventions (where the viewer is ostensibly distracted from the mechanics producing the image). Instead, preclassical cinematic "looks" are closely related to numerous traditions of spectacle and narrative, and the looks of the camera and the viewer can be both carefully planned and open to roaming. Jean-Louis Baudry suggests that the camera produces a "transcendental subject" who, as spectator, "identifies less with what is represented, the spectacle itself, than with what stages the spectacle, makes it seen, obliging him to see what it sees."[51] What is useful about Baudry's and other ideological critiques of the apparatus for the analysis of preclassical Black representations is not so much how the camera necessarily obliges the viewer to look in particular ways but the notion that the function of the apparatus is to encourage identification with the making of the scene/seen, and the sense of power and pleasure this identification is intended to produce for the "ideal" spectator. Without full formal recourse to staples of minstrel performance such as diegetic speech or song, or live direct address to the audience, a film like *Woodpile* supplements its use of blackface theatrical conventions (producing the dialectic of identification with and desire for "Blackness") with cinematic techniques that position the viewer to enjoy and identify with the camera's suspenseful, voyeuristic presentation of Black transgressive acts as well as the process of their inevitable exposure and disruption.

*A Nigger in the Woodpile* presents "stereotypical" Black figures within several performative, narrative, and representational modes (use of blackface, gag structure, play with white voyeuristic looks and Black visibility, and a "trick" of editing) to dismiss Black insurgence by comedically entrapping and punishing Black characters for a petty, but highly symbolic, crime. A multiple-shot film like *A Nigger in the Woodpile* signals the beginnings of the cinema's gradual transition from one-shot exhibitionist displays to multiple-shot narratives in which telling stories became the primary task of dominant cinematic discourse.[52] This shift presumed a different relation between film and viewer and required different methods of representing time, space, and character. Consequently, during the transitional era, Black figures continue to be informed by a variety of familiar discourses on racial difference, but formal and stylistic changes opened up new methods of presenting the anxieties associated with Black mobility and visibility.

Unlike early films, which relied heavily on audience foreknowledge (e.g., the plots of preexisting stories like *Uncle Tom's Cabin*, popular songs, news events, fairy tales, or expressions like "a nigger in the woodpile"), later ones gradually began to articulate narratives from "scratch," elaborating characters and story lines as if for the first time. To make such freestanding narratives legible, filmmakers developed techniques to make temporal and spatial relationships clear when depicting actions taking place at different times and/or in different settings in more than one shot, such as the repetition and/or continuation of actions and characters across separate shots. For example, in the heavily exploited "chase" genre, the same characters enter, pass through, and exit the frame in a series of shots representing a succession of locations, often moving in the same screen direction (left to right, background to foreground).[53] A variation on the chase, the linked vignette film, features the same character in a series of shots/settings engaged in corresponding actions.[54] A linked vignette film like *Laughing Gas* (Edison, 1907), in which a Black female domestic engages in a series of parallel activities, illustrates how continuity techniques place individual Black spectacles within larger structures of narrative coherence. In contrast to early cinema, with its sometimes jarring visual gags and tricks—such as the explosion-induced fall of the old Black man in *Woodpile*—later films de-emphasize disruptions caused by edits by bridging continuous action, at the story level, across different shots. *Laughing Gas* and other transitional-era films indicate how seemingly familiar Black types (like Black "mammies") actually produce and reflect tensions in the construction of the "ideal" viewer's look as stories and characters become developed rather than "presented," and as African Americans demonstrate more social and geographic mobility on and off screen.[55]

In *Laughing Gas* a large Black woman (named "Mandy" in the Edison catalogue) goes to the dentist to have a tooth pulled. In great pain, she insists on receiving nitrous oxide, and after the tooth is removed, she begins to laugh uncontrollably. Her laughter is infectious, causing the dentist and his assistant to begin laughing as well (fig. 11). She proceeds to move through a series of public spaces in which she continues to laugh and spreads her laughter to everyone she encounters. As I discuss in more detail in the next chapter, Black female domestics were a common feature of turn-of-the-century American life, and domestic work became a kind of cultural shorthand for Black women and their social position in the United States.[56] Black female characters appear in a large number of preclassical films set in a variety of locations (South and North, urban and rural, contemporary and antebellum), as indicated by the number of surviving examples along with catalogue descriptions of films that are not extant.[57] Although these Black female figures are typically ridiculed or marginalized on the basis of their low position in racial and gender hierarchies (e.g., their social and moral inferiority, their unattractiveness), their formal staging often raises illuminating questions about what kinds of spectatorial looks they anticipate in light of the class, ethnic, gender, and other divisions within the dominant "white" audience to whom such films were addressed.

The representation of the Black female domestic in *Laughing Gas* is striking in comparison to earlier films for her seeming authenticity and agency. She is played by a Black actress, not a white actor in blackface. Before we see her working as a domestic, we see her at the dentist, on a

FIGURE 11. The dentist's nitrous oxide sends Mandy into an extended, raucous laughing spree that infects everyone she meets. *Laughing Gas* (Edison, 1907, dir. Edwin S. Porter). Library of Congress, Motion Picture, Broadcasting and Recorded Sound Division.

streetcar, and in several street scenes in which she travels unaccompanied. She carries no groceries or basket of laundry to mark her occupation or to motivate her circulation in white public spaces. In many ways, she appears to enjoy a considerable amount of autonomy viewers might not expect for a Black woman in turn-of-the-century America. She travels alone in the same section of public conveyances as whites; she patronizes a white dentist; she presses him to administer the laughing gas; she causes a series of accidents and disruptions—causes a white artist to drop his sculptures, pours soup in the lap of one of the white diners, and even ends up surrounded by white officers at the police station in the middle of the film— only to laugh herself out of trouble every time. Thus, *Laughing Gas* draws on some dominant but seemingly contradictory expectations of Black female social roles (subservient employees) and behavior (untamed physicality).

Structurally, *Laughing Gas* is anomalous in the degree to which its narrative organization depends on the movements of a Black female character.

The seeming independence and unchecked mobility of this character produce the central tension in understanding the film's mode of address. One interpretation might suggest that the representation of this Black woman in a leading role is a radical break from the brief, seemingly marginalizing representations of most Black female domestics. The inclusion of two close-ups of Mandy—emblematic shots at the beginning and end of the film—might further indicate a rare effort to bring this character closer to the (white) viewer, to enlist audience sympathy for and/or identification with a Black subject. On the other hand, each of the qualities that would seem to indicate that Mandy is a progressive departure from previous Black female domestics can be read in the opposite direction to suggest how the film uses continuity and other techniques to extend and rework long-standing stereotypes, producing a character that seems to unify a white spectatorial gaze at her expense. For example, the fact that her persistent laughter is produced by the nitrous oxide administered by the dentist suggests that Black/female bodies are particularly susceptible to intoxication, and it potentially undermines her role as agent of goodwill, since she is not in control of her own faculties. The emblematic shots—first a close-up of her bandaged face writhing in pain, finally a close-up of her continuous laughter—may not bring us closer to her consciousness but instead highlight her function as spectacle disconnected from the white worlds in which she circulates in the main body of the film.[58]

This sense of Mandy's proximity to but disconnection from her white observers can also be read diegetically in her travels across shots, where she creates or discovers a series of social disruptions among whites from different national backgrounds, including run-ins with a German street band, an Italian artist, and two arguing Irishmen. Through her laughter she brings disorder, then harmony, to each of these white ethnic types, enabling a kind of melting pot reconciliation via her boisterous Blackness. It is Mandy who, over the course of the film, links these and other conflicting white individuals and segregated white ethnic groups both across separate spaces and within single public settings populated by diverse constituencies (the street, the train). But in doing so, does she facilitate the process of white ethnic assimilation into American culture and society, and/or does she disrupt such discourses? It seems that Mandy's Blackness consolidates the figures she encounters as "white," and at the same time her racial difference highlights the distinctions between these white immigrant groups (and between them and "native" whites represented by Mandy's ethnically unmarked dentist and employers). What is more, her Blackness (especially as constructed through close and distant framing) posits both Mandy and the film's white characters as available for (white) viewer identification and as similarly superficial, broadly drawn comic attractions.

These contradictions demarcate the ambiguous, undertheorized space created by and for Black representations during the first steps toward narrative integration and the development of American film culture. Transitional films are still bound up with early and precinematic traditions of racial stereotyping, and they foreshadow a classical flattening of representational modes for nonwhite figures (in contrast to the development of white "characters"), even as they use those very nonwhite figures to navigate the gaps between the cinema's increasingly diverse white audiences and between two stylistic systems—attractions and narrative.

The stakes of representing racial difference in shifting modes of address—from presentation to narration—are also outlined in *Laughing Gas* through the linking of Black circulation in public space and Black female sexuality. This is set in motion in the opening scene at the dentist. The removal of the Black female domestic's tooth is presented as a visual gag— the dentist has to sit on her lap to pull out the stubborn tooth, with his assistant helping to pull from behind. When, after much effort, the dentist finally dislodges the offending tooth, we see that it is gigantic, as if pulled from a large animal. The visual presentation of the white male dentist mounting the Black female domestic (indeed, the need for two white men to complete the job) clearly taps into familiar discourses on interracial sex (voluntary and forced) and black women's bestial sexuality.[59] This scene is followed by her physical interactions with a number of other white men (e.g., falling into the laps of white men on the streetcar; delighting clusters of white men on the street, in the police station, in the home where she works). However, this series of moments of sexualized interracial contact is disrupted toward the film's end.

After her escapades with whites, it is evening, and Mandy is approached by, and rejects, an ostentatious Black male "masher." Then the film's penultimate shot completes the folding of Mandy into an all-Black world after she has been established as moving confidently through white society. After dismissing the Black dandy, she goes to an African American church service, where the congregation is swaying back and forth to the minister's sermon.[60] By showing that this Black female domestic is, at day's end, a member of a Black community, the film attempts to segregate her safely away to achieve narrative closure. At church, Mandy's laughter rocks her fellow Black worshipers out of their pews, disrupting the service. The culminating joke of the church scene—that Mandy's uncontrollable laughter is virtually indistinguishable from the gesticulations associated with Black religious ecstasy—suggests a connection between sexual and spiritual pleasures as registered by Black bodies. The wild physical motions she displays throughout the film (rolling on the floor, bumping into whites, kicking into the air) come to be naturalized by her color/cultural difference and to be disruptive within her own community. In the final close-up shot, when Mandy laughs into the camera, she can be read as a potentially autonomous (and anomalous) Black subject. But she is also presented as a representative of an entire Black population held up to ridicule for a viewing population constructed as "white" and as diverse in contrast.

As *A Nigger in the Woodpile* and *Laughing Gas* demonstrate, early filmmakers were challenged to represent Blackness in both visual and social terms. Quite often their constructions of Black-white social and looking relations operate together to produce Black figures as sites of confusion and contradiction, despite the fact that racial difference would seem to be clearly constructed and policed by physiological markers, segregationist practices, and performative traditions. For instance, in terms of visual presentation, preclassical cinema almost always renders Black characters as very dark-skinned—practicing what James Snead has called "marking"—so as to make them readily distinguishable from and identifiable by whites.[61] As we shall see in the next chapter, however, many films feature scenarios in which Blackness is misrecognized by white characters within the diegesis (e.g., white mothers accidentally bring home Black babies, and, in an interesting variation, white characters are "blackened," rendering them unrecognizable to their families and communities). In social terms, Black figures are usually placed in familiar, subservient relation to whites, often conveyed by their economic relationships (e.g., thieves of white property, faithful house servants, West Indian natives scrambling for money thrown by white tourists). But, as in *Laughing Gas*, they frequently appear in situations in which white characters are deprived of the power to (fore)see their seemingly unlikely social transgressions. In a climate of shifting racial relationships, preclassical cinema stages a wide variety of scenarios in which Black visibility and mobility are both exploited and contained. Reading this tension in terms of form and content enables us to recognize the complexity of the many representational traditions informing Black cinematic images. This approach also reveals the range of viewing positions preclassical films enable for the sake of providing innovative entertainment, positions these films also seek to coalesce in the name of producing a normative white audience.

Although the cinema presented African Americans with a new field of Black representation in which they initially had difficulty intervening (as demonstrated by the challenges Ida B. Wells faced with *The Birth of a Nation*), African Americans did exert some influence on Black cinematic images, even before they began to make their own films in the early 1910s. Though the white-dominated cinema clearly manipulates Blackness for its own political/psychic/entertainment purposes, one could argue, as Arthur Knight does in relation to Black cinematic musical performance, that "white appropriations of black culture, along with their blackface marker, did not only or always indicate *absence* of (and for) African Americans; rather, they indicate a complex, relational, multivalent, though virtually always constrained and unequal *presence.*"[62] The African American presence in preclassical cinema was registered not only by Black screen appearances and the minstrel tradition but also by broader Black efforts to refute their "misrepresentation" and exclusion. African Americans protested, created alternative media images, and also, significantly, modified their lifestyles and labor roles via urban migration. As I elaborate in a broad survey of preclassical films in the next chapter, the Black image problem was not the burden of Black people alone. In distinct but related ways, early white filmmakers struggled with the complexities of Black image making as a result of growing white awareness of, and anxieties about, the permeation of African American voices, and bodies, into previously closed social, economic, and political arenas.

# CHAPTER TWO

# Mixed Colors

## Riddles of Blackness in Preclassical Cinema

Proceeding from the discursive and apparatus-based approaches outlined in chapter 1, this chapter surveys Black images in a wide variety of preclassical films to explore more broadly how the complex issues surrounding Black image production developed as Black northern and urban migration gained momentum. I describe how the Black image problem in preclassical cinema is frequently organized around Black-white looking relations and the visibility of Blackness in many cinematic contexts.[1] Preclassical films repeatedly foreground questions about the ability of whites to see and recognize Blackness—and thereby control and contain it—at a moment when African Americans were vocally and visibly challenging their prescribed roles in American society. This preoccupation not only suggests the range of turn-of-the-century anxieties about what to do with a "colored" population in motion but also destabilizes claims we might make about a uniform "white" gaze or racist sensibility that structured the production and reception of these images.

Although racial difference is seldom discussed in scholarship on the constitution of preclassical cinema audiences, diversity among white audiences (along class lines in particular) has been researched and debated quite extensively and linked to major developments in film production and exhibition practices.[2] For example, whereas white middle-class viewers made up a significant portion of the early cinema audience (when moving pictures were featured at variety theaters, fairgrounds, and other multimedia venues), by the nickelodeon era (1905 to 1907), low-priced venues dedicated to film exhibition flourished on a clientele of immigrants (notably from southern and eastern Europe) who were flowing into American cities. Nickelodeons appealed particularly to white immigrant, working-class, youth, and female viewers, causing alarm among municipal officials, religious leaders, and social reformers who questioned both the moral and physical cleanliness of these cheap, darkened public spaces and the suitability of the films they exhibited. One way the transition from early to classical representational practices has been read, then, is in relation to the industry's efforts to uplift its working-class audiences with stories designed to edify and educate as well as entertain, and also to attract middle-class viewers with stories organized to correspond with stylistic features found in literature and legitimate theater, such as coherent spatiotemporal relations, engaging characters, and the production of a self-enclosed aesthetic/entertainment experience. In addition, production companies (led by Edison's formation of the Motion Picture Patents Company in late 1908) sought not only to regulate the production and distribution of films but also to assume editorial control over the conditions of exhibition, thereby shaping the moviegoing experience that had largely been in the hands of film exhibitors (who included variables such as live, sometimes ethnic, musical performance).

As with class and white ethnicity, the question of where race fits into these key shifts in the cinema's business and representational practices is crucial for more fully understanding the complex appeals the cinema was making during these formative years of American mass culture. How, for example, might the use of racist imagery and the rigorous racial segregation of film exhibition venues work in tandem with the move to guide the viewer carefully through an uninterrupted, self-contained, and universally intelligible diegetic experience? Also, we might look to preclassical cinema to explore questions raised in scholarship on the historical construction of "whiteness" as a social and biological marker tied to modern discourses on Americanization, class consciousness, gender identity, and cultural expression.[3] For example, how thoroughly could preclassical cinema bridge ethnic, class, and gender differences among white viewers by standardizing the ideal spectator as "white"?

While the cinematic institution was taking shape during the 1890s and early 1900s, Black people were responding with a number of strategies to intensified Jim Crow segregation, lynching, and disfranchisement, as well as inadequate wages, limited housing and educational opportunities, and negative media imagery. They emphasized self-help and racial solidarity, migrated to southern and then northern cities, and organized for racial advancement. In light of these African American geographic and political movements, preclassical cinema participates in a larger effort on the part of a dominant and diverse white population to suppress and ignore rising Black voices of self-determination, politicization, and protest. These films (along with newspapers, literature, drama, and other media produced during this period) register fears about Black empowerment, assurances that racial hierarchies will remain firmly in place, and a range of beliefs and claims in between. These tensions are expressed not only in familiar, negative Black stereotypes but also in the staging of numerous plots of racial misrecognition and subversion, in which Blackness steps outside its traditional boundaries when, significantly, white vision is impaired. Preclassical films frequently foreground their ability to visually organize and manipulate signifiers of racial difference, but they also reveal the instability and artificiality of these very differences. Though the images I examine in this chapter were produced during the years just before the massive wave of Black northward migration around World War I (the Great Migration), they indicate how the preliminary signs of an insurgent Black presence (gradual migration into cities, film audiences, public discourses) influenced the cinema's developing signifying systems. Although preclassical films often attempt to figure "Blackness" as a fixed sign of natural inferiority to "whiteness," they also struggle with its slippery status as something both known and unknown, essential and constructed, docile and dangerous.

This chapter examines three problematics of Black representation in preclassical cinema: the performance of "Blackness" by both Blacks and whites in blackface (raising issues of Blackness as "authentic" versus fabricated); the use of the camera as an instrument for Black surveillance (thus positioning the "white" viewer in a role of voyeuristic mastery); and the dangers of representing different forms of Black/white intimacy (particularly in scenarios involving racial substitution and masquerade). As preclassical films move from "documenting" Black subjects to more elaborate fictionalizations of Blackness, they continuously circle around these clusters of issues. I emphasize films in which seeing and marking Blackness are dominant themes in order to demonstrate how preclassical films play with a variety of scenarios and modes of representation (e.g., nonfiction, fiction, comedy, drama, "genuine Negroes," whites in blackface) within a still-developing economy of cinematic looking relations and performative conventions. As preclassical films struggle to assimilate Black representations from older media (e.g., from literature, live performance) and to create their own representational codes in the face of a radically changing racial landscape, they exhibit numerous ruptures and inconsistencies that become more carefully concealed with the codification of classical cinema. Thus, although these films are undoubtedly structured by racist ideologies and social practices, warranting Black criticism and protest, I suggest that the variety and alterity of their Black representations indicate how they continually maneuver between a host of desires, presumptions, challenges, and fears. This diversity signals how the conditions of modernity, and particularly the cosmopolitanism of urban modernity, required new ways of looking at racial identity and difference, and how the cinema both responded and contributed to these new racialized looking relations.

## Reading Blackness, Blackface

Translating Black representations from various precinema discourses and media, especially from vaudeville and minstrel shows, proved to be more complicated than film historians have suggested. Although early filmmakers could and did draw freely on a clearly articulated set of stock characters and situations (i.e., faithful Toms and mammies, dancing Sambos, watermelon-eating coons), early cinema also sought out new material to present to its audiences, and it gradually developed its own distinct set of narrational and representational strategies. One aspect of preclassical cinema's representation of Blackness that has been largely overlooked is the logic of its casting Black actors and/or white actors wearing blackface in various "Black" roles. My reading of these images suggests that while filmmakers seemed to follow some clear rules about how Blackness could be represented most appropriately in different formal and generic contexts, there were numerous instances in which the decision seems to have been quite arbitrary, raising questions about the function of "realism" versus "theatricality" in preclassical Black representations. For example, how would early film audiences be expected to read "Blackness" in a Caribbean travelogue next to a blackface slapstick comedy, since these different genres could easily have been projected in the same program? How did expectations of photographic realism shift to accommodate obviously fabricated (theatrical) representations of Blackness? Perhaps the cinema's debt to the vaudeville aesthetic (blackface performance, variety format) bridged these discontinuities for early viewers. What is clear is that while preclassical cinema features both actual Blacks and blackfaced figures, it was quite strict about visibly distinguishing between different forms of cinematic Blackness and marking the difference between Blackness (however depicted) and whiteness.

The earliest moving pictures featuring Black representation tend to use actual Black people in roles that, ostensibly, whites could not imitate to the same effect. For example, during the 1890s Edison's kinetoscope films featured popular Black dancers performing their stage acts such as *The Pickaninny Dance—From the "Passing Show"/The Pickaninnies* (Edison, 6 October 1894); Black music hall performer Elsie Jones (in *Elsie Jones [no. 1]* and *Elsie Jones [no. 2]* [both Edison, 26 November 1894]); and Black vaudevillian James Grundy *(James Grundy, [no. 1]/Buck and Wing Dance* and *James Grundy, [no. 2]/Cake Walk* [both Edison, January 1895]).[4] Other production companies also featured Black dance performance among their earliest films, such as American Mutoscope's *A Coon Cake Walk* (April 1897) and Lubin's *Cake Walk* (May 1898).[5] Although white performers had long presented "Black" dance in live minstrel performance, during the 1890s African American performers were becoming increasingly popular in vaudeville and burlesque houses and were, therefore, among the earliest theatrical performers to be filmed by motion picture producers.[6] Most of the earliest Black dance films consisted only of the dance performance, but at least one early dance film, Edison's *The Tramp and the Crap Game* (1900), foreshadows later films by incorporating African American dance into a framing scene or story. According to the Edison catalogue description, the film features a short, superficial narrative that provides minimal motivation for Black dance performance: "A number of darky boys and street arabs are engaged in a crap game just outside of the back entrance of a theatre. The darkies suddenly give up the game of craps for the purpose of indulging in a Southern break down."[7] This sort of presentation of Black dance was to persist in preclassical cinema—Blacks require little motivation to engage in one of their natural pastimes, and Black dance functions as a self-contained spectacle creating a break in the narrative.

Representations of Black movement are cast in the form of jokes that seem to present authentic, "everyday" practices in two extremely popular early genres—the baby-washing film and the watermelon-eating film. In films like *A Hard Wash* (American Mutoscope, September 1896) and Edison's copy, *A Morning Bath* (Edison, October 31, 1896), Black mothers vigorously scrub Black babies with white soap, playing on the joke that "no matter how hard the mother scrubbed, she would never get [her baby] 'truly clean' (i.e., white)."[8] Of course, these bath scenes could not work with white actors in blackface because the makeup would wash off, spoiling the illusion and the joke. In addition to functioning as humorous displays of Blackness ("the bathing of the black baby who kicked and struggled brought the house to a fever pitch"), they were among many early films featuring babies and children (mostly white), which were staged but enjoyable for the natural and unpredictable quality of youth performance.[9] The exclusive use of "authentic" Black babies in these films may also be in keeping with early filmmakers' almost consistent use of Black children in Black youth roles. Blackface is rarely used on babies and children in early cinema, a practice that holds throughout the silent era.[10] Black babies and children are valued as curiosities in their own right.

In films of the popular watermelon-eating genre, such as *A Watermelon Feast* (American Mutoscope, 1896) and *Watermelon Eating Contest/Watermelon Contest* (Edison, September 1896), Black men quickly and sloppily devour melons with a passion that, presumably, could not be rendered as humorously and realistically by white performers. This genre became so popular that by 1903, Lubin advertised its contribution, *Who Said Watermelon?*, as a refreshing variation: "The usual watermelon picture shows darkey men eating the luscious fruit. We have an excellent one of that kind of which we have sold quite a number, but the demand for a new watermelon picture has induced us to pose two colored women in which they are portrayed, ravenously getting on the outside of a number of melons, much to the amusement of the onlookers."[11] These films not only tap into discourses on Black animalistic behavior and revive southern iconography (returning Blacks to the plantation) but also experiment with different camera distances (close-ups, medium shots) to present a range of views, some replicating theatrical staging, some exploiting the cinema's capacity to present details of movement, texture, facial expression, and skin tone.

Scenes of "authentic" Black dance, baby washing, and watermelon eating recurred during the next few years of motion picture production (declining around 1903–4), seemingly reserved for Black actors.[12] These films, along with nonfiction presentations of Blacks such as those depicting activities of Black soldiers (e.g., *The Ninth Negro Cavalry Watering Horses* [Edison, 1898]), life among Blacks in the Caribbean (e.g., *Native Women Coaling a Ship at St. Thomas, DWI* [Edison, 1903]), and Black prizefighters (e.g., *Dixon-Chester Leon Contest* [American Mutoscope & Biograph, 1906]), were not as dependent as later films on theatrical conventions for Black representation. Instead, these brief Black attractions provided nonthreatening, exotic, and topical content for early moving picture audiences who enjoyed familiar but seemingly spontaneous performances.

By 1903–4, an increasing number of Black roles were performed by white actors in blackface. Blackface film comedies, in particular, were among the first story films, adapting popular minstrel performance styles to the screen.[13] Numerous types of racial and ethnic performance were adapted from the stage, using many of the same performers and routines, as the cinema incorporated more narrativized scenarios. The fact that preclassical cinema continued to include nonfiction scenes of various racial and ethnic groups (e.g., in travelogues), along with staged, costumed depictions of these same groups, suggests that generally speaking the cinema did not need to adhere uniformly to realistic conventions when it came to racial and ethnic performance. Instead, the element of foreknowledge—the assumed audience familiarity with particular kinds of narratives, character types, and (theatrical) modes of presentation—operates strongly in early cinema's racial and ethnic representations. Although the theatrical convention of whites in blackface in Black roles would predominate with the rise of the story film, Black performers continue to appear in preclassical cinema under certain circumstances.

When looking at early narrative films today, it is often quite difficult to ascertain when Black characters are being played by white actors in blackface or by Black actors. The deteriorated state of many early prints and the distant framing used in many films of this period make some of these figures difficult to read. What is more, the identities of early film performers are not always easy to trace, especially in the case of African Americans. In narrative films in particular, Black characters are delineated with such performative consistency (gesture and movement, costuming) that it can be difficult to determine the race of the performer in the "Black" role. The consistency of theater-derived Black representational styles and scenarios is so profound that early Black film historian Henry Sampson deliberately includes a number of films featuring Black actors in his chapter cataloguing "Whites in Blackface," as if to equate all "truncated, stereotyped" Black images in silent film regardless of the race of the performers.[14] Therefore, we must look for patterns of Black representation (e.g., genre, leading versus supporting roles) and also consult production information and promotional materials to understand when and why particular casting decisions might have been made.

Early narrative films present a range of modes of Black representation, for different social and stylistic reasons. For example, very early films boasted the authenticity of their Black subjects. In its promotional materials *The Watermelon Patch* (Edison, 1905) played up the fact that it featured all "genuine negroes."[15] Veteran Black vaudevillian Tom Fletcher was hired as both talent and talent wrangler by the Edison company around 1900, providing Black players for films directed by Edwin Porter at the company's Manhattan studios and their location shooting in North Ashbury Park.[16] A decade later, Alice Guy Blaché directed an all-Black cast in her comedy *A Fool and His Money* (1912), and according to Henry Sampson, the Lubin film company "employed a small stock company of black actors for several all-black cast one-reel comedy films" released between 1913 and 1915. These examples suggest that "authentic" Black performance was still a selling point after years of cinematic blackface representation.[17] However, blackface predominated during the 1910s in part because most studios did not regularly employ Black actors, perhaps indicating discriminatory hiring practices and segregationist ideas about the social mixing of black and white actors.[18]

Some types of Black roles had long been performed interchangeably by Black and white blackfaced actors, such as comic figures or chicken thieves.[19] Other Black roles, however, were played almost exclusively by white actors, and these blackface roles predominate in fictional narratives produced after 1907 or so, as films begin to make the transition toward the classical paradigm, placing greater emphasis on developing individual character psychology and realistic motivation. For example, faithful Black house servants—butlers and maids—are played for the most part by white actors, as seen in most cinematic versions of *Uncle Tom's Cabin* and the other popular scenes of antebellum life that proliferated during the transitional period. It seems that filmmakers used white actors in Black roles when they wanted to elicit from their white audiences a sense of sympathy for or identification with Black characters. As Linda Williams has observed, melodrama has functioned as one of the primary modes of staging such moments of interracial sympathetic exchange, from stage to screen.[20]

Blackface as a dramatic (or comedic) theatrical convention did not entirely supplant Black actors, who continued to appear in nonfiction films and occasionally in minor, background roles in fiction films during the transitional period. In fact, many films feature both Black actors and white actors in blackface, often within the same frame. Blackfaced mammies appear with real Black babies and children (*Mixed Babies* [American Mutoscope & Biograph, 1908]), *Mammy's Child* [Powers, 1913]); blackfaced house servants appear with Black plantation extras *(For Massa's Sake* [Pathé, 1911], *The Birth of a Nation)*; blackfaced jungle kings/queens lead Black extras playing "natives" (*Missionaries in Darkest Africa* [Kalem, 1912], *Sammy Orpheus, or The Pied Piper of the Jungle* [Selig, 1912], *His Cannibal Wife* [LaSalle, 1917]). Again, it seems that "leading" Black roles, particularly in dramas, are reserved for white actors, not only to facilitate white audience identification with these "Black" characters but also because of the prevailing belief that Black actors could not carry off substantial, sympathetic, dramatic roles.[21] Conversely, white actors in blackface are used in major roles in which Black characters are incriminated (as rapists, for instance, as is Gus in *The Birth of a Nation*). In this case, the motivation for casting whites involves a more complicated process of white viewer "identification," in which the spectator enjoys the perverse pleasure of watching whites perform Black transgressive acts. In addition, these transgressive Black figures must be performed by whites to conform to the prohibition against staging sexualized, physical contact between Black male and white female actors on screen. These casting decisions demonstrate that viewers were supposed to recognize white actors behind the makeup and understand the privileged position of blackfaced figures in relation to any "real" Blacks within the story.

Combinations of white and Black actors and characters produced a number of representational tensions and discontinuities that distinguish preclassical film from later, more consistent classical practice. For example, Sampson notes one of the more unusual combinations: "In a few films of this era the same character was played by a black and white actor in different scenes of the same film." He cites *The Dark Romance of a Tobacco Can* (Essanay, 1911), in which "a black actress plays the leading female character in the beginning scenes and a white actress plays the same character in blackface in the climactic scenes of this film" after several years have passed.[22] In the film, a young Black girl working in a tobacco factory slips a note into a tobacco can indicating that she is looking for a husband. Several years later George M. Jackson, a white man, finds the note just before he learns that he needs a wife to receive an inheritance. He sends for the note writer, but when she arrives Jackson is horrified by the appearance of a Black woman and puts her out. This film adheres to the practice of using "authentic" Blacks in youth roles and then using blackface for the conclusion, in which the threat of miscegenation is presented, then comically subverted.

A different kind of switch occurs in *Mixed Babies* (American Mutoscope & Biograph, 1908), in which a white actress in blackface playing the character of a Black mother during the body of the film is replaced by a Black actress in the film's final shot. The plot of *Mixed Babies* involves the switching of Black and white infants and their eventual return to their proper parents. After the closing scene of the main action of the film (a group of parents chasing and punishing the man responsible for the mix-up), we see an emblematic shot in which two mothers—Black and white—sit side by side, each holding a baby in her lap (fig. 12). At first it seems safe to assume that this shot features the mothers we saw during the narrative part of the film. The Biograph description implies as much by explaining that in the final scene "each mother secures and folds her own toodlums to her bosom."[23] However, not only is the (white) blackfaced actress replaced by a Black actress here, but also it is not clear that the white mother in the

FIGURE 12. After a comic baby mix-up, the races are properly reunited, displayed, and contrasted in the emblematic concluding shot of *Mixed Babies* (American Mutoscope & Biograph, 1908). Library of Congress, Motion Picture, Broadcasting and Recorded Sound Division.

closing shot is the same white actress who appears throughout the film. This final, emblematic shot plays important narrative and symbolic roles, providing closure to the story (the babies are back with their natural mothers) and illustrating the quaintness of motherhood across the races. Also, the representation of light and dark values in this final scene visually juxtaposes white and Black motherhood. In addition to the women's striking differences in skin tone, the white mother wears a black skirt that sets off the paleness of her baby's skin, and the Black mother's lap is covered by a white cloth (which she has to keep pulling back into place), presumably intended to emphasize her baby's dark complexion. One could imagine this emblematic shot standing as a film in itself a few years earlier, with its humorous, staged display of babies and Black/white difference.

The combination of strategies used to render Blackness in *Mixed Babies* is unique, but it suggests the numerous, simultaneous impulses at work in preclassical cinema's overall attempts to render racial difference. Although Blackness can be performed in different modes, even within the same film, the overdetermination of skin color is almost always primary. Preclassical cinema insists upon the visibility of racial difference in part because it is responding to fears about racial mixing (social and sexual), particularly in increasingly multiracial, modern urban environments. As I will describe in more detail in the final section of this chapter, *Mixed Babies* and other baby-switching films represent the city as a place where races can mix in unprecedented ways, and where substitutions can take place because race might not be instantly recognizable. Preclassical cinema registers anxieties about interracial interactions, including most notably the threat of miscegenation, by playing with Black visibility, even as it almost always marks Black skin as dark as possible.

Uneasiness about misreading Black/white difference is evident in the rarity of light-skinned Black characters in preclassical films. Fair-skinned Blacks (who might be interpreted as racially mixed) are repressed in the earliest films; they do not appear regularly until the transitional period, when their appearance (the way they look *and* why they are featured) can be narrativized and explained, usually in a drama set during the remote but familiar context of slavery. There are, however, at least two exceptions to this practice that are notable for the way in which the inclusion of light-skinned Black characters signals diversity among African Americans within the context of Black nightlife and recreation. They are used to evoke the dangers and attractions associated with venues such as the café and the saloon.

Some of the earliest light-skinned Black characters I have located appear in a nightclub scene in the 1907 film *Fights of Nations* (American Mutoscope & Biograph, directed by G. W. Bitzer), in which various ethnic pairs are shown fighting in comic and dramatic situations.[24] This film is mentioned in histories of Black film representation because of the way it initially situates Black stereotypes among those of other ethnic groups (hot-blooded Mexican versus Spaniard; bribing Jews; drunk Irishmen), only to exclude Blacks from its allegorical finale, in which representatives from the other groups (and one Native American) are reconciled beneath U.S. flags, an American eagle, and Uncle Sam.[25] This aspect of the film seems to support the view that American cinema devalued Blacks more than white ethnic groups in its assimilationist project; but the film's rare depiction of skin color diversity among African Americans remains unexplored. The Black episode, set in Harlem but titled "Sunny Africa," presents a love triangle in which a light-skinned and a dark-skinned man compete for the affections of a dark-skinned woman. The episode features Black actors of a range of skin tones (instead of white actors in blackface) and seems in this regard to

FIGURE 13. This "Harlem" scene features a rare range of African American skin tones, if only to center on a characteristic Black dance performance, and finally to pit light-skinned and dark-skinned male rivals against each other. *Fights of Nations* (American Mutoscope & Biograph, dir. G. W. Bitzer). Library of Congress, Motion Picture, Broadcasting and Recorded Sound Division.

deviate from traditions of representing Blackness as derived from blackface minstrelsy. But before the climactic fight, the light-skinned leading man performs an extended dance routine (with the accompaniment of a light-skinned piano player), an attraction intended to impress the girl as well as the film's audience, which is primed to expect a racially characteristic display similar to the ethnic stereotypes in the other episodes (fig. 13). The Harlem setting of this scene is significant because it references a visibly diverse Black urban community that is not only becoming well known for its nightlife and entertainment but also becoming potentially threatening in its changing relation to whiteness. That is, not only do the light-skinned figures possibly have "white blood" in their veins, but they (and the Black community they inhabit) could attempt to follow the immigration pattern suggested by the other groups presented in the film. In this way, the light-skinned figures signal the dangers of blurring the social and biological lines between whiteness and Blackness, particularly in urban contexts.

Similar anxieties are apparent in Griffith's *The Girls and Daddy* (Biograph, 1909), another rare depiction of a light-skinned Black character in preclassical cinema outside of a plantation setting. Susan Courtney describes how the film's Black intruder, who will break into the home of two white girls when their father is away, is coded as a mulatto. He is introduced in a Black bar among other patrons who are all noticeably darker, and where "a sign on the wall advertising an upcoming dance nominates 'Black/Tans.'"[26] Courtney reads this character, along with a light-skinned female character who enters the bar "ostentatiously," as signs of an "ambitious" and "dangerous" mulatto class whose members "both imply past acts of miscegenation and forebode future ones." Courtney also observes that publicity for *The Girls and Daddy* includes no mention of these "mulatto" characters; the same omission occurs in advertisements for *Fights of Nations.*[27] In both cases details about the featured "colored element" are not foregrounded in the films or their advertising. Although the source of these figures' (cinematically unique) light skin (i.e., family racial background) is not explained, perhaps audiences were expected to link certain characteristics or attach narrative significance to their visual presentation. For instance, perhaps both films use skin color to visually set apart the main Black characters (the thief, the competing lover) upon their initial appearance; and maybe in *The Fight of Nations* the Black lead's anomalous complexion helps to motivate the tensions that flare up between him and his darker-skinned rival. Although both films acknowledge some measure of diversity among Black people by picturing differences in Black skin color, in the end they reinscribe general attributes associated with Blackness (e.g., musicality, criminality, violence) despite the characters' visual exceptionality, and they link these characters with dangerous expressions of Black assertiveness, freedom in public/recreational spaces, and upward mobility. Even when white ethnic groups are ridiculed for similar attributes (the other scenes in *Fights of Nations*; white villains in other Griffith films), the imperatives of exclusion, segregation, and punishment are more pronounced for Black characters.

The problem of marking racially mixed characters seems to be less pressing in plantation films produced during the 1910s that, as mentioned previously, feature a number of light-skinned Black characters (played by white actors). Unlike the films just described, antebellum dramas like *A Southern Romance of Slavery Days* (Lubin, 1908), *The Debt* (Rex, 1912), and *The Octoroon* (Kalem, 1913) explain the origins of their mixed-race characters, implicitly or explicitly, as the result of interracial intimacy engendered by the peculiar institution (i.e., sexual liaisons between Black [female] slaves and white [male] masters). Many of these films encourage the viewer to feel some degree of sympathy for (if not identification with) mixed-race characters by presenting them in "tragic" tales of family separation or doomed romantic love. Although some of these characters are described in production company catalogues as being visually interchangeable with white characters *(The Debt, In Slavery Days)*, which might threaten the biological rationale for racial hierarchies, their appearance is fully explicated within the narrative.

For example, the visual binary of white and Black is complicated in *The Coward* (Triangle, 1915), a Civil War drama directed by Thomas Ince. The film advertised that it featured "a Negro servant" who is played in "darkened down" makeup as opposed to blackface.[28] This strategy suggests that the makers sought to improve on long-standing theatrical blackface conventions, even those associated with the ostensibly more sympathetic, abolitionist minstrelsy tradition, toward a standard of increased realism. This method of "darkened down" Black representation is indicative of the cinema's move toward classical narrative, in which theatrical conventions are no longer deemed best for conveying realism. Each of these exceptions to traditional representations of "Blackness" points up the theatricality and unrealistic uniformity of preclassical cinema's dark-skinned/blackface norm.

The obvious, self-conscious artificiality of cinematic Blackness is perhaps foregrounded most clearly in the significant number of moments in preclassical cinema in which a white character is "blackened" within the context of the narrative and then interacts with "Black" characters played by white actors in blackface. For example, in *The Subpoena Server* (American Mutoscope & Biograph, 1906), a blackfaced white actor playing an African American railroad porter helps to put blackface makeup on a white character in need of a disguise (fig. 14). In *A Close Call* (Biograph, 1912), a Black gardener played by a white actor in blackface exchanges hats with a white street performer who has applied blackface to enhance his act (fig. 15). In these films we see the interactions of two blackfaced white actors, one playing a character who is "really" white, and one who is supposed to be "really" Black. But their skin color and hair texture look exactly the same—they wear identical costumes of blackface minstrelsy. How were audiences expected to read the difference between these characters?[29] As I will discuss in more detail toward the end of this chapter, the plot of *A Close Call* relies on the indistinguishability of these two characters for whites within the story, but not for white viewers. I mention *A Close Call* here, though, because its use of blackface demonstrates an overwhelming

FIGURE 14. A "Black" waiter (played by a white actor in blackface) applies a blackface disguise on a white man on the run. *The Subpoena Server* (American Mutoscope & Biograph, 1906). Library of Congress, Motion Picture, Broadcasting and Recorded Sound Division.

confidence in the preclassical film viewer's ability to read crucial racial distinctions across multiple modes of Black representation.

Films like *The Subpoena Server* and *A Close Call* also show how preclassical cinema enables the viewer to confirm essentialist notions of Blackness even after it has exposed its own process of fabricating Blackness for the screen (i.e., showing whites apply the blackface mask). Although preclassical cinema features various and overlapping racial representational techniques, viewers are always supposed to be able to recognize Blackness, particularly when characters within the diegesis do not. As my later discussion of racial masquerade as a plot device will suggest, many of these films depend on the ability (or inability) of white characters to recognize "real" and "fake" Blackness at crucial moments, constructing Black identity as a complex negotiation between authenticity and fabrication or performance. Preclassical films openly play with this ambiguity and make the confusion itself a locus of fascination.

FIGURE 15. Jasper the gardener (left, in checkered pants) reluctantly provides the perfect top hat to complete the white salesman's impromptu minstrel costume. The Black and white characters wear the same blackface makeup. *A Close Call* (Biograph, 1912). Library of Congress, Motion Picture, Broadcasting and Recorded Sound Division.

I should also note that while white audiences were supposed to be able to read blackface as a representational convention, the scenarios in which these images were staged were still expected, at least by some viewers, to maintain some degree of narrative realism. For example, a reviewer of Edison's comedy *The Colored Stenographer* (1909) takes issue with the disrespectful treatment of the white "faithful stenographer" who is replaced by a Black scrubwoman, claiming that the film's comic situations "are none of them true and they are but poor attempts at fun."[30] In another generic context, Selig's temperance drama *The House of His Master* (1912) is criticized for its unconvincing rendition of the well-worn tale of Black sacrifice for white familial stability: "The situation seems rather carelessly (easily) developed, and fails to come to grips with real life more than once or twice."[31] The film's writer is criticized for creating a "salable scenario" rather than a "work of art," suggesting that although *The House of His*

*Master* features a fundamentally unrealistic mode of representation (blackface), by this time films are nonetheless expected to meet aesthetic expectations of artistry and realist credibility as distinct from theatrical practices. These kinds of criticisms suggest some of the ways in which a complex web of generic, stylistic, and performative expectations produced Black images that were highly variable. These films do not conform to a consistent set of expectations of Black behavior on the part of either white characters in the films or white audiences. This variability points to a diversity (if not flexibility) in the ways in which Blackness could be read by the imagined viewers of these films. I will now turn to films that seek to secure white visual mastery over knowable Black subjects by using the cinematic apparatus to "expose" Black difference and inferiority as natural facts.

## Observing "Natural" Blackness: Voyeurism and Surveillance

Early cinema features a number of Black representations in ostensibly nonstaged, unrehearsed scenes in which Black people "act natural." Thomas Cripps suggests that early nonfiction "actualities," like Edison's *Colored Troops Disembarking* (1898), present more realistic portraits of Blacks than later narrative films because at the time they were produced, "moviemaking consisted of no more than a single camera upon a tripod, recording the objective reality before it without artifice, staging or editing."[32] In Cripps's account, it was the institutional division of labor (scriptwriting, directing, and editing), and the increasing emphasis on contriving fictional narratives and characters, that brought about racist depictions of Blacks in the burgeoning cinema of narrative integration. For Cripps, the "unformed image" of Blacks in early film reflected an open, "primitive" mode of representation in which an "authentic," unaltered Blackness could reach the screen. In this way, Cripps does not acknowledge the structuring and "typing" of Blackness that was already being practiced in these early nonfiction films, such as the intended comedic effect of Black baby-washing films or the colonialist objectification of "natives" in Caribbean travelogues.

Following Cripps's lead, we must consider the alterity of these very early films in relation to the treatments of race in narrative films of the later transitional and classical periods. But we must also take into account the representational models and historical circumstances that influenced the production of these early, "nonfiction" images, while avoiding the pitfalls of simply assessing their "authenticity" or verisimilitude. As I have argued earlier in this chapter, even these earliest images are heavily informed by Black representations in literature, vaudeville, newspapers, and cartoons and by Black iconography on postcards and other commercial products, among other sources. Early cinema immediately adapted "Black" activities like the cakewalk, buck-and-wing, and other dances, as well as broad grinning, watermelon eating, and chicken stealing to the screen because these films sought to provide their (white) audiences with proven, familiar imagery and forms of entertainment. Many of these very early films are often classified as "nonfiction" because they are shot on location or lack formal plot structures. As Charles Musser has shown, however, the publicity materials for many early nonfiction films demonstrate that racist discourses regularly made their way into ostensibly "objective" Black cinematic representations.[33] The subjects featured in these films, the locations in which they are shot, and the ways they are framed are all conscious choices made by the filmmakers, creating images that are neither simply authentic nor reflective of a uniform white gaze or consistent views of Blackness.

Even though many early filmmakers claimed otherwise, nonfiction films did not function simply to educate or to introduce new information about Black life to white viewers. Instead, they typically provided yet another opportunity to rearticulate racist discourses. However, early film audiences probably did not fully buy into the notion that these films were purely objective or authentic, but rather read them as views of real-life subjects that were staged and presented in an entertaining manner. With this in mind, I contend that the appeal of many early nonfiction films (and, as I will show, fiction films as well) was the way in which they were structured to enable fantasies about voyeuristically observing Black activities that were typically not visible to a white gaze (such as the activities of Blacks in other parts of the world or in private, concealed spaces closer to home). This "surveillance" impulse functions as one of the most obvious ways in which preclassical cinema seems to limit the scope of Black character and potential within the white viewing imagination. But as steeped as these films are in white supremacist discourses, their explicit and implicit racism takes many shapes to counter the modern indications of Black diversity, progress, and returns of the gaze that they also acknowledge and display.

In the previous chapter, I suggested that Laura Mulvey's elaboration of the complex structure of looks in the cinema—the looks of the camera, the spectator, and the characters—suggests ways to denaturalize early Black images. Here, I want to explore how Mulvey's breakdown of cinematic looks helps to explain how a racialized voyeuristic look in preclassical cinema addresses many levels of white curiosity and anxiety about racially marked "others." I refer to the voyeuristic look in a modified sense here because I want to suggest that the visual pleasure voyeurism provides in the face of the castrating threat of woman in classical cinema bears some relation to the look of surveillance in response to Blackness in early cinema. Of course, almost every mode of cinematic representation and address can be described as enacting some form of voyeurism on the part of the viewer and exhibitionism or active complicity on the part of the figures on screen. I invoke these operations here because I want to describe how preclassical films work to enable a sense of white, visual mastery over Black objects by confirming their knowability, policing their difference, and exposing their transgressions despite opening up many potential holes in these processes, such as displaying the self-consciousness of the makers and subjects.

One of the primary frameworks in which early nonfiction films depict Black people is within the context of performing some kind of work, such as coaling ships and picking and spinning cotton, as soldiers, and even, I would argue, as performers (usually dancers). In many of these films, the camera seems to act as an ostensibly neutral observer, recording what Blacks would do naturally whether or not whites observed them. For example, the series of films recorded by the Edison company during Caribbean cruises in September 1902 and April 1903 show Blacks (mostly women) performing domestic tasks such as bathing their children (*Native Woman Washing a Negro Baby in Nassau, BI* [Edison, April 1903]) and washing clothes (*Native Women Washing Clothes at Fort de France* [Edison, September 1902], *Native Women Washing Clothes at St. Vincent, BWI* [Edison, April 1903]).[34] Certainly these films, like other travelogues, depict aspects of life in foreign locations in order to educate audiences, exposing them to peoples and places that many will probably never encounter firsthand.[35] The series of films illustrating work performed by Martinican women is advertised as providing "a clear idea of the manual labor performed by the sex and other native customs . . . showing how the native women are compelled to toil for a living."[36] The "authenticity" of such scenes is complicated by the range of looking relations that travelogues can elicit. As E. Ann Kaplan has observed, travel creates conditions for exchanges of looks that not only raise consciousness of national identities but also provoke "conscious attention to gender and racial difference."[37] On the one hand, these films might encourage a sense of sympathy and identification, particularly from white women viewers (watching these films in the United States or perhaps in Europe), who may recognize analogous aspects of female "toil" from their own lives. On the other hand, these films reinforce notions of Black suitability for manual labor as ubiquitous and universal. By presenting the observed Black cultures as primitive in comparison with the "modern" cultures of the observers (where, presumably, women are not "compelled to toil"), these films attempt to posit immutable racial and cultural differences between the Black subjects and white viewers. These films thus would have complex implications for viewers in the United States, where black women were limited to domestic service (as maids, cooks, washerwomen) but, paradoxically, were also the objects of racist beliefs about Black uncleanliness.[38]

Such discourses, framed as Black domestic scenes, are also in play in the popular early genre of Black baby-washing films.[39] Poor Black hygiene was a prevalent stereotype, as well as a political issue, at the turn of the twentieth century. Booker T. Washington emphasized physical cleanliness as part of his program to uplift rural southern Blacks into productive roles in the New South. Preaching "the gospel of the toothbrush," Washington incorporated standards of personal cleanliness as a fundamental part of the educational system he developed at his Tuskegee Institute: "Absolute cleanliness of the body has been taught from the first."[40] Washington's emphasis on cleanliness was intended not only to instill students from poor, country districts with a new sense of self-respect but also to make them presentable and inoffensive to whites (e.g., neighboring townsfolk, visiting philanthropists). Washington was responding to long-standing associations between Blackness and filth, as evoked by Lubin's *Whitewashing a Colored Baby* (January 1903), which suggests that Blackness, like dirt, could be washed off. In the filmed versions of this joke, the depiction of Black mothers washing their babies indicates both Black desires to be "white" and the absurdity of this desire. Another selling point for these films was their visual juxtaposition of white suds and Black skin. A catalogue description of Edison's *A Morning Bath* (1896) notes: "This is a clear and distinct picture in which the contrast between the complexion of the bather and the white soapsuds is strongly marked. A very amusing and popular subject."[41] By deploying racist discourses and boasting cinematographic attractions, Black baby-washing films combine the aesthetic qualities of Black cinematic display and performance with the claims of presenting typical private scenes (e.g., mother-child interaction).

Nonfiction films that seem to acknowledge some measure of progress and aspiration within the Black world are frequently inflected with countering discourses that cushion the political potential of Black upward mobility. For example, two films—*A Muffin Lesson* and *Physical Training* (American

Mutoscope & Biograph, April 1903)—were shot at the Lincoln School in Washington, D.C., illustrating a variety of school activities for Black youth.[42] Although picturing classrooms full of Black students was certainly rare in early cinema, one might argue that showing them engaged in a cooking lesson and physical exercise supports limited views of Black talents and social roles. Images of these students reading or writing may not have seemed as visually interesting as the activities the filmmakers chose to capture. But by illustrating Black girls in training in the kitchen and "colored children taking exercise in the school-room, using their desks and chairs as apparatus," these films fail to evoke any academic instruction the students might also receive.[43] In addition, like most nonfiction films with Black subjects, *A Muffin Lesson* is described as a "somewhat amusing view," though there is nothing immediately comic suggested in the film's subject matter. These films demonstrate that while early cinema never completely abandons condescending treatment of Black subjects, it also appeals to white viewers by capturing and presenting scenes that seem to be novel and unfamiliar. In this way, many nonfiction films confirm stereotypes by enabling white viewers to seemingly happen upon them, by providing views of Black inferiority in new and unexpected contexts.

Among the new contexts, as I have already suggested, is the travelogue, which was presented with claims to scientific and educational value, as well as the entertainment of viewing unfamiliar landscapes and human types. For example, the bare-breasted women washing clothes in *Native Women Washing Clothes at St. Vincent, BWI*, suggest an erotic appeal contained within the film's ethnographic premise and enact a film-viewer relation that is voyeuristic in the more traditional sense. The type of voyeurism and visual mastery suggested in early nonfiction films is not the same as that which characterizes the classical cinema, in which the characters within the diegesis operate as if they are unaware of the viewer's gaze, as maintained by the taboo against the actor's look into the camera. Instead, performers in early films frequently look into the camera (in both nonfiction and fiction films). For example, in the extant prints of *Native Woman Washing a Negro Baby in Nassau, BI*, and *Native Women Washing Clothes at St. Vincent, BWI*, it is clear that the "natives" wash more vigorously upon receiving instructions from the invisible cameramen. After they begin to wash the baby and the clothes, they look up toward the camera and then scrub and lather with much more energy. In these films, the demonstration of the performers' awareness of the camera/audience does not preclude voyeuristic pleasures on the part of the viewer. Rather, there is a different mode of voyeurism at work, in which spectatorial pleasure derives from the object's more obvious exhibitionist behavior. The Black figures in these films do not simply act naturally but are presented as if they enjoy displaying themselves for the camera.

This kind of complicit Black exhibitionism can also be seen in *West Indian Girls in Native Dance* (Edison, April 1903), in which five St. Thomas youths look directly at the camera as they perform. Clearly, these girls are not captured unknowingly in the midst of their daily activities. They dance for the camera because the cameraman has solicited this "representative" form of cultural expression. In *Laughing Ben* (American Mutoscope & Biograph, May 1901), in close-up an elderly Black man with white hair and beard and few teeth talks and shakes his head with a wide grin. But this film and *On the Old Plantation/Cotton Spinning* (American Mutoscope & Biograph, May 1901), which were advertised as illustrating authentic southern types reminiscent of antebellum life, were both shot at the Pan-American Exhibition in Buffalo, New York, and were promoted as such. Thus these films contain a combination of authenticating and fabricating gestures—their close framing enables them to pose as "authentic" southern scenes (without taking in the context of the exhibition grounds), while their promotional discourses make it clear that these are already types on (live) display for a viewing public. These and other nonfiction films demonstrate that many early films did not disguise the viewers' or the subjects' awareness of their participation in a highly mediated representational exercise.

This would help to explain how nonfiction films could appeal to viewers even as they show unmistakable signs of manipulation on the part of the men behind the cameras or suggest hesitation or agency on the part of the filmed subjects. For example, the final moments of the single-shot film *Native Woman Washing a Negro Baby in Nassau, BI,* consist of a surprising camera movement in which the camera pans to the left from the main action at the washtub to reveal that a group of "native" children and women were watching the filming take place. But as the camera turns toward them, these onlookers flee from its moving gaze (fig. 16). Tom Gunning captures the complex interplay of looks in this otherwise typically condescending travelogue/baby-washing film when he observes that the "spectacle makers themselves become a spectacle, the tables turned with the camera's pivot," followed by "a sublime moment as this witnessing audience refuses to become a spectacle in turn and takes off, escaping the frame and the camera, running off into unimaged space."[44] But the exchange does not stop there. As the onlookers-turned-subjects flee from the moving lens, we see the cameraman's hat wipe across the bottom left edge of the frame as he gestures to the reluctant subjects to reenter the scene (fig. 17).

FIGURE 16. The camera makes an unexpected turn from its ethnographic subject, revealing a group of onlookers who quickly flee from the camera's gaze. *Native Woman Washing a Negro Baby in Nassau, BI* (Edison, 1903). Library of Congress, Motion Picture, Broadcasting and Recorded Sound Division.

The cameraman persists in trying to orchestrate the shot, and his efforts are visible to the spectator. This film demonstrates that the appeal of many nonfiction films lies not simply in the way they confirm Black stereotypes (as reflective of some externally verifiable "reality") but also in the display of their own efforts to stage these "nonfiction" scenes.

To be sure, this film's unusual ending was probably retained in part because it illustrates a frequent trope of colonialist discourse—natives fearful of modern, white technology. But along with this joke, we have the willingness of the film's primary subjects (who, as noted, look into the camera) and the persistent gaze of one of the "native" girls revealed by the camera's movement (who, unlike the others, decides not to flee the scene), illustrating two sides of the processes of looking and staging here. Although these Caribbean travelogues are structured by an unequal power relationship between their Black subjects and those who film/view them, they also demonstrate that those who seem to manipulate and benefit from the apparatus can be surprised by what it might reveal, including a return of their

FIGURE 17. The cameraman waves his hat in an effort to recompose the "natives" in his shot; one girl directly returns the camera's look. *Native Woman Washing a Negro Baby in Nassau, BI* (Edison, 1903). Library of Congress, Motion Picture, Broadcasting and Recorded Sound Division.

gaze. Maintaining the illusion of authorial and spectatorial control over the Black image is an ongoing process.

A white voyeuristic look is perhaps more conventionally structured in fiction films that explicitly enable fantasies of surveillance by constructing scenarios in which Black subjects are diegetically unaware of watching white eyes watching them. Many fiction films produced during this period situate the camera as a recorder of typical Black activities, which can catch Blacks stealing white property—most frequently chickens and watermelons—and then record their apprehension by whites within the diegesis. Notions that Blacks routinely engaged in criminal activities were widespread and dated back to slavery, but this stereotype was reanimated after emancipation, as southern racists argued that crime among Black people had escalated because their needs were no longer met by their masters and they were no longer being closely monitored.[45] This stereotype was so pervasive that numerous preclassical films do not feel compelled to show the criminal act but can imply Black criminality merely by showing Blacks enjoying items that they are assumed to have stolen (e.g., films in which Blacks eat watermelon) or by including criminality as a character trait that is purely incidental to the plot (e.g., in *The Snowman* [American Mutoscope & Biograph, 1908], as a frightened black man runs away from a moving snowman, he drops a sack full of chickens he presumably stole earlier, off camera). Even if Black characters are not shown in the act of stealing, various other aspects of their representation support the notion that Blacks are up to no good when whites are not able to see them.

Those early films that do show Blacks in the act of stealing frequently conclude with the thieves' violent punishment. In *The Chicken Thief* (American Mutoscope & Biograph, 1904), two Blacks are chased through the woods by a mob of gun-toting white farmers—one tries to escape with a bear trap biting into his ankle, the other "gets a charge of bird shot in a tender section of his anatomy."[46] In many ways, these cinematic scenes reproduce the dynamics of lynchings, which were common occurrences during this period. Practiced in the South and throughout the country, the lynching of African Americans (particularly men) served as a graphic warning to Black communities to remain in their subservient social, economic, and political positions. These films perform a function that is strikingly similar to "spectacle" lynchings, those less frequent but highly publicized, grotesque displays of torture and murder that were staged by and for large white crowds, sometimes numbering in the thousands. Like spectacle lynchings, which were frequently captured by cameras and sound recorders, films like *The Chicken Thief* serve as cathartic, entertaining, mass-mediated assertions of white supremacy.[47]

The sadistic pleasures of watching violent forms of Black punishment on screen are enhanced by other forms of visual pleasure provided by film as a medium. For example, advertising for *The Chicken Thief* celebrates its particularly impressive cinematographic, compositional, and projection quality. The Biograph catalogue boasts: "The opening scene is a triumph of photography, something that has never been done before; that is, a moving picture of the interior of a big hen-coop at night, showing over one hundred chickens asleep on the roosts as the thieves enter." And of further interest to exhibitors and audiences: "The film throughout is without a flaw photographically, and projects as steady as a lantern slide."[48] Seven years earlier, Edison's *Chicken Thieves* was also advertised as an aesthetic achievement of cinematic presentation:

> Both darkies start to run when the farmer and his hand appear in the foreground, one with a scythe and the other with a gun. Just as the marauders disappear 'round the corner, the farmer, back to, but still shown at life-size in

FIGURE 18. Inside the Black cabin, an extended dance performance (frontally oriented to the camera) before the eating of the stolen melons. *The Watermelon Patch* (Edison, 1905, dir. Edwin S. Porter). Film Studies Center, University of Chicago.

the picture, aims and fires twice. The smoke effect from the gun at this close range is startling and *beautiful,* and the entire picture is one of the best composed and most ingenious we have made [emphasis mine].[49]

Both of these films supplement the pleasures of reinscribing long-standing discourses on Black criminality and anti-Black violence with the celebration of the visual marvels of moving picture technology.

Multiple forms of visual pleasure are combined in Edison's *The Watermelon Patch* (1905), which draws on stereotypes, previous modes of Black cinematic representation, and the elaboration of cinematic time and space within and between shots. In *The Watermelon Patch* the camera allows white viewers to witness Black criminality, as well as scenes of Black domestic life (performed by "genuine negroes"). In the film, directed by Edwin S. Porter, several Black men steal watermelons, then reach safety in a modest cabin filled with other Blacks (men, women, and children). They quickly forget all danger and celebrate by dancing and devouring the illicit melon (figs. 18 and 19). The series of shots illustrating the Black celebra-

FIGURE 19. Devouring the illicit melon. *The Watermelon Patch* (Edison, 1905, dir. Edwin S. Porter). Film Studies Center, University of Chicago.

tion replicates a number of previous, extremely popular one-shot films that displayed Black dance performance (discussed earlier in this chapter), including numerous films featuring the cakewalk.[50] Some scenes also replicate one-shot watermelon-eating films (also described earlier, such as *A Watermelon Feast* [American Mutoscope, 1896], *Watermelon Contest* [Edison, June 1900], and *Who Said Watermelon?* [Lubin, 1902]). Unlike these earlier films, however, *The Watermelon Patch* connects these scenes, and several others, to produce a longer, narrative structure. The dancing and watermelon-eating shots are framed by a lengthy opening chase sequence, "through fields and over fences," and a closing punitive gag involving the Blacks inside the cabin and their white pursuers on the outside.[51] The film's elaboration of these narratively motivated spatiotemporal relationships produces a complex dynamic of racialized looking in which the visibility of the Black figures shifts back and forth between the voyeuristic viewer and the whites within the film—that is, until their looks are joined through an awkward but telling device to force the Black characters out of hiding.

FIGURE 20. As smoke enters their cabin, the panicked watermelon eaters try to flee through a small window. *The Watermelon Patch* (Edison, 1905, dir. Edwin S. Porter). Film Studies Center, University of Chicago.

At the film's comic climax, the Blacks' watermelon-eating party is interrupted by the arrival of white farmers with dogs. The farmers board up the cabin window and door, then place a piece of wood on top of the chimney. Smoke fills the cabin, forcing the inhabitants to reveal themselves to their white pursuers.[52] As they try to flee, one of the Black characters, a fat woman, opens a window at the back of the set and tries to crawl through it (fig. 20). Apparently her girth gets her stuck halfway, and a Black man and woman grab her legs as they dangle frantically for about twenty seconds, her stockings and petticoats exposed to the camera. But when Porter cuts to the film's final shot, an exterior view of the cabin, we see the window open (again), and the same Black woman slides through in one quick move, followed by the others.

The temporal discontinuity between the inside and outside views of this action (an indication of preliminary gestures toward classical continuity editing) enables Porter to tell different kinds of jokes based on the looks that coalesce around the figure of the large Black "mammy." The first joke, depicted from inside the cabin, "exposes" her typically desexed body in a racist reworking of popular early films in which white women's underwear is exposed both to the camera and to a salacious white male character.[53] Another joke is conveyed in the way in which her body prevents the other Blacks from escaping—the spectacle of dancing and melon-eating darkies is replaced by the spectacle of Black panic and entrapment. A third joke, illustrated from the second vantage point, outside of the cabin, joins the looks of the white farmers with that of the viewer, as the stream of exiting Blacks is comically swatted and kicked as they run out of the frame. Thus, *The Watermelon Patch* first enables the viewer to witness how Blacks behave behind closed doors (surveillance), then orchestrates their exposure to white onlookers within the narrative, terminating the Blacks' covert celebration of their successful procurement of white property. Here the mammy figure works not only as a visual bridge between shots but also as a visual gag that brings together white looks in order to disavow any Black threat to the proper social order. Thus Black criminality, sexuality, and autonomy are captured and contained by the film's methods of Black concealment and exposure, which in turn serve its delineation of temporal, spatial, and looking relations.

In fiction and nonfiction films, preclassical cinema places Blackness under staged surveillance as one strategy to demonstrate Blacks' natural inferiority and predictability. But this strategy also reveals serious concerns about Black progress out of familiar stereotypical roles by illustrating a high degree of self-consciousness in the construction and performance of these images. The many formal and stylistic strategies preclassical cinema uses to mark Black figures (by using either Black performers or whites in blackface) and to place a "white" viewer in a position of voyeuristic mastery over the Black image demonstrate the importance of making Blackness visible, if not always consistent. In the final section of this chapter, I examine films that explore the dangers that can ensue when Blackness is not properly recognized.

## Watching Out for Interracial Intimacy:
## Substitutions, Masquerade

While many early films encourage a spectatorial posture of surveillance, indicating white interest in, and anxieties about, what Blacks do in their own segregated environments, another large group of Black images in preclassical cinema involves the unexpected entrance of Black bodies into previously closed or highly regulated white spaces. These films are often set in

FIGURE 21. Large, Black, and gaudy, Nellie arrives by train and heads to meet her new white employers. *Nellie the Beautiful Housemaid* (Vitagraph, 1908). Library of Congress, Motion Picture, Broadcasting and Recorded Sound Division.

urban environments, where long-standing racial hierarchies risked being refigured as African Americans migrated to cities with a new, postbellum, post-Reconstruction measure of social confidence and independence. This growing Black presence created increased opportunities for interracial mixing, as well as interracial mix-ups.

Preclassical cinema frequently figures the "problem" of modern, urbanized Negroes around their changing and/or improper relation to their roles as laborers. Preclassical films register the fact that African Americans circulate more freely in the marketplace and in various work spaces. In Edison's *The Colored Stenographer* (1909), for instance, the skirt-chasing white boss switches the beautiful white typist he has recently hired with the Black scrubwoman to make his wife believe he has given up his womanizing ways. But the Black woman's reluctance to give up her newly acquired position at the film's conclusion suggests the problems that can arise when Blacks display increased assertiveness in the workplace. In *Nellie the Beautiful Housemaid* (Vitagraph, 1908), three elderly white men place an ad in the newspaper for a maid, which is answered, much to their surprise, by a Black woman (fig. 21).[54] These characters stand in sharp contrast to the devoted Black maids and butlers who appear in nostalgic antebellum films of the transitional period. Such faithful, servile characters display undying loyalty and a commitment to preserving white families, facilitating white romances, and defending white supremacy, sometimes sacrificing their own lives for the Confederacy.[55] What is striking about many of these plantation films is the level of intimacy these "Black" and white characters share. This reflects the almost/often familial bonds that characterized many relationships between masters and their slaves. However, many other films produced during this period illustrate the dangers of the interracial intimacy of servant/employer relationships now that African Americans no longer feel tied to a subservient "place" in American society. While Black subservience is easily read and understood in antebellum contexts, many films set in contemporary times show that the workforce and related public spaces were opening up in new ways to African Americans, particularly Black women, who were seeking increased social and occupational opportunities.

During the decade before the massive Great Migration of southern Blacks to northern cities around World War I, African Americans began a slow but substantial migration to cities south and north. John Hope Franklin notes that although African American men often had difficulty finding employment in cities during this period, Black women "easily found employment as household servants," which "attract[ed] a larger number of women than men to the cities."[56] The Black maid, then, was a common, if not conspicuous, figure in the turn-of-the-century urban landscape. Therefore, it is not surprising that she surfaces in a number of early films characterizing contemporary city life.

For example, in *A Bucket of Cream Ale*, a Black maid (in blackface) pours a glass of ale for her white male employer (a Dutchman, according to the studio description), but it is all froth. As he expresses his dissatisfaction with her pouring, she sneaks a few sips from the bucket behind his back. When he catches her, he throws his glass of ale in her face. As he enjoys a hearty laugh, she responds by dumping the bucket of ale over his head (see fig. 10). This short comedy clearly pokes fun at both ethnic types, the Dutchman and the colored maid. It also contains a generally popular slapstick display. But this scene is also humorous because the Black maid's behavior is so exceptional given her subordinate status as employee, and so unlikely given her social identity as a Black woman. Perhaps we can read a new kind of Black assertiveness in her retaliation. What is clear is that her behavior takes the antiauthoritarian premise of many early comedies (chil-

FIGURE 22. The misdirected kiss in *What Happened in the Tunnel* (Edison, 1903). Film Studies Center, University of Chicago.

dren versus adults, wives versus husbands) a step further by suggesting the possibility that Blacks—a subordinate population these films never directly address—are forgetting their proper, subservient place.[57] Her employer (and presumably the viewer) is so busy laughing at her, expecting her to accept her role as the butt of the joke, that he fails to see her vengeance coming.

Black maids also surface in an important set of films in which white men accidentally kiss them instead of the white women these maids serve. In films like *What Happened in the Tunnel* (Edison, 1903), *The Mis-Directed Kiss* (American Mutoscope & Biograph, 1904), and *A Kiss in the Dark* (American Mutoscope & Biograph, 1904), the proximity of these Black maids to whites is supposed to be rigidly circumscribed by their labor function, as it had been for centuries under slavery. In these films, however, white men's vision is obscured (by their lack of glasses, by the darkness in a tunnel, etc.), and they are unknowingly tricked into kissing Black women (fig. 22). This racist joke works on a number of levels. The white men react with disgust, as Black women are clearly inferior and completely undesirable substitutes for white women. Cinematically, these comic situations are staged as visual gags—it is ridiculous that these white men cannot see the overdetermined markers of Blackness (darkness of skin, costume) that are immediately apparent to the spectator.

For obvious reasons, these films have attracted a great deal of critical attention from feminist film scholars. Miriam Hansen and Judith Mayne point out that they stage a reversal of the male gaze at the woman as object.[58] The two women turn the objectifying male look against him and share both a look and a laugh at his gullibility. Lynn Kirby argues that this shared look/laugh further supports the film's racist gag: "The women can laugh at the man because everyone can laugh at the black woman—an assumption entirely taken for granted by the film and the society in which it was produced."[59] Lauren Rabinovitz adds that depictions of men losing their "visual mastery" are actually quite conventional during this period. Citing this group of films, she asserts that "what is important is how widespread and exemplary is this syntactical employment of gendered, classed, and racial elements for the empowerment, not of a generalized but of a highly particular kind of female gaze"—that is, a gaze of desire and pleasure.[60] Rabinovitz speaks primarily of the white female gaze here. But is the Black woman's gaze completely recuperated in these scenarios? I would add to previous feminist critiques questions about how we might account for the ways in which changing racial arrangements (i.e., Blacks as confident city dwellers, as owners of their own labor) figure into the representation of intimate relationships between the white mistresses and their Black maids in these films, as well as others in which Black women subvert traditional racial, gender, and labor relationships.

For example, Hansen notes that What Happened in the Tunnel ends with "the maid's direct glance at the camera suggest[ing] not only that she was not merely a prop but that she, rather than her mistress, might have authorized the substitution."[61] This reading suggests that Black women characters may enjoy a significant measure of knowing confidence in these scenarios, despite attempts to render them simply as objects. However, the catalogue descriptions of these films stress the agency of the white women, not the Black women, in these substitutions. The Edison summary of What Happened in the Tunnel states, "Upon emerging he is hugging and kissing the colored maid, the [white] young lady having changed seats with her while in the tunnel, much to the young man's disgust" (emphasis mine). The description of A Kiss in the Dark points out that "she [the white woman] plays a joke on him [the suitor] by causing a colored maid to take her place" (emphasis mine).[62] Although catalogue descriptions rarely correspond exactly to what we see in the films, these extrafilmic materials tell us a great deal about how these films were expected to be read. In these cases, we must ask why is it that these filmmakers seem perfectly willing to stage reversals of white male-female looking relations but are reluctant to ascribe agency to the Black women who enable these substitutions, especially when this agency seems to be so apparent in the films themselves?

Eileen Bowser notes the suggestion of Black female agency in these films when she observes, in her extensive viewing of racial identity gag films, that "the black woman is usually quite amused at the consternation of the white person who has made the mistake. If not amused, the black woman may be indignant. I have not seen one example in which the black woman appears to have been embarrassed or humiliated by the error."[63] What accounts for this lack of embarrassment on the part of these Black women characters? I would argue that they are depicted as if they are enjoying or participating knowingly in these switches (even though officially they are not supposed to) because in doing so they speak of and to a new set of racial problems created by African American social and geographic mobility. For example, in her reading of *What Happened in the Tunnel,* Susan Courtney points out the significance of the action taking place on a train, which served both as the locus for the legalized segregation of public accommodations (*Plessy v. Ferguson,* 1896) and as the primary mode of transportation of southern Black migrants to northern cities. Thus, like the cinema itself, the train as a public space and as a relatively new technology "come[s] to signify mobility and constraint, play and rigidification."[64] The transgressive maids in *What Happened* and other early films perform and are performed upon in ways that suggest that African Americans, like white women, are falling out of the personal and social control of white men and, therefore, pose threats to traditional gender and racial hierarchies.[65] Although the Black maids in these films are supposed to function simply as vehicles for a joke between white men and women, their assertive mediating presence puts the problem of seeing Blackness squarely within the films' discourses on white female empowerment, white male sexual desire, and the maintenance of a white-controlled social order.[66]

Clearly, the threat of miscegenation underwrites the comic operations of these films, indicating how proper (i.e., segregated, hierarchical) interracial relationships can be subverted in white public and private life when Blacks are not appropriately recognized and monitored. For instance, many of the films that depict interracial kissing take place in settings in which distinctions between public and private space are blurred. *A Kiss in the Dark* details the Romeo-like courtship of a man on the street and a woman inside her home via the window. *What Happened in the Tunnel* takes place on a sparse-looking train, a public space where the white couple (or, rather, the interracial trio) appears to experience a certain measure of privacy. These films suggest that the boundaries between white public and private spaces could now be blurred and transgressed by Black people, potentially creating unpleasant interracial interactions.[67]

Taking miscegenation anxieties a step further, the popular comic plot of Black-white baby switching explores the dangerous implications of breaches in the distinction between public and private spaces and in traditional social hierarchies. In films like *Mixed Babies* (American Mutoscope & Biograph, 1908) and *Mixed Colors* (Pathé, 1913), babies are switched when their caretakers are distracted, much like the unforeseen switches of Black and white female love interests.[68] Although there are significant variations in the plots and settings for baby-switching scenarios, the comic, surprising appearance of a Black baby where a white one is expected gives the general impression that social controls are not working properly and that embarrassing interracial mix-ups can take place by pure accident or prankster design. These dangers are particularly acute in films that are set in the city.

Many baby-switching films demonstrate that both traditional racial and gender roles are changing in ways that threaten the stability of the white family and, by extension, the social order. For instance, in *Mixed Babies*, mothers check their babies at the door of a New York City department store as they enter to shop during a big sale. One notable element in *Mixed Babies* is the extreme confidence displayed by the Black woman shopper (played by a white actor in blackface), who aggressively grabs for bargains and clearly holds her own in a predominantly white environment (fig. 23). The mothers are so preoccupied with their purchases that they do not notice that the claim tags have been switched on their baby carriages (by a young prankster) and that they take the wrong infants home. In *Mixed Babies* the white mother/shopper accidentally brings a Black baby home in part, it seems, because she makes the questionable decision to go shopping just after acquiring her new white baby from the orphanage. Presumably unable to bear a child of her own, the white woman adopts a baby in a speedy transaction after seeing a notice in the newspaper. Here the baby carriage is likened to a shopping cart, and the modern urban white woman is mocked for becoming distracted from what should be her natural domestic duties and priorities.

Although some of these films blame the switches on white women who fail to fulfill their maternal or nursing functions properly (e.g., the flirtatious white nannies in *Mixed Colors* and *A Close Call* who take their eyes off their white charges), in several others the appearance of a Black baby

FIGURE 23. The department store manager tries to settle an argument between a white and a Black female shopper. *Mixed Babies* (American Mutoscope & Biograph, 1908). Library of Congress, Motion Picture, Broadcasting and Recorded Sound Division.

exposes the dishonesty of white bachelors. In *The Valet's Wife* (American Mutoscope & Biograph, 1908), New York playboy Reggie Van Twiler must produce a wife and child to substantiate the stories he has been telling his benefactor uncle.[69] Unfortunately, the nurse who is dispatched to the orphanage to procure a baby brings home a Black one, exposing Reggie's deception. In these films, the unexpected appearance of Black babies illustrates the potential confusion that can ensue in a modern, urban, multiracial environment. Such babies are the proverbial "niggers in the woodpile" that would have been familiar but disavowed in southern and antebellum contexts. When whites in contemporary and urban settings fail to carry out their proper social, family, and occupational roles (i.e., responsible mothers, fathers/husbands, caregivers, inheritors), they risk misrecognizing, and being surprised by, crucial racial differences.

Finally, misrecognitions of Blackness are staged in films in which white characters are blackened in a variety of narrative contexts.[70] These films are notable because they represent the process of blacking up, as distinct from the illusionist use of blackface found in most other films produced during this period. What is more, they suggest that the risks of fabricating and misrecognizing Blackness far outweigh any potential benefits, such as a better understanding of the struggles of those who cannot wash off their Blackness. In some films, whites deliberately blacken themselves to avoid unpleasant situations. For example, in *Advertising for a Wife* (Pathé, 1910), a young white man blackens himself when his ad for a wife is answered by a mob of anxious would-be brides; in *The Subpoena Server* (discussed earlier in this chapter), a wealthy white man disguises himself as a Black railroad porter to evade the server. However, plots in which Blackness serves as a (temporarily) effective disguise seem to be few in number compared with those in which whites are blackened unknowingly or unwillingly (i.e., when they are drunk or asleep) with much more comic and negative consequences. In films like *Drawing the Color Line* (Edison, 1909), *Burnt Cork* (Vitagraph, 1912), *Black and White* (Crystal, 1913), *A Change of Complexion* (Crystal, 1914), and *A Mix-Up in Black* (Edison, 1916), white characters experience race prejudice, even from members of their own families, until the "Black" mask is discovered and removed.[71] In some ways, these representations of crossing the color line reinforce notions of essential racial difference by rendering the act of boundary crossing humorous and unthinkable in the real world. I would also argue, however, that these films illustrate an open recognition of the virulent racism running rampant in American culture, complicating the essentialist premises on which their humor is based.

For example, in the comedy *A Close Call* (discussed briefly in the section on blackface earlier in this chapter), a white banjo player who performs in blackface is almost lynched by an angry white mob that mistakes him for the disgruntled Black gardener Jasper, who has been falsely accused of kidnapping a white baby girl. At the climax of the film, our blackfaced hero has a noose placed around his neck, is marched to a tree, and is about to be strung up before his innocence and true identity are revealed (fig. 24). Significantly, the banjo player is mistaken for the impertinent Negro gardener when he begins to flirt with a white woman on the street, a moment in which he seems to have forgotten that he wears blackface. It is this combination of purported offenses against white womanhood/girlhood that necessitates his capture and lynching. Thus, lynching, rape, and interracial sexual desire are clearly connected in this film and are worked into a farcical scenario in which the violence and pervasiveness of white racism take on different meanings than in Griffith's epic, *The Birth of a Nation*, which mobilizes similar themes and scenarios. Whereas *The Birth of a Nation* urgently calls white supremacy to action to oppose Black social, political, and

FIGURE 24. Mistaken for a Black kidnapper, the blackfaced white salesman is nearly lynched. *A Close Call* (Biograph, 1912). Library of Congress, Motion Picture, Broadcasting and Recorded Sound Division.

sexual threats, *A Close Call* illustrates the fatal errors that white racism can make, turning white mob rule into a comic situation with a happy ending—the white child returns home, the white banjo player is vindicated.

*A Close Call* brings together many of the key issues concerning Black representation treated in this chapter—multiple uses of blackface, presumptions of Black criminality, representations of interracial social and labor relations, and concerns about interracial intimacy. Most significantly, it illustrates how preclassical cinema figures the extreme dangers of racial transgression and misrecognition, and the complex ways in which these films locate white viewer identification and sympathy in relation to "Black" images. *A Close Call* features two white actors who play "Black" roles—one consistently throughout the film (as Jasper), the other only temporarily (as the banjo player who applies blackface). As I argued earlier, viewers were expected to remain fully aware of the white identities behind blackfaced characters, to facilitate their identification with the blackfaced characters, and to understand that transgressive Black roles (such as the predatory Gus and Silas Lynch in *The Birth of a Nation*) are safely within the protective custody of white actors. But when Jasper/the banjo player is falsely accused of threatening white girlhood/womanhood, the film would seem to expose the faulty premises on which its own rationale of racial casting is based. Race is shown to be a social (as well as visual, cinematic) construction—a white man can be mistaken for a Black one. Black men are shown not to be universal threats to white females, because Jasper did not kidnap the girl or accost the white woman. Hence, the film offers pleasures not by confirming Black bestiality but by flaunting the misleading nature of racial markers and stereotypes.

The racial representational politics in *A Close Call* clearly draw on the dynamics of theatrical blackface minstrelsy, which according to Eric Lott contained "an unsteady but structured fluctuation between fascination with (or dread of) 'blackness' and fearful ridicule of it, underscored but not necessarily determined by a fluctuation between sympathetic belief in the authenticity of blackface and ironic distance from its counterfeit representations."[72] These fluctuations, and their implications for white viewer identification, are particularly visible in *A Close Call*, as the film transposes two "Black" figures who are never entirely sympathetic or authentic. Certainly, one of the appeals of the film is that it enables the textually constructed white (male) viewer, through the "ironic distance" of blackface, to vicariously experience the position of a Black male rapist. As Clyde Taylor has argued with reference to Griffith's use of obviously blackfaced white actors in Black roles (such as Gus) in *The Birth of a Nation*, "the identifiability of whiteness beneath the surface of bestiality of Blackness was a libidinal requirement," that is, it allows for the playing out of "hidden desires," such as the rape of white women and then the ritualized "lynching of a Black alter ego."[73]

In *A Close Call*, however, the viewer is not presented with a scenario in which a diegetically "Black" character is punished for a transgressive act he performed or even attempted to perform (Gus does not rape Little Sister, but he wanted to). Instead, *A Close Call* dramatizes (or, rather, makes comic) the horror of being mistaken for a Black man and nearly lynched for a crime that was never committed. This vicarious experience of transgressive Blackness is mediated in numerous ways—not only because the "Black" victim is played by a white actor in blackface but also because the viewer understands that the victim is "really white" within the terms of the story and, furthermore, because he is accused of a crime that was never actually committed. Here there is no rape and, in the end, no punishment (Gus is killed, but the banjo player is released). Thus, unlike a more elaborate dramatic narrative such as *The Birth of a Nation*, which combines theatrical conventions (i.e., blackface) and cinematic devices (i.e., parallel editing) to distinguish Blackness from whiteness and to offer the white viewer a melodramatic confirmation of racist ideologies, *A Close Call*, as a preclassical comedy, flaunts the dangers of becoming implicated, as proponent or victim, in erroneous and illusionist racial discourses in themselves.

While preclassical films try to contain Blackness, it always comes across as a contradiction—familiar but foreign, innate but imitable. Preclassical cinema staged Blackness in ways that would be commercially viable as well as socially, politically, and psychically useful for a diverse white viewership. This viewing public included both "native" white Americans and a large proportion of recent European immigrants who, in their efforts to enter the American cultural mainstream, sought to construct themselves as "white" over and against nonwhite others. The presentation of Black film images in preclassical cinema attempts to confirm a measure of power and (visual) mastery for whites of many class and national backgrounds seeking to gain or maintain cultural authority. But for filmmakers based in cities like New York and Chicago, and audiences in these and other urban centers, anxieties about seeing and recognizing Blackness become more pronounced as Blacks move into new social and political positions via urban migration. For example, as African Americans migrated north, northern whites frequently responded by enforcing greater spatial (residential) separation between the races than was practiced in the South. Thus, preclassical films' efforts to define, recognize, and reproduce Blackness are heavily informed by desires to claim visual dominance over and privileged knowledge about Black people, but also to maintain distance from the real thing.

A close examination of the looking relations in preclassical films reveals that contrary to previous assertions, binaries of real Blacks versus whites in blackface, realist versus theatrical, nonfiction versus fiction, attractions versus narrative do not always line up neatly. Instead, preclassical cinema demonstrates an astonishing eclecticism in its visual, generic, and performative methods of Black representation, which speak to the many discourses about racial difference in general, and Blackness in particular, that had to be mobilized in light of the rapid processes of migration, mixing, and modernization. The largely unquestioned sense of consistency that has been attributed to preclassical cinema's racial politics (particularly its use of stereotypes) can be complicated by thinking about the proliferation of labels used to mark "Blackness" in preclassical film titles, reviews, and publicity materials. The terms "dark(y)," "colored," "black," "negro," "coon," "nigger," "dusky," and "smoke" are used interchangeably in preclassical film culture, as they are in other turn-of-the-century American discourses.

What is notable about the use of these words in cinematic discourse is the way in which they are applied and combined without refinement or qualification to describe any "Black" images, regardless of the race of the performers.[74] These multiple labels can have the effect of flattening the distinctions between many different treatments of Blackness in preclassical cinema, particularly for scholars who must depend heavily on written descriptions of lost films. However, these terms also suggest a recognition of the numerous modes of Black performance operating within and outside of mass culture.

When a reviewer of Pathé's interracial baby-switch comedy, *Mixed Colors* (1913), praises the Black actors in the film by stating that "the colored people are the best as real darkies," we can read the complicated status of performance and authenticity, as well as visibility, within preclassical cinema's racial representational politics.[75] Despite this proclamation, there was never any clear consensus during the preclassical era on the "best" methods for representing Blackness on screen. Instead, Black images in preclassical cinema were defined by their very multiformity and instability. As the cinema developed ways to codify and amplify particular visual representations of Blackness, African Americans continued to express concerns about their public "images" and tried to distance themselves from popular stereotypes. The efforts to contain and ridicule Blackness displayed in preclassical films illustrate the profound impact African Americans had on the cinema's development by constituting social and representational problems. Even the earliest Black film images show that Blackness is not just an immediately recognizable and duplicatable display but also a potentially subversive threat to America's racial and social hierarchies that must be controlled through performance and policed by the camera. Throughout the cinema's shift from "primitive" to "classical" modes of representation, it maneuvers—sometimes awkwardly, sometimes violently—to simultaneously exploit, examine, and contain "Blackness" as a visible sign.

In another review of *Mixed Colors* that appeared in *Moving Picture World*, the (presumably white) writer noted with some surprise that despite the fact that "there have been more jokes perpetrated on the colored race than on any other," it seems that "our darker brethren never complain."[76] In the following chapters, I will describe how various members of the African American community (leaders and migrating masses, audiences and filmmakers) did indeed challenge racist cinematic representations by establishing their public presence in urban centers, and by developing critical reading and production practices that spoke volumes to the elaboration of modern American mass culture.

# PART TWO

# Into the Audience

CHAPTER THREE

# "Negroes Laughing at Themselves"?

*Black Spectatorship and the Performance*
*of Urban Modernity*

On screen, preclassical cinema treats Black figures as complex and contradictory reflections of white anxieties about Black mobility and visibility. In contrast, the dominant film industry's treatment of African Americans as viewers may seem to be more straightforward and consistently discriminatory—it excludes Blacks from its textually inscribed, imagined audience and adheres to prevailing segregationist policies in its exhibition practices. As the cinema formalized and standardized its modes of representation, address, and exhibition, more and more commentators questioned the attraction of moving pictures for African Americans, particularly in light of the kinds of Black images they featured, which seemed to anticipate a white audience. For example, in 1918, Chicago's Black political newspaper, the *Broad Ax*, ran an item entitled "Negroes Laughing at Themselves," which chastised Black viewers for patronizing films that ridicule the Race: "In a moving picture show the scenario unfolds a story in which a Negro is merely used to add color to the situation and peradventure tickle the risibility of a race that seems to laugh at itself, and to take special pardonable pride in appreciating the damnable contempt some other races exercise for their insane and uncanny hilarity."[1] Similar concerns have been echoed over the decades by a variety of cultural critics and film scholars. Why have Black moviegoers patronized films that seem to place "people of their kind in a degrading light" or that do not represent Blacks at all?[2] Does Black enjoyment of such films necessarily signify a posture of self-deprecation? As a result of representational marginalization, is Black spectatorship a qualitatively different (and more problematic) cultural practice than that of other groups?

In this chapter, I approach the oft-discussed "problem" of Black spectatorship by considering how the multiple discourses informing images of

*93*

Blacks on film (e.g., progress vs. stasis, New Negroes vs. Old Negroes) also shaped the images and practices of Black people as spectators. To get at this wider set of discourses, I shift the emphasis from individual films and psychological processes to issues of collectivity, performance, and public space suggested by the *Broad Ax* editorial. I foreground the intersection of two phenomena that profoundly shaped Black spectatorship practices but are rarely discussed together in a systematic way—urban migration and the development of the classical cinematic paradigm. As African Americans poured into cities during the late 1910s, transforming public life and their understanding of their own roles in it,[3] the cinema was simultaneously undergoing major institutional transformations as a public sphere—film producers were working to subordinate the social space of the theater to the perceptual power of a self-enclosed film text on screen. While urban centers have long been prioritized in studies of film exhibition and of Black "modernity," and the classical (Hollywood) cinema has long been posited as the bad object of African American spectatorship, I want to explore how the nexus of the city and the classical as performative paradigms shaped both the ways in which many African Americans saw movies (e.g., accessibility of theaters, types of films screened) and how Black people came to understand their public roles as spectators.

With these issues in mind, I offer an alternative conception of Black viewing practices that I call "reconstructive spectatorship," a formulation that seeks to account for the range of ways in which Black viewers attempted to reconstitute and assert themselves in relation to the cinema's racist social and textual operations. I read Black spectatorship as the creation of literal and symbolic spaces in which African Americans reconstructed their individual and collective identities in response to the cinema's moves toward classical narrative integration, and in the wake of migration's fragmenting effects. I am especially interested in how the public dimension of spectatorship (which is explored in greater detail in the next two chapters) persisted for Black viewers, complicating the presumed pleasures (and limitations) of classical absorption and distraction for the "ideal" spectator.

To recover this public dimension, I draw on a range of accounts of Black spectatorship, including fictional ones that describe Black responses during the classical period. Although some of these accounts reach beyond the Great Migration of the World War I era (the end point of this study), they help to supplement the limited historical archive on Black spectatorship practices during the era of segregation in general and enable us to see the limitations of reading spectatorship exclusively within the framework of the Hollywood feature. I juxtapose various types of accounts to construct an appropriately layered conceptual model for understanding how African American spectatorship worked both as a set of fleeting encounters with mass culture and as an enduring feature of Black urban modernity.

## African American Spectatorship: Myths and Models

Black spectatorship is typically characterized as an activity fraught with social, psychological, and political contradictions for Black viewers, who are subjected to films that privilege white (racist, hegemonic) values and perspectives. Critics like Manthia Diawara, James Snead, and bell hooks have discussed Black spectatorship in relation to films such as *The Birth of a Nation* (1915), *King Kong* (1933), and *Imitation of Life* (1934) that, in different ways, seem to pose obvious representational and ideological problems for Black viewers.[4] Focused on the politics of the image, neither contemporary Black film criticism nor traditional sources of historical documentation (e.g., the Black press, trade journals, autobiographies) offer accounts of early Black spectators experiencing senses of wonder, shock, or liberation in response to motion picture technology and the virtual, mobilized gaze it is said to have enabled for white (European, American, immigrant) viewers. Representations of African American spectatorship in Black fiction offer brief glimpses of such fascinated responses, but in general they tend to support the prevailing view that most film images restrict Black spectators to temporary and shallow moments of pleasure at best. However, those moments of pleasure and engagement described in creative works also problematize theories of Black spectatorship offered by academic film scholarship because they are couched in rich descriptions of the material conditions in which African Americans have watched films, and they emphasize how spectatorship relates to other aspects of Black public and private life.

My turn to fiction in an effort to recover and describe the dynamics of Black spectatorship is not made lightly; it is intended to foreground the methodological difficulties of studying spectatorship in any context. What kinds of "evidence" can we mobilize to understand what happens in the minds of viewers as they watch films? How widely can we extrapolate from the experiences of particular viewers—as constructed in fictional accounts, as reported in the press, interviews, or oral histories, or even based on our own personal observations of audience behavior? The following chapters in this part struggle with these very questions. I do not presume that accounts of Black spectatorship produced by artists, because of their seeming immediateness and vividness of detail, are more accurate or reliable than those offered by historical sources and film scholars. Rather, I want to explore how fictional descriptions of spectatorship, which abound in African American film and literature, open up facets of the moviegoing experience that tend to be overlooked by academic film criticism. These texts help to map out what Yuri Tsivian calls the "cultural reception" of cinema, the set of "active, creative, interventionist, or even aggressive" responses that *reflect* on films and their meanings rather than simply *react* to them.[5] They suggest ways to bridge the gaps between "spectator" as textual point of address and "viewer" as empirical unit. While grounded in a tradition of social observation and historical documentation, they offer imaginative mediations between the realms in which the academic study of spectatorship tends to become fragmented—between the analysis of ethnographic/historical "facts" and (psychoanalytic) theoretical speculation.

For instance, in creative works, Black spectators are frequently characterized as members of the working-class "masses," prominently including southern migrants living in the urban North. Characters such as Pauline Breedlove in Toni Morrison's *The Bluest Eye* (1970) and Bigger Thomas in Richard Wright's *Native Son* (1940) exemplify unsophisticated Black spectators who uncritically enjoy Hollywood cinema despite the films' illusionist incongruity with the "realities" of their Black lives. In different ways, these fictions work as historicist sources to be read productively against historical materials. That is, both Wright and Morrison reference specific aspects of African American migration as a historical movement to reflect on how migration not only structures the past lives of their characters but also plays a continuing, significant role in shaping their everyday lives and worldviews. In *Native Son*, set on the South Side of Chicago, Wright's social realism (including his naming of specific streets, films, the Regal Theater) offers a scathing analysis of the oppressive social map that confines young, Black working-class (male) migrants at the moment the novel was written. Morrison's *The Bluest Eye*, set in the author's hometown of Lorain, Ohio, looks back several decades from the vantage point of 1970s Black Nationalist and Black Feminist movements to explore the lives of Black women trapped by white racism and Black patriarchy. Though Wright and Morrison employ markedly different fictional techniques (not least of which is Wright's effort to write a novel that replicates the visual and temporal immersion of classical cinema), they share a concern to historicize and imagine how and why African Americans are attracted to, but ultimately alienated by, the "glitter" of American popular culture.[6] Although Black spectatorship (of films, live performance, and other visual spectacles) appears in numerous other works of Black fiction written during and about the segregationist era, I draw on Morrison and Wright because they so prominently feature the tensions that result when Black migrants' social and physical beings get caught between the fantasy world on screen and the public space of the theater.[7]

While both authors use the movies as part of a larger web of external and psychological factors that circumscribe their African American characters, they also linger momentarily in their fictionalized theaters—generating descriptions of the darkness, the seats, the ushers, the refreshments—to describe how such extradiegetic elements inform the characters' moviegoing experiences. These aspects of "cultural reception" can be extremely difficult to trace historically and to incorporate theoretically. I consider some of the phenomenological details that Morrison and Wright present, alongside theoretical work and other forms of evidence (e.g., discourse in the Black press), with the expectation that these different modes of representing Black spectatorship will address, contradict, and illuminate each other. This kaleidoscopic approach seeks not to reconstruct actual moments of Black spectatorship but to conceptualize the shifting combinations of factors that structured the appeals of moviegoing for African American viewers (particularly during the preclassical era), factors left out of text-based, classical-centered models of pleasure and identification.

In Morrison's *The Bluest Eye*, Pauline Breedlove is a working-class, southern migrant employed as a maid in Lorain during the 1930s. Reflecting on her meager home and her unhappy marriage to Cholly Breedlove, she observes, "The onliest time I be happy seem like was when I was in the picture show."[8] One of the primary reasons Pauline is attracted to the movies is the extreme loneliness she feels up North, away from her southern home and familiar way of life. Cholly secures a job in the local steel plant, but Pauline is left alone days in their two-room apartment. Her social isolation is compounded by her class position and gender; she cannot compensate for her unstraightened hair and southern speech with her awkward efforts to wear makeup, new clothes, and high-heeled shoes. Thus, a combination of factors arising from Pauline's status as a migrant—homesickness, isolation, an inability to remake herself through northern urban fashion and commodity culture—lead her to the movies for comfort and distraction.

Pauline's "education in the movies" erodes her sense of self and her relationships with others by leading her to fetishize "romantic love" and "physical beauty" (*BE* 97). At one point, the pregnant Pauline even tries to style her hair like Jean Harlow's in an effort to emulate and embody white Hollywood beauty and desirability.[9] Thus Pauline's experiences as a motion picture spectator are shown to exacerbate her already-damaged sense of self-esteem, a problem that also afflicts other Black female characters in the novel.[10] Pauline submerges herself in white screen fantasies in order to be transported away from her lonely, modest existence: "The screen would light up, and I'd move right on in them pictures" (*BE* 97).

Bigger Thomas, in Richard Wright's *Native Son*, also goes to the movies to escape momentarily the pressures and limitations of his everyday life on the South Side of Chicago. Just after Bigger and his friends discuss their plan to rob Blum's Delicatessen at gunpoint, he seeks a diversion to "hide his growing and deepening feeling of hysteria," and "a stimulus powerful enough to focus his attention and drain off his energies" until the appointed time of the robbery.[11] Ultimately he decides to see a movie at the Regal Theater with his friend Jack to calm his nerves.

Bigger and Jack watch a romantic drama, *The Gay Woman*, featuring scenes of white millionaires engaged in "cocktail drinking, dancing, golfing, swimming, and spinning roulette wheels" (*NS* 33). The film's characters live entirely in a world of leisure, with no financial cares, and Bigger and Jack admire the lavish, wealthy white lifestyle pictured on screen. Like Pauline, Bigger and Jack also admire the white female film star, but they openly view her with a sexual desire that is strictly prohibited outside of the theater. As a Black young man raised in the South, Bigger understands that white women are strictly off-limits. As moviegoers in a Black urban neighborhood theater, however, Bigger and Jack not only are able to express their attraction to the white starlet but also feel empowered to make broad, lewd comments about the sexual proclivities of white women: "Them rich white women'll go to bed with anybody, from a poodle on up" (*NS* 33). Bigger and Jack talk back to the screen, suggesting that they enjoy a critical distance from the images that Pauline does not seem to achieve. However, Bigger and Jack's intense reaction to the film's climax indicates that even in their vocal participation they shift between aggressive and vulnerable spectatorial positions.[12]

While these fictional representations of Black spectatorship are rich with particular motivations and behaviors, they ultimately characterize the cinema as a medium of absorption and distraction. Many film critics begin with this assumption and, within the framework of cultural studies, attempt to address it by ascribing some measure of control or autonomy to Black viewers by emphasizing their resistance to problematic mainstream (white, racist) films. For example, Manthia Diawara describes the Black spectator as a "resistant spectator"; bell hooks characterizes the Black woman's look at the screen as an "oppositional gaze." By charting Black spectatorship in relation to the negative and "negating" representational politics of particular films, scholars have made a variety of claims about how Black viewers have worked to subvert an otherwise degrading viewing experience in relation to individual cinematic texts.

The limitations of analyses like these based entirely on close readings of individual film texts become apparent when read alongside our fictional examples. For instance, most critics do not consider how spectatorship might be affected by the organization of multiple films in a single program. In his brilliant reading of racial codes in *King Kong* (1933), James Snead significantly recognizes the fluidity of spectatorial identification: "It is not true that we identify only with those in a film whose race or sex we share. Rather, the filmic space is subversive in allowing an almost polymorphically perverse oscillation between possible roles, creating a radically broadened freedom of identification."[13] However, Snead's notion that Black viewers would identify most strongly with the "Black" images appearing on screen (Kong, the natives of Skull Island), however, is challenged by Wright's representation of Bigger's reaction to the colonialist fantasy, *Trader Horn*, which is screened immediately after *The Gay Woman*. Bigger ignores the images of naked Black savages in *Trader Horn* because he is still thinking about the opulent lifestyle pictured in the previously screened film as he imagines what it will be like to go to work for the rich white Dalton family: "He looked at *Trader Horn* unfold and saw pictures of naked black men and women whirling in wild dances and heard drums beating and then gradually the African scene changed and was replaced by images in his own mind of white men and women dressed in black and white clothes, laughing, talking, drinking and dancing" (*NS* 35–36).

Is Bigger assimilating to white models and values here? Is he resisting any claims to realism made by either of these racialized Hollywood fantasies? Is he negotiating between these positions? Wright's representation of the juxtaposition of multiple films within a particular program (a mix of feature attractions, B movies, newsreels, and serials was standard during the classical period he describes) opens up possibilities of spectatorial pleasure and interpretation that might not be apparent when we focus our analysis on the operations of a single film text—that is, the Hollywood feature. What is more, the actual Regal Theater to which Wright refers (located in the heart of Chicago's Black Belt), and other theaters like it, also regularly featured live musical and dance performances between films. When we consider that a mix of film genres and types of live performance (e.g., jazz, vaudeville) would have been common during the preclassical era as well, Wright's scene suggests that the variability of theater programs would have also shaped early Black "moviegoing" experiences in general, and readings of individual films in particular.[14] Spectators can read across different films or between films and other elements of the "show," or, like Morrison's Pauline, they can engage in multiple viewings of the same film during one trip to the theater. These reception contexts can produce many kinds of spectatorial "fluidity," suggesting pleasures beyond limited single-text-based notions of "identification."

A few scholars, including Snead, have moved away from the rigid "assimilationist versus resistant" model in productive ways. For example, Jacqueline Bobo's interview-based work on Black female spectatorship employs the model of "negotiated reception" to explain how "Black women sift through the incongruent parts of [a] film [like Steven Spielberg's adaptation of Alice Walker's novel *The Color Purple*] and react favorably to elements with which they could identify and that resonated with their experiences."[15] Similarly, Michele Wallace suggests that African American spectatorship can be heterogeneous and complex, even in relation to "mainstream" products. Recalling her own childhood admiration of white movie stars, Wallace suggests that Black fandom "may have been about problematizing and expanding one's racial identity instead of abandoning it. It seems crucial here to view spectatorship not only as potentially bisexual but also multiracial and multiethnic."[16] Turning his attention away from the exclusive emphasis on dominant cinema, Mark Reid offers a notion of "polyphonic" spectatorship, in which he imagines that viewers (of any race) can read "black-oriented" films from a number of social and psychic (and not simply *racial*) positions.[17]

My conception of reconstructive spectatorship draws on the notions of fluidity, negotiation, heterogeneity, and polyphony offered by these models. However, I seek to broaden these formulations along another axis, the cinema's public dimension. Even the notion of "negotiated reception," despite its repeated references to the social and political standing of marginalized viewers, excludes the public aspects of spectatorship. These more nuanced accounts are still predicated on the psychic activities of the *individual* viewer rather than a consideration of the viewer as part of a viewing public, a member of a variously constituted group that can mediate engagements with the text and/or exert pressures on individual viewers to perform in particular ways.

Reconstructive Spectatorship

By moving beyond an emphasis on the individual, the textual, and the psychic to include a consideration of the collective, the contextual, and the physical dimensions of Black spectatorship, we can develop a fuller picture of how African Americans have positioned and expressed themselves in relation to the cinema under particular historical conditions. According to Miriam Hansen, the "public dimension of cinematic reception" is a useful mediating concept that is distinct from both textual and social determinations of spectatorship because it "entails the very moment in which reception can gain a momentum of its own, can give rise to formations not necessarily anticipated in the context of production."[18] During the era of de jure and de facto segregation in the United States, this public dimension took particular forms for Black viewers: they might be segregated in balconies, in separate Blacks-only showings, or in all-Black neighborhood theaters. Given these conditions, we must imagine that the potential pleasures offered by the cinema extend far beyond the viewer's capacity to identify with (or resist) particular characters or ideologies, or her ability (or refusal) to lose herself within the story world on screen. In addition, there is a range of possible responses, including those aspects of spectatorship that are shaped by the viewer's experience of inhabiting and interacting with others within the space of the theater.

During this period, Black viewing practices can be read as a reconstructive process, whereby Black viewers could reconstitute themselves as viewing subjects in the face of a racially exclusionary cinematic institution and social order.[19] Though marginalized as a social group, African Americans constituted a dynamic, variable, interpretive public in venues such as theaters, churches, lodges, and jazz clubs. By placing movie theaters in this constellation, we can imagine how the cinema as a public space functioned as an important corollary (or alternative) to other spaces in which modern Black life was experienced (including, for many working-class urban migrants, austere factory floors, crowded kitchenette apartments, and dangerous street corners).

Black spectatorship was structured not only by limitations imposed by dominant practices but also by expectations and pressures Blacks created for each other. These intraracial dynamics are particularly visible in urban centers that attracted waves of Black migrants. For example, during the Great Migration of 1916–19, "between fifty and seventy thousand Black southerners poured into Chicago."[20] The sharp, alarming rise in Chicago's Black population resulted in various expressions of white racism, including routine discrimination in public accommodations and restrictive covenants limiting the areas in which Black people, regardless of income, could find housing. Eventually, the bulk of Chicago's diverse African American population was hemmed into a narrow strip of the city's South Side known as the Black Belt. Despite the neighborhood's racial homogeneity, the Great Migration created and exposed many lines of fragmentation within the city's rapidly growing Black community.[21] Those African Americans who had struggled for years (or even generations) to attain some semblance of social standing and political influence in Chicago feared that the flood of rough, unlettered migrants would adversely affect the public image and social status of the Race as a whole.

Thus, a concerted effort by the *Chicago Defender*, Black churches, the Chicago Urban League, and the Young Men's Christian Association (YMCA) was organized to instruct new migrants in acceptable urban deportment. Flyers, palm cards, lectures, and door-to-door visits stressed the importance of thrift, cleanliness, sobriety, and respectability, emphasizing issues of public appearance.[22] For example, on May 25, 1918, the lead story of the *Defender*'s women's page warns, "WAR DECLARED ON APRONS AND CAPS IN STREET CARS." In a long list of admonishments, Betsey Lane chides "newcomers" for brushing their dirty work clothes up against neatly dressed women on streetcars and urges everyone to "stop the young miss who chatters like a parrot during a lecture or a program. By doing this you not only help the Race, but all humanity." Lane makes clear her preference for middle-class norms of silent reception rather than the more participatory modes (e.g., those practiced in Pentecostal churches and jazz and blues clubs) that characterize working-class audience behavior.[23]

In this context the streetcar functions as the exemplary stage for Black urban performance, an important corollary to the theater. James Grossman points out that many Black migrants ritualistically tested their new social freedoms by sitting next to a white person on a streetcar. Although for some migrants this act was a quiet, symbolic gesture of their new social standing, others were accused of making nuisances of themselves by talking too loudly and being rude to white conductors and passengers.[24] Black newspapers repeatedly instructed Black migrants on streetcar deportment, demonstrating its central importance as a site of interracial interaction, and therefore a defining space for the public perception of the Negro. For example, the *Chicago Broad Ax* editorial cited at the beginning of this chapter, "Negroes Laughing at Themselves," describes improper streetcar behavior, linking it with the embarrassing public behavior of Blacks in moving picture theaters. "Scene 1" takes place in a theater where Blacks inappropriately patronize films with "contemptible" Black screen images. "Scene 2," which takes place on a crowded streetcar, describes multiple forms of crude Black behavior— "loud talking"; young people refusing to relinquish seats to older riders; and, worst of all, Black boys flirting with white girls: "We noticed two little white girls who seem to be greatly amused at the treat they were getting outside of a circus, and two little Negro upstarts had the nerve to be quite familiar with a worn out kind of dignity, assuming that these white girls were laughing other than at the merriment they were getting, and so they dove in to make hits or mashes."[25] The editorial presents these observations as if describing a (cinematic or theatrical) show with "scenes" in order to position Black readers as spectators of their own embarrassing daily performances.[26] In the struggle for public respectability in the multiracial city, interventions like these clamp down on Black behaviors and desires that suggest inappropriate (conspicuous, sexual) appeals for white notice and approval. Although the editorial does not mention migrants explicitly, their growing presence clearly informs these scenes.

While the Black press, the voice of "Old Settlers" and the middle class, bemoaned the embarrassing migrant adjustment period, many migrants in turn celebrated the significant differences they encountered in Chicago as opposed to the restrictions on public circulation in the South. The Thomas family, who had migrated from Seals, Alabama, in 1917, related to an interviewer for the Chicago Commission on Race Relations (CCRR) that "the freedom and independence of Negroes in the North have been a constant novelty to them and many times they have been surprised that they were 'not noticed enough to be mistreated.' They have tried out various amusement places, parks, ice-cream parlors, and theaters near their home on the South Side and have enjoyed them because they were denied these opportunities in their former home" (*NC* 96). The Thomas interview, along with many others, indicates that the opportunity to engage more freely in these kinds of leisure activities was a crucial new aspect of life in the urban North for southern migrants, along with increased salaries, voting rights, and educational opportunities.[27]

Black migrants faced the shocks and ruptures of modernity in their new city lives in ways that resonate with accounts of other newly urbanized populations. Urban experiences such as industrial labor, streetcar travel, and entertainments like the cinema reshaped the im/migrant's sense of time and space. In addition, members of the recently urbanized working class had to create new contexts in which to express their individual and collective cultural lives in the city, where they could not always maintain the social and cultural practices and institutions they had developed in their former homes, and where (despite having more leisure time and disposable income) they were denied access to many arenas of public life. Several social historians have suggested that the cinema offered a space where marginalized, alienated, fragmented social groups could reconstitute themselves in(to) new public formations.[28] But how could the cinema perform this function for Black viewers, who, unlike white ethnic immigrants, were not included within the cinema's imagined audience?

African Americans developed ways to negotiate the problems of moviegoing just as they developed strategies for addressing racism in various other arenas of public life. By developing public spheres like the Black press, race theaters, and race movies, African Americans intervened in the racist patterns of dominant cinema. But what kinds of spectatorial responses can we imagine took place in the "very moment" of reception, enabled by the variable Black publics constituted inside the space of the theater?

We can imagine that in urban theaters catering to Black clienteles, African Americans could posit themselves as the subjects of cinematic address, and, if offended or alienated by what appeared on screen, they could withdraw their attention from the film to consider aspects of the public context of exhibition, where Black migrants in particular could feel connected to a group identity that was both familiar and new. This movement between the imaginary space of the screen and the social space of the theater can account for an array of cinematic pleasures—from an individual spectator's complete identification with the film, to modified readings of mainstream films mediated by the live performance of Black music, to an audience's collective rejection of the images presented on screen, which could be registered with theater managers and reported to/in Black newspapers.[29] In addition, the composition of Black audiences (like that of other audiences) could vary along lines of class, age, and gender, producing different combinations that could alter the sense of the Black public of which spectators formed a part. Youth audiences might feel licensed to be boisterous; the presence of "ladies" might curtail crude behavior. This range of spectatorial contexts and potential responses suggests how Black spectatorship is better characterized as a set of numerous complicit and resistant possibilities for Black agency and activity, and for the reconstruction of the negated Black viewing subject on psychic, social, and public levels.

Since Black spectatorial responses are also shaped by the viewer's sense of public self, this would include the viewer's sense of herself or himself as an embodied subject. The status of the Black body within the social space of the cinema, and the degree to which viewers assert and/or sublimate this body, is of particular importance when imagining the social, psychological, and political valences of Black spectatorship. When we consider Black spectating bodies, our attention is drawn to the politics of Black circulation in public spaces, and the unrelenting ways in which these bodies have been socialized into racial regimes (e.g., of surveillance, of segregation).

One of the values of the literary representations discussed earlier is their delineation of some of the ways in which the Black body can hinder and complicate seemingly "assimilationist" modes of African American spectatorship. For example, in *The Bluest Eye*, Pauline styles her hair like Jean Harlow's, only to have her efforts at emulation fail in the most painful, and painfully embarrassing, physical terms. When Pauline bites into a piece of candy she purchases during an intermission, one of her teeth unexpectedly pulls out of her mouth, further destroying her attempt to approximate movie star beauty and ending her love affair with the picture show. Pauline recalls: "There I was, five months pregnant, trying to look like Jean Harlow, and a front tooth gone. Everything went then. Look like I just didn't care no more after that" (*BE* 98). Here we see Pauline's desire to escape numerous aspects of her bodily self—including her skin color and hair texture, and her impending motherhood—only to be reminded of the physical limitations that shape her existence. This is, without question, a negative representation of Black spectatorship, revealing the incongruity between Black lives and the fantasies on screen, echoing what cultural critics have long argued. Morrison emphasizes the tragedy and absurdity of Pauline's desire to resemble Jean Harlow by graphically depicting how her working-class Black body fails her at the very moment when she attempts to embody the positions of both the classical Hollywood star and the classical Hollywood spectator.

Richard Wright also suggests how the physical presence of the Black spectator problematizes Bigger Thomas's reading of the films he views. While watching *The Gay Woman*, Bigger wonders what it would be like for him to interact with the rich, glamorous whites in the nightclub scene he sees on screen. When Bigger tells Jack that he would "like to be invited to a place like that," Jack responds, "Man, if them folks saw you they'd run. . . . They'd think a gorilla broke loose from the zoo and put on a tuxedo" (*NS* 33). Bigger and Jack laugh at the absurdity of this image, but their exchange demonstrates how Black cinematic pleasure can be enhanced (enabling a joke) and/or destroyed (confirming one's segregation and demonization) when African American spectators try to insert their physical selves, unchanged, into the fictional world of the classical cinema text. Bigger would have the same terrifying effect as King Kong if he were to appear before these fictionalized white socialites; his body would signify the kind of bestiality and hypersexuality later ascribed to him by the press when he is charged with the rape and murder of Mary Dalton.

For Bigger and Pauline, such body-based interruptions do not produce the same kind of pleasurable virtual viewing experiences that are associated with nomadic urban viewing practices such as flânerie, the movement through urban space with a wandering gaze (Benjamin), or the surrealist technique of moving randomly between film screenings "at the first sign of boredom," thereby constructing a montage of visual effects via continual motion (Breton).[30] These modernist practices center around bourgeois, white male subjects who enjoy a freedom of physical movement, and an affective anonymity in public space, unavailable to most African American leisure seekers in segregated urban America.[31] At the same time, the ways in which Black spectators like Pauline and Bigger experience disjunctive engagements with the cinema as show (physical and mental engagement and withdrawal) suggest some important affinities between Black working-class modes of modern looking via the cinema and those of bourgeois white flâneurs.

Certainly, in light of the new (though limited) mobility that they experienced both in the act of migrating and in the mechanics of urban life, Black migrants would experience some cinematic pleasures akin to what Giuliana Bruno has called forms of *transito* in metropolitan film spectatorship. *Transito* connotes the "many levels of desire as inscribed in both physical and mental motion," including notions of "traversing, transitions, transitory states and erotic circulation."[32] I would argue that Black spectatorship is elaborated within the contradictions of the modernist promise of urban mobility, and the persistence of racial hierarchies and restrictions impeding smooth transitions into and through urban modernity. African American spectators share with the flâneur, the surrealist, and Bruno's (Neapolitan) female "streetwalker" a kind of cultivated distance from the immobile spectator-in-the-dark position imposed by the classical cinematic apparatus and its attendant theories of the gaze. But for Black viewers this distance can prove unpleasantly isolating (calling forth reconstructive collective viewing practices); it is not always voluntary (imagine the Black viewer forced to move into the Jim Crow balcony); and it risks the consequences of challenging mainstream cinema's racial and sexual economies of desire and identification.

This is evident in the cases of Pauline and Bigger when, by calling attention to their bodies, they both try to imagine/perform themselves as desiring and desirable subjects within the space of the theater. In Morrison's Black female version of this dynamic, Pauline suffers for her misguided desire to look like the white female star (and presumably to be a universal object of attraction and affection). After a pathetic display of Pauline's physical inferiority, movies are no longer a viable form of recreation for her; this passage to urban fascination and circulation is closed off.[33] In Wright's Black male version, Bigger and Jack's desire to demonstrate some form of mastery—if not over their destinies in a white-controlled world, then over images of white women—produces several displays of physical masculinist assertion. Not only do they speak their desire for white women, but, as Chris Looby has pointed out, in the original, uncensored version of the scene Wright depicts Bigger and Jack masturbating as soon as they take their seats at the Regal, before the show begins. Upon entering the theater, Bigger and Jack are primed to enjoy the unique combination of active physical exertion and passive mass cultural reception that the cinema provides.[34] But without the flâneur's affected freedom of unchecked social/geographic mobility, Bigger's gaze is always tethered. In his viewing behavior he bristles at these restrictions, seeking to construct and synthesize fragments of images and sensations into coherent, satisfying wholes, or goals—the opposite of the flâneur/surrealist's deliberately aimless, partial, disintegrative viewing. Bigger dreams of flying airplanes and of socializing in lavish white nightclubs, signs of equal opportunity and upward mobility. But his desire for exhilarating circulation can manifest itself only as violent acts, a run from the law, and illicit fantasies within the walls of his neighborhood movie palace.

By illustrating how the public space of the cinema participates in the construction of Black spectatorship (and by extension Black urban modernity), Morrison and Wright suggest that even "assimilated" Black readings of films can involve many layers of desire, fantasy, and interpretation. As laborers as well as leisure seekers, in the urban landscape, Pauline and Bigger engage in reconstructive spectatorship practices, in which they use the cinema to fill spaces in their lives that result from their status both as working-class African Americans with few social options and as migrants struggling to (re)construct themselves—physically and metaphysically—in new and often hostile urban environments.

## The Migrants Are Coming!
## Primitive Spectators, Classical Cinema

Discourses circulating around the Black presence in the city played a major role in determining the contours of Black motion picture spectatorship, particularly (as we have seen) when newly arrived migrants were instructed in proper public (audience) behavior. Conversely, the interpretive, participatory, and public practice of reconstructive spectatorship helped to alleviate the sense of social and psychic fragmentation within and among African Americans who were seeking to reconstruct what Henry Louis Gates Jr. has called the "Public Negro Self," despite the classical cinema's racist social and representational politics.[35] For African American viewers, the impulses both to control and to flaunt their physical presence produced significant conflicts with the developing classical cinematic paradigm, which anticipated white viewers even as it worked to pull spectators' attention away from their social identities and into the fictional world on screen.

Although most social and leisure activities in urban Black communities during the Great Migration were organized by churches and social clubs, Blacks in cities became increasingly interested in emergent forms of commercial and mass culture, like the movies. In Chicago, many Blacks sought to patronize downtown theaters, but they were frequently sold tickets in segregated sections, or ushered to seats far away from white viewers. The CCRR interviews with white owners of downtown theaters reveal that they attempted to seat Negroes in balconies or on aisles next to the walls, "even when there are center seats empty," because white patrons often "object to sitting next to them for an hour, or hour and a half. Offensive odor reason usually given" (NC 319).

Complaints about foul-smelling Black stockyard workers on streetcars were common during this period, substantiating claims that unkempt laboring migrants were undeserving of sharing social space with whites or respectable Negroes.[36] Racial discrimination in "places of public accommodation and amusement" had been illegal in Illinois since the passage of the Civil Rights Act in 1885. But de facto segregation persisted.[37] When theater managers and white patrons used the complaint of "smell" to justify segregated seating practices, they extended stereotypes about Black uncleanliness and undesirability into places of leisure to exclude or discriminate not only against members of the Black working class but against African American theatergoers as a whole. Although the CCRR concluded that white patrons rarely objected "to the actual presence of Negroes when they are well-mannered, well-dressed, and appreciative auditors," it is clear that the Negroes who were deemed to be "well-mannered" were the ones who quietly accepted seats away from whites or otherwise remained inconspicuous.[38] Thus, the centralization and celebration of whiteness that characterize film on screen were reinforced by the spatial arrangement of theaters, which deliberately kept Black audiences out of sight (and beyond the broader field of sensory perception) of whites.

The issue of racial segregation of public amusements raises important questions about the implications of Black embodiment at the movies during this period because cinematic pleasure, as it was being shaped according to the emerging classical paradigm during the late 1910s, required that the spectator transcend the limitations of his or her public self during and through the motion picture experience. Unlike early cinema, classical cinema sought to minimize audience awareness of theater space and to encourage the absorption of the spectator into the narrative space of the film text. Classical narrative and its attendant systems of style, along with increasing film lengths and changing exhibition practices (such as the elimination of live performances between films), attempted to "convey narrative through careful manipulation of audience attention."[39] Devices like continuity editing, tight causal chains, and thorough motivation were developed to carefully guide the viewer through an uninterrupted, self-contained, and universally intelligible diegetic experience. Hansen argues that rhetoric about the cinema as a "universal language" coincided with this shift from early to classical modes of filmmaking, as film producers attempted to standardize narration and address and thereby determine a textually prescribed spectatorship experience.[40]

According to Kristin Thompson, the codification of classical narrative and stylistic systems in American filmmaking was complete by 1917.[41] I want to emphasize that this is precisely the moment when the Great Migration was exerting new, highly visible pressures on public urban spaces and mass entertainments like the cinema. Although film producers were seeking at this time to wrest editorial control away from individual exhibitors and diminish audience awareness of the space of the theater, I would argue that for Black spectators the practice of segregated seating complicated the process of forgetting one's social self and becoming completely absorbed into an increasingly self-enclosed narrative. Thus, in terms of the cinema's development as a social institution, rhetoric about cinema as a "universal language" or "democratic art" (as propounded by D. W. Griffith and others) did not fully extend to Black spectators.[42]

I do not mean to suggest that the exclusion of African Americans was the primary objective in the development of the classical model, nor do I raise Griffith's name simply to demonize him further in African American film history. I do argue, though, that the codification of the classical paradigm (which is indebted to Griffith's development of what Tom

Gunning has called his "narrator system") functioned alongside other exclusionary practices to support racial hierarchies at a moment when they were being seriously challenged (e.g., by massive Black migration). Though no group of spectators became consistently and fully assimilated into the classical model of spectatorial absorption and distraction, classical practices sought to homogenize ethnically diverse but "white" spectators, while marginalizing Black spectators from the realm of cinematic "universality."

The pressure Black audiences felt to remember their social selves could contribute to an exhibition context that could keep Black viewers at what we might describe as a level of "primitive" reception. I use the word "primitive" here deliberately, to evoke the loaded and often condescending ways in which it has been used to describe both people of color and preclassical cinema. Early cinema, to paraphrase Noel Burch and Tom Gunning, is characterized by "externality," "non-closure," and a "willing[ness] to rupture a self-enclosed fictional world."[43] Much like early cinema audiences of the previous decade, Black spectators at the dawn of the classical era were not meant to be fully integrated into the developing narratives on screen, in large part because they were not fully integrated into American theater audiences. As segregated exhibition conditions persisted throughout the classical period, the conspicuousness of Black bodies did not disappear in darkened theaters; rather, segregation facilitated classical spectatorship for white viewers and complicated it for Black viewers.[44] But while Black spectatorship may be described as "primitive" in its relation to the classical model of narrative integration and viewer absorption, this term does not specify the limits of Black spectatorial experience. Indeed, as our fictional examples suggest, the conditions of segregation (not to mention poverty or social discomfort) might even encourage marginalized spectators to seek absorption into the projected image more vehemently. I would argue that "primitive" looking relations are among many modes of African American spectatorship, understood as a multiply determined, contradictory, modernist form of Black urban performance.

For example, many Black viewers patronized classical films in theaters catering specifically to African Americans, where many of the overt problems of inhabiting a Black body at the movies (visibility, smell, proximity to whites) would seem to be less of a problem. As I discuss in the following chapters, Chicago's Black neighborhood theaters not only welcomed Black moviegoers but also tried to construct an experience of race pride while exhibiting mainstream and, on occasion, Black-produced films. But even in their consumption of "white" films, Black audiences developed numerous

FIGURE 25. Owl Theater advertisement, *Chicago Defender,* 29 June 1918.

reconstructive strategies that need not be read simply as assimilationist "identification" or as primitive "externality" or disidentification.

Consider, for instance, Black engagements with the Hollywood star system. Ads and reviews in the *Defender* during the late 1910s celebrated Black Belt screen appearances by Dorothy Gish, William S. Hart, Charles Chaplin, and a particular favorite, vamp actress Theda Bara (fig. 25).[45] Given the absence of Black actors from most of the films seen by Black audiences, admiration for white stars is not particularly surprising. What is interesting is the way in which Black audiences, as Michele Wallace suggests, might have enjoyed these actors "not because they were 'white,' but because they were 'stars.'"[46] Instead of an effacement of the racial (Black) self, this interest in movie stars may have enabled a complex process of subject positioning and interpretation.

The complicated dimensions of Black fandom are particularly interesting in the case of Noble M. Johnson, a Black actor who starred as a hero in a number of Black-cast race films made in the late teens by his own Lincoln Motion Picture Company (discussed in chapter 6), as well as in numerous Hollywood films in roles of various racial types. African American audiences hailed Johnson as "America's premier Afro-American film star" (fig.

FIGURE 26. Noble Johnson, a popular actor in white- and Black-produced films, as a "race" hero carrying a wounded white soldier in *The Trooper of Troop K* (Lincoln Motion Picture Company, 1916). George P. Johnson Negro Film Collection, Department of Special Collections, University of California at Los Angeles.

26).[47] But in Hollywood films Johnson played diverse racial roles (including Native Americans, Mexicans, Arabs, and even whites); in fact, Johnson almost never played Black characters in his Hollywood film appearances.[48] Black audiences celebrated and patronized Johnson's films, regardless of the race of his characters and despite the fact that he played villains in many Hollywood productions. For Black audiences, Johnson's star text undercut the classical diegetic world of mainstream films. In relation to a variety of film stars, Black moviegoers could read alternately with and against the disparate racial identities being performed on screen.

What survives of the debates and discourses around African American spectatorship during the late teens, such as concerns about the public circulation of Black bodies and engagements with movie stars, points to a number of fissures in the classical cinema's totalizing veneer. During this period (and in the classical/segregationist decades that followed), Black spectatorship did not revolve entirely around expectations or experiences of complete "identification," uninterrupted narrative engagement, or visual mastery, cornerstones of classical practices and psychoanalytic film theory. Instead, it may be more useful to regard the cinema as a stage for modernist Black performance, and as a field for the continuous interpretation of the Black subject's highly contested public roles, rights, and responsibilities. In the next two chapters, I consider more fully the public dimension of early Black moviegoing, in light of heated debates about Black migrants and leisure in Chicago.

CHAPTER FOUR

# "Some Thing to See Up Here All the Time"

## Moviegoing and Black Urban Leisure in Chicago

Given the dearth of evidence documenting specific instances of Black film spectatorship, but the survival of early Black protest against the cinema's racist and exclusionary practices, many scholars have assumed that most African Americans did not want to patronize preclassical cinema any more than white audiences wanted to share theater space. Film historian Thomas Cripps has argued that during the early years of film production, African Americans were not particularly interested in moviegoing:

> Negroes, both intellectuals and urban masses, shared an indifference to the cinema. Because of their deep puritan fundamentalist roots, black churches eschewed film as needless frivolity. Organized Negro groups such as the Afro-American Council and the American Negro Academy struggled for survival against injustices. . . . [N]ot until 1915 would [the NAACP's] house organ, the *Crisis*, speak to a national black audience on the subject of cinema.[1]

In addition to these purported religious prohibitions and political preoccupations, Anna Everett has pointed out that segregation may have prevented many potential Black audiences and critics from viewing and commenting on preclassical films.[2] Indeed, African American newspapers and other Black writing of the late 1890s and early 1900s include scant references to the emergence of cinema or discussions of Black patronage of kinetoscope parlors or nickelodeons, making it extremely difficult to characterize the very first interactions between Black audiences and moving pictures.

Despite these early restrictions, evidence suggests that by the second decade of moving picture production, African Americans were going to the movies in appreciable numbers, particularly in their own communities. Julie Lindstrom found that during the nickelodeon era in Chicago, for ex-

ample, "the south side Black Belt supported a substantial number of five-
and ten-cent theatres, usually at transfer points between mass transit systems and along business strips."[3] Dan Streible cites an item that appeared
in the Washington, D.C., Black newspaper, the *Bee*, in 1910, which states
"matter-of-factly that 'there are separate motion picture theaters among
the whites and blacks in this country.' "[4] By 1910, there were at least one
hundred venues across the United States presenting films to African
American audiences, often along with live vaudeville performance.[5]

In light of these contradictory accounts of early Black moviegoing—
racial and cultural barriers, on the one hand, and evidence of numerous
"colored" theaters, on the other—this chapter and the next attempt to reconstruct early Black moviegoing practices as they were shaped by both
the challenges and the opportunities presented by the conditions of urban
modernity. During this period, African Americans weighed the options of
urban and northern migration, transplanted to cosmopolitan, industrial
centers, monitored the behaviors of recent migrants, managed reconfigured
(but persistently repressive) interracial relationships, and negotiated intraracial pressures to perform as New Negroes. Dominant discourses,
prominently including mass media, consistently attempted to limit and
control the terms of Black imagery, movement, expression, and citizenship
that were potentially expanded by African American migration and modernization. In response to these activities and restrictions, Black people developed new modes of living and looking—including the reconstructive
spectatorship practices discussed in the previous chapter—that redefined
African American culture and identity for modern, urban contexts. We
have seen how migration intensified anxieties about African American mobility and visibility as pictured in white-produced film images of Blacks; I
will now explore how migration heightened concerns about Black social
freedoms and respectability in and around sites of film exhibition, concerns
expressed not only by whites but also by members of the African American
community.

I focus on the role moviegoing played within a particular African Amer-
ican community in a city where movie theaters, along with other commercial amusements, occupied a major place in the urban landscape—Chicago's
Black Belt (map 1). Informed by city-specific studies of film exhibition to
Black audiences by Streible (Austin, Texas), Gregory Waller (Lexington,
Kentucky), Robert C. Allen and Douglas Gomery (Durham, North Carolina), Matthew Bernstein and Dana White (Atlanta), Alison Griffiths and
James Latham (Harlem), and particularly Mary Carbine (Chicago), these
chapters shift attention from generalizations about a "national black audi-

ence" to the ways in which early Black moviegoing was structured by the social, economic, and political factors defining Black public and private life at a local level.[6] I describe how the movies fit into the evolving cultural life of African Americans living in Chicago from the turn of the century through the Great Migration of 1916–19, a period that witnessed a dramatic increase in the number of Black Chicagoans in search of recreational activities, as well as an intensification of long-standing debates about the nature and scope of Black leisure in urban settings. Chicago is a fruitful site for the study of these debates not only because of its sheer number of African American migrants and entertainment venues but also because it is a major industrial center characterized by especially rigid racial segregation. Many of the experiences and debates I describe reflect those in other locales, particularly northern cities (e.g., New York, Philadelphia, Cleveland, Detroit). But Chicago enables us to see, in dramatic and relatively well-documented form, the high stakes of defining the racial boundaries of urban leisure for migrants seeking new "modern" freedoms and opportunities, for whites seeking to maintain racial hierarchies, and for Black "Old Settlers" seeking to police and distinguish themselves from recent arrivals from the South.

At the turn of the twentieth century, Black Chicagoans enjoyed a wide range of leisure activities—a world of things to see and do—that were unavailable or highly restricted in other parts of the country, particularly the South. Migrants to Chicago frequently cited increases in leisure time and disposable income and the wider choice of recreational activities as major improvements in their daily lives, alongside the better educational opportunities and greater political participation this northern city afforded. Even before the Great Migration of 1916–19 swelled Chicago's Black Belt with a massive influx of southern newcomers, however, African Americans expressed what Waller describes as "public concern over how to fill and manage leisure time and whether to tolerate or even condone cheap amusements," including moving picture theaters.[7] Black and white reformers alike voiced concerns about the use of leisure time among the newly industrialized and urbanized immigrant and migrant working classes. These concerns were perhaps heightened with regard to Black leisure because in many cities, including Chicago, the proximity of Black residential areas to urban vice districts linked many of the commercial entertainments available to African Americans to disreputable forms of recreation (i.e., gambling, drinking, prostitution). This prompted Black moral leaders (like their white counterparts) to condemn cheap amusements such as the movies, particularly for the lower classes, recent migrants, women, and children.[8]

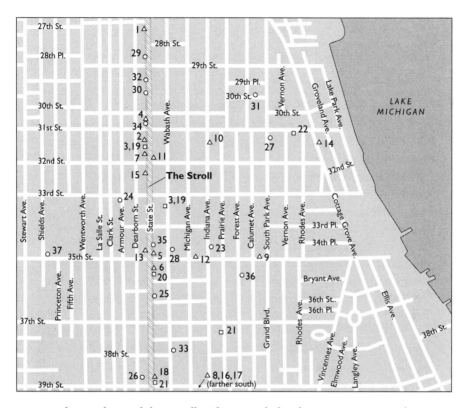

MAP 1. Along and around the "Stroll": Chicago's Black Belt, 1906–1920. Drawn by Bill Nelson.

△ **THEATERS**

1. Pekin Theatre, 2700 S. State St.
2. "Old" Grand Theater (later the Phoenix Theater), 3104 S. State St.
3. "New" Grand Theater, 3110–12 S. State St.
4. "Old" Monogram Theater, 3028 S. State St.
5. "New" Monogram Theater, 3451 S. State St.
6. States Theater, 3507 S. State St.
7. Lincoln Theater, 3132 S. State St.
8. Owl Theater, 4653 S. State St. (not pictured)
9. Fountain Theater, 344 E. 35th St.
10. Elba Theater (later the Blue Bird Theater), 3115 S. Indiana Ave.
11. Vendome Theater, 3141–49 S. State St.
12. Pickford Theater (previously the Lux Theater) 106 E. 35th St.
13. Washington Theater, 3440 S. State St.
14. Roosevelt Theater, 3125 S. Cottage Grove Ave.
15. Byron's Temple of Music, 3230 S. State St.
16. Chateau Gardens, 5318–26 S. State St. (not pictured)
17. Atlas Theater, 4711–17 S. State St. (not pictured)
18. Star Theater, 3835–37 S. State St.

□ **BLACK FILM COMPANIES**

19. Foster Photoplay Company, 3110 S. State St. (Grand Theater Bldg.) and 3312 S. Wabash Ave.

20. Unique Film Company, 3519 S. State St.
21. Peter R. Jones Photoplay Company, 3704 S. Prairie Ave. and 3849 S. State St.
22. Royal Gardens Motion Picture Company (Royal Gardens Café), 459 E. 31st. St.

○ **OTHER SITES**

23. Chicago *Defender*, 3435 S. Indiana Ave.
24. Armour Institute of Technology, 3300 S. Armour Ave.
25. Binga Bank, 3633 S. State St.
26. Institutional Church and Social Settlement, 3825 S. Dearborn St.
27. Olivet Baptist Church, 3101 South Park Ave.
28. Appomattox Club, 3441 S. Wabash Ave.
29. Negro Fellowship League, 2830 S. State St.
30. Jordan's Century First-Class Billiard and Pool Room, 2958 S. State St.
31. Edward Felix's Ice Cream Parlor, 368 E. 30th St.
32. Sandy W. Trice & Company Department Store, 2918 S. State St.
33. Wabash Avenue YMCA, 3763 S. Wabash Ave.
34. Elite Café No. 1, 3030 S. State St.
35. Elite Café No. 2 (Teenan Jones' Place), 3445 S. State St.
36. Eighth Regiment Armory, 3533 S. Forest Ave. (now Giles Ave.)
37. Comiskey Park, 324 W. 35th St.

In addition, although Black Chicagoans enjoyed relatively greater social freedom than their southern counterparts, they encountered racism in many areas of urban life in the North, including de facto segregation of public accommodations. Therefore, moviegoing for Blacks in Chicago was heavily informed by heated debates concerning accessible and acceptable leisure activities for a diverse and rapidly growing African American community.

Reading some of the earliest Black interactions with the cinema in Chicago, I argue that the tenuous cultural legitimacy of the movies both mirrored and exacerbated the tenuous social standing of African Americans in turn-of-the-century urban centers. This tension produced a range of dismissive, anxious, and contradictory African American responses to the cinema. For example, the seeming ambivalence of African Americans toward early cinema reflects not simply a general lack of interest in this new entertainment but, rather, the biases of the Black commentators who sought to depict a Black-centered, positive image of the South Side's leisure activities and commercial amusements. The Black press emphasized the activities of members of the Race—such as church and club events, live Black performance (and later the activities of Black filmmakers, theater owners, and managers)—over moving pictures produced primarily by and for whites, until the cinema evolved from a questionable novelty to an undeniable cultural institution drawing large Black audiences. Also, attempts by those African Americans who left a written record (e.g., professional men and club women, church and race leaders) to define and monitor the boundaries of Black recreation, including efforts to curtail Black patronage of cheap movie theaters, revealed intraracial fissures along lines of class, gender, and age, and often contradicted their arguments against discrimination against the Race as a whole in the city's public accommodations and amusements. In addition, Black Chicagoans projected a conflicting image to potential migrants, boasting about the city's astonishing array of commercial amusements (such as movie theaters) that Black people could not patronize in the South, while insisting that up North new migrants must focus on work, not play, and engage in more wholesome forms of recreation. In these and many other ways, moviegoing exemplified fundamental contradictions regarding Black urban leisure, as both the cinema and African Americans had to fight for legitimacy in the modern city.

The wide range of reported Black responses to the cinema during this period—endorsement and condemnation, incidental acknowledgment and exhaustive description, support for Black film entrepreneurs and advocacy of alternative recreational activities—illustrates that moviegoing played a complex and changing role in the construction of modern Black life in the city. Though Black moviegoing was shaped by many of the contemporary issues and debates regarding the circulation of white women and European immigrants in modern urban public spaces, dominant cinema's segregationist and exclusionary practices toward African Americans produced conditions that were potentially more hostile and alienating, not to mention more difficult for historians to trace. But while the apparent dearth of surviving Black commentary on specific films prior to the 1915 release of *The Birth of a Nation* might seem to indicate African American "indifference" to early cinema, I observe that Black Chicagoans had long expressed serious concerns about the impact of commercial entertainments and particular films on their communities. Then, after *Birth* and during the Great Migration, the contradictory nature of Black moviegoing became even more pronounced as the cinema soared in popularity despite its continued racist exhibition and representational practices. By examining Black moviegoing within a constellation of leisure activities in Chicago, we can reconstruct the cinema's place in the changing social, cultural, and political lives African Americans were building in the face of modernity's prospects and disappointments.

## Black Leisure Activities in Turn-of-the-Century Chicago

From the very beginning, moving picture exhibition in Chicago, like other public attractions and entertainments, was structured by segregationist discourses and practices. Protocinematic exhibits were featured at the World's Columbian Exposition of 1893, a massive, elaborately constructed celebration and display of science, technology, and commerce as signifiers of America's national progress into a modern age. Lauren Rabinovitz notes that historians have described the exposition as "a signal event representative of a shift or rupture in American society that characterized the origins of modern experience and particularly of experience rooted in a new mode of vision." However, these historians "all ignore the centrality of gender in making up that vision"—that is, the ways in which the World's Fair produced a safe space for women to engage in a mobile urban spectatorship.[9] Rabinovitz focuses on the ways in which white women overcame their exclusion from the public sphere to become modern flâneuses, female versions of Walter Benjamin's flâneur, the nineteenth-century figure who moved through the streets of Paris directing a distinctively modern "mobilized gaze" at his urban surroundings.[10] These white flâneuses enjoyed with new freedom sights staged in the palatial pavilions in the "White City" section of the exposition, such as Edison's peephole kinetoscope in the Electricity Building, along with fairground attractions, including Eadweard Muybridge's lecture-demonstrations of animal motion studies, on the Midway.[11]

But how did African American fairgoers—male and female—negotiate their exclusion from the construction of the exposition and the racial politics of the new, mobilized modes of looking it produced? In the previous chapter, I argued that Black film spectators, who were not anticipated by the dominant cinema's modes of address, engage in a restricted form of flânerie, moving between a modernist state of visual distraction and a persistent self-conscious awareness of their social limitations based on race. In many ways, the fair sets up a similar (if not foundational) contradiction of modernist looking from the racial margins. People of color were imagined more as spectacles than spectators by the exhibition organizers, as illustrated by the display of Javanese, Dahomeyans, South Sea Islanders, and Native Americans in "villages" located in the sideshow environment of the Midway. These ethnological displays, along with other anthropological exhibits, not only exacerbated the sense of powerlessness and exclusion to which Black and Native Americans were relegated but also codified white supremacist notions of racial difference and human evolution espoused in the name of modern science. As Robert Rydell has argued, "The [fair's] vision of the future and the depiction of the nonwhite world as savage were two sides of the same coin—a coin minted in the tradition of American racism, in which the forbidden desires of whites were projected onto dark-skinned peoples, who consequently had to be degraded so white purity could be maintained."[12] The carnivalesque ethnic displays on the Midway and the utopian future imagined by the White City functioned together to deny the progress of nonwhites, as well as their contributions to American modernity. We can imagine that the thousands of African Americans who visited the fair practiced a type of flânerie that foreshadowed the range of reconstructive practices that characterized Black spectatorship in moving picture theaters; that is, a mode of looking with complicit and resistant possibilities shaped by the exposition's racial (and racist) politics of organization, display, and public circulation.

Although African Americans had been marginalized by the exhibition's organizers, many participated as spectators, performers, and activists. Efforts to exclude Americans of color from significant organizational and representational roles in the fair were not accepted without complaint. The omission of African Americans from official participation was protested by

Black leaders, including journalist Ida B. Wells, who, with Frederick Douglass, published a pamphlet detailing "The Reason Why the Colored American Is Not in the World's Columbian Exposition."[13] After the exposition closed, Wells decided to relocate to Chicago, as did many other Blacks who had visited the fair.[14] African Americans who "came to look" and "stayed to work" included a number of figures who would become leaders in Chicago's Black community. Jesse Binga came to the fair from Detroit and worked as a door-to-door salesman; eventually he became the most successful Black real estate entrepreneur on the South Side and founder of the celebrated Binga State Bank (3633 S. State Street) in 1908 (see map 1). Attorney Louis B. Anderson came to the exposition from Virginia; in Chicago he rose to prominence as a Republican Party regular, and in 1917 he became the city's second Black alderman (after Oscar DePriest). Robert S. Abbott came to the fair "as a member of the Hampton (Institute) Quartet" and moved to Chicago four years later; in 1905 he founded what would become the nation's leading Black newspaper, the *Chicago Defender*.[15] These and other Black visitors came to Chicago from across the country (including the South), gathered at the exposition's Haitian Building, where "Mr. Douglass held high court," participated in (or protested) the last-minute "Colored American Day" Douglass was asked to organize, and took in sights that may have included moving pictures.[16] According to Rydell, Black visitors "experienced little overt discrimination in public facilities at the Fair," suggesting that Black fairgoers enjoyed some measure of autonomy, and perhaps a mobility of spectatorship similar to that which Rabinovitz identifies for white women taking in the exposition.[17] Thus, in different ways, the exposition actually enabled a number of African Americans to claim Chicago as home, as a location in which they could participate in a new regime of visual culture and take advantage of the numerous social, economic, and political challenges and opportunities the city presented.

In addition to the wonders (and insults) of the exposition, Black visitors found a small but diverse Black community in Chicago that had been growing significantly since the mid–nineteenth century. In their landmark study, *Black Metropolis: A Study of Negro Life in a Northern City*, St. Clair Drake and Horace R. Cayton describe Chicago's Black population during the 1870s and 1880s as being employed largely as servants, working "as coachmen, butlers, cooks, and maids in the homes of the wealthy; as servants in stores, hotels and restaurants; as porters on the increasingly popular Pullman coaches; and as maids and handymen in white houses of prostitution." There was also a very small number of Black Chicagoans who belonged to the politically active "business and professional classes."[18] Extrapolating from the pages of the *Conservator*, Chicago's first Black newspaper, founded in 1878 by a prominent attorney, Ferdinand L. Barnett, Drake and Cayton describe the Black community of this era as composed of three socially stratified groups—the refined, the respectables, and the riffraff:

> The "respectables"—church-going, poor or moderately prosperous, and often unrestrained in their worship—were looked down upon somewhat by the "refined" people, who, because of their education or breeding, could not sanction the less decorous behavior of their racial brothers. Both of these groups were censorious of the "riffraff," the "sinners"—unchurched and undisciplined. The "refined" set conceived themselves as examples of the Negro's progress since slavery. . . . They had an almost religious faith that education would, in the long run, transform even the "riffraff" into people like themselves.[19]

I cite this oft-quoted passage at length because it illustrates some of the ways in which Black Chicagoans would continue to distinguish themselves from one another in the decades to come, particularly in their social and leisure activities. Black people in Chicago were stratified not merely by differences in their economic positions but, more important, by notions of refinement, progress, and respectability.

As Chicago's Black population grew during the late nineteenth and early twentieth centuries, it became increasingly conspicuous and diverse. According to U.S. Census reports, in 1890, there were 14,271 Blacks in Chicago, making up 1.3 percent of the city's population; by 1900 this number had more than doubled to 30,130, and by 1910 Chicago's Black population had increased to 44,103. As historian Allan Spear points out, "Although this growth was overshadowed by the massive influx of Negroes during and after World War I, this was nevertheless a significant increase."[20] Many who migrated to Chicago during the 1880s and 1890s, including those who arrived for the Columbian Exposition, came "in what has been called 'the Migration of the Talented Tenth,'" which included "prominent preachers and politicians who, for a brief spell after the Civil War, sat in southern state legislatures and in Congress; less distinguished individuals who occupied minor political posts in country and town; and all the restless educated and half-educated, who were not content to live life on southern terms."[21] Most African Americans in Chicago continued to be "confined to the domestic and personal service trades" during this period, and Drake and Cayton estimate that by 1890, the city's Black community was large enough "to sustain twenty churches, a dozen or so lodges, three weekly newspapers, and several social and cultural clubs."[22]

The turn of the twentieth century witnessed major changes in the social and political leadership of Chicago's Black community. Informed by the work of August Meier, Spear describes these changes in terms of the different racial ideologies subscribed to by Chicago's "Negro elite," on the one hand, and a "new leadership" of professional men with business and political interests, on the other.[23] Prior to 1900, the "refined" or elite class of African Americans controlled the Race's major social and civic activities. Some members of this class belonged to families that had been in Chicago for generations, and most of them distinguished themselves in professional arenas in which they came into frequent, close contact with whites. Individuals like John G. Jones (an attorney elected to the state legislature), Rev. Archibald J. Carey (politically active and powerful pastor of Quinn Chapel, then Institutional Church), and Daniel Hale Williams (the most celebrated Black surgeon in the country and cofounder of Provident Hospital) subscribed to W. E. B. Du Bois's notion of the "talented tenth," which appealed to their elitist social and cultural sensibilities. Although members of Chicago's Black elite would hold differing ideological positions on particular issues during this period, for the most part they shared the belief that their high levels of education, their leadership experience, and/or their long tenures of residence in the city authorized them to serve as spokesmen for the Race as a whole.

In the militant, abolitionist tradition, many of these elite Black Chicagoans—like most other northern Black leaders at the time—were vehemently opposed to segregation of any kind, and they shunned the establishment of separate Negro institutions.[24] After 1900, however, the philosophies of self-help and racial solidarity popularized by Booker T. Washington became quite attractive among nonelite segments of the Black community in light of the deteriorating state of U.S. race relations. Thus, the first decade of the twentieth century saw a new leadership arise on Chicago's South Side. These "self-made men" were relatively new to the city; they did not have the same educational and cultural attainments of the "refined" group and did not always verbalize a racial ideology. Rather, "they left their mark not by writing or speaking but in business ventures, institutions, and organizational politics."[25] Unlike the old elite, men like Dr. George Cleveland Hall (whom Daniel Hale Williams rejected because of his "inadequate" medical training), businessmen Theodore W. Jones and Jesse Binga, professional politicians Edward H. Wright and Oscar DePriest, and *Defender* publisher Robert S. Abbott did not benefit primarily from direct professional, social, or political ties with whites.[26] Instead, they built their financial and power bases upon the developing socially segregated Black community. Their clients, readers, and constituents were the Black laborers in the city's service industries, whose numbers were growing rapidly after the turn of the century. This mass Black population needed and sought out goods, information, and social services, as well as educational, social, and leisure activities, which were routinely denied them by Chicago's de facto segregation as well as the closed circles of the city's Black elites.

By this time, most of the city's African American population had already been hemmed into a narrow residential area on the city's South Side known as the Black Belt, in which poor and middle-class Blacks were charged high rents for the worst housing stock in the city.[27] Although Chicago's Black elite opposed the idea of separate Negro institutions, the vast majority of the African American community needed hospitals, banks, churches, stores, restaurants, amusements, and other establishments that would not show them second-class treatment or turn them away entirely. Thus, as Spear observes, while white hostilities created the "physical ghetto" on the South Side—confining Blacks residentially—between 1900 and 1915 the new middle-class leadership built the "institutional ghetto," comprising "a complex of community organizations, institutions, and enterprises" in which the doctrine of self-help rather than integrationism encouraged the loyalty of Blacks to their own "city within a city."[28] Although whites continued to have a significant impact on the lives of Black Chicagoans (e.g., as politicians, employers, landlords, police), it was within a rigidly segregated "Black Metropolis" that most African Americans lived their daily lives and engaged in the majority of their leisure activities.

Not surprisingly, many social activities for African Americans were organized by its longest-standing institutions—churches and lodges. At the turn of the twentieth century, Chicago's Black churches made concerted efforts to provide social services and activities in addition to religious services. For example, as early as 1905, one of Chicago's largest Black churches, Olivet Baptist, offered secular programs, including boys' and girls' clubs, a literary society, and athletic activities. The Institutional Church and Social Settlement, founded in 1900 by Rev. Reverdy Ransom (see map 1), was modeled after Jane Addams's Hull House and offered activities and services ranging from a day nursery and kindergarten to cooking and sewing classes to lectures by "leading white and Negro figures."[29] Although most of Chicago's Black churches were stratified by class, some, like Institutional, created opportunities for different segments of the community to worship and interact with each other socially.

Chicago's Black elite enjoyed civic and leisure activities organized by their own lodges and fraternal organizations like the Good Samaritans (organized in 1859), the Prince Hall Masons, the Illinois Grand Lodge, and the Odd Fellows. Other exclusive elite clubs, like the Ladies' Whist Club and the Prudence Crandall Club (a literary society organized in 1887), excluded members of the rising Black middle class, who in turn created their own social organizations, such as the Appomattox Club.[30] The *Chicago Defender* regularly reported on the functions held by the elite and middle-class organizations, often on the front page, detailing who was in attendance, what they wore, prizes awarded, and gifts exchanged.[31] These clubs functioned primarily as networking opportunities for their members. The balls, lectures, dances, picnics, and concerts they sponsored provided members with opportunities to confirm their refined tastes, as well as their financial and social standing among members of their own set. They also functioned, by highly publicized example, to model acceptable forms of Black leisure for members of the lower classes.

Working-class Blacks had developed a number of formal and informal leisure activities of their own, many of which were frowned upon by the upper and middle classes. Historian James Grossman observes that "enthusiastic worship" in storefront churches and a "lively nightlife" of gambling, saloons, and rent parties offered Black laborers "respite from their backbreaking, low-status jobs."[32] These "boisterous" forms of leisure did not project the image of the Race that Chicago's Black leadership wanted to convey. But these kinds of activities persisted and proliferated in the years to come, particularly during the Great Migration of the late teens, as members of Chicago's growing Black laboring class devised ways to spend their precious leisure hours in environments free from middle-class pretensions and prohibitions.

Black Chicagoans of all classes had access to a variety of noncommercial activities and amusements, many of which were tied to religion, education, and/or uplift. In 1912 the *Defender* advertised the "2nd Annual Chautauqua Assembly," featuring "speaking, lectures, musical and religious exercise."[33] The Negro Fellowship League (headquartered at 2830 S. State; see map 1), like other settlements, presented speakers at its weekly meetings and offered "one of the finest reading rooms in the city, especially for men and boys," where they could "find the leading magazines and newspapers and the best books, also tables at which they can write letters."[34] Occasionally settlement-sponsored lectures featured projected photographic images, such as a free talk at the Fellowship League illustrated with "stere-opticon views on 'The Industrial Development of Cuba.'"[35] These kinds of activities were offered not only as wholesome alternatives to street life but also as nondiscriminatory alternatives to the city's white-owned commercial amusements.

African Americans also controlled a wide variety of commercial entertainment venues during the first decade of the twentieth century, many of which advertised themselves as appropriate for families, children, and seekers of good clean fun without racial discrimination. For example, the Chateau de Plaisance, located south of the Black Belt at 5318–26 State Street, advertised in 1908 as a "Summer Resort for Ladies and Gentlemen who will find the desired spot at the only Amusement Park Pavilion and Stadium owned and controlled by negroes in the world." Visitors to the Chateau de Plaisance, which was easily accessible by streetcar, could enjoy a variety of "Open Air Attractions," including "Band Concerts, Vocal Solos, Roller Skating and the Best Meals procurable" for the low admission price of ten cents.[36] The Chateau advertised regularly in the *Defender* and *Broad Ax* newspapers, noting visits by luminaries such as Mrs. Booker T. Washington and vaudeville legend Bert Williams. Visitors could also come to the Chateau to meet and congratulate members of the extremely popular Leland Giants baseball team.[37]

The Chateau was, in fact, owned and operated by the Leland Giants Base Ball and Amusement Association, headed by businessmen Robert R. Jackson and Beauregard F. Moseley. Baseball enjoyed tremendous popularity among African Americans, and Jackson and Moseley fielded the Giants to provide opportunities for Black players, who were excluded from major league baseball. The Leland Giants was Chicago's first successful Black baseball enterprise, playing games weekly at Seventy-ninth and Wentworth. In addition to the Chateau, Jackson and Moseley attempted to open an amusement park and summer hotel; they also sought to organize the National Negro Baseball League. Although enthusiasm for these ventures was high, they could not raise enough capital to realize them.[38] For several years, though, the Leland Giants and the Chateau Gardens provided Black Chicagoans with comfortable venues that allowed them to support Black entrepreneurs.

The 1908 edition of *Rhea's New Citizens' Directory*, a guide to Black Chicago compiled by advertiser H. W. Rhea, includes ads for a number of Black-owned enterprises, and the individual and business listings indicate dozens of Black proprietors and employees of confectioneries, saloons, restaurants, and pool rooms. Businesses like Jordan's Century First-Class

Billiard and Pool Room at 2958 State Street and Edward Felix's ice cream parlor (featuring notions, cigars, tobacco, candies, and sweetmeats) at 368 E. 30th Street catered to the diverse segments of Chicago's growing Black population. For a brief time, Black Chicagoans could shop at Sandy W. Trice & Company, "The Largest Negro Department Store in the West," located at 2918 S. State Street (see map 1). Although some African Americans lived in and owned businesses in other parts of the city (e.g., the North Side Ice Cream Parlor, located at 307 Orleans Street and operated by Blacks who lived outside of the Black Belt), the establishments on and near South State Street served as the primary locations for Blacks to spend their leisure time and money.[39]

Black Chicagoans also enjoyed a city boasting an extremely active theater scene. In October 1900 the *Chicago Broad Ax* announced in an "Amusement Notes" item that "twenty theaters will compete for the patronage of the amusement-seeking public in Chicago this season."[40] Although this article probably counts theaters both inside and outside of the Black Belt, the writer refers to the array of venues where African Americans could potentially see live musical and theatrical performances without racial restrictions. Whereas the *Broad Ax* rarely detailed entertainments, the pages of the *Defender* were consistently filled with notices and reviews of appearances by vaudeville performers—singers, dancers, comedians, and many specialty acts—in venues along South State Street, popularly known as the Stroll. The *Defender*'s focus on Black Belt entertainments, though, did not preclude its writers from agitating for access to amusements citywide, or from commenting with increasing frequency on dominant mass cultural forms like the cinema.

## *Defender* Critics and Moving Pictures

Prior to 1915, theatrical discussions in Chicago's Black press emphasized live performance, without much attention to film exhibition or the film industry in general.[41] Discussions of movies are few and far between both in the entertainment pages and in the general news columns during this period, largely reflecting the biases of theatrical critics, rather than an absence of moving pictures from theatrical bills. For example, Sylvester Russell, theater critic for the *Defender*, observed in April 1910 that Blacks and Jews in Chicago are avid moviegoers: "The moving picture theater craze has developed a wonderful stampede among [Chicago's] Negro and Yiddish theater goers."[42] But rather than discuss the kinds of films these audiences enjoy, or describe the theaters themselves, Russell uses this occasion to make broad, essentialist comparisons between Jews and Blacks, and to lament the fact that unlike Chicago's Blacks, Jews are not forced to mix across social classes. Describing his visit to Halsted Street, near Taylor and Van Buren— "the most congested district of the Hebrew population"—Russell writes that most of the Jews he sees at the theaters are poor, unkempt, and "uncouth." But while "the same noisy condition exists on State street, near 31st street [the heart of the Black Belt theater district]," Russell notes the primary difference for Black audiences is that "the best class of people of the colored race are compelled to be mixed with the undesirable or remain at home in seclusion." As Mary Carbine points out, this item reveals that African Americans of all classes attended Stroll theaters and reflects the *Defender*'s authoritative, middle-class position regarding appropriate audience behavior. But this rare, brief mention of film exhibition by Russell, who regularly described live vaudeville performers and their acts in great detail, also demonstrates Russell's lack of interest in conveying the specifics of films screened to Black audiences.[43]

Black critics were not unique in this regard. Other contemporary commentators on Chicago's theaters neglected to describe venues exhibiting films, or the films they presented, in detail. For example, Moya Luckett found that the white reformer Louise de Koven Bowen of the Juvenile Protective Association, who conducted many studies of Chicago's movie houses, "does not record any details of the actual places she visited, their location, or the conditions she found inside the theaters." Noting that most reformers "seemed to find it sufficient to note that the conditions were just as bad as expected," Luckett concludes that the absence of specific theater descriptions "suggests that their authors felt that they did not have to go into detail because their readers would already know as these details were part of everyday life."[44] I would add that in the case of Black theatrical critics, details about movies and movie theaters were rarely noted because films were not yet seen as something that engaged Black agency or artistry. Films that were shown in Black Belt theaters did not yet, in the minds of Black critics, carry significant cultural value for Black audiences. Also, Black critics were not privy to inside or background information about mainstream films, whereas they had close ties to the Black entertainment industry and often knew Black performers and Black Belt booking agents and theater owners personally. Therefore, Black critics could write about the live theatrical scene with a firsthand knowledge that they did not yet possess in relation to moving pictures.

The *Defender*'s next theatrical critic, Minnie Adams, continued Russell's practice of detailing live performance to the exclusion of the films that were occasionally screened on the same bills. Occasionally Adams notes at the very end of her substantial reviews that films were shown during a particular program, particularly at the Grand Theater (see map 1, and more detailed discussion of the Grand in the next chapter). For example, in a piece from February 1912 she gives a lukewarm review to the Grand's current offerings (including an aerial act, comedians, a singer, and a comedy sketch), coolly noting that "the 'Photo Plays' were interesting and the orchestral numbers up to 'par.'"[45] A month later, she briefly states at the end of a more positive Grand review that "some excellent pictures were shown to conclude the performance."[46] While Adams does mention the titles of films screened at the Grand at least twice—"The photo play of 'The Ranchman's Mother-in-law' was fine"; "The photo-play of 'East Lynee' [sic] was one of the best pictures seen at the Grand in some time"—she almost never even acknowledges that moving pictures were featured along with the live performances at this and other Stroll venues she reviews.[47]

From mid-1913 through April 1914, the *Defender*'s "Musical and Dramatic" column featured no byline. Anna Everett reads this absence during this period as an indication that Adams, unlike her predecessor, Sylvester Russell, was not the sole writer of the *Defender*'s theatrical column.[48] Though it is not as clear to me that Adams was still writing during these months, it may be that her eventual successors, Columbus Bragg and Tony Langston, were already contributing substantially to the *Defender*'s entertainment pages. Whoever actually authored the columns, the *Defender* continued to try to put the cinema behind live African American theatrical and musical performance, despite important developments in local film culture. During this period movies screened in the Black Belt are described slightly more frequently, as the States, Lux, Star, and reopened Pekin theaters offered Black audiences a variety of special cinematic attractions (see map 1). These included the first films by a Black producer (William Foster), screenings of spectacular features (such as *Quo Vadis*) direct from their first runs downtown, and the opportunity to patronize a theater owned and operated by a member of the Race (the Star, discussed in the next chapter).[49]

Everett observes that Adams's style and editorial persona differed considerably from those of Russell, Bragg, and Langston, indicating key distinctions in her response to cinema's growing popularity and what it should mean to *Defender* readers. Adams's writing, Everett contends, was "circumspect and reportorial," consisting mostly of "description and pré-cis," and therefore reflected matter-of-factly "the decline of theatrical productions brought about by films." In contrast, the male critics who preceded and followed Adams produced more "personalized" and "author-centered" criticism, and their "interpretive" voices responded more cautiously to the cinema.[50] Indeed, Russell's and Langston's weekly columns were accompanied by photographic portraits, and these writers, like Bragg with his "On and off the Stroll" column, constructed recognizable, authoritative critical personalities that sought to both inform and instruct readers about developments in the theatrical world. These men expressed a combination of expertise and skepticism when addressing moving pictures, playing up their personal knowledge and opinions, but also displaying their concerns about the cinema's encroachment upon the local (not to mention national and international) entertainment scene.[51] Adams occasionally acknowledged moving pictures, but she kept them at the margins of her reviews. By the time Bragg and Langston start their (signed) columns, however, they must engage in a more complex negotiation with the cinema's increasing influence on the Stroll's theatrical, social, and business cultures, in which they had substantial personal and public investment.

For example, when critic Tony Langston inaugurates his weekly "Review of the Theaters" for the *Defender* in May 1914, he not only regularly lists the titles of films shown in Black Belt theaters but also notes other places of amusement, like the Elmwood Café (a jazz club at Thirty-second and State Streets) and the Palms Ice Cream Café, featuring food and entertainment for a Black clientele. Beginning in 1915, Langston includes notices for individual moving picture theaters (now including the Phoenix, Lincoln, and Washington) and their weekly bills, along with reviews of live performances at the Grand and Monogram (see map 1). This increased attention to movies both reflects Langston's wider view of the Stroll's theatrical offerings and registers the moment when movies evolved from a novelty to a social institution. By 1915, the film industry is impossible for any theater critic to downplay or ignore, and the Black press is following a general trend in American newspapers of describing movies more frequently and with more specificity. Discussion of live performance continued to dominate the *Defender*'s entertainment pages, but these acts no longer completely overshadowed the movies, which clearly enjoyed a growing Black audience.

Langston's reviews provide a broader picture of Black patronage of commercial amusements. He not only indicates an increase in Black participation in these kinds of activities but also legitimizes this participation by describing it in print. By the time Langston began his tenure at the *Defender*, notions of acceptable Black leisure had expanded beyond elite and middle-class club and social functions and church activities. Places of amusement for the Black working class could be more fully described, and even elevated to the same level as previously sanctioned, noncommercial recreational activities. Thus, although films had been screened for many years to Black Chicagoans, by the midteens the *Defender* began to register Black film culture in more detail. Movies became a major cultural force in American life in general, with implications for the Black community that were now deemed worthy of description. As the *Defender*'s entertainment pages illustrate, this film culture was inextricably linked to a host of commercial amusements, particularly live theatrical performances, available to African Americans along the Stroll.

## "The State Street Bugaboo": Policing Black Leisure

Given the wide array of entertainments available to African Americans in Chicago, many Black leaders and institutions (e.g., churches, the Black press) attempted to monitor and regulate the Race's leisure activities, indicating which amusements and venues were worthy of Black time and money. During the early 1910s, the *Defender* served as a major advocate of Black Belt amusements. The newspaper ran occasional features that extolled the virtues of the Stroll, the commercial strip of cafés, dance halls, poolrooms, and theaters along South State Street, which attracted seemingly ever-increasing numbers of African Americans seeking to see and be seen during their leisure hours.[52] For example, an article about the intersection of "31st and State Streets" that appeared in the *Defender* in 1910 describes the vibrant social interaction that took place outside of the Stroll's places of amusement:

> Every man of color in Chicago, young or old, if he has any leisure time generally wends his way to this interesting corner. Why? Because here he can meet all of his friends and here he can talk "shop" to his "hearts content" and learn in an hour everything of interest that has occurred during the last day, week, or year. Here congenial souls in all walks of life meet in a happy half hour's chat.[53]

In some ways, this description of the typical character strolling through the Black Belt recalls Benjamin's flâneur. However, unlike the white male dandy, with his individualized, distracted, and dreamlike gaze, these Black Belt strollers are depicted as participants in community interaction, with an emphasis on collectivity and verbal communication. As Shane White and Graham White observe, "What was valued highly on the Stroll was not only the stylish way young black men-about-town presented their bodies but also their verbal agility and quickness of wit."[54] The Stroll certainly provided a unique space for the elaboration of a modern, African American experience in a stretch of urban sidewalks replete with amusements, commodities, and other sights, similar to the dynamics described by Rabinovitz for white women. But the new, mobilized modes of looking and modern subjectivities that were developed along the Stroll (and within its cinemas) were never completely divorced from a sense of engagement and participation in a new Black public, and a heightened personal and political awareness of how one performs and interacts with others within that public.

In addition to serving as a center for Black community dialogue and display, the Stroll was also a "magnet" for "progressive pleasure seekers," including whites, from across the city. In a 1912 *Defender* article, J. Hockley Smiley carefully describes the appearance of whites seeking entertainment (not "slumming") when he reports that "Pleasure-Bent Residents of Both the North and West Sides Contribute to the Nightly Throngs." His account emphasizes the sheer numbers of visitors who are drawn to South State in search of nighttime amusement:

> At the hub of all this gaiety, 31st street, you find the bulk. You find, as it were, the masses going north and the masses going south. They meet at this corner as a bag of shot drawn to a powerful magnet, and it takes strength to pull them away.
>
> But, like the shot, they are harmless unless supercharged with force, and the late hour (the force) generally disperses them without friction. Where they go is another story.[55]

These articles are revealing not only because they provide a picture of the people and atmosphere that characterized South State Street but also because they indicate the kind of image advocates of the Stroll wanted to promote and the kind they wanted to overwrite. Smiley notes that the Stroll is so popular, in part, because Black Chicagoans have few other choices in their places of amusement: "The discrimination at several amusement parks tend [sic] to make this miniature midway more profitable and enjoyable—and why not?" At the same time, Smiley's reference to the "harmless" crowds indicates his attempt to convince "those opposed to the great crowds that nightly congregate" on State Street that there is "No Undue Unpleasantness or Crime 'Along the Stroll.'"[56] Smiley may tip his hand, however, when he suggests that members of these crowds, including whites, may pass through the "hub" of the Stroll on their way to unspeakable locations: "Where they go is another story." In Smiley's characterization, the Stroll itself may be free of elements that have been accused of "leading your child astray," but those who congregate on this thoroughfare may include the kinds of people who go on to engage in less "progressive" pleasures.

Fears about these large, pleasure-seeking crowds stemmed from concerns about the danger, immorality, and negative effects of State Street's active nightlife on Black families—especially women and children—who lived near the Stroll. For years, Chicago reformers, Black and white, had castigated places of amusement on the South Side because this area was home to much of the city's vice activity. According to Drake and Cayton, after the Chicago fire of 1871 destroyed the city's infamous "red-light" district, most of the gamblers and prostitutes relocated to the Black community and never left.[57] Vice "resorts" thrived near and within the Black Belt because white authorities were not concerned about their impact on Black residential life and did not fear community protest.[58] Hazel Carby points out that the South Side of Chicago was not unique in this regard. In areas like East St. Louis, the tenderloin in Kansas City, and Harlem in New York, "Black urban life was viewed as being intimately associated with commercialized vice because Black migrants to cities were forced to live in or adjacent to areas previously established as red-light districts in which prostitution and gambling had been contained."[59] This made Black residential areas playgrounds for white Chicagoans, as well as white visitors to the city. The popular practice of white "slumming" on the South Side encouraged disregard for African American community life among politicians, police, and patrons.

The proximity of vice created a "moral panic" within Chicago's Black community regarding the safety of women and children.[60] While singing the praises of the Stroll, Smiley tries to make light of reformers' studies of the area when he writes that "a careful investigation—or, I might say, visit—to many places . . . along State street will show less that tend to be bad than in any other section of the city."[61] However, reformers' investigations repeatedly revealed that the Black Belt was home to many vice activities, including, perhaps most notoriously, prostitution. The 1911 report of the Vice Commission of Chicago found that prostitution—"the social evil"—was rampant in the Black Belt, through no fault of the African American residents:

> The history of the social evil in Chicago is intimately connected with the colored population. Invariably the larger vice districts have been created within

or near the settlements of colored people. In the past history of the city, nearly every time a new vice district was created down town or on the South Side, the colored families were in the district, moving in just ahead of the prostitutes. The situation along State street from 16th street south is an illustration.

So whenever prostitutes, cadets and thugs were located among white people and had to be moved for commercial or other reasons, they were driven to undesirable parts of the city, the so-called colored residential sections. A former Chief of Police gave out a semi-official statement to the effect that so long as this degenerate group of persons confined their residence to districts west of Wabash avenue and east of Wentworth avenue they would not be apprehended. This part of the city is the largest residence section of colored families. Their churches, Sunday schools and societies, are within these boundaries. In this colored community there is a large number of disorderly saloons, gambling houses, assignation rooms and houses of ill-fame. An investigation shows that there are several thousand colored people in the First, Second and Third Wards where these vicious conditions obtain. Under these conditions in the Second and Third Wards there are 1,475 young colored boys and girls.[62]

Black girls, in particular, were viewed as being endangered by a combination of their inescapable residential proximity to houses of prostitution and their limited employment opportunities due to racial discrimination. Because young African American women could not always find work in "legitimate" domestic service, "they are eventually forced to accept positions as maids in houses of prostitution." In fact, the commission reported with alarm that "employment agents do not hesitate to send colored girls as servants to these houses. They make the astonishing statement that the law does not allow them to send white girls but they will furnish colored help!"[63] As cited earlier from Drake and Cayton's *Black Metropolis*, many of the domestic service jobs available to African Americans—men, women, and children—during the late nineteenth century were in white houses of prostitution.

The persistence of this practice into the twentieth century continued to arouse fears not only about the moral and physical safety of these Black workers but also about the possibility of miscegenation. The commission reveals its anxieties about interracial intimacy when it links the following observations about Black employees in the vice district: "It is an appalling fact that practically all of the male and female servants connected with houses of prostitution in vice districts and in disorderly flats in residential sections are colored. The majority of entertainers in disorderly saloons on the South Side are colored men who live with, and in part upon, the proceeds of white women."[64] Thus it was the proximity of Blacks and whites in sexually charged spaces (i.e., brothels, saloons, black-and-tan resorts) that concerned the commission as much as (perhaps more than) the well-being of the young Black women forced to work there as domestics. The commission echoes the outrage expressed by Black reformers when it concludes that the city's discrimination against African Americans is unconscionable: "Permitting vice to be set down in their very midst is unjust, and abhorrent to all Fair minded people. Colored children should receive the same moral protection that white children receive."[65] But houses of prostitution, saloons, gambling houses, and pool halls continued to operate in the Black Belt, lending the area an aura of danger and excitement that angered moral leaders but attracted pleasure seekers of both races.

The *Defender* often played a dual role in debates about Black Belt amusements, voicing conservative, middle-class reservations about the use of Black leisure time, on the one hand, and advocating the variety of Black Belt amusements (including many businesses that regularly bought advertising in the *Defender*), on the other. The *Defender* frequently tried to put a positive spin on the Stroll by emphasizing how South State Street functioned as an important gathering place for upstanding members of the Race, as opposed to slumming whites or Black shadies. For example, the 1910 article about Thirty-first and State Streets cited earlier describes the congenial atmosphere of the Stroll as follows: "Sometimes old cronies renew friendships over a game of billiards, but as a rule the evening out is spent along the curbstone in the enjoyment of the 'after-dinner' cigar."[66]

Although these "old cronies" are described as belonging to different social classes ("congenial souls in all walks of life"), the columnist clearly codes this vibrant Black street life as masculine. The article continues: "The Keystone Hotel and the Elite [Café] are the favorite meeting places. There is a bar in both of these places, but they are establishments of the highest class. The best of decorum always prevails and women are ABSOLUTELY barred." By excluding women, these establishments sought to avoid being accused of harboring prostitution. But this policy also meant that the "famous" Keystone Hotel, "the Mecca of all that is bright and best in the colored race," and the popular Elite Café were oriented primarily to a male clientele (see map 1, and discussion of the Elite's controversial owner, Henry "Teenan" Jones, in the next chapter). Along with the poolrooms, cigar shops, and barbershops in the Black Belt, these saloons provided men with exclusive recreational spaces.[67] For Black men, then, the corner of Thirty-first and State was "the regular meeting place, the center of interest, the only place when you want to seen [sic] and be seen."[68]

But where could Black women see and be seen in public? The article quoted earlier suggests that women were not participants in the Stroll's street corner conversations. And women were barred from some of State Street's most fashionable saloons not only because they might be (taken as) prostitutes but also because they might make spectacles of themselves by appearing drunk in public: "Intoxicated women (the bane of civilization) and equally soused men are never encountered in the select places 'along the stroll.' "[69] The role of a Black flâneuse who openly engages in the new looking and social relations made possible along the bustling Stroll seems, in these discourses, unsavory, if not unthinkable.

African American women seeking to promenade along South State Street certainly knew that they would be looked at, even if the *Defender* did not foreground the new subjectivities they were developing in modern urban contexts. Women were visually inspected and verbally accosted on a regular basis by Black men gathered along the Stroll. Shane White and Graham White note that "one could always see women on State Street" but that "the Stroll became a byword for an aggressive display of masculinity," including "a type of behavior that frequently amounted to what nowadays would be labeled sexual harassment and, even when it did not, was sufficiently raucous and unruly to be an affront to many middle-class African Americans."[70] Strolling functioned as a mode of performing one's racial, gender, and class identity, a practice that could be, depending on one's position and attitude, liberating and/or embarrassing, seductive and/or objectifying, empowering and/or unpleasant.

Some of these dynamics are suggested in a cartoon depicting a Stroll encounter featured on the cover of sheet music for "Take Your Time" (1907), composed by Joe Jordan (fig. 27).[71] Jordan served as orchestra leader and musical director at the landmark Pekin (2700 S. State Street), and the cartoon depicts two African American men ogling a Black woman as she walks past the popular saloon, music hall, and theatrical venue located at the Stroll's northern tip (see map 1, and more detailed discussion of the Pekin in the next chapter). The images of Black Chicagoans in this drawing are similar to the yearbook caricatures of Black Belt male and female types drawn by white students at the neighboring Armour Institute of Technology, as discussed in the introduction (see figs. 8 and 9), especially in their depictions of Black (male) fancy dress. However, the humor of the "Take Your Time" illustration derives not primarily from minstrel traditions or fears about Black invasions of white spaces but from Black community settings for and discourses about everyday city life. Black street deportment is rendered here not as a comic display of imitating white manners but as part

FIGURE 27. Cartoon depicting two men watching a woman walk past the Stroll's popular (but controversial) Pekin Theatre. Detail from the sheet music cover of "Take Your Time," music by Joe Jordan, words by Harrison Stewart (Pekin Publishing Company, 1907). From the collection of Terry Parrish.

of a Black urban world in which Black-owned businesses (like the Pekin) and African American cultural production (like the theater's inaugural, Jordan-penned musical *Man from Bam*) are thriving. We can certainly imagine how both the yearbook and the sheet music images would be embarrassing to Black Chicago elites and reformers seeking to distance the Race from crude stereotypes and lewd behavior. But the "Take Your Time" cartoon references popular and street culture to capture a different kind of emblematic Black performance than what the middle class might want to present. It illustrates the interplay of the visual and the verbal, of display and dialogue among Black Belt types, specifically how Black men and women look at and speak to each other on the Stroll. The man on the far left may be telling the woman to "take her time," or to slow down so that he can take in a longer view of her body; he may be advising the other man to "take his time" as he tries to make time (flirt) with the woman; or, as the song's second verse suggests, he may be warning his Stroll brother about where such a flirtation may lead:

Familiarity breeds contempt is what folks do say
Got acquainted with a girl day fore yesterday
She said I was the finest man dat she'd ever seen
She commenced talking 'bout marrying so naturally I scream'd
Take your time, take your time
Dat's the best way to do you will find
When you take a wife it's the same as jail for life
Take your time

The lyrics and illustration depict public life as open and attractive for Black men, particularly for bachelors. In contrast, the experience and meanings of strolling for Black women seeking to circulate in city streets (those who, like the woman in the drawing, may or may not be looking for a date or a husband) are not as easily interpreted or recuperated.

Like African American men and white women, African American women struggled with the question of what kinds of attention they could and should attract in the city. But their behaviors (particularly those of working-class Black women) were alternately highlighted (in terms of moral panic) and overshadowed (by emphasis on the public culture for Black men) in discourses about the dangers and opportunities of urban life. The Stroll's function as a stage for Black masculinist behavior was especially pronounced during and after the Great Migration, when, as I discuss later in this chapter, tensions flared across race and class lines regarding appropriate public Black behavior with the massive influx of working-class Black southerners. If African American women (older settlers and newer migrants) wanted to take advantage of the cultural and expressive opportunities offered in northern and urban contexts—not just access to a wider network of spaces but the display of fashion and sophistication that city life was supposed to enable—they had to negotiate the constant sexualization of their public appearances (by Black men and whites, by strollers and reformers), as well as traditional prohibitions on women's public roles, and modern anxieties about how those roles would have to change as African Americans in every class position pressed for public freedoms for the Race as a whole.

Although Black women faced a number of race-, gender-, and class-based restrictions on their public behavior, they were directly solicited by a number of the Stroll's commercial amusements, including movie theaters. Film exhibitors frequently played up their advertising to women, in part because women constituted an important part of the expanding African American market. The Phoenix Theater, for example, located at the nerve center of Thirty-first and State Streets (see map 1), stressed in its advertisements that it "cater[ed] to ladies and children" by showing "selected high class motion pictures."[72] Judging from the pages of the *Defender*, it seems that even though women were barred from certain forms and venues of public recreation, they were encouraged to participate in a variety of other commercial amusements depending on how their presence would affect indices of profitability and respectability. The presence of women could damage the credibility of saloons, for example, but increase the propriety of movie theaters. In some instances, women were welcomed to entertainments that would seem to be open to men only. A front-page *Defender* item announcing a wrestling exhibition at Odd Fellows Hall features a large, erotic photo of the muscular wrestler Illa Vincent and quotes another wrestler, "Sampson, the German Hercules," as saying that "he hopes to see the ladies as well as the gentlemen out on Saturday night."[73] Perhaps this appeal to female fans was primarily an advertising ploy to get more men to attend—the exhibition would offer male spectators both a wrestling display and, perhaps, a coterie of available women. Thus Black women could signify many things when they appeared in different public places, and Black Belt venues took advantage both of women's desire to enjoy safe, comfortable leisure environments and of their function as magnets for other potential patrons across lines of gender, age, and class.

A significant number of Black women created leisure activities for themselves by establishing a network of women's clubs. Chicago's elite and middle-class Black women participated in social, literary, economic, arts, dancing, and matrimony clubs, among others, and their activities were well documented in the Black press. These women hosted whist parties, musicales, luncheons, and charity balls, often using these events to flaunt their comparative wealth and refined sensibilities. In her detailed study of African American club women's activities in turn-of-the-century Chicago, Anne Meis Knupfer describes the many ways in which these women organized clubs not only to amuse themselves and to stage "genteel performances" but also to achieve social equity, political reform, and racial uplift. Certainly many Black club women took pleasure in the superficial trappings of their social activities, but at the same time they offered a few material benefits for Black women outside of their social set. For example, Knupfer points out that while these women enjoyed displaying their cultural capital at extravagant social events, the events also "supported the predominantly female business of dressmakers, milliners, chiropodists, hairdressers, and manicurists," thereby providing "alternative forms of employment to African American women who faced discrimination in the workforce."[74] Club-sponsored social events could generate income for Black women entrepreneurs while also raising money for less fortunate members of the Race, but they did so by maintaining the markers of class stratification among these groups (i.e., those who wore the ball gowns, those who made the ball gowns, those unfortunates in need of uplift for whom the ball was staged).

Although most Black women's club activities were rigidly segregated by class, some of these women also participated in uplift activities designed to connect them directly with the lower classes and others in need. Club women were particularly concerned about providing for the elderly, for poor Black children, and for young working girls, and they established activities and institutions to mentor and care for these underserved groups.[75] Knupfer frequently notes that Chicago's Black club women, like their white counterparts, were concerned about the effects of unwholesome work and living conditions, as well as leisure activities, on children and young women in an urban environment. The Chicago Vice Commission noted in its 1911 report that "the prejudice against colored girls who are ambitious to earn an honest living is unjust. Such an attitude eventually drives them into immoral surroundings. They need special care and protection on the maxim that it is the duty of the strong to help the weak."[76] Long before the commission made this declaration, African American club women recognized their responsibility for steering young people in the right direction in the absence of effective municipal action.

Knupfer notes that "to alleviate delinquency, wholesome recreational activities, such as youth clubs, dances, lyceums, and picnics were organized and chaperoned by the club women to lure adolescents away from neighborhood saloons, dance halls, and pool rooms."[77] Club women organized debates, essay contests, and other activities as positive distractions from the city's tempting, disreputable amusements. Despite their often elitist and highly religious approaches, the club women organized youth group and settlement activities that were intended not only to "uplift" young people but also to appeal to their particular interests and desires. Engaging them "in the popular culture of dances, songs, and sports," for example, these youth clubs differed from "the middle-class youth clubs, which reflected the cultural capital of evening gowns, promenades, and whist and bridge games." Instead, club women created activities that offered the less privileged teenager opportunities to "forget about his or her impoverished home or neighborhood, without the moral overtones often accompanying

YMCA or YWCA programs."[78] Thus Black club women, who experienced regulation of their leisure activities based on racial and gender difference, performed some policing of their own with regard to the uplift activities they devised for Black youth and the lower classes.

As Chicago's African American community continued to grow in numbers through the midteens, Black club women and institutions like the Black church and the African American press functioned as cultural arbiters, attempting to model, provide, and promote acceptable forms of Black leisure. While some of these spokespeople celebrated the range of activities available to African Americans in Chicago, and sometimes attempted to do "away with the State Street bugaboo, away with the odium against 31st and State streets,"[79] other cultural observers tried to circumscribe the scope of Black leisure within boundaries of class, gender, and age. In some ways, it would seem that these efforts to define and monitor the boundaries of Black recreation for certain segments of the community would contradict the larger political project of securing the right of the Race as a whole to patronize the amusements of their choice. Notions of class, in particular, enabled African Americans higher up on the social scale to distinguish between themselves and less affluent, less educated Blacks who, in their view, needed protection from disreputable amusements and a redirection of their desires to patronize such amusements. However, during the late teens, attempts to monitor and police African American leisure activities along the Stroll and elsewhere were further complicated by the arrival of huge waves of Black migrants to Chicago's South Side. This Great Migration intensified long-standing debates and problems regarding Black leisure in an urban environment.

## Urban Attractions and Distractions: Black Leisure and the Great Migration

Years before the Great Migration of 1916–19, many Black observers were skeptical about the impact of urban living on the future and well-being of the Race. For instance, during a lecture at Chicago's Bethel A.M.E. Church delivered in January 1900, Booker T. Washington admonished Black parents to keep a close and constant eye on their boys and girls to "prevent them from keeping company with the vile and vicious associates—prevent them from roaming the streets at all hours of the day and night—keep them out of saloons, gambling hells and brothels," because these kinds of people and places would lead to their eventual downfall and incarceration. Washington recognized that "it is an admitted truth that more vice and crime surrounds our race in the large centers of population in the North than in the South" and went on to claim that "doctors state that owing to their dissipation and criminal practices they are dying off more rapidly than the whites."[80] Washington dramatically asserts that the physical health of the Race is endangered by the unseemly side of northern, urban life, despite the numerous social and economic advantages the industrial North claims to offer. Although Washington encouraged African Americans to stay put and build capital and character in the South, thousands of Black southerners took their chances and moved to the North.

Chicago was a particularly attractive destination for southern migrants during the late teens not only because of the economic benefits (particularly higher-paying industrial work), but also because Black southerners already felt a familiarity with the city's meatpacking firms, Black-owned businesses, society happenings, and entertainments from reading the *Chicago Defender*. James Grossman notes that Robert S. Abbott's militant newspaper was promoted and distributed in the South by Black Pullman porters, eventually becoming "the most widely read newspaper in the black South, afford[ing] thousands of prospective migrants glimpses of an exciting city with a vibrant and assertive black community." Chicago was easily accessible from many points south via the Illinois Central Railroad. Grossman estimates that from 1916 to 1919, "between fifty and seventy thousand black southerners relocated in Chicago, and thousands more passed through the city before moving on to other locations North."[81]

Many southerners wrote directly to the *Defender* regarding job advertisements they saw in its pages and seeking financial assistance for transportation (usually train fare) to the North. In their letters, potential migrants insist that they want to come north to work and not to play. A man from Pensacola, Florida, responded to a *Defender* ad seeking laborers for a foundry in 1917: "I am a working man I am not sport or a gamble or class with them. . . . But I am study evry day working man of family wife and one child 9 years old."[82] Another writer, from Atlanta, says he would like to come to Chicago "as a workman . . . not a loafer" and describes himself as a "good strong *moral religious* man no habits" (emphasis in original).[83] Still another writer, from West Palm Beach, Florida, vouches not only for his own character but for that of his children as well: "I don't drink al all [sic] any thing like whiskey I am a church man and all the children belong to the church too."[84] These individuals, and many others, tried to present themselves as models of industriousness, sobriety, and respectability, in keeping with the ideals espoused by their beacon, the *Defender*. "We are not coming for pleasure," wrote a man in New Orleans, "we are looking for wirk and better treatment and more money and i ask your aid in helping us to secure a good position of work as we are men of familys and we canot aford to loaf."[85]

Migrants who found jobs and settled in cities like Chicago had to acclimate themselves to many aspects of northern, urban life, including a new sense of work and leisure time. As numerous historians have pointed out, those migrants who worked as "farmers, handymen and personal servants" in the South were not accustomed to the fast and rigid pace of industrial labor in factories and stockyards. In addition, as Grossman explains, "Black southerners' hours of work had depended as farmers and rural laborers not upon the clock, but upon the sun, the calendar, and the vicissitudes of a crop."[86] This meant that a migrant's conception of completing a day's work or a particular task was linked to larger, seasonal crop cycles, not mechanized and regulated on a daily basis by an employer. In the rural South, Black workers had much more flexibility in their individual schedules than industrial work allowed. As a result, many Chicago employers complained that recent migrants failed to report to work every day and often arrived late. These criticisms were incorporated into the orientations provided to new migrants by Black service organizations such as the Wabash Avenue YMCA (3763 S. Wabash Avenue; see map 1). Spear quotes A. L. Jackson, the YMCA's executive director, who reports a conversation with a migrant who complained that he had lost his job: "Had he gone to work every day? . . . 'Goodness no. . . . I had to have some days of the week off for pleasure.'"[87] Migrants had to make adjustments to their conceptions of leisure time relative to their new industrial work schedules. Whereas in the South, "sharecroppers would take full days off and turn weddings and funerals into prolonged social occasions, especially during seasons of less intensive labor," in northern cities industrial employers who oversaw a "continuous production process" had little tolerance for "such spontaneous and unilaterally declared 'holidays'" on the part of their laborers.[88]

Although Black migrants had to structure their leisure time differently, rest and recreation constituted significant portions of their new, urban lifestyles. Black migrants experienced a dramatic shift in their conceptions of "spending time" when they moved into northern cities. Many reported that industrial work ultimately provided them with more leisure time and, because they received higher salaries, more disposable income than they ever had in the South. Industrial labor and crowded living conditions could be difficult to bear in cities, but there was time and money to seek diversion outside of the home. Thus, in many respects Black life in Chicago stood in stark contrast to the southern agrarian life, such as that described by Du Bois in *The Souls of Black Folk* (1903). Du Bois paints a bleak portrait of life among Blacks in Dougherty County, Georgia, at the turn of the century, emphasizing their lack of leisure time: "Among this people there is no leisure class. . . . here ninety-six per cent are toiling; no one with leisure to turn the bare and cheerless cabin into a home, no old folks to sit beside the fire and hand down traditions of the past. . . . The toil, like all farm toil, is broken only by the gayety of the thoughtless and the Saturday trip to town."[89] Du Bois defines "leisure" here not simply as a marker of class distinction and economic privilege but as any time free from labor that would be most productively used to enjoy and cultivate domesticity, family interaction, and the transmission of culture and traditions. But because of the physically, emotionally, and economically draining nature of southern agricultural work, rural Blacks have little energy or opportunity to make productive use of what little free time they manage to spare. Many of the parameters of Black leisure in the South were established during slavery, when Black activities like going to town, dancing, drinking, and participating in religious worship were allowed but monitored by whites. E. Franklin Frazier points out the significance of keeping antebellum Black leisure visible and legible when he notes that while overseers and masters would permit certain forms of Black "merriment," such as religious activities, they were suspicious of Blacks using leisure time for "meditation or reflection."[90] In the decades after emancipation, southern, rural Black leisure continued to be limited to fleeting, conspicuous, and heavily policed distractions.

However, Black migrants in Chicago in the late teens found new possibilities in the changed structure of their work and leisure time, as well as their new standing in public and private spaces. When migrants were interviewed by the Chicago Commission on Race Relations (CCRR) about their migration experience, fourteen out of twenty respondents reported that life in Chicago was easier, and many credited it with shorter workdays and increases in salary. "I get more money for my work and have some spare time," one migrant stated. Another concurred, adding that he had "more time for rest and to spend with family."[91] Thus, it would seem that despite the warnings of Booker T. Washington and others, in some ways an urban setting could be beneficial for Black domestic life, enabling African Americans to spend more leisure time at home and with family than might have been possible in the South.

But it is also clear that urban Blacks spent large amounts of their newly won leisure time patronizing public, commercial amusements. The southern "Saturday trip to town" was replaced in northern urban life by more frequent leisure activities in much closer proximity to Black residential areas. Thus the hearthside transmission of culture that Du Bois imagines may not have actually occurred more frequently among Blacks who enjoyed more leisure time as a result of northern and urban migration. Numerous cultural commentators, Black and white, expressed concerns about the impact of commercial amusements on family and community life, in light of the radical changes precipitated by urbanization and industrialization. For example, John Collier, a member of the National Board of Censorship of Motion Pictures, told an audience at the Economic Club of Providence in 1912 that as a result of "free government" and mechanized production "we have today in America more leisure time than we have proved ourselves able to use well,"[92] particularly in urban areas. Under these conditions, Collier argues, factories, public schools, and outside leisure activities pull families apart, leaving them little time or reason to be together at home. Collier is most concerned about the damaging effects of unregulated, irresponsible commercial entertainments: "We cannot leave recreation to commerce. Commercialized recreation means dissipation; dissipation means that leisure time, no longer the great creative agent of society, has become a social destroyer instead. Commercialized recreation means saloons, it means the commercial dance-hall, it means the theatre dominated by financial speculation and the moving picture reduced to the general level of yellow journalism."[93] Although Collier's discussion is limited to a consideration of leisure for white (Anglo-Saxon, Irish) subjects, his words resonate with those expressed by many others during the first decades of the twentieth century with regard to monitoring the activities of other European immigrants, and African American migrants, when they are not working.

As I have already begun to indicate, despite the fact that many Black southerners stressed their desire to work when they sought northern jobs and rail passes, after they got to Chicago, leisure activities became an extremely important part of their new lives away from "the darkness of the south."[94] Interviews conducted by the CCRR illustrate the tremendous significance of the new sense of public freedom experienced by southern migrants. For example, as cited in the previous chapter, the Thomas family from Seals, Alabama, reported their surprise at being able to move unmolested through Chicago's public spaces. Migrants like the Thomas family indicate that the opportunity to patronize "more places of attraction" complemented the economic, political, and educational opportunities offered by northern cities.[95] Another migrant registers both the array of amusements in Chicago and the time one could take to enjoy them: "Place just full of life. Went to see the sights every night for a month."[96]

The choice of amusements for African Americans increased dramatically during the Great Migration, as entertainments for a rapidly growing, segregated Black population became increasingly profitable. Business along the Stroll was booming, and the Black press reflected this in its columns and advertisements. For example, in 1918, the *Chicago Broad Ax,* which rarely featured entertainment news, praised the jazz and ragtime performances at the Dreamland Café, "one of the most pleasant places of amusement on the South Side."[97] As a primarily political (Democratic) newspaper that circulated within Chicago, the *Broad Ax* never demonstrated much of an interest in commercial entertainments, but by the late teens the Stroll's places of amusement found their way to its pages.[98] The *Defender,* on the other hand, prominently featured entertainment news and advertising in each weekly issue (particularly the Stroll's vibrant theatrical scene; fig. 28), not only for the information of local readers but also to project an image of the Black Belt to readers across the country, including potential migrants throughout the South. In this way, the *Defender* (and, to a lesser extent, the *Broad Ax*) sent mixed signals to prospective migrants and new arrivals in Chicago. They stressed the importance of perseverance and hard work to migrants, while also painting a picture of Chicago as a place with so many entertaining ways to enjoy one's leisure hours. They emphasized the virtue of working steadily and saving one's earnings, while promoting establishments where African Americans could quickly spend their newly acquired disposable income.

Some migrant accounts make it seem as if the world was open to them in Chicago, in contrast to the South, not just because they had more money and time to spend amusing themselves but also because of reduced racial discrimination. One migrant reported to the CCRR, "At home did not earn much money and did not have any left to go what few places colored people were allowed to go. Here, Negroes can have whatever they want."[99] Migrants appreciated the fact that so many amusements were available to them, even if they did not choose to patronize them all. One migrant observed that Blacks in Chicago can "spend money anywhere you want to, go anywhere you have money enough to go; don't go out very much but like to know I can where and when I want to."[100] Other migrants noted that in the absence of southern-style Jim Crow segregation, they "can go to the parks and places of amusement [without] being segregated"; enjoy improved "conditions on the street cars and in movies"; and "don't have to

FIGURE 28. Advertisements for Black Belt theaters illustrating a vibrant, race-proud (and patriotic) urban entertainment culture. *Chicago Defender,* 22 February 1919.

look up to the white man, get off the street for him, and go to the buzzard roost at shows."[101]

These observations bear out the comparative images of the South and North conveyed by the *Defender*, even before the Great Migration began. For instance, the front page of the May 23, 1914, issue carried two stories, one about a mob of two hundred whites in Jackson, Mississippi, who forcibly closed the "No Name" movie theater when its new owners converted it to a Black-only venue, and another announcing that Chicago's Stroll was expanding its southern boundary from Thirty-fifth Street to Thirty-ninth Street.[102] While Blacks in Jackson witnessed the violent destruction of the only movie house open to them ("the mob cut the wires, disconnected the moving picture apparatus, and finally locked up the place"), Black Chicagoans enjoyed a commercial strip in their community that expanded to offer them an increasing array of leisure activities. Gradually ads appearing in the *Defender* for amusement venues in the South (e.g., the opening of the Douglas movie and vaudeville theater in Macon, Georgia, in 1917) indicated that commercial entertainments were becoming more available for southern Blacks, perhaps as part of southern white efforts to stem the outflow of Black labor to the North.[103] But clearly Chicago offered an unparalleled array of venues serving Black patrons. The Great Migration expanded the city's Black clientele and therefore increased the number of public accommodations to serve them. In addition, migrants reported not only that they enjoyed amusements in their own neighborhood but also that they could participate in mainstream entertainments outside of the Black Belt. For example, in addition to their own amateur and professional athletic teams (e.g., church baseball leagues and the Leland Giants baseball team), African Americans could attend major league White Sox games. In a letter sent back home, a recent migrant to Chicago writes to a friend:

> I wish you could have been here . . . to those games. I saw them and beleve me they was worth the money I pay to see them. T.S. and I went out to see Sunday game witch was 7 to 2 White Sox and I saw Satday game 2 to 1 White Sox. Please tell J—— write that he will never see nothing as long as he stay down there behind the sun there some thing to see up here all the time.[104]

Grossman notes that letters like these, in which migrants reported their firsthand experiences of urban life to friends and family down home, were circulated widely in southern Black communities, doing more to convince people to migrate than "any advertisement, agent or publication."[105]

Not only did the range of available amusements give migrants a new sense of social freedom and equality in the urban North, but commercial entertainments could also help migrants to overcome feelings of homesickness and isolation. Sociologist Donna Franklin has argued that the transition to northern urban life fragmented the sense of Black community because people did less visiting and had fewer friends, and the intimacy that characterized Black relations in the South was replaced with "the detached and impersonal social relations of the city."[106] Franklin's account of southern community relations differs in important ways from Du Bois's description of the rural South, in which agricultural "toil" makes such intimate, meaningful home and communal relationships seem impossible, as well as from migrant reports that urban lifestyles actually provide more time to spend with family. Still, Franklin echoes observations many of these same migrants make regarding the difficulty of adjusting to their relative social isolation in northern cities, away from familiar networks. Whereas some migrants relocated in groups (such as extended or multiple families, entire congregations) or connected with church members, friends, or relatives when they got to the city, many others came alone or as single families, had no connections in Chicago, and felt like strangers in an intimidating new environment. For example, the Thomas family (mentioned earlier), which consisted of "Mr. Thomas, his wife and two children, a girl nineteen and a boy seventeen," had belonged to a church and several fraternal orders back home, where they "took part in rural community life." Upon arriving in Chicago, however, they became ashamed of their southern manners and speech. As a result, "[all] the family were timid and self-conscious and for a long time avoided contacts, thus depriving themselves of helpful suggestions."[107] Perhaps their patronage of "various amusement places" helped to make up for the community life they left behind. The Thomases' experience suggests how migrants had to redefine their identities and practices as individuals and as families in northern cities, producing new "community" relations. Community life in Chicago was enabled, for better (as related by many satisfied migrants) and/or for worse (in Collier's and Franklin's views), by public spheres that were more commercialized but also more "free" than the traditional structures of social life in the South. As another migrant describes his or her first impressions of Chicago: "Didn't like it; lonesome, until I went out. Then liked the places of amusement which have no restrictions."[108]

But Black life in Chicago was by no means completely free of racial restrictions. Although migrants were optimistic about improvements in their social, economic, and political status outside of the South, once they arrived in cities like Chicago they quickly discovered a different set of social practices. The dramatic increase in Chicago's Black population resulted in a variety of discriminatory practices in housing, employment, and public accommodations. Segregation of public facilities (including "inns, restaurants, eating houses, hotels, soda-fountains, saloons, barber shops, bathrooms, theaters, skating rinks, concerts, cafés, bicycle rinks, elevators, ice-cream parlors" and public conveyances) had been outlawed by the Illinois Civil Rights Act of 1885.[109] Still, African Americans were barred from, or received bad treatment in, many public places, even some located within the Black Belt. For example, the CCRR reported that an L-shaped restaurant located at the corner of Thirty-first Street and Indiana Avenue catered to whites on the Thirty-first Street side and to Blacks on the Indiana Avenue side. The "white" side was "neatly arranged and well-kept" and staffed with white waiters. The "Black" side featured "colored" waitresses and was "narrow," "dark," "not kept neatly," and "not so well supplied." The two dining rooms were served by the same kitchen but had different names. If Blacks entered the Thirty-first Street room designated for whites, "they [were] given indifferent service, [were] required to wait long and the service given them [was] reluctant and discourteous."[110] Even within the Black Belt many white proprietors continued to maintain rigid racial segregation in an effort to preserve social hierarchies that the migration and empowerment of African Americans were threatening to rearrange.

Thus the public and personal experiences of African Americans in Chicago were often paradoxical. The social and political freedoms they enjoyed up North were tempered by instances of racial discrimination, both inside and outside of the Black Belt. An interview with the Jones family, who migrated to Chicago from Texas in 1919, illustrates how migrants' urban experiences, as well as their accounts of these experiences, could be contradictory. The CCRR investigator reports: "They had been told that no discrimination was practiced against Negroes in Chicago; that they could go where they pleased without embarrassment or hindrance because of their color. Accordingly, when they first came to Chicago, they went into drug-stores and restaurants. They were refused service in numbers of restaurants and at the refreshment counters in some drug-stores."[111] Despite these negative experiences in public accommodations, the Jones family still claims that their "greatest satisfaction" in coming to Chicago is "escape from Jim Crow conditions and segregation," as well as better work conditions. Here the Jones family maintains that life in Chicago offers them freedom from segregation, after acknowledging that they have been refused service at various places of business.

Perhaps the "escape from Jim Crow" they describe is comparative—in the South they would have been uniformly barred from public accommodations, whereas in Chicago, racial discrimination was "unofficial, informal, and uncertain."[112] According to Spear, the discrimination that African Americans faced in downtown restaurants, theaters, and department stores like Marshall Field's was sporadic; many white establishments "served Negroes with courtesy" or "had no policy at all but simply allowed individual clerks to follow their own inclinations."[113] This kind of inconsistency seems to have characterized the treatment of African Americans by theaters located outside of the Black Belt. For example, in March 1912, the *Defender* reported that white ushers at the Columbia Theater on North Clark Street near Division instructed a Black woman to take a seat in the gallery or be refused admission.[114] But the very next week the *Defender* ran an item in its "Musical and Dramatic" section praising the fine pictures, talented vocalists, and courteous service offered at the Orpheum Photo Play House located in downtown Chicago, on State Street near Monroe.[115] Thus, both before and after the Great Migration, Blacks "could never be certain when they might be embarrassed or humiliated by discriminatory practices."[116]

The uncertainty and inconsistency of racial discrimination in the urban North certainly had a tremendous impact on Black migrants' conceptions of leisure and amusement, since they always had to be prepared to face discrimination, even though they had made the move north, in large part, to escape racial restrictions. Perhaps it was the very irregularity of racist treatment in Chicago's public accommodations, and the freedom to voice complaints in venues like the *Defender,* that gave migrants an overall sense that segregation was less of a factor in their lives up North. Farah Jasmine Griffin has argued that while racist white power in the South was "immediate" and "identifiable" (usually taking the form of physical assaults such as "lynching, beating, and rape"), in the North Black southerners confronted new "mechanisms of power," which were "more subtle and sophisticated."[117] The different contours of race relations in the North could be disappointing and difficult to recognize, but they were not as consistent and inflexible as those in the South. Therefore, while racism continued to shape Black public life, Black migrants could learn to navigate discrimination in the city (identify which theaters to attend, which stores to patronize) while they simultaneously opposed all racial segregation and experienced the North as a dramatic improvement over their lives in the Jim Crow South.

Migrants were not the only ones who expressed contradictory views about the Black experience in the urban North. Many African Americans who had lived in Chicago prior to the Great Migration claimed that before the large influx of Black southerners, race prejudice was not a major factor in their lives. Drake and Cayton quote a number of "Old Settlers" who nostalgically recall the prevalence and acceptability of Black-white personal and professional relationships, ranging from interracial marriages to Black doctors serving white patients. Old Settlers claimed that before the Great Migration, they could work and patronize businesses freely in any part of the city. "There was no discrimination in Chicago during my early childhood days," according to one woman who came to the city in the 1890s, "but as the Negroes began coming to Chicago in numbers it seems they brought discrimination with them."[118] Certainly Chicago's race relations did undergo dramatic changes as the Black population increased, and perhaps these Old Settlers found that it was easier, and safer, to blame the new migrants, with their southern ways, than to condemn white Chicagoans for their discriminatory treatment of the entire Black community during this period. Despite their complaints, however, racial discrimination was hardly a new development occasioned only by the Great Migration. The pages of the *Defender*, for example, clearly demonstrate that African Americans had faced racist treatment before the Great Migration, particularly in public amusements.

In addition to the "dastardly conduct" of white ushers at the Columbia Theater just described, the *Defender* reported numerous cases during the early 1910s in which African Americans were discriminated against in downtown theaters. In June 1910, a pair of stories detailed how two Black men, George A. Wilson and Frank D. Donaldson, were refused admission to the lower floor of the Colonial Theater.[119] Wilson, an insurance agent, took the Colonial to court, where an all-white jury denied his request for $200 in damages. Donaldson, in contrast, won his case, perhaps because he engaged the services of militant Black attorney Edward H. Morris, who, as a member of the state legislature, had helped to construct Illinois's civil rights law. Reportedly, Morris's persuasive closing argument was convincing to the jury, which included a white man who stated during jury selection that "Negroes should go to the Pekin [the prominent Black Belt venue], and not to the downtown theaters."[120] Later that year, Mrs. Monroe L. Manning, the wife of a railroad porter, refused a seat in the Jim Crow section of the Globe Theater. Mrs. Manning complained to the manager, who begrudgingly gave her a better seat in a section reserved for whites. Manning told the *Defender* that African Americans are routinely subjected to this kind of discrimination because "many of them don't know that a theatre, restaurant, department [store?], and a church are public places and as such, no person should be barred."[121] All three of these stories demonstrate that African Americans faced racial discrimination in Chicago's public accommodations years before the Great Migration began. In addition, they illustrate that Black and white responses to such discrimination could be just as inconsistent as the instances of discrimination themselves. White juries were as likely to absolve offending theaters as fine them; Black theatergoers like Wilson, Donaldson, and Manning protested racist treatment, but many others (as Manning suggests) silently suffered illegal segregation.

Black migrants not only faced the possibility of racial discrimination in Chicago but also had to watch out for the many real and alleged dangers of urban living, including illicit and criminal activity. New migrants were not merely potential victims of crime; they also could be seduced by the Black Belt's active underworld of gambling and prostitution. As one settled migrant told a CCRR investigator, southerners who had no connections when they arrived in Chicago were most at risk: "The danger lies in getting among the wrong class of people."[122] As I will elaborate further in the next chapter, during the late teens, the Black Belt continued to be home to numerous vice activities, and Black leaders continued to express concerns about the safety of African American women and children. For example, African American club women sought to address the problem by agitating for, among other things, more "playground and recreational facilities" for Black youths to provide alternatives to saloons, dance halls, poolrooms, and cheap theaters.[123] But while migrants and reformers responded to a number of serious urban dangers and to inequities in allocations of municipal resources, the image of the dangerous city was also conjured by members of the Black elite to justify their uplift activities and to maintain their roles as guardians of Black public life and the Black public image. Thus, while Chicago's vibrant social and entertainment life was part of the attraction for thousands of southern migrants during the late teens, upon their arrival they learned that Black urban leisure was shaped by vice, by racial discrimination, and by gender, age, and class differentiation within the Black community, all of which complicated their enjoyment of public amusements.

Between the turn of the century and the years of the Great Migration, Blacks in Chicago developed an active public life, including a world of leisure activities. Despite the discriminatory treatment they received from white Chicagoans, from the exclusionary World's Fair to the tightening of residential restrictions with the influx of southern migrants, African Americans created a diverse array of cultural institutions and practices growing out of their unique cultural interests, as well as their desires to mirror (and eventually gain access to) mainstream models. Although traditional Black activities and amusements (i.e., those provided by churches, lodges, clubs) held their central places in African American cultural life, by the late teens commercial amusements became increasingly important among the urban leisure activities that shaped modern Black experience. Patronizing movie theaters became an extremely popular method of participating in urban community life, even as race leaders and the Black press expressed ambivalence about the cinema. In the next chapter, I describe more specifically how theaters located in Chicago's Black Belt before and during the Great Migration attempted to capitalize on the cinema's rapidly growing popularity while negotiating its tenuous moral and cultural position within the Black community.

# CHAPTER FIVE

# Along the "Stroll"

*Chicago's Black Belt Movie Theaters*

During the first two decades of the twentieth century, moviegoing became one of the most popular and, therefore, hotly debated leisure activities for African Americans in Chicago and other cities. As a feature of a northern industrial landscape that was more "modern" than the South, but still structured by racial segregation, urban moviegoing could allow Black people, particularly migrants, to assume a range of evolving public rights and roles. For example, Mary Carbine persuasively argues that during this period movie theaters provided Chicago's African American community with "a space for consciousness and assertion of social difference as well as the consumption of mass amusements," particularly via culturally specific live entertainment by vaudeville, blues, and jazz performers.[1] But, as discussed in the previous chapter, early Black film culture was also heavily influenced by elements of vice that surrounded Black urban amusements in general and that informed discussions about movies and their places of exhibition in particular. This chapter describes how Black Belt theaters negotiated a wide variety of Black reactions to the movies' status as both an extremely popular entertainment and a cheap, disreputable amusement during a period of rapid growth in the city's African American population.

Black Chicagoans differed in their understanding of how theater space could be used for the expression of Black pride and progress, on the one hand, and to the distraction and detriment of the Race, on the other, as evidenced by the controversy surrounding the opening of the legendary Pekin Theatre in 1906. The Pekin was one of the country's first Black-owned and Black-managed theaters to feature motion pictures.[2] One of the shining stars in the constellation of venues along South State Street, the Pekin not only showed films but also was celebrated for its stock company of Black actors, for featuring appearances by the country's leading African American entertainers, for employing a large number of Blacks from the community, and for not discriminating against African American patrons. But this celebrated race theater opened under a cloud of controversy because it was housed in a building that had long been home to one of Chicago's most popular and notorious saloons. Located at the corner of Twenty-seventh and State Streets, between the southern boundary of Chicago's vice district and the northern edge of the Black Belt, the Pekin was converted from a saloon to a theater by owner Robert T. Motts, "gambling lord of the South Side" (fig. 29).[3]

Many of Chicago's race leaders denounced the Pekin as a disreputable venue, whereas others celebrated it as a symbol of race pride and Black entrepreneurial spirit. Black religious leaders in particular preached against the Pekin, urging their congregations not to support an establishment with such a scandalous past and infamous owner. Rev. Archibald J. Carey of Bethel A.M.E. Church called the Pekin a "low gambling dive," and both he and Rev. E. J. Fisher of Olivet Baptist Church spoke out against a benefit for the Frederick Douglass Center, a Black settlement, that was scheduled to be held there. In contrast, Ida B. Wells, who was organizing the benefit along with a number of Chicago's "representative women," selected the Pekin specifically to build community support for Motts's new venture. Wells was appalled by the inflexibility of those leaders who refused to accept the Pekin's new identity, such as Anna Morgan, a noted drama teacher whose students had been scheduled to present a play at the benefit. Morgan pulled out after she "learned of the Pekin's notorious reputation," because "the young ladies in her school of acting had come from the best families of the city" and "she could not afford to take them into such a place."[4] For many, the Pekin's history as a saloon overshadowed its efforts to provide Black Chicagoans with a comfortable, culturally specific environment in which to enjoy live performances and moving pictures.

Despite the protests, the Douglass Center benefit was a success. The Pekin went on to earn a national reputation for providing high-quality entertainment; movie and vaudeville theaters serving Black audiences across the country adopted the Pekin name. Dan Streible observes that the Pekin's tremendous popularity over the next few years "marked a progressive shift in the state of black theatrical enterprises" from "the level of honky-tonks" to venues offering legitimate entertainment.[5] But the controversy that the Pekin Theatre inspired demonstrates how questions of legitimacy consistently arose in connection with places of Black urban amusement. While such places were inextricably linked in public discourses with Black efforts to achieve social freedoms, political equality, and economic self-

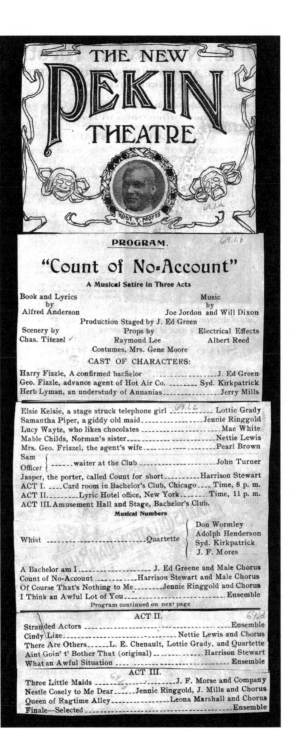

FIGURE 29. Portrait of owner Robert Motts on a program for a theatrical production at the new, "legitimate" Pekin Theatre (c. 1907). Special Collections and Preservation Division, Chicago Public Library.

determination, Black urban entertainments did not consistently adhere to traditional or middle-class definitions of respectability.

The Pekin and other theaters in Chicago's Black Belt addressed both the social and the imaginative desires of their clienteles. They were constructed (architecturally, and in promotional and community discourses) to attract African American patrons by appealing to progressive notions of race pride, cleanliness (physical and moral), and "high-class" pretensions, at the same time acknowledging the cinema's "low" cultural attractions, such as its connections to vice, sensationalism, and working-class tastes. This dual appeal can be read in the locations of these theaters, particularly those along the South State Street "Stroll," as well as in their management styles, types of entertainment, amenities, employees, and the clienteles they attempted and claimed to serve. Although the showing of films in the Black Belt has not been explored in much detail in the many rich cultural histories of the area (including those documenting jazz performance in many of the same venues), Stroll theaters serve as exemplary sites for considering the contradictory nature of urban New Negro performance. As venues of film exhibition, these theaters exploited various Black community notions of legitimacy, not only enabling reconstructive spectatorship practices but also reconfiguring the meanings of ownership, cultural expression, and class status in Black urban contexts. Stroll theaters attempted to validate a range of Black engagements with commercial entertainments (for exhibitors and musicians, for critics and patrons) as signifiers of a modern lifestyle, including those aspects of mass culture that were not deemed respectable or authentic by uplift orthodoxy.

## Cheap and Disreputable: Theaters Get a Bad Name

Reservations expressed by many African American leaders regarding the respectability of the Pekin and other places of amusement in the Black Belt were not unfounded. Mark H. Haller has shown that Black Chicago's lively entertainment scene was closely tied to underworld figures like Motts, his mentor, the legendary Black gambler John "Mushmouth" Johnson, and Johnson's successor, Henry "Teenan" Jones.[6] Given the limited opportunities and capital available to African American entrepreneurs in "legitimate" fields, these men and many others turned to the worlds of gambling and entertainment, in which they could achieve fame, fortune, and even political power while serving a segregated Black clientele. In addition to operating gambling houses, saloons, and policy syndicates, these men were connected to a number of the Black Belt's entertainments. For example, "Mushmouth" Johnson's brother and business partner, Elijah Johnson, opened the Dreamland Ballroom in 1912, which in later years, as the Dreamland Café, became a center of Black jazz and nightlife. "Teenan" Jones, who ran a number of saloons and cafés, managed vaudeville acts and purchased the Star movie theater in 1916. Even boxer Jack Johnson, who associated with many "sporting" figures of the South Side red-light district, opened the Café de Champion in 1911 on Thirty-first Street, "an elegant establishment for drinking, dining, dancing and entertainment."[7]

In addition to their financial successes, Chicago's major Black gambling figures also achieved a measure of political power on the South Side. Following the white models of "Bath-house John" Coughlin, Michael "Hinky Dink" Kenna, and other white gangster/politicians who controlled politics in Chicago's First Ward, Black "bosses" developed close relationships with police, judges, and the Republican Party machine in order to protect their business operations in the predominantly Black Second Ward. In these ways, African Americans involved in the underworld played a crucial role in the development of the Black Belt's commercial amusements, providing Black Chicagoans with an array of entertainments and activities—legal and illegal—as they carved out a central place for themselves in the economy and politics of the Black community.

While dance halls, gaming houses, and saloons were obvious targets of protest and concern because they provided and/or encouraged activities such as drinking, gambling, and prostitution, theaters featuring live performance and motion pictures were also held under suspicion because of their disreputable, underworld connections. As indicated by drama teacher Anna Morgan's concerns, cited earlier, regarding her young female students, the Pekin's history as a saloon was imagined to have negative implications for women who performed there. Although Ida B. Wells ridicules Morgan by suggesting that "her young ladies could not have a very secure hold on their reputations if giving one night's performance would cause them to lose them," Morgan feared that even one appearance at the Pekin would be enough to associate her students with the prostitutes and unsavory female performers who regularly appeared in such establishments.[8] Lauren Rabinovitz imagines that Black Belt theaters provided African American women with much-needed employment opportunities, but at the time Black moral and cultural leaders frequently criticized forms and venues of performance that called attention to Black women's sexuality.[9] For instance, *Defender* theatrical critic Sylvester Russell noted in a 1910 review of a performance at the Grand Theater that "there was a falling off of the respectable element when it was discovered that Miss Wallace was doing a disreputable dance that would not be allowed in any other city. It is no wonder that Dr. Fisher extols the people of his church not to go to those wicked moving picture theaters."[10] Here Russell links several disparate observations—a decline in respectability of Black entertainment, the inappropriateness of Wallace's presumably sexually suggestive dance, and the sinfulness of moving picture theaters—to create a sordid image of Chicago's Black theatrical scene.

Theaters were often lumped in with other degraded and degrading places of amusement that were considered to have a particularly bad influence on Black youth. For instance, Anne Meis Knupfer quotes a Black club woman associated with the Clotee Scott Settlement who celebrates the success of its Young Men's Glee Club in drawing young people away from inappropriate amusements: "Look at the well-behaved youth who before had only one or two disreputable saloons, a jim-crow theater and the pool room as the only place as a center."[11] Cheap, segregated theaters, particularly those showing movies, were regarded by many as unwholesome gathering places, encouraging delinquency and corrupting young people's health, tastes, and morals. In early 1910, the Black-owned Chateau de Plaisance compared its superior facilities for dancing and roller skating to the unhealthy environment of the increasingly popular nickelodeons: "Go where you will, pay what you may but the CHATEAU leads in real wholesome, health-giving entertainment. Come away from the stuffy, tubercular 5¢ death-giving, cheap theatre and enjoy the invigorating, health-giving atmosphere of the CHATEAU."[12] Although the Chateau also featured presentations of "pictures that move" on its grounds, it offered open-air areas and healthful food and activities that, according to its advertisements, provided Black patrons with a positive alternative to foul nickelodeons.

Black concerns about nickelodeons echoed many of those expressed by white reformers, who deemed movie theaters "unhealthy" both inside and out. In 1911 the Vice Commission of Chicago reported that while the movies shown in five- and ten-cent theaters were "generally clean," these establishments were considered to be dangerous because unsupervised children were "influenced for evil by the *conditions surrounding* some of these shows" (emphasis in original). The commission found that "vicious men and boys mix with the crowd in front of the theaters and take liberties with very young girls." Proprietors and stage managers were also found to "offer certain indignities" to girls and boys inside of darkened theaters. One social worker reported to the commission that "the nickel theater is a recruiting station for vice," and "a good many of my young girls have told me their first wrong came when they attended nickel theaters."[13] These observations about the dangers of moving picture theaters for young audiences in general, along with connections between certain theaters and vice activities near and within the Black Belt, contributed to the tenuous position of moviegoing as a legitimate leisure activity among Black Chicagoans.

The content of films screened in Black Belt theaters often mirrored the real and imagined dangers and appeals associated with their places of exhibition. During the middle to late teens Black Belt theaters regularly screened feature-length films advertised for "adults only" in addition to adventure serials and comedies. These features treated sensational topics, including murder, suicide, kidnapping, blackmail, abortion and birth control, unwed pregnancy, and illicit sexual relations. These "pink slip" films, for which theaters had to apply for a city permit and restrict admission to viewers over twenty-one years of age, came to the Stroll from first-run theaters downtown, where they were screened to white audiences.

The appeal of (and objections to) such fare across the color line is not particularly surprising. But the popularity of these films among Black audiences indicates some of the contradictions that the changing American mediascape could produce for the project of racial uplift as Black urban populations expanded. Pink slip films treated many of the same topics that appeared with increasing frequency in the white and Black urban presses during this period. During the mid-1910s the *Chicago Defender* began to be characterized by the reporting of shocking, scandalous, and violent stories, a practice it would continue for several decades. For example, the October 7, 1916, issue of the *Defender* features a barrage of startling headlines such as: "FIND LOST BABY"; "Finds Wife Murdered"; "Saved from Flames"; "Fired On from Ambush"; "Train Strikes Wagon, Mules and Owner Killed"; "Shoots Mother Accidentally"; "Woman Commits Suicide"; and "Badly Burned," among many others. In his survey of *Defender* headlines from 1910 to 1937, Ralph Nelson Davis found that "sensational news," including stories about crime, sex, divorce, suicide, and disasters, began to appear during the mid-teens "as the novelty of the sensational presentation of race problem news waned." This yellow journalism approach to news presentation provided *Defender* readers with entertaining human-interest fare alongside the usual updates regarding racial conflict and discrimination.[14] Although the Black press continued to agitate against segregation in its news stories and editorial pages, by the height of the Great Migration reporting on the "race problem" was increasingly supplemented by stories of sex and violence that highlighted the adventures of contemporary urban life in general.

The *Defender*'s modes of address changed, in part, in response to the demographic shifts produced by the migration. Just as the *Defender* presented a conflicting image to potential migrants by advertising the Black Belt's attractive array of entertainments while editorializing on the importance of thrift, industriousness, and propriety, it risked compromising its political agenda of racial uplift by following popular mainstream trends in news reporting that would be attractive to a growing urban working-class readership. Although sensational topics, both on screen and in the Black press, probably offended many Black Chicagoans with refined, religious, and/or conservative sensibilities, many others purchased the *Defender*, read its sensationalist news and entertainment pages, and patronized Black Belt movie theaters—including those with "underworld" affiliations— even though these activities were not always clearly consistent with a middle-class or "Old Settler" program of uplift and respectability.

Even while describing the seedy and gruesome aspects of life in the urban North, the *Defender* continued to claim that it projected a progressive "race" viewpoint. And many *Defender* readers viewed their consumption of the paper as an investment in race issues and in a Black-owned business. The increasing influence of dominant media did not preclude Black-serving publications and entertainments from professing cultural pride and authenticity. In terms of film exhibition, Black Belt theater owners and managers attempted to bridge conflicting views about the movies as legitimate and low, as alien to Black culture and an entitlement of urban living, by selling an experience of race pride.

Most Stroll theaters were owned and operated by whites, but, as Mary Carbine points out, "theaters were identified as belonging to the 'Race' because of the composition of the audience, not the race of the owner."[15] Some theaters attempted to make African American audiences proud and comfortable by hiring Black employees. The *Defender* highlighted theaters with Black personnel, such as the States, which featured "member[s] of the Race in every position, from the box office to the operating room."[16] In theaters like these, Black audiences did not have to fear the unpleasant treatment by white ushers and managers that they often experienced in downtown theaters. Black Belt theaters programmed the handful of Black-cast "race films" that were produced to redress the marginal and degrading treatment of Blacks in the predominant mainstream fare. In addition, Black Belt theaters occasionally hosted benefits for race causes, such as raising legal and medical funds for community members, supporting institutions like the Old Folks' Home and the Phyllis Wheatley Home, and buying Christmas gifts for Black soldiers.[17] Although these strategies were intended to provide Black viewers with a sense of race pride and agency as they spent their leisure time and money, Stroll theaters did not completely deny or overcome the many negative qualities being ascribed to movie theaters, inside and out. Instead, as the film industry's ever-increasing popularity was interpreted through Black discourses on entrepreneurship, self-determination, and class mobility, theaters enabled African Americans to perform both the progressive and the plebian dimensions of urban industrial life.

Between the opening of the Pekin Theatre and the end of the Great Migration wave in 1919, at least eighteen different venues exhibited motion pictures to Chicago's Black population (see map 1). Looking at several of these establishments in detail, I describe how they solicited African American audiences in light of the questionable status of both Black Belt commercial amusements and urban movie theaters. My discussion moves roughly chronologically, beginning with theaters that incorporated films into their much more highly publicized live performance programs and then describing those theaters dedicated to moving picture exhibition. Much of the surviving data about these theaters is inconsistent, and their exhibition of films has been obscured by attention to the ostensibly more authentically "Black" forms of entertainment they featured (e.g., descriptions of jazz and vaudeville performance in the press at the time, as discussed in the previous chapter, as well as in cultural histories).[18] In light of these gaps and discrepancies, my overview suggests how the actual and discursive spaces of Black Belt theaters contributed to the development of a Black urban film culture that consistently struggled with notions of social and cultural legitimacy but thrived as the African American population and the dominant film industry expanded.

## The Pekin

Built in 1892 at the corner of Twenty-seventh and State Streets (2700 S. State), marking the northernmost point of the Stroll, the Pekin served for many years as a cultural institution within Chicago's Black Belt despite (and because of) its controversial history (fig. 30). Tracing the Pekin's central place in the development of Chicago jazz, William Howland Kenney describes how it evolved from a beer garden serving an interracial clientele to a "night club, gambling hall, theater, and political hot spot called the Pekin Inn."[19] As a music hall, the Pekin featured musical entertainment supervised by Motts's friend, ragtime composer Joe Jordan, who wrote a tribute to

FIGURE 30. Exterior of the (in)famous Pekin, 2700 S. State Street. *Chicago Daily News*, 1920. Chicago Historical Society, DN-0072231.

the venue, "Pekin Rag," in 1904 (fig. 31).[20] Robert Motts was motivated to convert the Pekin into a theater not only because of the increasing profitability of presenting African American musical entertainment but also because Chicago was cracking down on the city's gambling operations, and local clergy were intensifying their opposition to the venue.[21] Motts reconfigured the Pekin from a Continental-style music hall in which drinking and dining patrons (as seen in fig. 31) were seated around a central performance space (featuring "short plays, musical selections, and variety acts") to a more conventional theatrical stage and seating arrangement. Tim Samuelson reports that in February 1906 Motts added a fireproof brick auditorium to the back of his two-story, wood frame saloon.[22] With this increased space, the Pekin mounted its first theatrical production, *The Man from Bam* (see fig. 27). The Pekin, which was celebrated in the local and national Black press for featuring legitimate entertainment and employment opportunities for African Americans, holds a central place in music historiography as one of the first venues to feature "jass" performances.[23] But the Pekin's offerings, as well as its location, patrons, and ownership, produced complicated relationships between the theater and members of Black Chicago's "refined," "respectable," and "riff-raff" classes.

FIGURE 31. A full house of Black patrons seated at tables on the floor and balcony of the well-appointed Pekin, enjoying entertainments, including the house orchestra under the direction of Joe Jordan (foreground). "Pekin Rag" composed by Joe Jordan (Pekin Publishing Company, 1904). From the Collection of Terry Parrish.

With a seating capacity of around 610, the Pekin drew patrons, Black and white, from across the city, including the interracial "sporting" crowd Motts had cultivated as a saloon keeper. Throughout his ownership of the Pekin, Motts walked a fine line between serving the interests of the (largely working-class) Black neighborhood in which the venue was located and profiting from the patronage of whites with more disposable income.[24] In addition to its Black stock company, Motts sought to book white as well as Black performers on the Pekin stage. *Defender* theatrical critic Sylvester Russell noted in 1910 that Motts "caters much at present to white people," but Russell anticipates that the Pekin will draw larger Black audiences and praises Motts for "booking with the vaudeville association and playing actors, white and colored, who appear first on the big time," enabling Black audiences "to see all the best performers without a trip downtown."[25] The exhibition of "mainstream" moving pictures, then, would have been consistent with the Pekin's mixed-race entertainments and diverse audience tastes.

While the Pekin drew mixed crowds for its various entertainments, it also served for many years as an important social and political gathering place specifically for Black Chicagoans. Motts used the Pekin as a base for organizing the Black vote in his activities as a Republican Party operative.[26] During and after Motts's reign, Black Chicagoans used the Pekin for meetings and benefits. For example, representatives of Chicago's four leading Black publications—the *Defender, Broad Ax, Chronicle,* and the *Illinois Idea*—met at the Pekin café in 1912 to form the Colored Press Association and to endorse Black candidate Beauregard F. Moseley for Cook County commissioner. Leading Black club women held many benefits at the Pekin, including the annual performance of the Chicago Women's Amateur Minstrel Club in 1916.[27] Thus in addition to enjoying its reputation as "the meeting place of the gay boulevardiers and the chosen rendezvous of chorines and tired business men," the Pekin was a central space within the Black Belt for African American social gatherings, fund-raising, and political organizing.[28] The Pekin's multiple uses across the spectrum of respectability (benefits and booze, race dramas and ragtime, political activism and patronage), along with its appeals to neighborhood Blacks and "slumming" whites, suggest the contradictory public context in which Chicago's Black film culture originated.

After Robert Motts's death in 1911, the Pekin's future was uncertain. Motts's sister, Lucy, inherited the theater. In early February 1912, the *Defender* reported that the Motts's estate was tied up in litigation, but later that month the theater reopened under new management (fig. 32).[29] Dis-

FIGURE 32. Pekin advertisement after the death of owner Robert Motts. *Chicago Defender* (c. 1911).

satisfied with the Pekin's new "prices and style of theatrical ventures," *Defender* theatrical critic Minnie Adams suggested in March 1912 that the theater needed not only a physical "cleaning" and "renovating" but also "a rigorous sifting out of those who have control of the theatre in every department" in order to remove "those who seek to get rich quick at the expense of the other fellow."[30] Although the Pekin would continue to offer theatrical presentations, and presumably moving pictures, during the midteens, it gradually faded from the *Defender's* theatrical notices, mentioned occasionally with a tone of nostalgia for its glorious past. In late 1912 *Defender* readers were encouraged to come see a production of the play *Tallaboo,* and in doing so "make the Pekin look like days of yore."[31] Subsequently the Pekin was owned and operated by a succession of whites, contradicting Motts's reported deathbed request that it "remain always under black ownership."[32] In 1916 the theater seats were removed to make room for a dance floor. In 1918 the Pekin reopened as a dance hall featuring the New Orleans Jazz Band and serving soft drinks instead of alcohol, as manager Walter K. Tyler attempted to conduct the establishment "in a more law-abiding manner or method than what it was in the past."[33] But this new clean image did not last long; by the early 1920s the Pekin was a black-and-tan joint selling alcohol during Prohibition and was the site of numerous raids and violent confrontations between gangsters and police.[34] By the height of the Great Migration, the Pekin was no longer the Stroll's leading Black theatrical venue, no longer a shining national beacon of legitimate Black entertainment, as it began to return to its roots as a "disreputable" saloon.

## New Temples of Amusement:
## The Grand(s) and the Monogram(s)

As the Pekin fell from prominence on the Black Belt theatrical scene, two sets of Stroll theaters, the Grands and the Monograms, rose from behind its shadow to become the leading venues for live performance and, though rarely noted, moving pictures. While Sylvester Russell observed in 1910 that Pekin manager Motts "has thus far outclassed the managers of the Grand and Monogram in the proximity of a racial amusement problem," by 1912 the *Defender*'s theatrical reviews began with long blurbs about offerings at the Grand and the Monogram, with relatively little mention of the Pekin.[35] The original Grand (3104 S. State) did not receive much critical attention in the press until a new, larger Grand theater building opened on State Street just south of Thirty-first Street (3110–12 S. State) on March 20, 1911 (fig. 33). The *Defender* featured long, detailed descriptions of the new theater, lauding it not only as an architectural "work of art and a great addition to the neighborhood" but also as a comfortable place of amusement for Black theatergoers: "No expense or pains have been spared to make the New Grand the finest theatre in the country and it is designed to give the Colored people of Chicago the best accommodations for theatre going that it has been possible to devise. There are 800 comfortable seats and every patron will be treated with the utmost courtesy and made to feel at home." The new Grand offered Black Chicagoans vaudeville and dramatic entertainment in "a new temple of amusement where they can while away the hour and drive dull care away."[36]

Owned by the white-controlled Grand Amusement company, the Grand had an interior that was designed, and described, as beautiful, luxurious, and safe in an effort to ward off persistent concerns about the cheapness, disreputableness, and unhealthiness of older Black Belt theaters. As Sylvester Russell describes it:

FIGURE 33. Exterior of the Grand Theater. Photograph by Harold Bretz. By permission of University Archives, Paul V. Galvin Library, Illinois Institute of Technology, Chicago.

The building is of fire proof and amply supplied with exits. The stage is of good size with a full set of scenery and equipments *[sic]*. The walls and decorations are of pink with gold trimmings. There are four boxes each box seating ten people. Brass rails sub-divide the different sections and heavy maroon plush curtains adorn the boxes. There is but one balcony, including the manager's office, which can be reached on each side by a long or short stairway. All the chairs are of morocco leather and people can see the full stage from any section of the house. . . . That which adds to the beauty tone and shade of atmospheric splendor is the electric light jets which hang in bowl-like circled white globes of different sizes held by heavy brass chains.[37]

The new Grand also provided clean air with its "modern combination ventilation" system, through which "torrid heat, hygienic moderation or compressed air is projected in which all scents of odoriferous flavor is evaporated." In addition to these modern and elegant amenities, the Grand departed from common practice by hiring female ushers. The presence of these women elicited very different reactions from two *Defender* critics. Whereas Russell wrote, perhaps jokingly, that "something strange and unspeakable is the introduction of lady ushers and that's a plenty," the following year Minnie Adams remarked that "one of the greatest pleasures that the Grand Theatre gives to its patrons is that of meeting the four little ladies who have charge of seating the audience." Adams names these women and explains that while they are "polite," "pretty," and "ladylike," they are also "decided" in their duties: "Their power is respected by all who enter the theatre, and this is demanded of the patrons by the management."[38] Thus, these attractive female ushers were both a provocative novelty and an additional effort to lend the Grand an air of safety, order, and respectability.

Like the Pekin and the Monogram Theaters (discussed later in this section), the Grand was best known for the live acts that appeared on its stage. The Grand has been celebrated as the theater that introduced New Orleans jazz to the North.[39] As noted in the previous chapter, *Defender* theatrical reviews in the early teens rarely described films that were screened in Black Belt theaters in much detail. For instance, in 1910, Russell wrote an item on "The Vaudeville and Picture Houses" in which he reviews programs at the Monogram and the Grand. However, he describes only the live performers that appeared on their stages. Russell's review of the new Grand's opening night program describes the live acts featured (including comedians, singers, acrobats, and a roller skate dancer) but does not indicate that moving pictures also were screened. However, an advertisement in the same issue proclaims that the Grand is the "finest small theater in America, Built for the Colored People," featuring "continuous vaudeville [and] moving pictures" (fig. 34).[40] Also, in 1916, the (presumably white) managers of the new Grand (Mr. Johnson) and the two Monograms (Mr. Klein) joined with managers of theaters that showed moving pictures exclusively in an agreement not to screen racially offensive films. Not only is it clear

The New Grand
Continuous Vaudeville and Moving Pictures

Change of Program Monday and Thursday
FINEST THEATRE IN AMERICA
3110-12 State St.,     ·     Chicago, Ill.
Performers Send in Your Open Time

FIGURE 34. Advertisement for the New Grand Theater. *Chicago Defender,* 9 January 1915.

that films were included on the programs of these vaudeville theaters with some regularity, but it also seems that Black patrons (with allies in the Black press) exercised considerable influence over the kinds of films that could be shown in their neighborhood.[41]

The Monogram Theaters were owned by Harry B. Miller, a white businessman who opened the first Monogram around 1905 and the second one around 1913.[42] Although the Monogram Theaters became staples of the Stroll's theatrical scene, they often seemed to struggle in the shadow of the Pekin and the Grand. For example, Russell defended the "old" Monogram (3028 S. State) against unfair representation by a critic in another Black publication: "In a theatrical review last week in a colored newspaper there appeared a little comment on the Monogram Theater, which spoke of that house being in the slumming district, when in truth that house is in the best locality on State street and the same class of people go there that go to the Grand and the Pekin Theaters."[43] The Monogram and the New Monogram (located farther south, at 3451 S. State) held approximately 432 and 376 patrons, respectively, smaller capacities than the Pekin or the Grand. Still, by the late teens, when the Great Migration flooded the Black Belt with African Americans seeking places of amusement, the Monogram Theaters did very good business.

While Russell attempts to defend the old Monogram's respectability, the recollections of two African American women—one who was a spectator and one who performed there—indicate that the new Monogram was hardly a classy establishment during the late 1910s. After 1915, the new Monogram was one of only three Black Belt theaters featuring vaudeville performance, as the old Monogram stopped hosting live entertainment and eventually showed only moving pictures.[44] In one of her autobiographies, dancer, choreographer, and anthropologist Katherine Dunham describes her childhood memories of Chicago's theatrical scene, recalling the new Monogram theater in particular. Dunham's account of being taken to the Monogram when she was a small child illustrates why reformers were so concerned about the physical and moral cleanliness of theaters and their potentially negative impact on children.

Growing up poor on Chicago's South Side, during one period in the late 1910s Dunham was left in the care of a thirty-five-year-old, stagestruck, distant cousin who worked as an usher at the new Monogram and attended innumerable vaudeville shows there. This woman frequently took young Dunham to the theater during the height of the Great Migration, when it was packed to the rafters with newly migrated southern Blacks in search of entertainment.[45] Dunham recalls that "the entrance fee at the Grand was slightly higher than that of the Monogram, which—having no history of past glories before the decline of the neighborhood—allocated what funds might have gone into improved sanitation and creature comforts to securing the best entertainment that could be offered," indicating the Monogram's lower status and its attempt to make up for it by featuring acts that were particularly attractive to a working-class clientele. Dunham goes on to describe in vivid detail the new Monogram's shabby conditions and the audience's crude behavior:

> The unknowing would not have given the nondescript assembly that gathered to wait in the littered vestibule, muddy with trash and dirt ground into melted snow, credit for enough discrimination to appreciate the subtle distinctions that made the stage show at the Monogram superior to that at the Grand. But the management had learned, at the expense of wrecked seats and fistfights and performers forcibly ejected from the stage, that the seasoned act, the perennial joke disguised only enough to give the impression of newness while retaining the comfort of familiarity, the bawdy song full of double meanings sung in a folk code language, were what the audience wanted. Those waiting in the vestibule for seats would make insulting remarks to each person who opened the street door on either side of the glassed-in ticket cage, cursed at the cold knife of air that entered with them, and spat noisily, as though thereby casting out physical discomfort. In this setting the child made her first acquaintance with the residuum of the minstrel era and with forerunners of the Broadway revue.[46]

Here we see that elements of violence, raunchiness, and hostility were very much a part of the sense of "familiarity" and community Black patrons experienced at the Monogram, one of the many sites where African American performers transformed American entertainment. Although she was extremely young at the time, Dunham vaguely remembers seeing vaudeville luminaries like Cole and Johnson, Buck and Bubbles, Bessie Smith, Ida Cox, Florence Mills, and others, recalling the sometimes vulgar nature of the performances and the audience's reactions:

> Most of the time she [Dunham] would have to sit on the second cousin's lap, and after about an hour she would fall asleep, her dreams uncomfortable because of the stale air, the fetid breath on either side, the raucous laughter, the comments hurled at the stage and bounced back in kind to the delight of the squealing, squirming audience; the banging of an out-of-tune piano punctuated the guttural rasp of the blues.[47]

One of the performers Dunham dimly recalls seeing at the new Monogram, Ethel Waters, seconds Dunham's impression of the raunchiness and squalor of the venue. Waters performed there in the late teens when she was a teenager embarking upon her career as a traveling vaudevillian. She describes touring in 1917–18 through Baltimore, Detroit, Pittsburgh, Cincinnati, and across the South, playing in "ramshackle" theaters owned by whites who held themselves "responsible neither for your property nor your life." Waters describes her experiences at Chicago's new Monogram theater in the most detail:

> Of all those rinky-dink dumps I played, nothing was worse than the Monogram Theatre in Chicago. It was close to the El, and the walls were so thin that you stopped singing—or telling a joke—every time a train passed. Then, when the noise died down, you continued right where you left off.
>
> In the Monogram you dressed away downstairs with the stoker. The ceiling down there was so low I had to bend over to get my stage clothes on. Then you came up to the stage on a ladder that looked like those on the old-time slave ships.
>
> Ever since I worked at the Monogram any old kind of dressing room has looked pretty good to me so long as it had a door that could be closed.[48]

This observation is particularly poignant in Waters's narrative, which describes the constant threat of sexual assault to which young Black women are subjected in the closely associated theatrical and "sporting" worlds. Dunham's and Waters's descriptions of the new Monogram at the height of the Great Migration convey what newspaper advertisements and reviews do not. Certainly the Monogram featured an incredible range of Black entertainment, from stage legends to up-and-coming acts, and, like other Black Belt theaters, it provided audiences with an all-Black venue free from

racial discrimination. But it was also a loud, raunchy, and unseemly establishment that could be unpleasant and inappropriate for young people (especially women and girls) as performers and as spectators.

## Moving Pictures Only: States, Lincoln, and Owl Theaters

While live entertainment maintained its central place on the Black theater
scene, during the midteens a number of theaters opened in the Black Belt
that showed moving pictures exclusively. The States Theater, near the intersection of Thirty-fifth and State Streets (3507 S. State), was one of the
most prominent and highly publicized of the establishments catering to
Chicago's Black audiences. Seating almost seven hundred, the States
opened around 1914, and in addition to shorts and serials, it booked many
of the major features after they completed their runs in downtown theaters.[49] The States specialized in sensational, multireel dramas screened in
the Loop months before, from war spectacles like *The Battle Cry of Peace*
(1916) to sex-themed dramas for adults only like *Damaged Goods* (1916)
and *The Common Law* (1916) to epics like *Joan the Woman* (1917) and the
Theda Bara vehicle *Cleopatra* (1918). For really big features, such as D. W.
Griffith's *Intolerance* (1916), the States raised ticket prices from fifteen
cents to twenty-five cents for adults and all evening showings (fig. 35).[50]

Occasionally, the States, like other Black Belt theaters, showed films by
African American filmmakers, including the first Black-produced film, *The
Railroad Porter* (1913), by Chicago-based William Foster, and Lincoln Mo-
tion Picture Company releases such as *The Trooper of Troop K* (1916) and *A
Man's Duty* (1919). The States also presented Oscar Micheaux's first film,
*The Homesteader* (1919), as it toured Black Belt venues, emphasizing its "9
Reels of Action," including a "murderess and a suicide!"[51] Micheaux appealed to Black audiences by combining elements of race pride and sensationalism in his films and their advertising. For example, Jane Gaines
reports that in the advertising for *Within Our Gates* (1920), Micheaux
represented controversial racial themes like rape and lynching as sensationalist spectacles for a Black audience seeking racial justice: "As his publicity asserted, this 'Preachment of Race Prejudice and the Glaring Injus-
tices Practiced Upon Our People' was to 'Hold you Spellbound' and offer
you details that would make you 'Grit Your Teeth in Silent Indigna-
tion.'"[52] While the *Defender* was scaling back on its sensational representation of race news, Micheaux's films combined the violent and sexual con-

FIGURE 35. Advertisement for D. W. Griffith's *Intolerance* (his follow-up to *The Birth of a Nation*) at the States Theater. *Chicago Defender*, 3 November 1917.

tent of white-produced films with graphic, incendiary accounts of racist abuses.

Although the States brought Black-produced films and high-profile features to the Black Belt, African American moviegoers occasionally registered complaints about films shown at the theater that they found to be racially offensive. In 1914 the *Defender* reported that Stroll patrons were fuming because the States was showing Lubin's *Tale of a Chicken*, featuring "an illiterate going into a coop and stealing a chicken," and *Mother of Men*, which shows "a slave stealing a white child."[53] In 1918 the States screened *Son of Democracy*, a biographical serial about Abraham Lincoln, which included in the first episode a "youthful member of the Race's inclination to pilfer poultry."[54] In both cases, States manager George Paul was not held responsible for presenting these offensive scenes to Black viewers; the *Defender* blamed the censor board for passing *The Tale of a Chicken* and *Mother of Men* in the first place, and Mr. Paul was out of town and reportedly unaware of the chicken-stealing episode in *Son of Democracy*. By responding quickly and sympathetically to Black complaints, the States management worked to avoid alienating Black viewers and remained popular throughout the teens.

The States also appealed to its Black clientele by hiring African American employees, like Helen Greene, "the pleasant and accommodating ticket seller at the States," and numerous Black musicians who played there over the years under the direction of orchestra leaders Edward F. Bailey, Will Bailey, and E. M. Wyer.[55] As Tony Langston noted with great enthusiasm: "A member of the Race fills every position from the box office to the operating room—fifteen people in all—and the advertising is handled exclusively through the Langston Advertising Bureau."[56] By hiring Black employees and cultivating a private business relationship with the *Defender*'s theatrical reviewer, the States management put its money in the right places and, therefore, enjoyed great popularity among Black moviegoers and positive representation in the Black press.

*Defender* coverage of the States emphasizes its status as a classy establishment, bringing the finest films to Black Belt audiences at reasonable prices. Langston frequently praises George Paul and his partner, Mr. Stone, for catering "exclusively to the most refined tastes of the high class trade which the States enjoys."[57] When the States was forced to close during late 1918 due to an influenza epidemic (along with the Lincoln, Owl, and many other theaters), Paul and Stone reportedly used the opportunity to make improvements. The theater reopened in November, having been "entirely renovated and redecorated throughout," with overhauled ventilation and heating systems. In addition, manager Paul announced that the States had an "exclusive contract on all Fox features." This combination of enhancements was intended to ensure that "the handsome photoplay house will be the center of attraction in the future, the same as it has been in the past."[58]

The Lincoln and Owl theaters also sought to present themselves as "high-class" establishments, using many of the same tactics as the States. The Lincoln Theater (3132 S. State) attempted to cater to refined moviegoers by booking "productions of the better class." Although the Lincoln was a smaller house, with a seating capacity of around three hundred, it advertised as "the cosiest little theater in Chicago," giving itself an air of intimacy and exclusivity.[59] Managed by Henry Salken and then Nathan Josephs, the Lincoln booked many of the same films that were shown at the States, giving Black Belt patrons another opportunity to see major features in their own community. Like the States, the Lincoln would raise admission prices when it screened special attractions. "We have a big feature booked for Sunday," the Lincoln announced in early 1916, "on which day we have advanced our price to ten cents."[60]

The Owl Theater similarly presented itself as a classy venue, richly appointed specifically for Black Belt patrons (see fig. 25). The Owl's location, on State Street near Forty-seventh Street (4653 S. State), indicates the southward expansion of the Stroll during the late teens, as the Great Migration increased the need for and profitability of amusements aimed at Black Belt residents. The Owl was a large theater, seating around a thousand patrons. When Tony Langston toured "the new $100,000 Owl theater" just before its opening in January 1917, he called it the "finest movie house on the south side," remarking especially on its "big, roomy, regular seats; not the kind that doubles you up in a knot and spoils your enjoyment, but wide, comfortable seats, such as are found in the theaters of the better class." The Owl also featured "a specially built Kimball pipe organ, installed at a cost of $10,000."[61] Langston described the Owl's interior as a "dream": "The lobby is a thing of beauty, and aside from it there is a spacious rotunda reaching clear across the rear of the theater, the walls of which are decorated with oils of some of the world's greatest movie stars." The Owl boasted "the largest screen" of all Black Belt theaters.[62] The Owl's (presumably white) owners, Myers and Flowers, assured Langston that the theater's expensive facilities would be offered along with "courteous treatment and the glad smile of welcome" to everyone who entered the theater, anticipating Black concerns about confronting racial discrimination.

Like the States management, Owl manager Mr. Solomon promised to "employ as many members of the Race at this house as it is possible for him to use."[63] One month later, Langston reported that "all employees are members of the Race, with one exception, and that the operator is a member of local 110, which means that one of our boys is responsible for the proper showing of the offerings on the screen."[64] This is an extremely rare reference to an African American projectionist, not to mention a Black union projectionist. The Owl featured vaudeville as well as moving pictures during its first year of operation, but in December 1917, it announced that vaudeville would be discontinued, and "nothing but the best of first-run and feature pictures will be shown."[65] Live performance was still a big attraction in the Black Belt, but apparently the Owl management decided that it could do better business by presenting movies only.

In February 1918, the Owl changed hands, and George Paul of the States and Nathan Josephs of the Lincoln took over its management. Thereafter, Paul and Josephs frequently booked the same big features at all three theaters, one after another, offering Black Belt patrons numerous opportunities to see these films close to home.[66] The consecutive booking of the same films at theaters in such close proximity suggests that they served a substantial audience, and perhaps also that Black Belt moviegoers went to see the same films several times. Although the films shown at these theaters usually had been run downtown months earlier, in their Black Belt exhibition runs they could be promoted and experienced as special events in exclusive, Black-oriented venues.

## The Hammond Chain:
## Phoenix, Fountain, Elba, Vendome, and Pickford

Another group of Black Belt theaters, the Phoenix, Fountain, Elba, Vendome, and Pickford, were all eventually owned and operated by white proprietors, O. C. Hammond & Sons (fig. 36). Scattered along and near the Stroll, these theaters did not present the big-name feature films that were shown at the States, Lincoln, and Owl, but they offered dozens of comedies, westerns, serials, and many features to Black Belt moviegoers. The Phoenix, located at the bustling hub of Thirty-first and State Streets at the former site of the "old" Grand (3104 S. State), was a small theater (holding roughly 321 patrons) designed by architects Newhouse and Burnham, and was originally managed by O. C. Hammond. In 1914, Hammond hired a Black manager, Al Gaines, making the Phoenix, for a time, "the only theater on the Stroll that has a member of the race as manager."[67] Gaines became a notable figure on Chicago's Black theatrical scene when he took charge of booking films at the Phoenix. For many years he was mentioned by name in the *Defender*'s weekly announcements of the Stroll's theatrical programs.

Like several of the theaters described earlier in this chapter, the Phoenix tried to cultivate an air of respectability by presenting itself as a venue for discerning audiences. In its early days, O. C. Hammond offered a selection of films, illustrated songs, and, of course, live musical performance that "cater[ed] to refined people in favor of the patronage of ladies and children."[68] While many race leaders expressed concerns about the effects of cheap movie theaters on young and female patrons, the Phoenix worked to provide programming and a physical environment that were suitable for these audiences. Sylvester Russell proclaimed that "the Phoenix theatre is the place for the children, and we are glad to see them go" because "the picture plays are moral and humorous." In a later column, he claimed that the Phoenix showed films of "high moral character" and remarked on the "good class of young people who attended."[69] As Anna Everett points out, Russell seeks "to disabuse dubious parents of the notion that film theaters

FIGURE 36. Advertisement for the Hammond chain of Black Belt moving picture theaters. *Chicago Defender,* 22 December 1917.

FIGURE 37. Advertisement for the mammoth, Hammond-owned Vendome Theater. *Chicago Defender,* 21 June 1919.

were equivalent to those other notoriously amoral dens of iniquity littering the crowded tenement districts of Southside Chicago."[70] I would add that by remarking on the "good class of young people," Russell suggests that the Phoenix attracted respectable, well-behaved youths who could model appropriate behavior for lower-class Black children.

Other Hammond-owned theaters in the Black Belt, the Fountain at Thirty-fifth Street and Grand Boulevard (344 E. Thirty-fifth Street) and the Elba at Thirty-first Street and Indiana Avenue (3115 S. Indiana, later the Blue Bird Theater; see fig. 48), both a few blocks east of the Stroll, were managed by O. C. Hammond's sons, Frank and John, respectively. In late 1917, the Hammonds announced that they were building a sixteen-hundred-seat "New MOVIE PALACE to Be Erected at a Cost of $250,000" on a large lot at 3141–49 S. State Street. This theater, the Vendome, opened more than a year later, on the site of the South Side Turners' Hall, which had been destroyed by fire (fig. 37).[71] The large new structure featured a thirty-foot domed ceiling, a balcony, stage, and pipe organ, as well as storefronts adjoining the main entrance.[72] Frequently cited in jazz histories for featuring an outstanding live band directed by Erskine Tate, the Vendome specialized in the kinds of big, sensationalist features that appeared at the States and Owl theaters. It was also the first theater to screen Oscar Micheaux's debut film, *The Homesteader,* after its premiere at the Eighth Regiment Armory in early 1919.[73] The Hammonds found that operating Black Belt theaters could be an extremely lucrative enterprise, enabling them to construct a massive new venue at the heart of the Stroll.

After its run at the Vendome, *The Homesteader* was shown the following week at the Pickford Theater at Thirty-fifth Street and Michigan Avenue (106 E. Thirty-fifth, two blocks west of the Stroll), which the Hammonds acquired from (Jack) Weihoffen & Parsons during the influenza epidemic of 1918. In earlier years, the Pickford had been the Lux Theater, a large venue (seating 754) showing "high-class pictures" like *Quo Vadis* under the management of Mr. Zurawski.[74] As the Pickford, the theater boasted the only "Bartola orchestra" in the Black Belt, playing a "fine class of music" along with "high grade photoplays," and drawing the patronage of "a great many of Chicago's most prominent people of color."[75] When the Pickford was purchased by the Hammonds, it was redecorated "and put into first-class working order."

By controlling five of the Black Belt's movie theaters, O. C. Hammond and his sons played "a prominent part in the amusement life of the South Side."[76] The Hammonds were among many white entrepreneurs who owned successful businesses in the Black Belt. By acquiring so many theaters and developing strong name recognition in the community, they became well-known personalities among Black Chicagoans but kept a large segment of the film exhibition business out of the hands of local Black entrepreneurs. Anna Everett argues that the increased popularity of dominant cinema among segregated Black audiences was "secured uneasily at the expense of black cultural workers, including writers, theatrical impresarios, drama critics and thespians."[77] Movie theater ownership was also on the list of enterprises from which Blacks were precluded as film exhibition became big business.

The relationship between actual and figurative ownership of Black Belt theaters is one of the structuring tensions of Black film culture. White theater owners worked continuously to demonstrate the cultural legitimacy of their venues even though they had a relatively captive audience, and Black patrons were inclined to claim "ownership" of neighborhood theaters even though they could only respond retroactively to their business and programming decisions. Black spectators (and other "cultural workers") were not merely victims of the film industry's increasing presence on the African American entertainment scene. Interactions between white owners and Black consumers (of films and other forms of commercial amusement) could involve genuine dialogue regarding appropriate material and conditions for entertaining minority audiences. But the dominant cinema's runaway business also enabled owners and patrons to maintain a fiction of shared financial and political investment in Black neighborhood film exhibition as a corrective to the indignities of urban life. White theater owners like the Hammonds, through the Black press, played up aspects of film consumption that evoked "high class" and comfort, even while much of the cinema's appeal in the Black Belt stemmed from its low cultural status (as an inexpensive, accessible entertainment) and the potential for community protest.

## Black Celebrity Ownership Returns: The Star

By boasting quality films and fine musical performances, as well as modern conveniences and amenities in beautiful surroundings, Black Belt theaters promoted themselves as refuges from squalor, exclusion, and discrimination. The Washington theater (3440 S. State) remodeled its interior "in a very beautiful manner"; the Roosevelt (3125 S. Cottage Grove) showed early works by Oscar Micheaux; venues like Byron's Temple of Music (3230 S. State), Chateau Gardens (5318–26 S. State), and the Airdome (with its "dance pavilion" and "canopy covered picture department") presented movies within presumably more culturally authentic contexts of Black music and dancing and/or respectable contexts of open-air healthfulness.[78] The Atlas theater, at Forty-seventh and State Streets (4711–17 S. State) was an "ornate structure finished in green and white" featuring "an improved ventilating system," a "$5,000 organ," a "sanitary bubbling drinking fountain," and "washrooms with hot and cold water." The Atlas sought to attract the patronage of women and children in particular: for "the lady beautiful," there were well-appointed toilet rooms with a number of "conveniently located" mirrors; and children reportedly exclaimed at the 1914 opening that the "'movies' are great," and "Gee, that place looks like heaven."[79] Much like the ornate movie palaces of the 1920s that would attempt to extend the fantasy space of cinematic narratives into theater spaces occupied largely by working-class patrons (of all racial and ethnic backgrounds), Black Belt theaters boasted (in print if not in fact) clean, healthy, beautiful spaces in which African American viewers could feel validated, even if Blackness was not represented (positively) on screen.

These strategies to legitimize the movies within an African American exhibition context may have elevated theaters in the estimation of some Black leaders, and may have contributed to their tremendous popularity among Black Chicagoans by the mid-1910s. Whether or not Black Belt theaters actually lived up to the "well-appointed" image they advertised, it seems that many African American moviegoers were not preoccupied with the cultural status or physical trappings of movie theaters. Black Belt moviegoers patronized theaters across the scale of respectability, as illustrated by the history of the Star Theater. The Star, located on State Street just north of Thirty-ninth Street (3835–37 S. State), opened in 1913 boasting the same clean and classy qualities advertised by other theaters, such as "electric lights," "new pictures," "polite attention," and "pure air."[80] But in 1916 the Star was purchased by Henry "Teenan" Jones, successor to the legendary John "Mushmouth" Johnson in leadership of the South Side's gambling operations.

Although one might expect that this underworld connection might threaten the Star's respectability, the theater successfully continued to present itself as a legitimate establishment, in large measure because Jones enjoyed a positive reputation within the Black Belt as a successful amusements entrepreneur. During the early 1890s, Jones co-owned the Turf Exchange at 474 State Street in downtown Chicago, a saloon catering to white patrons from the horse-racing crowd and those seeking "the reliable turf news."[81] Then in 1895 he established a saloon and gambling house in the affluent white Hyde Park neighborhood called the Lakeside Club, which also catered primarily to whites. Here Jones staged a complete floor show and operated successfully for fifteen years until a neighborhood reform group drove him out of their midst. Jones moved his operations to the Black Belt, where he opened two venues on State Street. The Elite No. 1 (3030 S. State), next door to the old Monogram Theater, was a fashionable bar and restaurant at the bustling hub of Thirty-first and State Streets (discussed in the previous chapter). In 1915 Jones opened The Elite No. 2 (3445 S. State), also known as Teenan Jones' Place, a "café and cabaret" situated next door to the New Monogram Theater. The Elites "became centers of Negro night life between 1910 and 1915." They featured classical and popular vaudeville music and served as fashionable meeting places for men of the Race and for performers who appeared at the Monograms and other Stroll theaters.[82] Jones was an extremely popular figure in the Black Belt, where he owned other establishments and even managed a vaudeville act, the Caroline Girls.[83] The Black political newspaper, the *Broad Ax*, ran a large photograph of Jones in 1918 with a caption indicating his popularity and staying power: "The shining light of the Elite Cafe No. 2, who is still in the ring and still stands ace high with his many friends and patrons" (fig. 38).[84]

Allen Spear notes that like the underworld figures who preceded him, Jones was "active in civic and political affairs," using his considerable wealth and influence to support Black cultural activities and Black politicians.[85] As Kenney reports, Jones served as president of the Robert T. Motts Memorial Association and the Colored Men's Retail Liquor Dealers' Protective Association and was an organizer in the Republican Party.[86] Even though Jones's "shady" business activities got him suspended from the

HENRY (TEENAN) JONES

The shining light of the Elite Cafe No. 2, who is still in the ring and still
stands ace high with his many friends and patrons.

FIGURE 38. Portrait of Star Theater owner and Black Belt celebrity, Teenan Jones.
*Chicago Broad Ax*, 7 December 1918.

Masons (and eventually indicted, but acquitted, for making payoffs to Alderman Oscar DePriest and police captain Stephen K. Healy), his places of amusement, including the Star Theater, continued to attract Black Belt patrons with race pride rhetoric. Under Jones's ownership, the Star was celebrated as "the only house in Chicago owned and operated entirely by members of the Race," assuming the place once occupied by Motts's legendary Pekin. In one of many moves echoing his late mentor Motts, in 1917 Jones hired pioneer Black filmmaker and entertainment writer William Foster to manage the Star, allowing Foster to reprise his role as the business representative and booking agent for Motts at the Pekin.[87] As Chicago's Black population increased, entrepreneurs like Jones could operate successful amusements for Black patrons without worrying too much about objections by Black moral leaders, such as those raised when the Pekin Theatre opened in 1906. As Spear observes, Teenan Jones's popularity and success indicate that "the standards of respectability of an earlier era were falling before the new ideal of economic achievement."[88]

By the midteens, with the attention of Black theatrical critics and the explosion of the film industry, movies had overcome their marginal and stigmatized status to become one of the most popular leisure activities for urban Blacks across lines of class, gender, and age. Chicago's Black community consistently experienced internal and external attempts to circumscribe its spheres of activity, especially as southern Black migrants adjusted to the urban North and as more established Chicago residents adjusted to the reconfiguration of their communities caused by the Great Migration. In light of these conditions, Black Belt theaters devised ways to validate moviegoing not only by asserting its respectability but also by appealing to audience tastes for sensationalism and support for Black entrepreneurship, even if tinged with moral impropriety. These theaters took both the high and the low roads in their appeals to African American patrons, reflecting Black responses to living in urban industrial environments in which opportunities for uplift and upward mobility coexisted with the freedom to participate in popular forms of commercial amusement as part of a growing and insurgent working class.

While moviegoing within the Black Belt thrived, African Americans looked beyond their neighborhood theaters for ways to participate equally and meaningfully in American mass culture and modern urban life. Black Chicagoans continued to agitate for equal access to and treatment in theaters outside of the Black Belt as part of their larger effort to enjoy in practice the rights guaranteed to them by law, rights for which many African Americans had relocated to the urban North. In addition, while African

American viewers, critics, theater owners, and managers attempted to create spaces for urban Blacks within the local public contexts of movie theaters, a small number of African American filmmakers sought to speak directly to segregated Black audiences across the country by developing production practices of their own.

Significantly, many of the earliest Black-owned film companies were headquartered along and around the Stroll, including the first African American production outfit, the Foster Photoplay Company (Grand Theater Building, 3110 S. State and then 3312 S. Wabash), along with the Unique Film Company (3519 S. State), the Peter P. Jones Photoplay Company (3704 S. Prairie and later 3849 S. State), and the Royal Gardens Motion Picture Company (459 E. Thirty-first Street), founded by Virgil L. Williams at his popular Royal Gardens nightclub with actor Samuel T. Jacks.[89] In many important ways, the possibilities and contradictions of Chicago's vibrant Black entertainment and theatrical scene influenced early African American film production, which, as I discuss in the next chapters, sought to respond to dominant cinema and to capitalize on a Black entertainment culture that was expanding with the migration of Black people into cities and film audiences across the country.

# PART THREE

# Behind the Camera

# CHAPTER SIX

# Reckless Rovers versus Ambitious Negroes

*Migration, Patriotism, and the Politics of Genre in Early African American Filmmaking*

As we have seen, by the early 1910s African Americans made up a conspicuous portion of the American film audience, patronizing moving pictures in a variety of contexts, including hundreds of theaters across the country that catered specifically to Black clienteles. Inspired by the expansion of this largely segregated market, which included growing Black urban populations with disposable income and race-conscious views, a handful of African American entrepreneurs began to form their own film production companies to respond in kind to the portrayal (or, more frequently, the absence) of Blackness in dominant cinema. Even before D. W. Griffith's inflammatory *Birth of a Nation* (1915) joined many Black voices in protest, several African American filmmakers pledged to represent the "better" aspects of Black life and character. But they continually struggled to manage the contradictions shaping the emerging Black film culture, including the politics of racial stereotypy, the cinema's high and low cultural appeals to largely working-class audiences, and Black moviegoers' increasingly sophisticated and diverse reconstructive viewing practices.

The first African Americans to enter the motion picture business recognized a unique opportunity to exploit a market that was hungry for more progressive Black images but that also enjoyed the comic and sensational popular cultural fare of the day. These men imagined that they could work toward racial uplift while turning a nice profit for themselves in a lucrative new industry. They learned very quickly, however, that they were at a significant disadvantage in relation to their white counterparts in terms of financing and experience. How could African American filmmakers carve out their own niche in an industry that was firmly in the control of white corporate interests, let alone develop a film aesthetic that would serve the purposes of both uplift and profit?

One after another, the early Black filmmakers met similar difficulties when trying to make, distribute, and attract Black audiences to their films, leading several of them to use the same metaphor to describe burgeoning Black film production—that it was in its "infancy." For example, Chicago-based William Foster, founder of the first African American–owned film company, wrote in 1913 that the Black motion picture business "is but a feeble infant, scarcely able to nurse its bottle."[1] A year later, Hunter C. Haynes, founder of the Haynes Photoplay Company in New York City, wrote: "The condition of the colored moving pictures and colored actors is in its infancy, but I am afraid it will get no further unless the colored exhibitors will give them more support."[2] As late as 1924, Oscar Micheaux, Black America's most successful film entrepreneur, described the plight of the Black filmmaker as follows: "He requires encouragement and assistance. . . . He is the new-born babe who must be fondled until he can stand on his own feet, and if the race has any pride in presenting its own achievements in this field, it behooves it to interest itself, and morally encourage such efforts."[3] These references to the newborn state of Black filmmaking were intended to elicit sympathy from members of an African American public that similarly required "encouragement and assistance" to overcome the tremendous obstacles they faced in their efforts to achieve social, economic, and political parity in a discriminatory society.

Although these men consistently expressed their infantile need to be nurtured by Black audiences, critics, and exhibitors, by the time Black producers started making films many Black viewers felt that they, along with the film industry in general, had reached a level of maturity. For example, in a 1917 *Chicago Defender* article condemning a Black-cast "low comedy" distributed by the Ebony Film Corporation, theater critic Tony Langston declares: "The moving picture business can no longer be considered in its infancy and patrons of modern houses should not be subjected to the humiliating experience of seeing things which lower the Race in the estimation of its own people as well as in the eyes of whatever members of the 'other' race who may happen to be in attendance."[4] Always under pressure to perform under the watchful eye of the dominant "'other' race," Black film producers were charged with the difficult task of pleasing demanding, discerning, and self-conscious Black constituencies with very few resources. As African Americans became an increasingly heterogeneous public—with communities located in the rural and urban South, the industrial North, and out West—their experiences and tastes were by no means monolithic, and it became more difficult to determine how best to enlist their interest and support.

This chapter traces how several early Black filmmakers attempted to develop production practices that would create cohesion among disparate African American communities, despite their social and geographic distance and differences. In competition with the dominant film industry, and with each other, early race film producers attempted to solicit nationwide Black support by echoing popular race rhetoric of the period, including the need to define and assert the "Americanness" of the Negro. Black filmmakers emphasized this national identity regardless of where in the country their characters and audiences lived, or what particular forms of racism they faced. To this end, early African American filmmakers frequently mobilized themes of migration and patriotism (in their films and promotional discourses) in order to create alternative narratives on "the nation" that challenged the racially exclusionary "America" constructed in white-dominated media (including *The Birth of a Nation*). Adapting, debating, and reworking mainstream generic conventions, race filmmakers produced city comedies, migration melodramas, and military newsreels that encouraged and reflected renewed assertions of American identity on the part of Black audiences.

But Black filmmakers hardly resolved the geographic and ideological differences that increasingly characterized modern Black life. Early race films reflect the fact that Black people had migrated to and settled in all corners of the country, broadly claiming America (not just the South or urban northern "Black Belts") as their home. Many feature story lines that trace the primary pattern of the Great Migration—from the South to the North. Some also feature movements to and from the West, not surprising given that two of the most successful race film companies, the Micheaux Book and Film Company and the Lincoln Motion Picture Company, were founded by Black men from western states. Some filmmakers tended to create moral and social hierarchies among their characters based on regional differences at the very moment when they sought to coalesce their dispersed Black audiences into a stable race film market. Micheaux and Lincoln, for instance, tended to celebrate the western frontier, representing cities as corrupt places where Black people lose touch with their nobler selves, despite the fact that a large percentage of their audience was choosing to settle in urban centers.

Many Black filmmakers address the rifts among Black populations by turning to the theme of patriotism, particularly in films produced during and just after World War I. They were keenly aware of the appeal of the argument that Blacks had consistently proved their loyalty to the nation in many ways, including military service dating back to the Revolutionary

War, and therefore deserved full American citizenship. Numerous films make patriotic gestures (e.g., heroic Black characters, nationalistic intertitles) in an attempt to show that Black people had earned their rightful, equal place in modern American society and to produce a pleasurable and pride-filled moviegoing experience for Black viewers. But the numerous stylistic contexts in which these gestures are staged (drama, newsreel, comedy) expose, in different ways, the limitations of using patriotism as a unifying discourse in Black mass culture.

Given the cinema's contentious legacy of Black representation and contested status as a space for Black leisure, themes of migration and patriotism could not smoothly bridge Black audience demands and desires for race pride and "low" amusement, realism and fantasy. African Americans continued to be subjected to racial discrimination (on and off screen) in the United States despite their moves into "modern" life and their participation in military campaigns waged in the name of "democracy." Thus, films that evoke Black patriotism and those that stratify Blacks geographically compound the contradictions of Black "American" identity and complicate any sense of pride, pleasure, and/or potential that African Americans might have associated with the cinema. This chapter outlines several early Black filmmaking practices—the problems of producing Black-themed comedies; the ambitious efforts of the Lincoln company to create a Black film studio around its "high-class" dramas; and the use of popular military themes in fiction and nonfiction films—to examine how these different generic frameworks test the cinema's capacity to simultaneously uplift and entertain Black audiences.

## New Negroes and Old Negroes: The Risks of Comedy

Several early Black filmmakers sought to make popular, inexpensive films by concentrating their efforts on producing short comedies. Although comedy certainly appealed to many African American viewers, it is the genre that would seem, superficially, to be most likely to feature offensive racial stereotyping, even in films produced by well-meaning, Black-controlled companies. As discussed in this book's opening chapters, early cinema is replete with slapstick comedies featuring a variety of broad racial and ethnic caricatures (of Blacks, Asians, Irish, Jews). In keeping with the broad popularity of African American vaudeville performance, many of the first Black-produced films used stage-derived comedy routines to render Black characters and locales. This meant that some Black-produced films repeated blackface minstrel conventions that white filmmakers had been using since the earliest days of the cinema. At the same time, comedy could open up opportunities for parody and critique that reflected on the changing contours of modern Black life.

For example, in many Black-produced comedies released during this period, humor is produced by juxtaposing different "types" of Black characters based on their geographic background and/or location. As a result of the dispersion of African Americans into different social and economic strata in their variously located communities, filmmakers could exploit the potentially humorous situations that result when disparate Black characters interact with one another, and most Black-oriented comedies seem to highlight intraracial conflict and alienation across class and regional lines.

One such film is the Hunter C. Haynes Photoplay Company's *Uncle Remus's First Visit to New York* (1914), which details the comic adventures of a southern Black rube and his wife as they navigate the big city.[5] The film starred some of vaudeville's most famous Black talent, including Abbie Mitchell and Tom Brown, potentially giving it audience appeal beyond an African American viewership.[6] Henry Sampson's description of the film's characters and plot suggests that *Uncle Remus,* like many Black vaudeville sketches of the period, features representations of Blackness that resemble those in numerous white-produced comedies of the era:

> The story of the play concerns Rastus, a successful New York colored businessman, sending for his Uncle Remus and his wife to come and visit them from their old cabin home in the South. The inexperienced daughter of Uncle Remus sends a telegram to Rastus informing him that the "Old Couple" will arrive in New York on a certain day, never mentioning what station or over what railroad. As expected Rastus goes to the wrong station and the old folks arriving in New York, afraid to trust anyone to tell them anything, start out in that big city to find Rastus.[7]

Although this film acknowledges the economic progress of African Americans by featuring a "successful New York businessman" among its characters, his respectability is compromised by giving him the name "Rastus," repeated here from the blackface vaudeville tradition that ridiculed lazy, henpecked, chicken-stealing Black men.[8]

The southern ignorance of the film's central comic figures—old Uncle Remus and his wife—provides regionalized and racialized humor. The story of a country rube's humorous experiences in the city is certainly not unique to Black-cast films.[9] However, the rubes in *Uncle Remus* speak to a Black audience about a variety of culturally specific issues regarding the social and historical status of the Negro. A reviewer for the *Indianapolis Freeman,* a

Black newspaper, points to some of these issues when he writes: "The mishaps and mixups which befell the old man and his wife from the time they left their delta farm to the close of their sojourn in Gotham, together with the embarrassment of the high-toned city nephew and his wife and stylish friends, form a series of situations that make for laughter, mingled with a bit of pathos."[10] This praise suggests that Black anxieties inform the construction and reading of the characters in this film, much as white anxieties structure references to Black movement in dominant cinema.

The *Freeman* reviewer claims that *Uncle Remus* is a "faithful portrait that contrasts the new Negro with the old and forges a chain of circumstances that vividly point out the progress the race has made in his fifty years of freedom." The writer goes on to say that this is a film in which "the modern and the ante-bellum Negro are shown in sharp differentiation."[11] This favorable assessment clearly comes from a northern, urban, "New Negro" perspective, since it unproblematically reads the representation of Uncle Remus as an "old Negro," an "ante-bellum" figure from the past, despite his circulation among "modern" Blacks in present-day New York City. Relying on the idea that Black "progress" is located in northern cities, the reviewer indicates that this particular film privileges urban Black sensibilities over the ostensibly persistently retrogressive "Old Negro" ways of the South.

Not every Black comedy filmmaker relied on staging this kind of Old Negro/New Negro conflict. Instead, the remarkable expansion of Black urban populations provided a backdrop for African American filmmakers to explore interactions among Black city types. For example, William Foster founded his Foster Photoplay Company in Chicago in 1913 in order to specialize in nondegrading comedies about urban Black life. Foster enjoyed a long career in show business, having worked as a vaudeville booking and publicity agent and as business representative for Robert Motts's Pekin Theatre before he formed his film company. With offices on the South State Street "Stroll," Foster produced at least a dozen films, including *The Railroad Porter* (1913) and the newsreel *The Colored Championship Base Ball Game* (1914).[12] None of Foster's films are extant, so it is difficult to determine the exact nature of the comparisons they staged between Black character types. Records indicate that Foster's films were shown primarily in theaters in Chicago (where they were shot) and eastern cities, and that they spoke to and about urban Blacks, suggesting that he had this milieu in mind when he expressed his belief in "the value of the motion picture as a medium for portraying the stronger features of [the Negro's] particular life."[13]

Mark Reid has argued that Foster represented segments of the African American community that had been largely ignored in white-produced films, notably the Black middle class of the urban North. Reid notes that "Foster photoplays altered the popular Rastus stereotype by using African-American socio-cultural realities as the content of his films."[14] Foster's familiarity with the African American entertainment scene suggests that his films not only reflected modern Black "realities" but also catered to prevalent Black popular cultural tastes. His unique combination of Black middle-class characters and the generic conventions of comedy enabled him to boast about the progressive, realistic, culturally specific nature of his work (in keeping with uplift ideology) despite the potential for (and long history of) unflattering caricature in comic Black representations.

For example, Foster's successful debut, *The Railroad Porter*, features a range of New Negro types. The action revolves around "a young wife who, thinking her husband had gone out on 'his run,' invited a fashionably dressed chap, who was a waiter at one of the colored cafés on State Street, to dine."[15] Both men's occupations in the film reflect exciting new opportunities available to African American men—uniformed, well-traveled Pullman porters were often treated as cultural heroes within the Black community;[16] the waiter (a "fashionably dressed" dandy) is employed at Chicago's Elite Café, which, as discussed in chapters 4 and 5, was owned by the well-known local businessman Henry "Teenan" Jones and extolled as one of the premier Black gathering places in the country.[17] Despite these gestures toward racial pride and celebration, the film's comedy derives from the disruptions posed by these attractive features of modern life—travel, consumer culture, and the glamour of the Stroll café scene can break up Black middle-class homes.

The deep resonances of these themes among Foster's audiences are suggested in a *Defender* report that the film's plot of infidelity forced Foster to seek a white producer for the project. The paper claimed that Foster "was refused support by the married men of the race," but "a white gentleman loaned him enough money to get the machine."[18] Whether this item takes a joking dig at Chicago's race men for not financing Foster's endeavor, or for their hypocritical moral standards (which are ostensibly higher than those of whites), or is stating fact, it demonstrates how issues of content and financing were foregrounded from the very beginning of Black film production. The *Defender* can joke about the morality and financial backing of Foster's film, while at the same time celebrating his achievement, because all these issues had long figured into debates about Black cultural production and reception.

Accounts in the *Chicago Defender* suggest that Foster's films enjoyed great popularity. The "Musical and Dramatic" column reported in August 1913 that Foster's debut, *The Railroad Porter,* "has surprised all of State street" by playing at the States Theater to "crowded houses, with matinees Mondays, Thursdays and Saturdays." As a result of this success, the States offered Foster an exclusive contract for the premieres of his subsequent films, including the forthcoming *The Butler.*[19] In October 1913, Foster's short comedy *The Fall Guy* also drew large audiences at the States. The reviewer notes that Foster's filmmaking skills had noticeably improved with this film, which "simply goes to prove that practice makes perfect."[20] Foster's success reached another peak the following month, when *The Railroad Porter* was screened to white audiences at the Majestic Theater, "the leading vaudeville house in Chicago."[21]

Whereas Foster was celebrated by the Black press for developing new urban realist contexts for Black comedy, the Chicago-based Ebony Film Corporation was accused of denigrating the Race, despite the company's claims to break away from the degrading stereotypes found in mainstream films. Founded in 1917, the well-financed Ebony company achieved rare box office success with its Black-cast comedies because they were marketed largely to white audiences. Short films like *When Cupid Went Wild* (1917), *Ghosts* (1917), and *Wrong All Around* (1917) were favorably reviewed in *Moving Picture World,* a mainstream trade journal, where Ebony ran advertisements exclaiming: "Colored people are funny. If colored people weren't funny, there would be no plantation melodies, no banjoes, no cake walks, no buck and wing dancing, no jazz bands, no minstrel shows and no black-face vaudeville. And They Are Funny in the Studio."[22] Ebony ads stressed the fact that the company featured the "novelty" of "Real Colored People" in their pictures, not white actors in blackface. Ebony comedies showcased the talents of a stock company that consisted of forty African American actors.[23] With their distribution handled by the well-established General Film Company in New York City, Ebony's Black-cast comedies reached a mainstream audience and made the company much more profitable than its Black-owned counterparts.

Ebony's status as a "race film" company has been questioned not only because of its appeal to white audiences but also because of its predominantly white management. In addition, Ebony gained a negative reputation in the Black community after distributing a series of Black-cast comedies that audiences in Chicago's Black Belt found to be highly offensive for their inclusion of stock stereotypes. Though Ebony did not make these films (*Aladdin Jones, Money Talks in Darktown,* and *Two Knights of*

*Vaudeville,* produced by the Historical Feature Film Company), their negative impact proved difficult to overcome, despite the efforts of Ebony's sole Black officer and spokesman, Luther J. (or "L. J.") Pollard, to build networks within Black film culture while maintaining Ebony's mainstream box office success.[24]

As the Ebony Film Corporation's most visible creative force, Pollard has been variously described as a strong advocate for positive Black images and as a colored "front man" for an exploitative white-controlled company.[25] In a 1918 letter to George P. Johnson, booking manager of the Lincoln Motion Picture Company, Pollard observes that "nearly all of the producing concerns owned entirely by colored people have specialized in the production of dramas" to respond to the routinely degrading treatment of Blacks in comedy films. However, Pollard expresses his pride in Ebony comedies because they "proved to the public that colored players can put over good comedy without any of that crap shooting, chicken stealing, razor display, water melon eating stuff that the colored people generally have been a little disgusted at seeing. . . . You do not find any of that stuff in Ebony comedies. It isn't necessary to put it in in order to make comedies that are full of laughs."[26] Indeed, those Ebony films that are extant do not include the kinds of traditional, offensive scenes Pollard describes. Instead, they construct contemporary scenarios in which to parody Black character types, particularly city dwellers.

For example, *The Comeback of Barnacle Bill* (1918) depicts the competition between Sam (Sam Robinson), a farmhand, and Hector, a city boy, for the affections of Skeeter (Yvonne Junior), the daughter of landowner Hiram Hayseed (Samuel Jacks).[27] Sam and Skeeter already have a flirtation going when Hector is sent to the farm from New York City by his father with a telegram that reads as follows: "The city has ruined my son's health. I am sending him to you to see if the country will build him up and make him forget the bright lights." Hector is represented as a citified milquetoast. He arrives in Podunk, New York, wearing a suit and large glasses, carrying a huge trunk, golf clubs, and a walking stick. Goofy but good-natured Sam humiliates Hector repeatedly in ways that demonstrate Hector's inability to adapt to rural life and, therefore, his unfitness as a mate for Skeeter. Sam ultimately wins the girl when he secures the money Skeeter's father needs to pay off his mortgage. Hector also attempts to come to the rescue by asking his wealthy father to wire the money, but his father promptly refuses to help. Sam, on the other hand, gives Mr. Hayseed a large sum of cash he obtained by accidentally shooting a thief. As Sam hands over the fortune to Mr. Hayseed, Skeeter gazes admiringly upon

FIGURE 39. Hector, the bespectacled city boy (lower right), fails to win the girl in *The Comeback of Barnacle Bill* (Ebony Film Corporation, 1918). Library of Congress, Motion Picture, Broadcasting and Recorded Sound Division.

him, while Hector pouts pathetically in the background (fig. 39). This film juxtaposes city and rural Black manhood, and the city men—Hector and his father—turn out to be the ineffective and selfish losers.

Another comic Black urban character is featured in Ebony's *A Reckless Rover* (1918), this time in a leading role that highlights the conflicts among urban types both within and across racial lines. The film's main character, Rastus Jones (Sam Robinson), is represented as a lazy, good-for-nothing prankster who sleeps all day and does not pay his rent. When the landlady comes with a policeman to Rastus's door, he escapes to "Charley Moy high grade Hand Laundry," where he engages in a series of disruptive activities like making a mess of the laundry, repeatedly kissing an attractive but unsuspecting Black woman customer (Yvonne Junior), and smoking the laundry owner's opium (fig. 40). When a group of police officers (Black Keystone Cops) come to arrest Rastus, he orchestrates his escape by placing a distracting shooting target on the laundry owner's rear end.[28] Although Rastus's laziness clearly evokes white-produced representations of Black

FIGURE 40. Rastus Jones (Sam Robinson, right) aims an iron at the head of a police officer, just the beginning of his disruptive antics in Charley Moy's Chinese laundry (Moy played by Black actor Samuel Jacks, left). *A Reckless Rover* (Ebony Film Corporation, 1918). Library of Congress, Motion Picture, Broadcasting and Recorded Sound Division.

men, his behavior is much like that of anarchic white figures found in silent film comedy, such as Charlie Chaplin and other Keystone actors who were popular among African American viewers. Rastus also invokes the African diasporic figure of the "trickster," who applies his cunning in ways that will benefit himself most directly. As Rastus's escape from the law demonstrates, the Black trickster seems to have greater subversive potential in a modern, urban context, where he can wreak havoc and escape unpunished. In addition, his mistreatment of his Black landlady, the Black woman client, and the Chinese laundry owner (who is represented stereotypically, waddling slowly and wearing a long ponytail and sandals) shows him to be an opportunist who manipulates other members of his urban community (notably women and people of color) for his own amusement.

A third Ebony comedy, *Spying the Spy* (1918), extends the comic treatment of Black urban character into the area of Black patriotism. *Spying the*

FIGURE 41. Sambo Sam (Sam Robinson) fantasizes about foiling German spies. *Spying the Spy* (Ebony Film Corporation, 1918). Library of Congress, Motion Picture, Broadcasting and Recorded Sound Division.

*Spy* features Sambo Sam (Sam Robinson), a Black man living in Chicago who unsuccessfully tries to capture German spies to assist in the war effort. Sambo Sam fantasizes about making headlines and constantly searches for suspicious-looking individuals or Germans who might be plotting attacks on American soil (fig. 41). Following a white man who drops frankfurters and a German newspaper, Sam locates the apartment of a Herman Schwartz, whom he captures from behind and covers with a laundry bag. Sam escorts his prisoner at gunpoint to "Headquarters," where three white officials remove the bag to find that Schwartz is a Black man—hence the twofold joke, "Schwartz" literally meaning "black" in German, and the absurdity of mistaking a Black man for a German spy. Schwartz insists that he is "a respectable colored gentleman," and the officials release him. The second part of *Spying the Spy* shows Sam investigating the mysterious activities of a "degree team" or secret society. The all-Black male group turns the tables on Sam by running him through a series of ghoulish "initiation" rituals. In the end, the terrified Sam runs away from the camera down the railroad tracks. Sam is by no means presented as a representative member of the Black community. Still, the way in which his dreams of serving his country are rendered completely absurd pokes fun at notions of Black patriotic feeling and service at the very moment when many Blacks are trying to demonstrate their support for the war effort as grounds for claiming rights and respect. If Pollard does indeed imagine African Americans as part of the audience for Ebony films, he anticipates that Black viewers can laugh at one of their own, even in relation to the almost sacred topic of Black patriotism.

On the other hand, perhaps Ebony films speak in two voices. They offer updated versions of broad comic Black types that might harken back to familiar minstrel figures, but they might also function as modernist critiques of Black stereotyping and Black middle-class norms of propriety and decorum. Sambo Sam, for example, takes patriotic rhetoric too far. He looks and functions much like other "coon" figures, but he is placed in context with noncomic Black figures, and his obsessive, outlandish behavior might be read as a commentary on the overuse of patriotic rhetoric among African Americans. We can see the dangers, then, that might be read into the production of Black-cast comedies, even those that claim to move forward from minstrel traditions of the past. The alternatives they offer to stodgy uplift posturing—both representational and spectatorial—not only potentially support continued racist beliefs held by white viewers but also might encourage self-deprecation or a rejection of political, religious, and/or middle-class orthodoxy (or leadership) on the part of Black viewers.

In many ways, Ebony's comedic representations of urban Black men like Hector, Rastus, and Sambo Sam seem to undercut claims that African Americans had made significant social progress in the urban North. These films indicate that Blacks are not necessarily more intelligent, proud, successful, or sophisticated just because they live in the city. But Ebony films do illustrate that the Black community was not monolithic (including rural farmers, urban property owners, and a variety of "respectable Negroes"). And the self-absorbed central characters, in keeping with the genre's conventions, provide comic relief precisely by creating discord in the diverse communities they inhabit. Race leaders deplored these kinds of representations because they seem to work against the projects of elevating the Black image, building bridges across Black communities, and presenting a united Black front in the face of white racism. But Ebony comedies also offer a view of modern Black life that authorizes the viewer to laugh at a variety of African American types. These representations are not necessarily just insulting stand-ins for Black people/viewers; they also are reflections on the often stifling expectations of Black behavior and expression in modern contexts.

L. J. Pollard may have honestly believed that Ebony comedies provided an important generic departure from the dramatic films that Black-owned companies produced almost exclusively. However, the comic, often parodic treatment of Black characters in Ebony films, along with Black representations in other white-controlled companies, impelled other African American producers to settle on drama as the appropriate genre for presenting the "positive" and unifying implications of migration and patriotism for African Americans.

## "See It and Be Glad You Are a Negro": The High-Class Dramas of the Lincoln Motion Picture Company

Two of the most successful Black-owned film companies, the Lincoln Motion Picture Company and the Micheaux Book and Film Company, appealed to Black audiences by focusing their efforts on producing "high" dramas rather than "low" comedies. African American moviegoers frequently made sharp distinctions between these two genres and their implications for Black representation. In 1916, for example, a woman identifying herself as "a member of the respectable class of theater patrons" wrote to *Defender* theatrical critic Tony Langston to complain about the "scenes of degradation" featured in the Historical Feature Film Company comedies distributed under the Ebony company's name which were being screened in Black Belt theaters.[29] Langston's reply, printed below the moviegoer's letter, reports that he has alerted the theater managers about the problem and has secured promises that they would no longer "carry 'comedy' that causes respectable ladies and gentlemen to blush with shame and humiliation." Langston extends his critique of both the genre of comedy and the claims of racial authenticity (via Black casts and perhaps claims of Black authorship) by urging Black moviegoers to be more discerning consumers: "I want to advise the members of the race to watch the booking advertised by the theaters in the 'belt,' and when you see one of these so-called 'all-colored comedies' advertised, keep your money in your pocket and save that dime as well as your self-respect. Some day we will have race dramas which will uplift, instead of rotten stuff which degrades."[30] Lincoln and Micheaux answered this call for uplifting dramatic Black-authored films.[31] Both companies relied heavily on a rhetoric of "race pride" in the production and the marketing of their dramatic films, advancing the idea that by supporting their serious productions, Black audiences were contributing positively to the advancement of the Race.

In a 1917 prospectus outlining the Lincoln Company's goals, the officers write that their company "was established in May 1916 in Los Angeles, California for the purpose of producing Negro moving pictures that will reflect merit and credit upon the Race, as well as opening up a field of employment to Negroes and an opportunity to make profitable financial investments."[32] Noble Johnson, a character actor at Lubin and Universal, founded Lincoln with a group of prominent Black businessmen and a white cameraman, Harry Gant.[33] Lincoln's goal was not only to make "respectable" race films but also to open up work and investment opportunities for Blacks in the growing field of motion picture production. It did so, however, on a much smaller economic base than a company like Ebony. Whereas Ebony was capitalized at $500,000, Lincoln was incorporated with a capitalization of only $75,000.[34] Still, between 1916 and 1917, Lincoln released three of the most highly acclaimed and widely distributed Black-produced race films of the silent era.[35]

Lincoln's first film, a two-reeler titled *The Realization of a Negro's Ambition* (1916), tells the story of James Burton (Noble Johnson), an enterprising Tuskegee graduate who leaves his father's farm to seek his fortune in the California oil fields. When he gets to California, Burton is denied an oil-drilling job because he is Black. However, he later saves the life of a wealthy white oil mogul's daughter and is given a job by the grateful father. While leading an oil expedition, Burton realizes that the geographic features of the California oil fields resemble those of his father's farm. He returns South, makes a fortune from his discovery of oil on his father's land, and marries his hometown sweetheart.

*Realization* met with tremendous praise from Black audiences and critics across the country. It was featured as the opening attraction at the National Negro Business League convention in August 1916 in Kansas City. A report from this screening noted that the film "marks the beginning of a new era in the production of Race pictures," in large measure because it presents Black characters in a dramatic (rather than comic) context:

> Feeling that the trend of public sentiment among the Race lovers of the silent drama is growing so antagonistic to the insulting, humiliating and undignified portrayal of the cheap burlesque slap-stick comedies so universally shown as characteristic of the Afro-American ideals, the Lincoln Motion Picture Co. of Los Angeles, Cal., a Race firm, has in their first release successfully eliminated these undesirable features and produced a really interesting, inspiring and commendable educational love drama, featuring the

business and social life of the Negro, as it really is and not as our jealous contemporaries would have us appear.[36]

Chicago's Black Belt theater owners testified to the film's quality and popularity. Teenan Jones, owner of the Star Theater, reported to the Lincoln management that "'Realization' proved the most popular feature shown here in a long time, and delighted record-breaking houses. To say our patrons were surprised and delighted is putting it mildly. You can put us down for your next and next releases." George Paul, manager of the States Theater, exclaimed,

> "Realization" proved to be all you claimed for it, and I made it a point to inquire of our patrons what they thought of it. They were unanimous in expressions of satisfaction. It is a clean-cut well-acted drama that has opened the eyes of many who have associated all colored pictures with the lowest of the low comedy. You can book me as far ahead as you please for all your future releases, not alone for the States but for the Washington and the Lincoln Theatres as well.[37]

*Realization* was applauded not just for the quality of the acting, writing, and photography, and for its uplifting representation of the finer qualities of the Race, but also because it featured a new setting for race films—the West. Burton's migration from the South to California reflected the westward migration of thousands of other African Americans. Since Lincoln's president and leading man, Noble Johnson, himself was born and raised in Colorado, he made films that exposed Black life west of the Mississippi to African American viewers in other parts of the country.[38] The representation of Black achievement via this westward trajectory of Black migration would be repeated in later Lincoln films.

For its second production, Lincoln turned to the topic of African American military service. *The Trooper of Troop K* (1916) was a three-reeler starring Noble Johnson as "Shiftless Joe," a directionless youth who joins the army, becomes a hero in battle, and returns home to the admiration of his community and his sweetheart (fig. 42). The film proved very successful because it dramatized the "Carrizal Incident," which occurred in June 1916. Well-known in African American communities, this incident involved Troops K and C of the all-Black Tenth Cavalry, in which "twenty-two Black soldiers were killed while on a mission pursuing a deserter."[39] The film attempted to faithfully reproduce the Carrizal Incident, and to replicate the style of Hollywood westerns, by featuring a number of ex-troopers from the Ninth and Tenth Cavalries, placed among "Mexicans, cowboys and horses" as well as "guns, uniforms, canon" and other supplies hired from

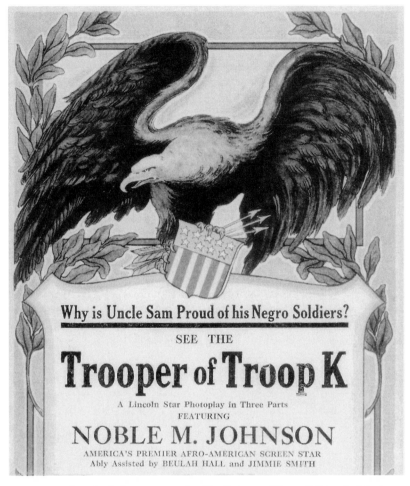

FIGURE 42. Detail of advertisement for *The Trooper of Troop K* (Lincoln Motion Picture Company, 1916). George P. Johnson Negro Film Collection, Department of Special Collections, University of California at Los Angeles.

the Hollywood firms that supplied the major studios, and by shooting on location in the sandy creek beds of the San Gabriel River to replicate the Mexican landscape (figs. 43 and 44).[40]

This combination of documentary and western generic strategies seems to have paid off, with positive responses from exhibitors, viewers, and critics, who praised the film's value within and beyond the African American community. A review of the film in the *California Eagle* argued that *The*

FIGURE 43. Portrait of an African American soldier serving in the celebrated twenty-fourth Infantry in Mexico, 1916. Library of Congress, Prints and Photographs Division, LC-USZ62-47383.

Noble Johnson in "Trooper Of Troop K"

FIGURE 44. Noble Johnson as a heroic cavalryman stationed in Mexico in a re-creation of the Carrizal Incident in *The Trooper of Troop K* (Lincoln Motion Picture Company, 1916). George P. Johnson Negro Film Collection, Department of Special Collections, University of California at Los Angeles.

*Trooper of Troop K* would have lasting historical significance because it documents that "our boys made such a good fight against overwhelming odds, sacrificing their blood for life and country."[41] A Lincoln advertisement for *Trooper* declared that the film should have appeal across racial lines: "Why is Uncle Sam Proud of his Negro Soldiers? See The Trooper of Troop K—Every Patriotic Person, White or Black, should see it." In this way, Lincoln attempted to code true "patriotism" as racially inclusive; there is no evidence, however, that the film was booked in theaters catering primarily to white audiences.

Reports from exhibitors indicate that *Trooper* struck a chord with Black viewers in a variety of contexts. It was exhibited in theaters, as well as churches, colleges, lodges, and high schools, in various parts of the country. Following a screening at the historically Black Wiley University in Marshall, Texas, the college's president, M. W. Dogan, wrote to the Lincoln Company: "Could Noble Johnson have heard the applause and the singing, 'My Country 'Tis of Thee' by the audience during the battle scene in the picture, he would have felt rewarded for his clever acting."[42] Reporting from Chicago, Lincoln booking agent (and *Defender* theatrical critic) Tony Langston wrote: "When Joe shot that greaser off the horse at the 8 o'clock show there was a yell let out that almost raised the roof."[43] These accounts represent vocal, participatory Black film reception as a testament to the film's effectiveness, even as it is performed at the expense of another "minority" group. Indeed, by aligning themselves against Mexicans, the Black makers and viewers of *Trooper* attempt to bolster their claims of patriotism and Americanism. Like the treatment of the Chinese laundry owner in Ebony's *A Reckless Rover*, this interaction between Blacks and other people of color is rendered as antagonistic; both anticipate visceral responses from Black audiences who, presumably, do not consider how alliances with Asians or Latinos might advance their struggles against white racism. In another striking report on the appeal of Lincoln films, A. B. McAfee, president and general manager of the Palace Picture Parlor in Louisville, wrote to the Lincoln Company about his exhibition of *Realization* and *Trooper*: "Even the Baptist ministers witnessed them, which is unprecedented; the Baptists here *never* attend theatres."[44] Lincoln's first two productions set a new standard in race film production, drawing even those segments of the Black community that typically ignored or opposed the cinema and creating a nationwide demand for more of their work.

Lincoln's third production, *The Law of Nature* (1917), was a three-reel drama that returned to the theme of African American western migration. Written by Noble Johnson, *The Law of Nature* took up the differences be-

FIGURE 45. Jess (Noble Johnson), a western ranch foreman, feels out of place in pretentious eastern high society. *The Law of Nature* (Lincoln Motion Picture Company, 1917). George P. Johnson Negro Film Collection, Department of Special Collections, University of California at Los Angeles.

tween city life in the East and rural life on the western frontier by depicting the failed marriage of an eastern society lady and a ranch foreman (fig. 45). Johnson underscores his notion of the "virile" West by characterizing his leading lady as being most susceptible to the city's demoralizing influences, while the manly ranchman, Jess, rightfully returns, with son, to the wholesome western frontier. Foreshadowing the work of Oscar Micheaux, *The Law of Nature* demonstrates that urban environments corrupt Black character, and that the West is a more wholesome, healthy environment for Black families. Again, the high quality of the Lincoln production—that is, both its "positive" Black representations and its acting, writing, and visual style—earned praise from urban audiences even though the film makes negative moral judgments about life in the city. *The Law of Nature* ran for four days at Chicago's Washington Theater in July 1918, and the manager, Chester Paul, wrote that Lincoln's films were "so far superior to the other all-colored productions that there is absolutely no comparison."[45]

Noble Johnson's brother, George P. Johnson, a postal clerk living in Omaha, Nebraska, served as booking and publicity manager, charged with expanding Lincoln's advertising and distribution network beyond its Los Angeles base. George Johnson learned the motion picture business quickly, picking up tips from *Defender* theater critic Tony Langston, whom he engaged as Lincoln's Midwest distributor and promoter. George Johnson established similar contacts in St. Louis (W. H. King), New Orleans (D. Ireland Thomas), Atlanta (Reuben Black), Philadelphia (Clarence Edward Wells), and New York (Romeo Dougherty). Under Johnson's management, Lincoln began a voluminous correspondence with Black newspapers, as well as white and African American distributors and exhibitors of Black-cast films across the country.[46]

George Johnson worked tirelessly to figure out how best to increase Lincoln's business. He developed detailed questionnaires for exhibitors in an attempt to learn the sizes of their venues, what kinds of films their clientele preferred, how and where they advertised, how many theaters they competed with, and how they wished to divide the box office take. Johnson's questionnaires also tried to ascertain whether Lincoln's star, Noble Johnson, was more attractive to Black audiences in Universal and Lubin films or in Lincoln productions.[47] George Johnson developed extensive advertising campaigns and consistently tried to solicit investors in the Lincoln company, particularly among Black audience members who had little to no investment experience. Always in need of capital, Johnson published letters and pamphlets such as "The Secret of Getting Rich!" and "Three Strong Reasons Why You Should Buy Lincoln Motion Picture Co. Shares," in which readers were encouraged to support a Black-owned venture while getting in on the ground floor of a booming new industry.[48]

The Lincoln officers had high hopes for their role in the race film business and imagined that they could take advantage of the numerous lucrative aspects of the moving picture industry. They aspired to produce "6 reels of Lincoln pictures weekly; one three reel drama; one two reel high class comedy and one reel Negro Pictorial News Features." After establishing a base with high-class drama, Lincoln looked to diversify, seeking

> to erect our own studio, printing establishment and laboratories, establish a Negro Movie Magazine and sell motion picture machines and accessories thru our Branch Offices. Producing 6 reels weekly for fifty two weeks for 250 Theatres at a conservative rental of $5 per reel means a yearly revenue of $390,000 from this source alone. Rebookings would double this estimate as practically every Theatre uses a Lincoln Photo-play two or three times.[49]

George P. Johnson even considered forging alliances with Lincoln's competitors, including the white-owned Ebony Film Corporation and the Reol Film Company, to secure a broader capital and audience base. This remarkable but unrealized vision of production and promotion (not to mention selling the means to exhibit films—projectors) seeks to replicate the tactics of the major studios in order to compete effectively with them.[50]

The Lincoln officers clearly understood that to compete with the mainstream film industry, as well as the growing number of race film companies springing up across the country, they would not only have to continue to produce quality films and broaden their distribution networks but also develop an audience base that was invested—emotionally and/or financially—in their enterprise. If Lincoln was to realize its ambitions, it would have to build stable, supportive relationships with distributors, exhibitors, critics, and patrons of race films from coast to coast. However, Lincoln's already difficult task of cultivating a thriving Black film culture was complicated by two events—the resignation of president and leading man, Noble Johnson, and the entrance of the United States into World War I.[51]

## Our Colored Fighters: Black Filmmaking and World War I

When the United States entered World War I on April 6, 1917, Lincoln, along with other race film companies, stepped up efforts to make and distribute films that would appeal to the patriotism of Black audiences. White and Black filmmakers had shot footage of Black soldiers in previous military action in Cuba and Mexico.[52] The Chicago-based Peter P. Jones Photoplay Company, founded by an African American photographer-turned-filmmaker, produced two such newsreels, *For the Honor of the 8th Illinois Regiment* (1914) and *Colored Soldiers Fighting in Mexico* (1916). Films about Black participation in World War I, however, enabled African American filmmakers to exploit to an even greater degree a topic that had unprecedented popularity among Black audiences. Exhibitors in Black communities recognized this and used references to the war in their advertising (see fig. 28). On screen, Black filmmakers featured positive representations of Black military service to counter racist images of Black men involved in war efforts that continued to appear in white-produced films, such as Griffith's *Birth of a Nation* and Ebony's comedy *Spying the Spy*. World War I–era documentaries are significant within the context of the burgeoning race film industry because they reflect many of the central issues that shaped the emerging Black film culture. These include questions about control over the production of Black images and the optimistic notion that the cinema—as both a representational medium and a public space—could potentially improve the social and political position of Black American citizens.

When the United States entered the war, pro-American feeling among African Americans ran high. Large numbers of Blacks flooded recruiting stations to volunteer their services, but most were turned away. However, after the passage of the Selective Service Act on May 18, which "provided for the enlistment of all able-bodied Americans between the ages of twenty-one and thirty-one," more than seven hundred thousand Blacks registered in the armed forces.[53]

Despite their enthusiasm, African American soldiers consistently faced various forms of extreme racial discrimination—from draft and registration to training to entering the war zone. After the Selective Service Act, draft boards, particularly those in the South, accepted a higher percentage of Black registrants than whites because they would not honor Black exemption requests. White officers routinely insulted and discriminated against their Black underlings. Black soldiers were not allowed to train as officers until they agitated for a separate training facility. White civilians barred Black soldiers stationed in their towns from restaurants, theaters, and other public places. White southerners objected vehemently to the training of Black soldiers from the North in their towns because of what they felt to be the "militant" disposition of northern Black servicemen. One result of such tensions was a race riot between white civilians and Black enlisted men of the Twenty-fourth Infantry in Houston in August 1917; another riot nearly erupted involving the Fifteenth New York Infantry stationed at Spartanburg, South Carolina. Once overseas, many Black troops were limited to work as stevedores and laborers, delivering supplies to the Allies. However, despite their general treatment as second-class soldiers, a number of Black combat troops did see action and distinguished themselves in battle. In the words of historian Herbert Aptheker, "The Blacks sent abroad fought so well that it proved embarrassing."[54] Four all-Black infantry regiments (the 369th, 370th, 371st, and 372nd) were awarded the Croix de Guerre, and the first American soldiers to be decorated by the French for bravery under fire were two Black privates.

Although there are numerous examples of African American bravery in battle—events that were celebrated by Blacks at home in the United States—some African Americans spoke out against Black involvement in an imperialist war effort.[55] The fundamental contradiction of disfranchised African Americans supporting a war for "democracy" fought in Europe was certainly recognized by many members of the Black community, even if race leaders (including such disparate figures as Emmett J. Scott, former secretary to Booker T. Washington, and W. E. B. Du Bois) advised that Afri-

can Americans "close ranks" with their white countrymen in order to secure victory.[56] German propagandists tried to point out American hypoc-
risy when they circulated a flyer asking Black soldiers:

> What is Democracy? . . . Do you enjoy the same rights as the white people
> do in America, the land of Freedom and Democracy, or are you rather not
> treated over there as second-class citizens? Can you go into a restaurant
> where white people dine? Can you get in the theater where white people sit?
> . . . Why, then, fight the Germans only for the benefit of the Wall Street rob-
> bers and to protect the millions they have loaned to the British, French, and
> Italians?[57]

Despite subversive messages like these, which pointed to the camouflaged
stakes and motives of World War I, publicly Black Americans showed
strong support for the war, purchasing millions of dollars of war bonds and
stamps and working at home and abroad to secure victory.[58]

The potential for exploiting war themes among Black audiences was
perhaps best recognized by George P. Johnson, booking manager of the
Lincoln Motion Picture Company. Johnson not only imagined that war
films could be used to entertain and motivate Black soldiers and civilians
but also saw the demand for war films as an opportunity to expand and
consolidate the race film industry, which at that time consisted of dozens
of companies competing for a limited, segregated Black market.

When Johnson learned that the federal government had appropriated a
large sum (he quotes $10 million) for the "production of propaganda
films," he devised a plan to request a population-based percentage of that
budget (10 to 12 percent) to make films "in behalf of the 12,000,000 colored
people who are true, loyal American citizens."[59] Johnson argued that the
War Service Advisory Board, which oversaw the film propaganda budget,
contained no Black members. Any films this board would authorize, Johnson asserted, would function "merely to enact some humiliating farce in
the way of a burlesque comedy staged by either white directors or inexpe-
rienced colored actors." Therefore, Johnson proposed a set of special offices
and advisory boards to allow Black filmmakers to participate in (if not take
complete control over) the production of war propaganda films for Black
audiences. These films would include documentaries illustrating "The Evolution of the Negro Recruit," "The Negro at Work" in factory and field, and
"The Negro as an Aid to the Administration."[60]

In his proposal, elaborated in a series of letters to government officials,
Johnson went so far as to suggest that the government provide this Black
production entity with "executive offices" in New York, Chicago, or Washington, and "that a studio be built in or near Los Angeles." Further, he rec-

ommended specific individuals for particular positions in this potential collaboration between the government and the race film industry. These included representatives from Lincoln, the New York–based Quality Amusement Company, and the Philadelphia-based Dunbar Amusement Company. In this way, "the Officers and Directors of the three largest and most successful firms of their kind catering to the colored citizens [Quality, Dunbar, and Lincoln] [should] be approached as to some form of consolidation or cooperation, not detrimental to the existence of their respective organizations, but of extreme value to the Government during the War period." Although Johnson was probably truly interested in using the cinema to serve neglected Black soldiers and audiences, he also took the occasion of the war to devise a way to cut down on competition among race film producers, encouraging them to join forces to draw Black audiences into theaters in larger numbers.

Johnson's tactics reflect what Leslie Midkiff DeBauche calls "practical patriotism," as employed by white wartime film producers and distributors like George Kleine and many others, who were both personally and professionally motivated to support the government's use of film in the war effort. Like Kleine, Johnson found it to be entirely "appropriate and reasonable to combine allegiance to country and to business."[61] His proposal might have created an unprecedented and successful network of race film concerns, ensuring more profits and increased longevity for the companies involved. Unfortunately, government officials turned him down flat, and no such alliance was built.

Despite securing meetings with Assistant Secretary of War Emmett J. Scott, in whom he hoped to find a Black ally, Johnson could not convince officials that his plan was viable or necessary. In a letter to Johnson, Frank R. Wilson, director of publicity for the Treasury Department, denies Johnson's charges of governmental discrimination against African Americans:

> To be perfectly frank with you I do not think that the charge you make to the effect that the various publicity departments of Federal organization invariably treat loyal colored American citizens in a humiliating way is correct.
>
> It may be that some of the motion pictures portray the colored Americans in a humorous way just as they do the Southern colonel, the Irish, the stupid Englishman with his monocle and cane, the dude, the Western cowboy, the New England prude and the bloated bond holder.[62]

Wilson's attempt to subsume Black comic stereotypes within the broad practice of "humorous" treatment of any number of white character types refuses to acknowledge the sensitivity of African American audiences re-

FIGURE 46. African American enlisted men in Alsace, France, during World War I. George P. Johnson Negro Film Collection, Department of Special Collections, University of California at Los Angeles.

garding Black media images, particularly in government-produced war-related discourse. Johnson's attempts to raise awareness about the particular issues of African American representation in propaganda films were trivialized and finally disregarded. His revolutionary idea of securing government support to finance the consolidation of a race film industry was summarily dismissed.

Still, through contacts he made during his letter-writing campaign to various government agencies, Johnson was able to secure documentary footage of Black troops in France from the French Pictorial Service (fig. 46). Showing it first in Chicago in September 1918, Lincoln distributed the one-reel film under the title *American Colored Troops at the Front*, circulating it to theaters, churches, colleges, and other Black institutions across the country.[63] Later, Johnson and cameraman Harry Gant shot documentary footage of the famous Tenth Cavalry (fictionalized in their *Trooper of Troop K*) at training camp in Fort Huachuca, Arizona, and circulated it under the title *A Day with the Tenth Cavalry*.[64] These were among the many nonfiction films about Black soldiers that circulated during and just after the war. In Chicago, William Foster planned to make a film recording the

FIGURE 47. Oscar Micheaux tied the promotion of his first film, *The Homesteader* (1919), to patriotic fervor and community pride by premiering it at the Eighth Regiment Armory in Chicago's Black Belt and featuring moving pictures of the victorious "Black Devils" back at home. Advertisement, *Chicago Defender*, 22 February 1919.

"glorious send-off" of the famous Eighth Regiment, and Oscar Micheaux may have shot footage of that regiment's triumphant return to the South Side, which was screened at its Armory (3533 S. Forest Avenue) in February 1919 along with the premiere of his first feature, *The Homesteader* (fig. 47).[65] Efforts like these occupy an important place in race film history because much of this footage was shot and produced by Black filmmakers, and it provided Black audiences with rare, "heroic" representations that deviated from the predominant mode of drama as the Black cinematic response to comic and "negative" portrayals.[66]

Films like *Our Colored Fighters* (1919) and *Our Colored Soldier Boys in Action Over There* (1921) also functioned to counteract negative perceptions whites held about Black loyalty and competence. When white film companies represented Black participation in war efforts, particularly in fiction films, they tended to render Black people in less than heroic terms. Griffith's treatment of Gus, the "renegade" Black soldier featured in *The Birth of a Nation* (1915), demonstrates the worst white fears about arming Blacks and allowing them to gain a sense of racial equality—that they will seek white women to consummate their newfound political power. On the opposite end of the spectrum is a figure like Sambo Sam from the Ebony comedy *Spying the Spy,* whose misguided efforts to capture German spies are rendered comic and absurd. Many Black distributors felt that if they could provide documentary proof of successful Black participation in the war effort, they could work toward dispelling false notions about Black people, particularly regarding their abilities and their patriotism.

The popularity and enthusiastic reception of World War I documentaries, as reported by the Black press, demonstrate that African Americans were greatly impressed by pictorials of Black soldiers in training and in action. Blacks turned out in huge numbers to see *From Harlem to the Rhine,* a five-reel War Department film that premiered at New York's Lafayette Theatre in May 1920. They cheered at the sight of celebrity Black servicemen like comedian Bert Williams and bandleader Jim Europe, and they applauded wildly when the "Hell Fighters" of the Fifteenth Regiment were shown in action on the firing line and making their historic victory march up Fifth Avenue and through Harlem.[67] During and after the war, Black filmmakers, distributors, and exhibitors tried to screen films that would enable Blacks to share pleasurable spectatorial experiences despite their routine marginalization by the government and the dominant film industry.

In a number of ways, World War I crystallized the paradoxical relations between Black American identity and the cinema. Films could address and inspire African American audiences across the country by documenting Black contributions to the war effort. However, the cinema and other social spaces would remain racially segregated during and after the war, and these films could not persuade white America (including government officials) to grant Blacks equal opportunities and full citizenship. In fact, interracial animosity increased during and after the war as whites tried to ensure that "there would be no wholesale distribution of the blessings of liberty."[68] The immediate postwar period saw a resurgence of the Ku Klux Klan and lynchings. Racial tensions mounted as Black soldiers did indeed return to the United States demanding their civil rights. These and other volatile elements in U.S. race relations exploded in bloody riots across the country during the Red Summer of 1919. The riots served as a most disturbing marker of the contradictory nature of the very notion of Black patriotism in a country that did not recognize Black humanity, let alone respect African Americans' rights or efforts on behalf of their country.

After the war, the Lincoln company produced three more films—a *Lincoln News Pictorial* (1919), featuring a variety of prominent Blacks, and two more melodramas set in the West, *A Man's Duty* (1919; fig. 48) and *By*

FIGURE 48. Advertisement for *A Man's Duty* (Lincoln Motion Picture Company, 1919) at Chicago's Blue Bird Theater. George P. Johnson Negro Film Collection, Department of Special Collections, University of California at Los Angeles.

*Right of Birth* (1920). Although the war did not enable Lincoln to substantially increase its operations or measurably impact the dominant film industry's treatment of African Americans (as subjects or producers), the company continued to refer to the war positively, as did most of the Black press. For example, an advertising campaign for *A Man's Duty* links the film (which does not seem to represent the war) with patriotic rhetoric like the following: "Attention Soldiers! You have done 'A Man's Duty' to your country and humanity. Do not fail to complete a soldier's duty by joining the American Legion. Your presence is requested at Headquarters."[69]

Despite its attempts to use the war (along with many other events and tactics) to build a stable, national Black audience, the Lincoln Motion Picture Company could not maintain the high costs and demanding labor of producing, advertising, and especially distributing Black-cast films; the company folded in 1923. In its wake, a number of Black film producers continued to seek ways to appeal to Black moviegoers' diverse tastes and physical circumstances, mostly by making dramatic films of African American life.[70] Among the most successful of the postwar Black filmmakers was Oscar Micheaux, whose early films responded in powerful ways to the key social, political, and representational issues facing the African American community, including the riots, the war, the migration, and *The Birth of a Nation*.

# CHAPTER SEVEN

# "We Were Never Immigrants"

## Oscar Micheaux and the Reconstruction of Black American Identity

George P. Johnson took credit for getting Oscar Micheaux started in the film production business. After reading Micheaux's third novel, *The Homesteader* (1917), Johnson approached Micheaux about the possibility of the Lincoln Motion Picture Company purchasing the film rights to his book. Correspondence ensued, and contracts were drawn up and ready to be signed when Micheaux demanded that the film be at least six reels in length and insisted on supervising the production himself. When Lincoln refused these terms, Micheaux produced the film on his own. He went on to make more than forty films between 1918 and 1948, becoming race film's most famous and prolific director.[1]

It is obvious why the Johnson brothers were attracted to *The Homesteader*. Like several Lincoln productions, Micheaux's novel is set in the wide-open spaces of the West, where a Black hero achieves personal and financial success that is prohibited in other sections of the country. Lincoln's and Micheaux's films demonstrate their shared conviction that the West was the ideal space for Negro self-improvement and self-definition. In this way, the West serves a mythic function for these Black filmmakers much as it does in white-produced western films (which enjoyed great popularity among African American audiences). Like Lincoln, Micheaux juxtaposed western spaces with those settings in the North, East, and South where the vast majority of African Americans lived. But even in his earliest work, Micheaux's narrative voice assumes a much more didactic tone than seems to have been the case in Lincoln films. As Pearl Bowser and Louise Spence have argued, Micheaux considered himself not so much a spokesman *of* African American viewpoints as "an instructive voice and an empowering interpreter of Black life *for* the community."[2]

Although Micheaux carries his moralizing literary voice into his film practice, his views about how African Americans should earn and enjoy their rights as full American citizens are presented in complex and often contradictory ways on screen. Micheaux's construction of setting, in particular, reflects the range of challenges facing diverse and migrating African American communities, as well as the multiple modes of Black representation that were available for representing and addressing those challenges. Micheaux's first four films—*The Homesteader* (1919), *Within Our Gates* (1920), *The Brute* (1920), and *The Symbol of the Unconquered* (1920)—sketch out Black life in the West, the urban North, and the South, as well as migrations between these spaces, illustrating how various geographically based "types" of Black characters function to help or hinder the projects of individual and race uplift.[3] Like the early race filmmakers discussed in the previous chapter, Micheaux presents migration and patriotism as vehicles for Black uplift; but his films also point to their limitations both as actual practices and as cinematic constructions. Micheaux's early melodramas leave open the contradictions of trying to uplift and entertain a national Black viewership by staging geographic conflicts and comparisons at the levels of content and style, as well as in the promotion of his films. Micheaux's aesthetic intentions can be difficult to determine given the incomplete, heavily censored, and inaccessible status of much of his work. Still, what survives of his films and records of their circulation, particularly in the case of *Within Our Gates*, indicates how his early efforts to represent Black American mobility and identity in cinematic terms not only respond to racism and race pride as expressed through mass culture but also raise questions about the reliability and efficacy of cinematic representation for Black subjects and viewers.

## West Is Best

Micheaux's first production, *The Homesteader*, released in Chicago in February 1919 (and shot, in part, at the Ebony studios in Chicago), was the first feature-length film produced by a Black-owned company. The eight-reel feature combined references to Micheaux's own early adult life in the West with an interracial love story. A young Black man, Jean Baptiste (Charles D. Lucas), moves from Chicago to South Dakota, where he becomes prosperous and falls in love with a woman, Agnes Stewart (Iris Hall), whom he believes is white. Thinking their love is doomed, Jean returns to Chicago, where he marries Orlean (Evelyn Preer), the daughter of

FIGURE 49. Jean Baptiste (Charles D. Lucas), the virile western frontiersman, with his soon-to-be-estranged wife, Orlean (Evelyn Preer). *The Homesteader* (dir. Oscar Micheaux, 1919). African Diaspora Images Collection.

a prominent Black minister (fig. 49). This marriage proves to be an un-happy one, and Jean returns to South Dakota, where he is reunited with Agnes upon discovering that she has Black heritage.[4]

*The Homesteader* seems to have been well received by urban audiences, despite its bias toward life in the West and against corrupt, hypocritical ministers who enjoyed positions of power in Black communities, not to mention the censorship his anticlerical themes elicited.[5] Micheaux staged an elaborate premiere, with live musical performances, at the Eighth Regiment Armory on Chicago's South Side as the all-Black unit made its triumphant return from Europe (see fig. 47). Micheaux's promotional materials cited O. C. Hammond, owner of Chicago's newly constructed Vendome Theater, remarking on the film's continued strong drawing power: "A line had formed at our box office and from 2pm to midnight 5700 paid admissions, at an advance price of 10c over our regular admission had been recorded."[6]

Micheaux solicited African American viewer interest by cultivating pride in his achievement as a Black artist and entrepreneur and by tying

*The Homesteader*'s release into Black patriotic feeling. But the film also drew audiences because it offered melodramatic juxtapositions of urban and western life that drew from both real life and cinematic fantasy. By the time *The Homesteader* was released, Micheaux was already well known to readers of the *Defender*, which published his letters advocating Black migration to the West and reported on his marital problems, which were related, in part, to the long distance between his wife's roots in Chicago and his homesteading enterprises in South Dakota.[7] Thus the film evoked comparisons between the city and the frontier that were familiar from Micheaux's biography (as rendered in the Black press) and from other Western films.

Although censor boards raised objections to *The Homesteader*, Micheaux's combination of appeals to race pride and popular western themes seems to have fostered Black support of the film across regional lines. A gushing review in the October 1919 issue of *Master Musician* magazine indicates that *The Homesteader* was a huge hit with Black Philadelphia audiences, who had begun to recognize that "[they] can be entertained to the fullest extent by [their] own movie actors and actresses."[8] As might be expected, *The Homesteader* was quite popular among Black audiences in the West. An advertisement in the July 29, 1920, issue of the *Monitor*, an Omaha weekly, announces that *The Homesteader* is returning for a repeat engagement at the Loyal Theater. As in the *Master Musician* review, the experience of patronizing Micheaux's film is described in terms of expressing a race pride that benefits other Blacks associated with the industry, this time including theater owners: "The management of the Loyal Theater is sparing neither expense nor trouble in their efforts to colored and white movie 'fans' who appreciate first class photoplays, courteous treatment and good order. If you appreciate our effort, come out and see a Negro Photo-play, written and produced by Negroes, acted by Negroes, owned by Negroes and shown in a Negro theater catering to Negro patronage."[9] Thus it would seem that Micheaux's treatment of westward migration in *The Homesteader* struck a chord with audiences in different parts of the country and provided an occasion for mustering up broad support for Blacks who worked in all areas of the race film industry (including theater owners who would welcome white viewers).

Micheaux would again take up the story of western migration in his fourth feature, *The Symbol of the Unconquered*. Released in November 1920 in Detroit, this eight-reel drama told the story of Evon (Eve) Mason (Iris Hall), a "quadroon" from Selma, Alabama, who moves to the Northwest to claim a mine that was willed to her by her grandfather. In the West she meets Black homesteader Hugh Van Allen (Walker Thompson), who is afraid to confess his love for Evon because he believes that she is white. When Hugh discovers oil on his property, he is harassed by a white swindler, August Barr (Louis Déan), and his cohort, Jefferson Driscoll (Lawrence Chenault), a Black man passing for white who hates his own race. Barr and Driscoll arrange for the Ku Klux Klan to attack Hugh and drive him off of his valuable land.[10] With Eve's assistance, however, Hugh effectively protects his property. Eventually Hugh and Eve can acknowledge their mutual attraction after her true racial identity is revealed.

The surviving, incomplete print of *The Symbol of the Unconquered* indicates that Micheaux has made some significant changes to his representation of westward migration, perhaps to expand its particular appeals to different segments of his audience—women and southerners. *Symbol* represents the movement of a woman to the Northwest. Eve's determination to travel alone to distant country makes her a uniquely strong and independent female character, and her bravery during the Klan attacks further distinguishes her from weaker, more dependent heroines found in other race films, and potentially more exciting to female viewers. All decked out in a buckskin cowgirl outfit, Eve jumps onto her rearing horse, determined to help Hugh fend off the Klan (fig. 50). Another important variation in this tale is that Eve migrates west from Selma, a southern city. For Micheaux, then, neither the North nor the South provided adequate opportunities for the Race's most enterprising young adults. As Bowser and Spence have noted, for Micheaux the western frontier is "the mythic space of moral drama and the site of opportunities seemingly free of the restrictive and discriminatory laws and social arrangements of the rural South and the urban metropolis."[11] Thus, whereas Micheaux shares Booker T. Washington's skepticism about Black urban migration, he revises Washington's program by advocating that Blacks plant themselves in western, rather than southern, soil. And while many southern Blacks were considering the appeals made by northern Black media, like the *Chicago Defender*, to migrate to industrial centers, Micheaux seems to advocate bypassing the city altogether.

The western frontier of *The Symbol of the Unconquered* also provides Micheaux with a novel setting from which to counter the heroic treatment of the Klan in *The Birth of a Nation*. *Symbol* exposes the fact that night riding is not limited to the seemingly more repressive southern districts. Micheaux's dramatic scenes of Klan violence directly addressed the sharp rise of Klan activity in many parts of the country, including New England and the Midwest as well as the South, after World War I.[12] *The Symbol of*

FIGURE 50. Eve Mason (Iris Hall) rides to warn Black frontiersman Hugh Van Allen of an impending Ku Klux Klan attack on his property. *The Symbol of the Unconquered* (dir. Oscar Micheaux, 1920). Frame enlargement by Charles Musser.

*the Unconquered* attempted to capture and capitalize on the sensational, real-life topic of Klan violence, which enhanced the film's popularity well after its initial release. A front-page story in the October 1, 1921, issue of the *Chicago Star* featured an interview with Swan Micheaux, Oscar's brother and business manager, who obliquely suggests that *Symbol*'s second run could prove to be more successful than the first: "Just what the harvest will be from the new demand for the 'Symbol of the Unconquered' bookings in America since the resurrection of the Ku Klux Klan can not yet be estimated. . . . [Swan Micheaux] stated that he cannot determine on the receipts abroad as to how the people in France and England will be attracted by their great Ku Klux Klan scene in all its haggard splendor."[13] Micheaux's threat to expose America's rampant, violent racism to a European audience, like his frequent use of interracial romance, was calculated to generate publicity. By broadening the scope of the setting in which Klan activity is represented—both within the film and in its potential viewership—Micheaux seeks to increase political awareness and his box office receipts.

In addition to films representing westward migration, Micheaux did produce a number of films set in northern cities such as Chicago and New York, where significant portions of his audience and his publicity were centered. Although most of his "city" films date from the sound era (presenting song and dance numbers associated with urban cabaret and nightlife), Micheaux's third feature, *The Brute* (released in August 1920 at Hammond's Vendome Theater in Chicago), is set entirely in the city. Shot in Chicago, *The Brute* depicts a young Black woman, Mildred Carrison (Evelyn Preer), who is forced to marry "Bull" Magee (A. B. Comanthiere), a brutal underworld gambling kingpin. *The Brute* depicts domestic violence as being directly linked to a depraved urban environment in which alcohol, gambling, and physical violence are the norm.[14] Micheaux drew fire from Black critics for his representation of the unseemly side of Black urban life (as he would throughout his career). *New York Age* critic Lester A. Walton complained, "As I looked at the picture I was reminded of the attitude of the daily press, which magnifies our vices and minimizes our virtues."[15] Micheaux's use of sensational topics, as discussed in chapter 5, reflected both "yellow journalism" trends in urban newspapers and topics covered in white-produced "pink slip" films. Though no print of *The Brute* is extant, descriptions and stills suggest that while the film criticizes violence against women, Micheaux's commentary on the cultural life African Americans were developing in urban centers also glamorizes many less "uplifting" aspects of fast city living, such as drinking, boxing, craps shooting, and the wealth one can accumulate, particularly by illegal means (fig. 51).[16] One can imagine that Micheaux's representations of urban life in *The Brute* and later films might accommodate a range of interpretations by his diverse audiences—as welcome reflections of urban (underworld) realities, as instructive preachments against greed and violence, and as warnings against city life altogether.

Although Micheaux frequently argued that the western frontier, not the city, was the ideal space where African Americans could succeed morally, financially, and socially and stake their most convincing claim to American citizenship, his filmmaking relied heavily on Black urban themes, audiences, and presses. Micheaux constructed dangerous but exciting urban landscapes in which young Black women are threatened by unscrupulous men and where promising Black men risk losing their integrity. In doing so, his films not only reflected many of the social and moral dilemmas Black urban audiences faced in their daily lives but also provided

FIGURE 51. In *The Brute* (1920), Oscar Micheaux depicts city life as materially opulent but morally impoverished. African Diaspora Images Collection.

Black newspapers with the contradictory material on which they thrived—opportunities to celebrate his artistic and entrepreneurial achievements and to attack his often scandalous and unflattering representational choices.[17] Micheaux's films may not have advocated Black migration to the urban North, but in many ways they depended on the markets, cultural practices, and debates that had been produced by the Great Migration.

## A Circuitous Journey to Citizenship: *Within Our Gates*

Micheaux may have privileged western spaces over both northern and southern ones for Black moral and material progress, but he always acknowledged the fact that most African Americans lived in the South or had migrated to urban industrial centers. Micheaux's second feature, *Within Our Gates* (released in January 1920 at Hammond's Vendome Theater in Chicago), concerns itself with the movement of its African American heroine between the South and the urban North. In *Within Our Gates,*

Micheaux stays within the dominant pattern of the Great Migration in order to address issues of racism, intraracial conflict, gender politics, and patriotism as experienced and recognized by the majority of his audience. *Within Our Gates* dramatically illustrates the significance of migration and patriotism not just as themes but also as key formal influences in Black filmmaking practices as they developed in relation to Black efforts to construct modern African American identities. In light of such recent events as the 1919 riots, the failure of World War I to bring about racial "democracy" at home, and the extraordinary popularity of Griffith's racist version of American history in *The Birth of a Nation*, Micheaux presents a picture of the country as deeply fragmented—regionally and racially—beyond complete political or aesthetic repair.

*Within Our Gates* represents Micheaux's most ambitious attempt to fashion a discourse on the meaning of Black American identity. The film features a large cast of Black character types, demonstrating that the Black population is made up of individuals from a wide variety of backgrounds and with very different goals and lifestyles. The film's heroine, Sylvia Landry (Evelyn Preer), is an educated southern belle who believes in doing what she can to uplift the less fortunate members of her race; Sylvia's cousin, Alma Pritchard (Flo Clements), and Alma's stepbrother, Larry (Jack Chenault), are dishonest city dwellers who misrepresent Sylvia's past in order to manipulate her; Conrad, Sylvia's fiancé (James D. Ruffin), is an educated man who holds a prestigious position that sends him to remote regions of Canada and Brazil; the Reverend Wilson Jacobs (Sam T. Jacks) and his sister, Constance (Jimmie Cook), are honorable Black southern teachers who run the impoverished Piney Woods School; Dr. V. Vivian (Charles D. Lucas) is a Boston physician-intellectual who intently studies race questions; Ned is a sellout southern Black preacher; Sylvia's adoptive parents, Mr. and Mrs. Jasper Landry (William Starks, Mattie Edwards), are struggling but upstanding southern sharecroppers; Efrem (E. G. Tatum) is an ignorant, gossiping southern servant who turns against members of his own race. Micheaux makes it clear that the environments from which these characters hail, and to which they migrate, say a great deal about what kinds of people they are and what impact their type will have on the progress (or failure) of the Race as a whole. But Micheaux presents no simple northern/southern, positive/negative, or New Negro/Old Negro dichotomies. Instead, by structuring *Within Our Gates* along a complex topography of narrative and character relations, Micheaux creates a film that mirrors the diverse but interconnected experiences of his African American characters and audiences.[18]

The meandering, melodramatic plot of *Within Our Gates* details the experiences of southerner Sylvia Landry as she moves between the North and the rural South in an attempt to figure out her rightful place in (Black) American society. The film opens in a northern city where Sylvia is visiting with her cousin Alma. After being spurned by her fiancé, Conrad, Sylvia returns to the South in response to a call for teachers at the Piney Woods School. Upon learning that Wilson and Constance Jacobs need $5,000 to keep the school running, Sylvia goes back up North, to Boston, to try to raise funds from the city's wealthy people. While in Boston, Sylvia meets Dr. Vivian, a "race man" with whom she grows quite close. One day Sylvia is accidentally hit by a car while saving a child's life. As luck would have it, the car belongs to a wealthy white woman, Mrs. Elena Warwick, who after much thought decides to donate not $5,000 but $50,000 to Piney Woods. Sylvia returns South with the funds but is forced to run away when Larry Pritchard, the criminal stepbrother of her cousin Alma, threatens to disclose unflattering information about Sylvia if she does not consent to a sexual relationship with him. Meanwhile, Dr. Vivian searches for Sylvia in the North, where he meets up with Alma. Alma recounts to Dr. Vivian the story of Sylvia's past, which, presumably, helps to explain why she has not committed to Dr. Vivian or any man since breaking up with Conrad.

Sylvia's painful southern story involves the false accusation of her adoptive father, Jasper Landry, of the murder of a tyrannical white landowner, Philip Gridlestone. The Landrys hide in the woods while a white lynch mob assembles to find them and exact revenge. As Sylvia's parents are captured, hung, and burned, Philip Gridlestone's brother, Armand (Grant Gorman), corners Sylvia in an empty house and tries to rape her. At the last minute, Armand stops his attack when he discovers a birthmark on Sylvia's breast, which indicates to him that she is his daughter, the product of his sexual relations with a Black woman.

Micheaux's revelation of Sylvia's interracial parentage helps to explain why she is repeatedly subjected to social, psychological, and moral dangers that prevent her from maintaining a stable family, home, and identity. This characterization of Sylvia draws on the long tradition of "tragic mulattoes" in Black cultural production, as well as the tradition of the African American migration narrative, with themes of exile, alienation, and reinvention.[19] In many ways, *Within Our Gates* resembles three roughly contemporary Black novels that combine mulatto and migration themes. Sylvia's multiple journeys north and south echo the movements of the title character of Frances Ellen Watkins Harper's *Iola LeRoy, or Shadows Uplifted* (1892), the protagonist of James Weldon Johnson's *The Autobiography of an Ex-Coloured Man* (1912), and Helga Crane in Nella Larsen's *Quicksand* (1928).[20] These characters similarly struggle with their interracial heritage, moving from place to place as they try to fit into different kinds of communities. The experiences of these characters serve as limit cases for the political and psychological status of the Race as a whole. Sylvia, Iola, the Ex-Colored Man, and Helga share a sense of estrangement in the urban North, as well as a complex relationship with the South as both "home" and the site of Black victimization and demoralization.[21]

Micheaux clearly marks the South as the source of far-reaching white racism and Black American trauma, which continue to have profound effects on Blacks despite their efforts to move forward with their lives via education and migration. In the restored Library of Congress print of *Within Our Gates*, it seems that Micheaux deliberately withholds pertinent information about Sylvia's southern experiences until the very end; the lengthy flashback does not occur until fifty-three minutes into the sixty-five-minute film. If this print reflects Micheaux's intended structure, he conspicuously extends the viewer's curiosity about the background and "true" character of his seemingly ideal Black heroine as they were shaped in the South. Indeed, when Larry warns Sylvia that he will tell her friends at the Piney Woods School "just what sort of person you are," it is not yet clear to the viewer what he means. Larry's threat seems to resonate with a brief scene very early in the film in which Sylvia's cousin, Alma, leads her fiancé, Conrad, to a room in which Sylvia is engaged in an emotional meeting with a white man whom we later learn is her father, Armand Gridlestone. At this early point in the film, we, like the enraged Conrad, are led to believe that Sylvia is having an affair with this unidentified white man. Micheaux does not explain Sylvia's relationship with him until the "rape" scene at the film's climax, and he never completely explains the circumstances of Sylvia's interaction with Armand Gridlestone in the North.[22] The "sort of person" Sylvia is, as represented in the main body of the film (an honorable woman dedicated to racial uplift), takes on different meanings when understood in the context of the flashback to her past, in which she is orphaned, rendered homeless, sexually attacked, and revealed to be biracial. She is the product, and victim, of illicit interracial relations, a southern legacy she can never escape. Placed at the end of the film, Micheaux's representation of southern life—characterized by sharecropping (which was an attempt to preserve the social and economic hierarchies of slavery), lynching, and the rape of Black women by white men—demonstrates that these are powerful and constant undercurrents of "modern" Black life, making it difficult for many

Blacks (including educated, upstanding migrants) to feel "at home" anywhere in the United States.

The flashback to Sylvia's southern past contains many of Micheaux's most scathing criticisms of American racism, particularly as it had been practiced and rationalized (or ignored) in a spate of romantic antebellum-themed films of the 1910s, culminating with *The Birth of a Nation*. For instance, several scholars have pointed out that the "rape" scene involving Sylvia and Armand Gridlestone is staged as a direct response to the "rape" scene involving Gus and Little Sister in *Birth*. As Toni Cade Bambara observes, Micheaux sought to "set the record straight on who rapes who."[23] Black men were regularly accused of raping white women in order to justify their lynching, when, in fact, white men routinely raped Black women as a form of social and political terrorism as African Americans expressed political and economic self-determination.

Certainly, Micheaux's film has broader aims and significance beyond its function as a critique of or corrective to *Birth*. Among its interventions, *Within Our Gates* provides an African American perspective on Black migration and citizenship that challenges southern white warnings and northern white paranoia about the transformation of the "race problem" from a regional to a national concern. Micheaux's film addresses both the kind of southern anti-Reconstruction sentiment represented by Thomas Dixon's novel *The Clansman* and the national appeal of Griffith's cinematic adaptation, which combined antebellum nostalgia with innovative visual and narrative styles. "Answering" *Birth* is not Micheaux's sole objective, but the film does mobilize Black American cosmopolitanism and patriotism to refute the racist discourses (and the powerful stylistic means of conveying them) that Griffith's landmark film represents.

Take, for instance, the way Micheaux constructs the coupling of Sylvia and Dr. Vivian as a union of South and North, a marriage that echoes and challenges the white Cameron/Stoneman union at the close of *Birth*. Sylvia has a number of suitors representing various Black male types as they perform in particular geographic contexts. Larry is obviously not the right mate for Sylvia because he is manipulative and dishonest. Whether he is running crooked poker games in the North or selling costume jewelry to Black laborers in the South, Larry exploits members of the Race, and he is therefore killed off. Conrad is not a viable husband for Sylvia because his job keeps him outside of the United States. If Sylvia were to live with Conrad in Canada or Brazil, she would not be in a position to claim her American birthright and work toward race equality at home. Finally, Reverend Jacobs, the principal of Piney Woods School, is eliminated from competition because, it seems, he is from the South. Although Jacobs is an intelligent man with honorable intentions, Micheaux chooses not to match southern Sylvia with a southern husband. She brings northern white capital down to Piney Woods (much like Booker T. Washington's method of financing his Tuskegee Institute), and that seems to fulfill her obligation to Reverend Jacobs.

The winner of Sylvia's hand is Dr. V. Vivian, the Boston physician who is never shown examining patients but is instead seen examining race issues in various highbrow publications. From his first appearance, when he recovers Sylvia's stolen purse from a thief, Dr. Vivian is revealed to be a rare, respectable Black urban man.[24] Micheaux deliberately chooses to match Sylvia and Dr. Vivian because they represent the educated elite of the Black South and North coming together to study and work for uplift. Perhaps one of the reasons Rev. Jacobs cannot become Sylvia's husband is that his southern, religious upbringing and his social position as a race educator would not allow him to fully and/or publicly accept her relationship with her white father/near-rapist. Though Sylvia's bespectacled fiancé, Conrad, has an adventurous professional life that might suggest his progressive New Negro status, we witness his violent reaction to finding her in "compromising" proximity to a white man—after seeing Sylvia with Armand Gridlestone, Conrad chokes her and throws her to the floor. Dr. Vivian, on the other hand, is represented as a sensitive, sophisticated, modern race man who can understand the contradictions of Sylvia's position. When he learns the whole truth about Sylvia, he is more convinced than ever that he wants to spend his life with her.

In light of Micheaux's attention to questions of racial uplift, community building, and Black American citizenship, his representation of Sylvia's impending marriage gestures both forward and backward in its political and stylistic construction. Like Griffith, Micheaux attempts to link traditional values and discursive modes with modern social and aesthetic possibilities. J. Ronald Green has argued that Micheaux's formulation of the Black "bourgeois marriage icon" in *Within Our Gates* rejects Griffith's conservative politics of white heterosexual coupling, in which marriage was "a reaffirmation of classical liberalism (the [male] individual as free agent) and of patriarchy" based upon "an old vision of racial purity and white supremacism."[25] But although Micheaux's representation of the uplift marriage may seem more "progressive," community-minded, feminist, and inclusive than Griffith's ideal couples, in many ways it is also decidedly more traditional (and optimistic) than representations of heterosexual coupling for "mulatto" characters in contemporaneous African American literature. Unlike the Ex-Colored Man, who opts to pass for white and marries a white woman, Sylvia's marriage confirms her proud Black identity. And unlike Helga Crane, who marries a southern Black preacher, Sylvia will not perish in the traditional, oppressive confines of wife and mother. Micheaux's treatment of Sylvia does not demonstrate the kind of modernist skepticism Johnson and Larsen exhibit regarding the impossible position of biracial characters in a racially polarized society. Instead, Micheaux reaches back to the melodramatic conventions of the sentimental uplift novel, like Harper's *Iola LeRoy*. The pairing of Sylvia and Dr. Vivian as a "race couple" is strikingly similar to Harper's pairing of Iola and physician-intellectual Dr. Latimer. Hazel Carby has argued that Harper presents Iola's marriage as an egalitarian one, "based on a mutual sharing of intellectual interests and a commitment to the 'folk' and the 'race.'"[26] Micheaux suggests that with the race man Dr. Vivian by her side, Sylvia finally will be able to settle down in one location and proceed to fulfill her role as a member of the African American educated elite.

Micheaux combines sentimental and modernist approaches in his attempt to redeem the mulatto figure as she or he had been slandered in white supremacist discourse (e.g., Dixon, Griffith). Since, as Michele Wallace reminds us, the mulatto figure's "real-life counterpart had, after all, played a central and pivotal role in Reconstruction politics," this figure was used by Black and white artists to reflect upon the troubling implications of interracial intimacy and biracial identity in both the southern past and the modern present/future.[27] Micheaux works to redeem Sylvia the mulatta not only by presenting her as the kind of educated and uplift-minded heroine who seems to step out of the pages of nineteenth-century Black fiction but also by fragmenting the film's narration in ways that attempt to convey the complex social, psychological, and political dimensions of Sylvia's mixed-race background. He presents Sylvia's marriage as precipitated by a jarring and lengthy temporal discontinuity—the southern flashback. Green argues that Micheaux's view of marriage, unlike Griffith's "old vision of racial purity and white supremacism," affirms "the social self," "mutuality," and women's rights to "free agency" and "racial hybridity and equality."[28] These oppositions are clearly staged in the southern flashback at the story level. But at the plot level, Micheaux takes advantage of some of the innovative cinematic narrative techniques Griffith develops in *Birth*.

For example, Griffith expands previous uses of parallel editing from showing two actions occurring at one time to, in the infamous "rape" sequence, combining three actions—Little Sister running, Gus the Black brute in hot pursuit, and her brother, the "Little Colonel," following them

FIGURE 52. Alma (Flo Clements) tells Dr. Vivian (Charles D. Lucas) the story of Sylvia's southern past. *Within Our Gates* (dir. Oscar Micheaux, 1920). Library of Congress, Motion Picture, Broadcasting and Recorded Sound Division.

both. Here, as in some of his previous work at Biograph (e.g., *The Girls and Daddy,* 1909), the rescue is delayed to suspenseful effect by keeping the white male rescuer at bay with a relay of cuts between him, the black aggressor, and the white female victims. In *Within Our Gates,* Micheaux not only intercuts the lynching and burning of the Landrys with the rape of Sylvia but also interpolates the framing narrative voice of Alma to draw out, in Griffithian style, Sylvia's ordeal. The "rape" of Sylvia is repeatedly "interrupted" (to use Gaines's term) by shots of the lynch mob's bonfire and, at the climax of the sequence, by a shot of Alma telling the story to Dr. Vivian (fig. 52) and a corresponding title card explaining that Sylvia is Armand's daughter. Micheaux's use of a third term here—a voice from the North/present—to rescue and redeem the mulatta victim suggests how his stylistic response to Griffith is not predicated on Griffith's aesthetic as simply an "old vision." Instead, Micheaux counters white supremacist accounts of Black character and race relations by acknowledging and adapting some of the narrative techniques from Griffith-dominant cinema.

Micheaux combines his interventions in dominant narrative film style with themes circulating in contemporary African American discourse. By joining the Black South and the Black North in matrimony, he produces an alternative narrative on national identity and belonging that resonates with Black patriotic expression. The white northern and southern characters who couple in *Birth* do so in defeat of African Americans who lust after power (and white women), thereby restoring white supremacy. The only Black characters in Griffith's epic who might be eligible for a second-class American citizenship are the loyal and submissive Black servants (or "faithful souls"). Micheaux, however, ends *Within Our Gates* with a speech delivered by Dr. Vivian asserting that African Americans have more than paid their dues and, as an entire race, are entitled to their rights as American citizens. Dr. Vivian offers as evidence a number of specific instances of Black military service, including battles in Cuba and Mexico and campaigns in France during World War I.[29] "Be proud of our country, Sylvia," Dr. Vivian exhorts, as he explains why African Americans should take their rightful place in American society.

Dr. Vivian's closing speech is notable for the ways it attempts to paper over deep cracks in the logic of Black patriotic rhetoric. At one point, he tells Sylvia, "We were never immigrants," thereby distinguishing African Americans from European immigrants who are more recent arrivals to the United States, and who presumably have less of a claim to American identity. At the same time, though, Dr. Vivian (as Micheaux's mouthpiece) seems to gloss over the contradictions of being a proud Black American in light of the radically different circumstances that brought Blacks to the United States—the slave trade. Bowser and Spence argue persuasively that while such expressions of Black patriotism may seem shortsighted from our current historical vantage point, at the time they played a major role in countering the erasure of Blackness from dominant commercial media. By expressing their patriotism, African Americans were "declaring their own identity" and thereby "writing their world into existence."[30] The conclusion of *Within Our Gates*, as with many of the patriotic films produced and circulated by African Americans during this period, strategically does not take up the obvious contradictions (or commonalities) raised by comparing Black and European immigrant claims to American identity.

Instead, Dr. Vivian's speech seeks to designate a form of patriotic expression that is viable for Black women—he delivers it at the end of the film as he asks for Sylvia's hand in marriage (fig. 53). Sitting by her side in a drawing room, Vivian acknowledges the difficulties Sylvia must face when trying to take pride in her American nationality given her experi-

FIGURE 53. Dr. Vivian makes a passionate patriotic proposal to the skeptical
Sylvia Landry (Evelyn Preer). *Within Our Gates* (dir. Oscar Micheaux, 1920).
Library of Congress, Motion Picture, Broadcasting and Recorded Sound Division.

ences with racial violence: "You . . . have been thinking deeply about this, I
know—but unfortunately your thoughts have been warped." Still, he concludes his proposal with: "In spite of your misfortunes, you will always be
a patriot—and a tender wife. I love you!" This dual proposal—asking
Sylvia to become a wife and patriot in the same breath—seems like an
awkward, hurried attempt to achieve narrative closure, heterosexual
union, and interracial harmony, all at once. But, more significantly, it attempts to create a positive, race-serving function for Sylvia at the precari-
ous intersection of her racial and gender identities to counteract the history of rape and terrorism she has experienced and that she represents. If
Micheaux can make a case for Sylvia to embrace her American identity,
then by extension any African American (regardless of gender, location,
family history, experience with racism) can make the same claim. To paraphrase Anna Julia Cooper, Micheaux is suggesting that only when and
where Sylvia Landry can enter the American citizenry, then and there the
whole Race enters with her.[31]

Dr. Vivian's speech suggests that Sylvia, like African Americans in general, honorably earned her patriotism through violence and victimization.

Jane Gaines argues that the film's culminating expression of "optimistic nationalism" depends on the representation, in the southern flashback, of "racial injustice as relegated to the past, not conceivable in the present of the film's contemporary story."[32] I would argue, however, that the revelation of Sylvia's family history late in the film actually emphasizes the grip that the southern past continues to have on its migrants, influencing their beliefs and actions as they attempt to shape themselves into New Negroes. Released not long after the bloody riots of 1919, *Within Our Gates* tries to demonstrate that African Americans will not endanger the security of the nation, despite (and possibly because of) all the pain and suffering they have individually and collectively experienced in their pursuit of U.S. citizenship. Their status as former slaves and their legacy of oppression trump claims to Americanism any white ethnic immigrant might make. And as a biracial woman, Sylvia has experienced, and represents, the most abject forms of racial discrimination, positioning her for the most sublime expression of American identity.

Perhaps Micheaux includes Vivian's patriotic speech, in part, to dampen the inflammatory potential of the lynching scenes presented earlier in the film. Indeed, *Within Our Gates* incited much controversy and was challenged (and cut) by numerous local censor boards that were concerned that its depictions of lynching and interracial rape might reanimate the racial antagonisms displayed during the 1919 riots.[33] But when Micheaux uses patriotism to try to rebury the traumas unearthed in the southern flashback, suggesting that Blacks can and should be well-behaved patriotic citizens, his rhetoric is hardly convincing. Sylvia's pained expression during Vivian's speech heightens the incongruity of this moment; her experiences in the North and South do not bear out the false promise of full American citizenship for Black people.

## Seeing and Believing

The unsatisfactory ending of *Within Our Gates* actually functions to emphasize what I would argue is the film's most compelling stylistic quality—its repeated demonstration that competing discourses about African Americans (as individuals and as a group) render Black representations, including Micheaux's, extremely inconsistent and unreliable. Although the film presents a thoroughly didactic message against white racism and in favor of African American uplift and equality, it also displays numerous ambiguities and misrepresentations, thereby calling modes of rendering Blackness, including cinematic realism, into question.

Some of the stylistic qualities I have in mind may not be intentional on Micheaux's part; we cannot know for sure how closely the print currently available for analysis reflects versions of the film that were shown at the time of its original screenings. This is always an issue with Micheaux's work because his films were so routinely censored and reorganized. Micheaux regularly made cuts, restored scenes, and changed the order of sequences, making it difficult to know what version(s) audiences saw when they were first shown. *Within Our Gates* was heavily censored, and newspaper accounts of screenings during the film's initial exhibitions suggest significant variations from what we see in the print currently in circulation. For example, Bowser and Spence cite a letter to Micheaux from George P. Johnson that describes a lynching occurring in the film's second reel, leading them to question the intended placement of the southern scenes.[34] In addition, the intertitles included in the surviving print are reconstructions—the print was located in an archive in Spain, and its Spanish intertitles had to be translated back into English by researchers who relied heavily on Micheaux's novels to make sense of narrative and character details. What is more, the current print is full of text. The intertitles include character and plot description, dialogue, letters, and print media stories. We must wonder if Micheaux intended to require so much reading (given the illiteracy rate among his primary audience), or if perhaps more explanatory titles were added in Spain for a European audience unfamiliar with many of Micheaux's culturally specific details. Gaines, Bowser, and Spence discuss one of the most glaring problems presented by the translated text—Sylvia is described in the Spanish titles as the product of a "legitimate" marriage between Armand Gridlestone and a Black woman, but evidence from viewers and advertisements (including references to "concubinage" not evident in the available print) suggests that she is the product, as well as the victim, of forced sexual relations.[35] With these inconsistencies in mind, I would argue that the footage we have displays major tensions regarding the reliability of Black media representation, in both textual and visual terms. By challenging the idea that one can believe what one sees, particularly with regard to Black character and actions, Micheaux's film points to the limitations of the very medium he is using, despite claims he (and other filmmakers) might make that cinema represents a powerful modern means of truth telling and intelligibility.

*Within Our Gates* contains various suspicious and contradictory elements at textual and visual levels. Corey Creekmur has pointed out that Micheaux, drawing from the writings of Charles Chesnutt, fills *Within Our Gates* with "white lies"—that is, white versions of events and perspectives on African Americans that deliberately misrepresent the "truth."[36] In a couple of instances, Micheaux demonstrates how such "white lies," told to maintain Black subjugation, circulate in print. Just after a scene in which we see Dr. Vivian reading an article about a prominent reverend seeking federal funding for Negro schools, Micheaux cuts to the prejudiced white southerner, Geraldine Stratton, reading a racist newspaper's account of the Negro's inherent ignorance and unfitness for the vote. Later in the film we see the restless southern white mob surround Efrem (the gossipy servant to Philip Gridlestone), with the intention of lynching him simply because he is the nearest Black victim. But later, when the town newspaper reports Efrem's death, it describes his murder as "an accidental death at unknown hands." While both scenes illustrate the powerful and historical role that white print media have played in sustaining racist policies and violence, the second is notable because the newspaper account clearly contradicts the visual representation of Eph's death dramatized earlier in the narrative. In fact, *Within Our Gates* features numerous moments in which the image presented on screen is later contradicted or is entirely misleading in its own right, providing a false picture of particular characters or events.

Creekmur describes Micheaux's repetition of events as representing the discursive demands of a segregated society, which "reinforced the regular construction of alternative *public narratives,* demanding at least two versions of every story" (emphasis in original).[37] What is particularly striking in *Within Our Gates* is the way in which Micheaux structures the relationships between how truth and lies are told (verbally or visually) and where they are staged and/or narrated (in the North or in the South). Sylvia's backstory, in particular, contains and is associated with various moments of misrepresentation and misrecognition. I have already indicated how the story of Sylvia's southern past, constructed through flashback, creates some extremely confusing moments in the film, such as her initially unexplained relationship with Armand Gridlestone. The confusion about what really happened in Sylvia's past, and how much of the truth various characters think they know, makes Sylvia's story (even if not intended as a last-minute flashback) a compelling statement about the unreliability of cinematic representation of Blackness in general, particularly how the South (its history and its contemporary representatives) obscures the picturing of Black truths.

For example, a striking instance of misrepresentation occurs when Sylvia's adoptive father, Jasper Landry, is accused of murder. The Landrys are lynched because the servant Efrem mistakenly accuses Jasper Landry of shooting white landowner Philip Gridlestone. The first time the murder is shown, it is represented from an omniscient narrative perspective that shows what really happened inside and outside of Gridlestone's office: a disgruntled white farmer shoots Gridlestone from a window; Gridlestone picks up his own gun to attempt to defend himself; Landry takes the gun out of the dead Gridlestone's hand. When the murder is actually committed, Efrem's head is turned away from his peeping vantage point, and when he turns his gaze back into the room, he sees only Landry holding a smoking gun. Landry then flees the scene in fear (fig. 54). Therefore, when Efrem recounts the murder to the white townsfolk, his version is based on circumstantial evidence. It is Efrem's account of Gridlestone's murder that is printed in the town newspaper. Micheaux graphically illustrates the power and pervasiveness of Black misrepresentation not only by conveying the false version of the murder in intertitles depicting the town's newspaper text but also by intercutting this text with a visual restaging of the murder. In this white reconstruction (informed by Black Efrem's false evidence), we see a drunken Landry pull the trigger (fig. 55). In this instance, as well as in the fleeting image of Sylvia with Armand Gridlestone, the film presents visual "evidence" that illustrates the manipulations of characters who bear false witness and precipitate violent consequences.

By visually restaging false versions of Black actions, *Within Our Gates* challenges rhetoric advanced by D. W. Griffith in *The Birth of a Nation,* in which the cinematic apparatus is imbued with the power to objectively and accurately represent life, including historical personages and events. Unlike live theater, Griffith claimed, "the motion picture is what technique really means, a faithful picture of life."[38] To be sure, Griffith's sense of realism was not a naturalistic or journalistic one; there was room for allegory, fantasy, and hyperbole in his cinematic practice. But Griffith's claims that the cinema could get at life's emotional truths were tied to his many gestures toward historical accuracy, particularly in *The Birth of a Nation,* which is filled with historical "facsimiles"—from Lincoln's assassination to the activities of newly elected Black state representatives. By inserting racist imagery into his facsimiles—like depicting Black legislators drinking alcohol and eating fried chicken while repealing laws against interracial marriage—Griffith amplified Black concerns about the cinema's damaging potential (as suggested by NAACP protests and Ida B. Wells's response to the film discussed in chapter 1). More than the Black spectacles in early

FIGURE 54. The murder of Philip Gridlestone (Ralph Johnson), as it really happened: Jasper Landry (William Starks) is a shocked, innocent bystander. *Within Our Gates* (dir. Oscar Micheaux, 1920). Library of Congress, Motion Picture, Broadcasting and Recorded Sound Division.

cinema, or the recirculation of minstrel figures in short comedies, Black representations in narratively integrated dramatic cinema (largely crafted by Griffith) were seen as politically dangerous because they were mounted in an aesthetic framework that gave the medium new artistic and cultural legitimacy. Micheaux foregrounds the deceptive (as opposed to the "faithful") representational potential of the cinema, demonstrating repeatedly that the dominant media can (and does) lie, and showing how such lies result in the demoralization, disfranchisement, and death of innocent Blacks.

But Micheaux does not restrict his critique to white characters and media practices. Significantly, he also implicates African Americans in misrepresenting the "Black" truth. Jane Gaines observes that the notion of betrayal—of wronging one's own—is a recurring theme in silent-era race cinema, and that "in Micheaux's world, the crimes committed against one's own people explain the failure of those people to rise higher and go further."[39] When Micheaux chooses to visualize the stories that unreliable

FIGURE 55. The murder of Philip Gridlestone, as told by Eph and the white press: Jasper Landry is a drunken murderer. *Within Our Gates* (dir. Oscar Micheaux, 1920). Library of Congress, Motion Picture, Broadcasting and Recorded Sound Division.

Blacks tell about upstanding ones, he stresses how obstacles to Black progress and mobility should be read as interracial constructions. For example, in a key scene Philip Gridlestone imagines that his Black tenants, the Landrys, are becoming too uppity because their daughter Sylvia has received some education. Gridlestone pictures the Landrys at home discussing their yearly account, with Mrs. Landry advising her husband: "[Sylvia] is as educated as white girls now—so when you go pay the boss you tell him that." However, another title card introduces "what they really said": we see the Landrys again at their table, and Sylvia advises her parents to "keep an account of all your purchases, sales, and debts so that . . . when you go to the Gridlestone house you can take the accounts and settle without argument." Here Micheaux again presents two visual stagings—one white and one Black—of the same event (fig. 56). And like the newspaper's false account of Gridlestone's murder, Gridlestone's false sense of the Landrys' audacity is instigated by his Black servant, Efrem. Efrem taunts his employer by telling him, "Dat Landry gal been ta school

FIGURE 56. The Landry family discusses its annual sharecropping accounts; the same discussion is rendered from conflicting white and Black perspectives. *Within Our Gates* (dir. Oscar Micheaux, 1920). Library of Congress, Motion Picture, Broadcasting and Recorded Sound Division.

'n' keeps her pappy's books now—so ya won't git ta cheat him no mo'." Thus, Micheaux illustrates repeatedly how Efrem enables white misrepresentations of the truth by fanning the flames of racial antagonism—first suggesting that Black sharecroppers will educate themselves out of subservient social and economic roles, and then falsely accusing a Black man of murder, inciting the retaliation of a white lynch mob. When Micheaux presents Eph imagining his own murder by lynching before it happens, and stages white fears about violent and educated Blacks, he marks the power of the visual to make even lies and fantasies "real," as supported by print media and facilitated by Black liars.

Micheaux implicates another Black character in the film's politics of truth and fabrication when he frames the entire flashback to Sylvia's southern past within the narrative voice of Alma, Sylvia's dishonest cousin. Micheaux invests considerable narrative authority in this unreliable character; there is never any diegetic reason, once the flashback starts, to disbelieve the events depicted. In some ways, Alma's role in keeping Sylvia running between North and South links her abuses with the revelation of those perpetrated by whites within the lengthy southern scenes framed by her narrative voice. Although Alma initially stood in the way of Sylvia's happy ending (orchestrating her breakup with Conrad), she introduces Sylvia's backstory to Dr. Vivian (and the viewer) by confessing her previous deceptions, so that her narration functions as an opportunity for her to redeem herself. Old Ned, the dishonest, white-serving Black reverend, gets a similar moment of redemption when he acknowledges his wrongs to himself (and the viewer), despite the fact that he is presented within the framework of racist Geraldine Stratton's myopic narration. At these awkward and striking moments, along with Eph's vision of his own lynching, Micheaux foregrounds his role as narrator, passing judgments and designating fates in ways that require some bending of the rules of classical narrative logic.

In these ways, *Within Our Gates* goes beyond criticizing the racist tendencies in white American filmmaking and the dominant society in general. The film also demonstrates stylistically that there are various and contradictory modes available for representing African Americans—textual and powerful new cinematic ones, for use by white people and Black people—complicating any claims that this mobile and diverse population can ever be represented entirely "realistically." Micheaux suggests that while Blacks were never immigrants, they are not completely innocent either. He implicates African Americans in the negative and positive directions that modern Black life and its representations are taking. Micheaux challenges his viewers to tell and to face the many truths about African Americans despite southern and northern temptations to put individual self-preservation before the advancement of the Race as a whole. What is more, his own narrative style betrays the difficulties of speaking to, speaking of, and particularly speaking for a Black population in the midst of dramatic social, psychological, and geographical transformations.

It was clear when *Within Our Gates* was released that the racial situation in the United States had reached an acrimonious state and that African Americans of all classes in all parts of the country were still the targets of virulent white attacks. Micheaux's attempt at the film's conclusion to construct proud Black American characters, unified in patriotism, certainly provides a compelling response to the racist and exclusionary image of America presented in *The Birth of a Nation*. But the film's use of patriotic rhetoric also reflects the often unresolved conflicts within and between diverse African American individuals and communities that were exacerbated by migration and persisted even as African Americans seemed to face a common enemy. Ultimately, the film cannot fully reconcile its controversial exposure of unspeakable white crimes (rape, lynching, media misrepresentation) and disgraceful Black betrayals (dishonest relatives, urban criminals, false religious leaders). By mobilizing the multiple appeals of migration narrative, patriotism, melodrama, and uplift tale, the film's awkward conclusion heightens our awareness of its contradictory discourses on the notion of Black progress and the variable nature of Black cinematic representation.

The inconsistent, fragmented narrative voices contained in *Within Our Gates* bear an important relation to the disharmonious Black environments and disruptive slapstick "heroes" featured in the comedies produced by the Ebony Film Corporation. Both reflect the new social possibilities that urban migration presented for Black individuals and communities. But they also illustrate the risks of subjective dispersion and instability in Black life and in African American cultural production. Micheaux, Luther J. Pollard at Ebony, and other early African American filmmakers attempted to take advantage of the cinema's uplift and commercial potential. However, the Black diversity they relied upon—that is, audiences in various regions, viewer tastes for different genres, models for numerous character types—also threatened their efforts to use the cinema to produce political consensus or a stable, national Black audience. By responding to pressing issues in modern Black life, such as migration and patriotic feeling, early Black filmmakers reached many segments of the African American audience, but they also broached the very topics that critics used against the movies, such as the breakdown of traditional values, the city's immoral temptations, and false media representation of the Race.

From their first filmmaking efforts and throughout the silent period, African American producers struggled with a series of financial and representational challenges. Although they often felt ill equipped to compete with the mainstream film industry, the comedies, westerns, nonfiction films, and melodramas they produced from the mid-1910s through the World War I and Great Migration years reveal the complexity of defining, claiming, and representing Black American identity at this historical moment. With the release of Micheaux's *Within Our Gates*, with its multilayered discourses on Black migration and patriotism, African American identity, and cinematic representation, we see an assertive post-*Birth*, postwar, post-riots Black filmmaking practice. By extension, this film announced the emergence of an African American film culture no longer in its "infancy" but exhibiting the acute self-consciousness of adolescence.

# Conclusion

Oscar Micheaux's misgivings about the quality of Black urban life would reverberate in African American art and political thought with subsequent waves of Black movement. So would the kinds of representational dilemmas he faced. Migration made African American subjects visible in unprecedented ways in (African) American intellectual and popular discourses. But this increased visibility heightened Black and white anxieties about how Black people could or should participate in the elaboration of a modern American society and its attendant visual, mass, and public cultures.

When Richard Wright was asked to write a short essay to accompany a collection of Depression-era photographs of African American life before, during, and after the migration experience, the images seem to have swept him away.[1] Heavily influenced by the fieldwork of Horace Cayton and the Chicago school of urban sociology, and drawing on his own experience as a migrant from Mississippi, Wright produced a passionate treatise that speaks in epic, and tragic, terms of the working-class Black migrants' quest for a better life. Wright characterizes Black urban experience as "death on the city pavements," referring not only to the physical demise of Black city dwellers (due to disease, malnutrition, violence, and other causes) but also to the public and visible disintegration of Black character, families, and communities under the exploitative, indifferent conditions of northern urban industrialism.[2] Moving more quickly than any other group in history from agrarian to industrial lifestyles, African Americans, Wright argues, were an "utterly unprepared folk" who would necessarily suffer major casualties "in the tall and sprawling centers of steel and stone."[3]

Micheaux's moralizing about urban hazards and Wright's grim portrait of the inhospitable cityscape (in his account of Black migration inspired by the photographs and in his characterization of Bigger Thomas's severely circumscribed existence in *Native Son*) raise important questions about how we might understand the growth of Black film culture, particularly in urban areas, between the world wars. To what degree did the increasing popularity of moving pictures in Black urban communities signal a new "freedom" for Black cultural producers and consumers gained through migration, over and against the development of unproductive new tastes for mass-produced commodities and commercialized experiences? Did the movies function as diversions from the important work of reconstituting Black lives and building counterhegemonic social organizations and political movements in urban environments? Did the cinema directly serve the purposes of the urban industrial complex, including its segregationist policies, by offering just enough superficial latitude for culturally specific expression (particularly at local points of exhibition) without making substantive structural or ideological changes in the ways in which films (along with other products and resources) were made, distributed, and consumed?

Any consideration of the development of Black urban film culture evokes long-standing debates about the relative "success" or "failure" of contemporaneous Black cultural practices and types of creative expression in relation to the social and political advancement of the Race. For example, Houston Baker has pointed out that the major critical accounts of the Harlem Renaissance have faulted this flowering of African American artistic production for failing to bring about any qualitative change in the lives of the Black "masses."[4] A similar argument could be made about the political efficacy of African American filmmaking and moviegoing, particularly for the largely working-class Black audience. Just as the Harlem Renaissance has been accused of failing to generate a succeeding, collective movement of Black artistic and literary activity, the race film movement has been faulted for its inability to build a stable, institutional framework for subsequent Black filmmakers.[5] The Great Depression dealt crushing blows to both movements, and in both cases it would seem that the gaps between Black artists and Black audiences, between Black creativity and white-controlled capital (cultural and monetary), proved extremely difficult to bridge for a sustained period of time.

Many of the grave social and political problems that race film and the Harlem Renaissance seemingly "failed" to address were the direct result of Black urban migration. Black movements into urban centers had cataclysmic repercussions, perhaps illustrated most dramatically by the racial violence that erupted throughout the country during the first two decades of the twentieth century. Race riots in New York City (1900), Springfield,

Ohio (1904), and Springfield, Illinois (1908) clearly demonstrated that America's race problem was not limited to the South. Indeed, interracial antagonisms in the North were heightened by an incendiary combination of ethnic, labor, and political tensions exacerbated by Black urban migration. William Tuttle explains that the particularly bloody riot that took place in East St. Louis, Illinois, in 1917, during the height of the Great Migration, was "fueled by bigoted and alarmist trade unionists, self-centered corporate managers, strikebreaking black migrants from the South, corrupt white politicians, inflammatory news reporters, and biased and lax police officials."[6] Clashes between Blacks and whites reached a dramatic peak in 1919 when riots broke out in twenty-five cities and towns across the country between April and October. Half of these occurred in northern and border states, including the infamous five-day riot in Chicago that took place in July.[7]

While these events forever disabused African Americans of the notion that the urban North was an unequivocal "promised land," northern white racism did not stop the flow of Black migration or the expression of a "New Negro" assertiveness. Indeed, Claude McKay's poem "If We Must Die" and Oscar Micheaux's film *Within Our Gates*—staples of the Harlem Renaissance and race film canons—were militant statements inspired by the events of the Red Summer of 1919.[8] The 1919 riots (particularly the one in Chicago) were notable for the degree to which African Americans fought back, refusing to passively accept racist assaults. They marked a point of no return in U.S. race relations. Though Blacks would continue to be perceived as a "social problem" and face numerous forms of discrimination in the future, they made it clear that they had come to the urban North to stay.[9] In different ways, the Harlem Renaissance and early Black film culture reiterated this claim.

Race film production reached its height during the early 1920s, demonstrating that the steady flow of urban migration continued to invigorate the development of Black film culture despite violent white efforts to repress African American participation in most arenas of American public life.[10] Then, after the setbacks of the Depression and the introduction of expensive sound technology during the late 1920s and early 1930s, race film production rose again in the late 1930s as segregated Black audiences across the country were targeted by producers (mostly white) of Black-cast musicals, thrillers, comedies, and westerns. After World War II, race filmmaking crumbled for the last time, as production costs soared, as Hollywood studios began to incorporate Black stars and themes (under pressure from civil rights groups like the NAACP), and as integration became the popularized goal of U.S. race relations. When mainstream, first-run the-aters became more accessible to Black audiences, the segregated market for race films dwindled.[11] African Americans still patronized neighborhood theaters and voiced their opposition to films they found to be offensive af-ter the race film era. But Black film culture took different forms as the mi-gration slowed and television (home viewing) replaced the movies (public consumption) as the predominant medium of American entertainment.

Through all these shifts, one consistent feature of Black film culture in the decades since the race film era has been its strong identification with urban experience, in terms of both content and audience.[12] For example, Paula Massood has shown that during the 1930s African American audi-ences craved images of modern Black sophistication, and "genre films like Ralph Cooper's *Dark Manhattan* [1937] obliged by conjoining the urban and the urbane, often through the use of contemporary fashions (not work clothes), urban slang (not rural dialect), and the performance of contempo-rary music (not spirituals)."[13] A few decades later, most of the action films of the "Blaxploitation" period were set in cities and marketed to the Black urban audiences who patronized downtown theaters abandoned by whites who had fled to the suburbs. Independent filmmakers like Haile Gerima and Charles Burnett (of the "L.A. Rebellion" group of Black independent directors) explored post–civil rights era urban disillusionment in films like *Bush Mama* (1976) and *Killer of Sheep* (1977). Spike Lee burst onto the scene with *She's Gotta Have It* (1986), a film about and addressing a "Bup-pie" (Black urban professional) culture that had been overlooked by both Hollywood and previous Black independents. Three years later, Lee's *Do the Right Thing* (1989) presented the racial antagonisms seething within a diverse Brooklyn neighborhood, generating massive media attention and a wave of widely released Black urban films. These included a cycle of ni-hilistic "boys in the 'hood" or "ghetto action" films in the early 1990s, in which young Black men come of age in urban jungles of violence and crime.[14]

Since the early 1990s, "Black film" production has been booming, as a steady stream of films by and about African Americans are being made independently and in Hollywood for theatrical release, (cable) television broadcast, and direct-to-video markets, typically taking up urban themes. On the exhibition front, new theaters have been constructed in Black urban communities abandoned by the industry decades ago, such as the Magic Johnson Theaters in the Baldwin Hills section of Los Angeles and 125th Street in Harlem, and the Inner City Entertainment chain on the South and West Sides of Chicago. Black-oriented film festivals proliferate in urban centers across the country, such as New York City's annual Urbanworld Film Festival, which presents the latest short and feature-length work to Black, Latino, and Asian American audiences and to industry representatives seeking to exploit "minority" markets. On the Internet, sites such as UrbanEntertainment.com and UrbanFilmPremiere.com showcase African American and "urban-themed" films, including independent shorts, animation, and discussions of current major studio releases. As these titles suggest, urban experience continues to be fetishized in the representation of Black life and prioritized in the marketing of "Black" films. But they also suggest how the entertainment industry (its dominant and independent strands) now expands the notion of the urban from its roots in Black content/audience to include broader multiracial demographics.

The appeals that many recent films and marketing strategies make to a Black viewing public bear an important relation to early Black urban film culture in that they target an African American niche market like the one William Foster, Noble and George Johnson, and Oscar Micheaux attempted to exploit. However, the current phenomenon of a separate Black marketplace is not the result of the exact same kind of hostile enforcement of segregation in movie theaters witnessed in the first half of the twentieth century. Instead, now there is an African American market that seems, in many respects, to choose to consume media produced specifically with Blacks in mind. The contemporary conflation of "Black" and "urban," while supporting a host of troubling stereotypes about African American taste and the translatability of Black identity, functions to designate story lines and markets (for films and related products like sound tracks and clothing) that have proved to be extremely profitable, and to have significant crossover appeal. The "urban" market now marks consumers of many cultural backgrounds and income brackets, particularly consumers of hip-hop culture and those who have begun the latest migration from the suburbs back to city centers.

Of course, many films produced from the race film era to the present have treated Black life beyond the city, and vibrant Black film cultures have developed outside of the urban North. Research into those areas of the South where segregated exhibition persisted much longer than in northern cities like Chicago offers important counterpoints to the history this book has described.[15] My efforts to trace the factors shaping the development of Black film culture in the urban North do not seek to displace these other film practices. Rather, I hope that my discussion of the origins of African American film culture offers new ways to think about how the first major waves of Black northern and urban migration reorganized America's social relations and media institutions, influencing the ways in which Black populations would experience the cinema in other local contexts, and in the years to come.

We know that the urban North was not the land of milk and honey that some migrants may have anticipated, and, certainly, many Black urban engagements with the cinema cannot be described as pleasurable or empowering. If we understand the founding relationships between African Americans, the city, and the cinema to be multiple and mutual ones, we can recover migration narratives that do not necessarily follow a straight path toward either empowerment or disillusionment. I have attempted here to describe and connect the web of fields offered uniquely by the cinema—representational and experiential, psychic and public, individual and collective—in which moving pictures and Black people in motion continue to encounter and interpret each other.

# Notes

1. See the screenplay in Julie Dash, *Daughters of the Dust: The Making of an African American Woman's Film* (New York: New P, 1992) 125. I discuss this stereograph scene in more specific relation to early African American spectatorship in "Negroes Laughing at Themselves? Black Spectatorship and the Performance of Urban Modernity," *Critical Inquiry* 29 (2003: 650–77).

2. Later in the film, the Unborn Child (who is invisible to most characters) appears suddenly in the viewfinder of a "mainland" photographer's camera. In another scene, Dash links the Unborn Child with visual signifiers of modern life—consumer culture and movies—when she shows the Child with a group of family members looking through a "wish book"—a Sears and Roebuck catalogue. The mail-order catalogue's display of commodities not only represents the rural Peazant family's idealized vision of the possibilities of modern life on the mainland but also functions something like a movie. The catalogue's succession of images presents a series of "wishes," appealing to the visual fascination of an audience constructed as spectator/consumers. See Alexandra Keller, "Disseminations of Modernity: Representation and Consumer Desire in Early Mail-Order Catalogs," *Cinema and the Invention of Modern Life*, ed. Leo Charney and Vanessa R. Schwartz (Berkeley: U of California P, 1995) 156–82.

3. Hazel V. Carby, "Policing the Black Woman's Body in an Urban Context," *Critical Inquiry* 18 (1992): 739. Revisionist migration histories that are important sources and models for my study are James R. Grossman, *Land of Hope: Chicago, Black Southerners and the Great Migration* (Chicago: U of Chicago P, 1989); and Carole Marks, *Farewell—We're Good and Gone: The Great Black Migration* (Bloomington: Indiana UP, 1989).

4. *Compensation* makes many references to *Daughters of the Dust* in both style and content. Dash and Davis are filmmakers associated with the "L.A. Rebellion" group of Black directors whose (mostly) independently produced films tend to take up self-consciously many historical, social, and representational issues that are overlooked in much "commercial" Black filmmaking. See Nton-

gela Masilela, "The Los Angeles School of Black Filmmakers," *Black American Cinema,* ed. Manthia Diawara (New York: Routledge, 1993) 107–17.

5. See my discussion of Foster and his debut film in chapter 6.

6. I am thinking of images like the portrait of a family of migrants who have just arrived in Chicago, posing with their baggage and wearing traveling clothes, and the crowd of whites and Blacks at Chicago's Twenty-ninth Street Beach just after the drowning of Eugene Williams, which reportedly precipitated the infamous race riot of July 1919. Both images have been frequently republished, first appearing in the report of the Chicago Commission on Race Relations, *The Negro in Chicago: A Study of Race Relations and a Race Riot* (Chicago: U of Chicago P, 1922).

INTRODUCTION

1. *Biograph Bulletin* 55, 27 Nov. 1905: 17, rpt. in Kemp Niver, ed., *Biograph Bulletins 1896–1908* (Los Angeles: Artisan, 1971) 207.

2. For more on the conventions of early comedy films see Tom Gunning, "Crazy Machines in the Garden of Forking Paths: Mischief Gags and the Origins of American Film Comedy," *Classical Hollywood Comedy,* ed. Kristine Brunovska Karnick and Henry Jenkins (New York: Routledge, 1995) 87–105; and Eileen Bowser, "Racial/Racist Jokes in American Silent Slapstick Comedy," *Griffithiana* 53 (1995): 35–42.

3. Henry Louis Gates Jr., "New Negroes, Migration, and Cultural Exchange," *Jacob Lawrence: The Migration Series,* ed. Elizabeth Hutton Turner (Washington: Rappahannock, 1993) 17. According to figures cited by historian Carole Marks, approximately 168,000 Black people moved from the South to the North between 1890 and 1900; 170,000 migrated between 1900 and 1910; 454,000 moved northward between 1910 and 1920; and 749,000 African Americans fled the South between 1920 and 1930. See Carole Marks, *Farewell— We're Good and Gone: The Great Black Migration* (Bloomington: Indiana UP, 1989) 2.

4. "A nigger in the woodpile" defined in *Oxford English Dictionary,* 1989 ed.; Eric Partridge, *A Dictionary of Slang and Unconventional English,* ed. Paul Beale, 8th ed. (New York: Macmillan, 1984); *A Dictionary of American English on Historical Principles,* ed. William A. Craigie and James R. Hulbert, 4 vols. (Chicago: U of Chicago P, 1942) vol. 3; *Dictionary of American Slang,* ed. Maurice H. Wessen (New York: Crowell, 1934); and Lester V. Barrey and Melvin Van Den Bark, *The American Thesaurus of Slang* (New York: Crowell, 1942) 165 (listed under "suspect; be suspicious"). The phrase "a nigger in the fence" is often used with the same connotations—see *Slang and Its Analogues: Past and Present,* comp. and ed. John S. Farmer and W. E. Henley (1902; New York: Routledge, 1965).

5. The essays collected in Daniel Bernardi, ed., *The Birth of Whiteness: Race and the Emergence of U.S. Cinema* (New Brunswick: Rutgers UP, 1996), represent important revisionist accounts of the complex function of race in

preclassical cinema, primarily in the area of representation. In his introduction, Bernardi argues for a comparative look at race and racial difference in relation to the cinema, because very few scholars stretch to look "beyond the experiences of any single group," such as African Americans, Chicano/as, Asians and Asian Americans, and Native Americans (see Bernardi 6). While I agree that this kind of analysis would be extremely fruitful, I still think there is much historical and theoretical work to be done to analyze how particular racial categories have been constructed, mobilized, and reproduced by the cinema as an institution. My focus on Black/white racial difference in this study does not seek to diminish the histories of other "nonwhite" groups in relation to the cinema. Rather, I hope to address the persistence of oversimplified "white" versus "Black" models of figuring racial difference in American society; the overwhelming popularity of "Black" representations in a variety of media (from postcards to cookie jars to minstrel shows) circulating in everyday American life during the period in question; and the consistent "marking" of Blackness in early cinema in the form of very dark skin (using dark-skinned actors and blackface makeup) to make a strongly visible distinction (I would go so far as to say an *opposition*) between white and Black. On the practice of "marking" in the cinema, see James Snead, "Spectatorship and Capture in *King Kong:* The Guilty Look," *White Screens, Black Images: Hollywood from the Dark Side,* ed. Colin MacCabe and Cornel West (New York: Routledge, 1994) 5.

6. Toni Morrison, *Playing in the Dark: Whiteness and the Literary Imagination* (1992; New York: Vintage, 1993) 6.

7. See, for example, Lewis Jacobs, *The Rise of the American Film* (New York: Teachers College P, 1939); and Judith Mayne, "Immigrants and Spectators," *Wide Angle* 5.2 (1982): 32–41. Judith Thissen charts Jewish grassroots opposition to the "Americanizing" function of the cinema in New York's Lower East Side in her essay "Jewish Immigrant Audiences in New York City, 1905–1914," *American Movie Audiences: From the Turn of the Century to the Early Sound Era,* ed. Melvyn Stokes and Richard Maltby (London: BFI, 1999) 15–28. In the same collection, Giorgio Bertellini argues that Italian immigrants in the United States watched Italian films that did more to connect them with an Italian nationalist identity than an American one. See "Italian Imageries, Historical Feature Films and the Fabrication of Italy's Spectators in Early 1900s New York," *American Movie Audiences,* 29–45. While such scholarship helps to deconstruct long-standing assumptions about the cinema's role in making a variety of ethnic whites "American," it is the mythic status of this presumption—part of the American cinema's myth of its own origins—and its resulting obscuring of issues around racial difference, that this book seeks to address.

8. Michael Rogin, *Blackface, White Noise: Jewish Immigrants in the Hollywood Melting Pot* (Berkeley: U of California P, 1996) 12. See also Eric Lott, *Love and Theft: Blackface Minstrelsy and the American Working Class* (New York: Oxford UP, 1995).

9. Motivations for the Great Migration are outlined in Marks 2–3 and passim. Other important studies informing my understanding of the migration

(its causes, effects, and representations) include Malaika Adero, *Up South: Stories, Studies and Letters of This Century's Black Migrations* (New York: New P, 1993); Alferdteen Harrison, ed., *Black Exodus: The Great Migration from the American South* (Jackson: UP of Mississippi, 1991); E. Marvin Goodwin, *Black Migration in America from 1915–1960* (Lewiston: Mellen, 1990); and essays in Joe William Trotter Jr., ed., *The Great Migration in Historical Perspective: New Dimensions of Race, Class and Gender* (Bloomington: Indiana UP, 1991). See also sections on the migration in John Hope Franklin and Alfred A. Moss Jr., *From Slavery to Freedom: A History of Negro Americans*, 6th ed. (New York: McGraw, 1988) 277–309.

10. Farah Jasmine Griffin, *"Who Set You Flowin'?": The African-American Migration Narrative* (New York: Oxford UP, 1995).

11. I realize that the word "modernity" (as well as the related terms "modern" and "modernization") has a complex etymology in social thought and aesthetic and cultural histories. I refer to "urban modernity" and "modern life" throughout this book in an effort to mark the experiential terrain opened up by the major economic, geographic, technological, and epistemological shifts that transformed American culture during the late nineteenth and early twentieth centuries (but that, of course, had international effects and longer histories). My understanding of the mutual relations between the cinema and American modernity owes much to Ben Singer's meticulous discussion of early film melodrama, the "meanings of modernity," and particularly the notion of "modernization" as it relates to the rise of mature capitalism and attendant "epic" socioeconomic phenomena (e.g., urbanization, e/migration, new visual and transportation technologies, nationalism, mass culture, heterosocial public circulation, industrial labor, disintegration of the extended family unit). My study seeks to understand the meanings of modernization through the lenses of African American representation and experience. Ben Singer, *Melodrama and Modernity: Early Sensational Cinema and Its Contexts* (New York: Columbia UP, 2001) 20–21.

12. Griffin 4–5.

13. Pearl Bowser and Louise Spence, *Writing Himself into History: Oscar Micheaux, His Silent Films, and His Audiences* (New Brunswick: Rutgers UP, 2000); J. Ronald Green, *Straight Lick: The Cinema of Oscar Micheaux* (Bloomington: Indiana UP, 2000); Betti Carol VanEpps-Taylor, *Oscar Micheaux. . . Dakota Homesteader, Author, Pioneer Film Maker: A Biography* (Rapid City: Dakota West, 1999); Pearl Bowser, Jane Gaines, and Charles Musser, eds., *Oscar Micheaux and His Circle: African-American Filmmaking and the Race Cinema of the Silent Era* (Bloomington: Indiana UP, 2001).

14. Jane Gaines, *Fire and Desire: Mixed-Race Movies in the Silent Era* (Chicago: U of Chicago P, 2001); Anna Everett, *Returning the Gaze: A Genealogy of Black Film Criticism, 1909–1949* (Durham: Duke UP, 2001); Everett, "Lester Walton's Écriture Noir: Black Spectatorial Transcodings of 'Cinematic Excess,'" *Cinema Journal* 39.3 (2000): 30–50.

15. James R. Grossman, *Land of Hope: Chicago, Black Southerners, and the Great Migration* (Chicago: U of Chicago P, 1989) 74.

16. Grossman 4.

17. "In the 1910s and 1920s, Chicago's 'Stroll'—the section of State Street between 26th and 39th—was the best known site for this behavior." Shane White and Graham White, *Stylin': African American Expressive Culture from Its Beginnings to the Zoot Suit* (Ithaca: Cornell UP, 1998) 225. White and White recognize the national reputation and exemplary status of Chicago's Stroll when they note that "every northern city had its equivalent of the Stroll" (such as Frankstown Avenue, called "Chocolate Boulevarde," in Pittsburgh, and Eighteenth Street in Kansas City), but "for all the vitality and vibrancy of these and many other locations there was, both in reality and in African Americans' imagination, only one serious rival to Chicago's Stroll, and that, of course, was to be found in Harlem, which by the 1920s had become the Negro Mecca." White and White 234.

18. These illustrations draw on long, complex traditions of representing Black/white (public) relations as cross-racial imitations, including the affected movements and extravagant dress of Black dancers of the cakewalk (which can be read as a Black imitation of white high-society manners), and white performances of the northern Zip Coon character in blackface minstrelsy. For an exceptional cultural history of Black "fancy dress," specifically the recurrent Black dandy as both a white response to Black mobility and a Black critique of the limitations placed upon race, gender, and class identity and performance, see Monica Miller, "Figuring the Black Dandy: Negro Art, Black Bodies, and African-Diasporic Ambitions," diss., Harvard U, 2000. See also White and White, esp. 85–124, and Brooke Baldwin, "The Cakewalk: A Study in Stereotype and Reality," *Journal of Social History* 15 (1981): 205–18.

19. Oskar Negt and Alexander Kluge, *Public Sphere and Experience,* trans. Peter Labanyi, Jamie Owen Daniel, and Assenka Oksiloff (1972; Minneapolis: U of Minnesota P, 1993) ch. 1. Negt and Kluge write in response to Jürgen Habermas's *The Structural Transformation of the Public Sphere: An Inquiry into a Category of Bourgeois Society,* ed. Thomas Burger (1962; Cambridge: MIT P, 1989). For a discussion of the limitations of Habermas's model for African Americans, see Michael Dawson, "A Black Counterpublic? Economic Earthquakes, Racial Agenda(s), and Black Politics," *Public Culture* 7 (1994): 195–223.

20. Negt and Kluge define a pluralistic notion of the "public sphere" as a "general social horizon of experience" in which "everything that is actually or ostensibly relevant for all members of society is integrated. Understood in this sense, the public sphere is a matter for a handful of professionals (e.g., politicians, editors, union officials) on the one hand, but on the other, it is something that concerns everyone and that realizes itself only in people's minds." Negt and Kluge 2. In this way the "public" is understood as a discursive rather than simply "social" construction. It also presents the possibility of a multilayered

alternative to both bourgeois and commercial constructions of the public sphere, offering a useful framework for understanding how African Americans shaped and understood their "public" lives from the bottom of America's social and political hierarchies.

21. Miriam Hansen describes this "complex theory of experience" (developed in the tradition of Adorno, Kracauer, and Benjamin) as "that which mediates individual perception with social meaning, conscious with unconscious processes, loss of self with self-reflexivity; experience as the capacity to see connections and relations *(Zusammenhang)*; experience as the matrix of conflicting temporalities, of memory and hope, including the historical loss of these dimensions." Miriam Hansen, *Babel and Babylon: Spectatorship in American Silent Film* (Cambridge: Harvard UP, 1991) 12–13. This conception of experience is useful for my purposes not only in its mediating function between social and psychic processes and between collective and individual spheres but also in its acknowledgment of the role of experience in the face of loss and erasure.

22. Morrison 5.

23. Rare acknowledgments of this usage appear in *Random House Historical Dictionary of American Slang*, ed. J. E. Lighter, J. Ball, J. O'Connor, vol. 2 (New York: Random, 1997), and Jonathan Green, *Cassell's Dictionary of Slang* (New York: Sterling, 2000).

24. Ann Lamott, *Traveling Mercies: Some Thoughts on Faith* (New York: Pantheon, 1999) 12. The phrase appears in Mark Twain's *Tom Sawyer* and other literary sources not referenced by the *OED*. Significantly, an Internet search of the phrase "a nigger in the woodpile" produced largely verbal, anecdotal references to the expression suggesting this sexual meaning. For example, in an address (c. 1978) by a member of the Peoples Temple in Jonestown, the ("white") speaker recalls that his father was so "proud of [his] family tree, but I, I smelled, as the old whites used to say nastily, I smelled sweetly, a nigger in the woodpile. . . . So I got that family tree. . . . I went to the courthouse and I searched and I searched and I went *way* back to South Carolina and I found that Grandma went out to somebody's back cabin." Jonestown Audiotape Primary Project, transcript of Tape Q 612 (www-rohan.sdsu.edu/~remoore/jonestown/tapes/Q612.html); Jimmy Carter is also rumored to have jokingly used the expression when speaking to a Black man also named Carter, suggesting that given his southern background they could indeed be related by blood.

25. Emmett J. Scott, comp., "Additional Letters of Negro Migrants of 1916–1918," *Journal of Negro History* 4 (1919): 440.

26. Philip Rosen, ed., *Narrative, Apparatus, Ideology: A Film Theory Reader* (New York: Columbia UP, 1986) 282.

CHAPTER 1

1. Wells, along with the *Chicago Defender*, charged that although there were several potential white suspects who had access to the warden's private

quarters, Campbell had been singled out because he was Black. Ida B. Wells, *Crusade for Justice: The Autobiography of Ida B. Wells*, ed. Alfreda M. Duster (Chicago: U of Chicago P, 1970) 337–39, 341; *Chicago Defender* 26 June 1915 and 3 July 1915.

2. Wells 338.

3. NAACP protests against *Birth* tended to call for the suppression of the film (rather than boycotts, for example), despite the fact that this would violate Griffith's First Amendment rights. Arthur Knight points out that W. E. B. Du Bois expressed his uneasiness with this method of protest, as well as his frustration with the Race's seeming inability to secure the resources to stage a cinematic reply: "We had to ask liberals to oppose freedom of art and expression, and it was senseless for them to reply: 'Use this art in your own defense.' The cost of picture making and the scarcity of appropriate artistic talent made any such answer beyond question." W. E. B. Du Bois, *Dusk of Dawn: An Essay toward an Autobiography of a Race Concept* in *Writings*, ed. Nathan Huggins (1903; New York: New American Library, 1986) 730, qtd. in Arthur Knight, *Disintegrating the Musical: Black Performance and American Musical Film* (Durham: Duke UP, 2002) 251n16.

4. Wells 343.

5. Henry Louis Gates Jr., "The Trope of a New Negro and the Reconstruction of the Image of the Black," *Representations* 24 (1988): 131.

6. Wells 341.

7. My understanding of the relationships between industrial shifts in the production, distribution, and exhibition of films, the transition to the set of film-viewer relations that came to be associated with classical narrative style and modes of representation and address, and debates about the makeup of preclassical audiences is drawn from, among other sources, Eileen Bowser, *The Transformation of Cinema: 1907–1915* (Berkeley: U of California P, 1990); David Bordwell, Janet Staiger, and Kristin Thompson, *The Classical Hollywood Cinema: Film Style and Mode of Production to 1960* (New York: Columbia UP, 1985); Ben Brewster, "A Scene at the 'Movies,'" *Early Cinema: Space, Frame, Narrative,* ed. Thomas Elsaesser (London: BFI, 1990) 318–25; Charles Musser, "The Nickelodeon Era Begins: Establishing the Framework for Hollywood's Mode of Representation," also in *Early Cinema: Space, Frame, Narrative* 256–73; and Miriam Hansen, *Babel and Babylon: Spectatorship in American Silent Film* (Cambridge: Harvard UP, 1991).

8. Michele Wallace, "*Uncle Tom's Cabin:* Before and after the Jim Crow Era," *TDR:The Drama Review* 44.1 (2000): 137. My attempt to survey both representations of Blackness in early cinema and the methodological frameworks used to understand these images is indebted to Wallace's astute description of the "impossible, inconceivable" and "insufficiently explored" intersection of the eras of silent cinema and Jim Crow segregation, as well as her assessment of the difficulties of conducting research in the ephemeral archives of silent film and her provocative cultural history of Harriet Beecher Stowe's *Uncle Tom's Cabin* and its major impact on dominant and "race" filmmaking.

9. For example, Manthia Diawara states that "the release of D. W. Griffith's *The Birth of a Nation* in 1915 defined for the first time the side that Hollywood was to take in the war to represent Black people in America." Manthia Diawara, "Black American Cinema: The New Realism," *Black American Cinema,* ed. Manthia Diawara (New York: Routledge, 1993) 3. In his historically and institutionally grounded study of Black representation in commercial narrative films, Ed Guerrero opens with a discussion of the centrality of the "plantation genre" in "the cinematic devaluation of African Americans," citing *The Birth of a Nation* as its "original hegemonic impulse." Ed Guerrero, *Framing Blackness: The African American Image in Film* (Philadelphia: Temple UP, 1993) 10.

10. Notwithstanding the poor showing in Chicago, the National Association for the Advancement of Colored People (NAACP) did launch a national campaign against the film, an effort that stands as the most visible and vehement early demonstration of Black film criticism. In an index to articles appearing in *Crisis* magazine (organ of the NAACP) between 1910 and 1960, the first nine entries listed under "movies" refer to protests against *The Birth of a Nation.* Articles written as late as 1938 and 1940 protest revivals of the film, and a 1955 article responds negatively to rumors about a remake. Rose Bibliography, American Studies Program, George Washington University, *Analytical Guide and Indexes to* The Crisis *1910–1960,* 3 vols. (Westport: Greenwood, 1975). For a detailed discussion of criticism and protest that appeared in the Black press against both *The Birth of a Nation* and its literary antecedent, Thomas Dixon's *The Clansman,* see Anna Everett, *Returning the Gaze: A Genealogy of Black Film Criticism, 1909–1949* (Durham: Duke UP, 2001) 59–106.

11. Wells 344.

12. Studies of this nature include Peter Noble, *The Negro in Film* (London: Skelton Robinson, 1948); V. J. Jerome, *The Negro in Hollywood Films* (New York: Masses and Mainstream, 1950); Edward Mapp, *Blacks in American Films: Yesterday and Today* (Metuchen: Scarecrow, 1971); Donald Bogle, *Toms, Coons, Mulattoes, Mammies, and Bucks: An Interpretive History of Blacks in American Films* (New York: Viking, 1973), and revised editions published in 1990 and 1994; James P. Murray, *To Find an Image: Black Films from Uncle Tom to Super Fly* (Indianapolis: Bobbs-Merrill, 1973); Daniel J. Leab, *From Sambo to Superspade: The Black Experience in Motion Pictures* (Boston: Houghton, 1975); Gary Null, *Black Hollywood: The Negro in Motion Pictures* (Secaucus: Citadel, 1975); Lindsay Patterson, *Black Films and Film-Makers* (New York: Dodd, 1975); Jim Pines, *Blacks in Films: A Survey of Racial Themes and Images in the American Film* (London: Studio Vista, 1975); Thomas Cripps, *Slow Fade to Black: The Negro in American Film, 1900–1942* (Oxford: Oxford UP, 1977); James R. Nesteby, *Black Images in American Films, 1896–1954: The Interplay between Civil Rights and Film Culture* (Washington: UP of America, 1982).

13. James Snead, "Spectatorship and Capture in *King Kong:* The Guilty Look," *White Screens, Black Images: Hollywood from the Dark Side,* ed. Colin MacCabe and Cornel West (New York: Routledge, 1994) 1.

14. Reid objects to the emphasis on Black images that appear in "white-directed, -written, and -produced films about black America" made by major Hollywood studios, to the exclusion of films in which "black people controlled the key aspects of production." See Mark Reid, *Redefining Black Film* (Berkeley: U of California P, 1993) 1–2. Ross, drawing on the work of Kobena Mercer, recognizes that "the constant reiteration of the evils of negative images and misrepresentation becomes circular and unhelpful." See Karen Ross, *Black and White Media: Black Images in Popular Film and Television* (Cambridge: Polity, 1996) 3–4. Smith offers an extremely thoughtful discussion of the drawbacks of stereotype-based analyses that revolve around notions of "positive" and "negative" Black images. Heeding Smith's warnings, this chapter and the next seek to consider "what kind of narrative or ideological work" Black images perform, and to avoid "essencializ[ing] racial identity and deny[ing] its dynamic relation to constructions of class, gender, sexuality, region, and so on." See Smith's introduction to *Representing Blackness: Issues in Film and Video*, ed. Valerie Smith (New Brunswick: Rutgers UP, 1997) 1–3.

15. Clyde Taylor, "The Re-birth of the Aesthetic in Cinema," *The Birth of Whiteness: Race and the Emergence of U.S. Cinema*, ed. Daniel Bernardi (New Brunswick: Rutgers UP, 1996) 16.

16. Homi Bhabha, "The Other Question: Stereotype, Discrimination and the Discourse of Colonialism," *The Location of Culture* (London: Routledge, 1994) 70. Bhabha also talks of his "shift from the ready recognition of images as positive or negative, to an understanding of the *processes of subjectification* made possible (and plausible) through stereotypical discourse" (67).

17. Ella Shohat and Robert Stam, *Unthinking Eurocentrism: Multiculturalism and the Media* (London: Routledge, 1994) 214.

18. Turning her attention away from the limited and stereotypical images of Blacks in films of this period, Mary Carbine has shown how live jazz and blues musical accompaniment for mainstream silent films provided segregated Black audiences (in Chicago) with culturally specific sound tracks or "voices" at the moment of exhibition. Mary Carbine, " 'The Finest outside the Loop': Motion Picture Exhibition in Chicago's Black Metropolis, 1905–1928," *Camera Obscura* 23 (1990): 9–41.

19. Eileen Bowser, "Racial/Racist Jokes in American Silent Slapstick Comedy," *Griffithiana* 53 (1995): 35–42; Daniel Bernardi, introduction, *The Birth of Whiteness: Race and the Emergence of U.S. Cinema*, ed. Daniel Bernardi (New Brunswick: Rutgers, 1996) 7.

20. George M. Fredrickson, *The Black Image in the White Mind: The Debate on Afro-American Character and Destiny, 1817–1914* (1971; Hanover: Wesleyan UP, 1987) xviii. See also Rayford Logan, *The Negro in American Life and Thought: The Nadir, 1877–1901* (New York: Dial, 1954), and Charles A. Lofgren, *The Plessy Case: A Legal-Historical Interpretation* (Oxford: Oxford UP, 1987), esp. ch. 5, "The Intellectual Environment: Racist Thought in the Late Nineteenth Century."

21. Fredrickson 271–82, 283–97.

22. Fredrickson 260.

23. Kenneth W. Warren, *Black and White Strangers: Race and American Literary Realism* (Chicago: U of Chicago P, 1993) 13.

24. Warren 108, 41.

25. Richard J. Powell, *Black Art and Culture in the 20th Century* (London: Thames and Hudson, 1997) 26.

26. Patricia A. Turner, *Ceramic Uncles & Celluloid Mammies: Black Images and Their Influence on Culture* (New York: Anchor, 1994) 12. See also Marlon Riggs's documentary *Ethnic Notions* (1986), which traces stereotypical Black images in American visual media back to the middle of late nineteenth century.

27. According to Michael Rogin, the half-century theatrical run of *Uncle Tom's Cabin* witnessed major changes in the story's representational strategies and political orientation: "Far from perpetuating antislavery . . . the play mourned a lost antebellum world. Plantation scenes took over the minstrel show after the Civil War. . . . [P]ostbellum productions of *Uncle Tom's Cabin* promoted national reconciliation by celebrating the plantation, on the one hand, and intensifying racial division." Michael Rogin, *Blackface, White Noise: Jewish Immigrants in the Hollywood Melting Pot* (Berkeley: U of California P, 1996) 42. Filmed versions of *Uncle Tom's Cabin* are numerous, including productions by Edison in 1903, Thanhauser in 1910, and World Film Corporation in 1914 (starring for the first time on film a black actor, Sam Lucas, in the role of Uncle Tom).

28. See Rogin; Eric Lott, *Love and Theft: Blackface Minstrelsy and the American Working Class* (Oxford: Oxford UP, 1995); Linda Williams, *Playing the Race Card: Melodramas of Black and White from Uncle Tom to O. J. Simpson* (Princeton: Princeton UP, 2001).

29. W. E. B. Du Bois, *The Souls of Black Folk* in *Three Negro Classics* (1903; New York: Avon, 1965) 207–389. For further discussion of Du Bois's use of the "sorrow songs," as well as a consideration of how Du Bois's ideological rival, Booker T. Washington, constructed a different Black "voice," or "sound" (particularly in his "speaking manual," *Up from Slavery* [1901]), see Houston A. Baker Jr., *Modernism and the Harlem Renaissance* (Chicago: U of Chicago P, 1987).

30. Anna Julia Cooper, *A Voice from the South* (1892; Oxford: Oxford UP, 1988) i.

31. Cooper 201–9. Kenneth Warren argues that Cooper's investment in "gentility" and class differences among African Americans actually aligns her more closely with Howells than she cares to admit. Warren 68.

32. Cooper 25.

33. Powell 26.

34. See Deborah Willis-Thomas, *Black Photographers, 1840–1940: An Illustrated Bio-Bibliography* (New York: Garland, 1985).

35. Attempts to address negative stereotypes by invoking the "progress" of the Race are multitudinous during this period. Books like Henry F. Kletzing and William H. Crogman, *Progress of a Race, or the Remarkable Advancement*

*of the Afro-American* (New York: Negro UP, 1897); Booker T. Washington, *A New Negro for a New Century: An Accurate and Up-to-Date Record of the Upward Struggles of the Negro Race* (Chicago: American Publishing House, 1900); and G. F. Richings, *Evidences of Progress among Colored People* (Philadelphia: Ferguson, 1902) describe the accomplishments of individual Blacks (e.g., in business, law, medicine, the arts), as well as their military contributions and educational and religious institutions. Anne Meis Knupfer describes numerous ways in which Black club women in Chicago mobilized against retrogressive images (such as Negro mammies in corn-meal advertisements) and sponsored lectures and essay contests on topics such as "What Has the Negro Contributed to the World for the Advancement of Civilization?" Anne Meis Knupfer, *Toward a Tenderer Humanity and a Nobler Womanhood: African American Women's Clubs in Turn-of-the-Century Chicago* (New York: New York UP, 1996) 59, 121.

Black responses to racist discourses were not without their own contradictions. For example, numerous elite and middle-class Blacks expressed their fundamental agreement with essentialist ideologies like social Darwinism to argue for the enfranchisement of an upper stratum of the Black community. Many also rejected elements of Black culture that lower-class Blacks developed and turned to for race pride and enjoyment precisely because of Black exclusion from and denigration in mainstream American life. In addition, some Black leaders mobilized stereotypes (as Booker T. Washington did in invoking the image of the "chicken stealing darky," such as his own slave mother, in the opening of his autobiography, *Up from Slavery*, and in his landmark Atlanta Compromise speech) to secure white favor and resources. See Baker's discussion of Washington in *Modernism* 15–31. In these and other ways, African Americans attempted to respond to racist Black "images," but in the process they exposed tensions within the Black community, as well as impulses to construct images of Blackness that were as misrepresentative (though for different reasons) as those produced by whites.

36. Gates 129. Gates points out that this New Negro rhetoric often overcompensates for negative white treatments of Blackness. Also, it posits an "Old Negro," an African American past that must be rejected, making this act of renaming also an act of self-negation.

37. Visual representations of the progress of the Race were also projected in the form of stereopticon slide presentations, which were extremely popular among African American audiences. G. F. Richings, white author of *Evidences of Progress among Colored People* (cited earlier), published his book after years of gathering information and presenting illustrated lectures, or "entertainments," on the subject of African American progress. In 1918, the *Chicago Broad Ax* reported on a lecture delivered by Kathryn M. Johnson at Olivet Baptist Church entitled "Birth and Progress of a Race," in which she illustrated "through stereopticon slides, the Colored Man's Claim to Egyptian Civilization; His Material Progress and Solution of His Economic and Employment Problems," *Broad Ax* 9 Feb. 1918: 3.

38. Gates 130.

39. Shohat and Stam 215.

40. Mary Ann Doane, Patricia Mellencamp, and Linda Williams, "Feminist Film Criticism: An Introduction," *Re-Vision: Essays in Feminist Film Criticism*, ed. Mary Anne Doane, Patricia Mellencamp, and Linda Williams (Los Angeles: American Film Institute, 1984) 6. See also Claire Johnston, ed., *Notes on Women's Cinema* (London: Society for Education in Film and Television, 1972).

41. Philip Rosen, ed., *Narrative, Apparatus, Ideology: A Film Theory Reader* (New York: Columbia UP, 1986) 282.

42. Laura Mulvey, "Visual Pleasure and Narrative Cinema," in Rosen 208. Originally published in *Screen* 16.3 (1975): 6–18.

43. Among the important reconsiderations and reformulations are Gaylyn Studlar, "Masochism and the Perverse Pleasures of the Cinema," *Quarterly Review of Film Studies* 9 (1984): 267–82; Carol J. Clover, *Men, Women, and Chainsaws: Gender in the Modern Horror Film* (Princeton: Princeton UP, 1992); Judith Mayne, *Cinema and Spectatorship* (London: Routledge, 1993); and Mulvey's own "Afterthoughts on 'Visual Pleasure and Narrative Cinema' Inspired by *Duel in the Sun*," *Framework* 15–17 (1981): 12–15.

44. Manthia Diawara, "Black Spectatorship: Problems of Identification and Resistance," *Black American Cinema*, ed. Manthia Diawara (New York: Routledge, 1993) 211–20.

45. Hansen 38.

46. Hansen 45; Charles Musser, *The Emergence of Cinema: The American Screen to 1907* (Berkeley: U of California P, 1990) 2.

47. Description of the deacon in *Biograph Bulletin 55*, 27 Nov. 1905: 17, rpt. in Kemp Niver, ed., *Biograph Bulletins 1896–1908* (Los Angeles: Artisan, 1971) 207.

48. Tom Gunning, "Crazy Machines in the Garden of Forking Paths: Mischief Gags and the Origins of American Film Comedy," *Classical Hollywood Comedy*, ed. Kristine Brunovska Karnick and Henry Jenkins (New York: Routledge, 1995) 90.

49. Mulvey, "Visual Pleasure" 208.

50. Tom Gunning, "The Cinema of Attractions: Early Film, Its Spectator and the Avant-Garde," *Early Cinema: Space, Frame, Narrative*, ed. Thomas Elsaesser (London: BFI, 1990) 56–62.

51. Jean-Louis Baudry, "Ideological Effects of the Basic Cinematographic Apparatus," *Narrative, Apparatus, Ideology: A Film Theory Reader*, ed. Philip Rosen (New York: Columbia UP, 1986) 295.

52. I take this account of the transition from the "cinema of attractions" to a "cinema of narrative integration" from Tom Gunning as outlined in, among other places, *D. W. Griffith and the Origins of American Narrative Film: The Early Years at Biograph* (Urbana: U of Illinois P, 1991) 6.

53. Chase films feature Black subjects as both pursued (*The Watermelon Patch* [Edison, 1905]) and pursuers (*The Snowman* [American Mutoscope & Biograph, 1908]).

54. On linked vignettes see Bowser, *Transformation* 57, and Tom Gunning, "Non-Continuity, Continuity, Discontinuity: A Theory of Genres in Early Films," *Early Cinema: Space, Frame, Narrative*, ed. Thomas Elsaesser (London: BFI, 1990) 92.

55. I discuss *Laughing Gas* and other films featuring Black female domestics made during the "transitional" era in "What Happened in the Transition? Reading Race, Gender and Labor between the Shots," *American Cinema's Transitional Era: Audiences, Institutions, Practices*, ed. Charlie Keil and Shelley Stamp (Berkeley: U of California P, 2004) 103–30.

56. According to historian Elizabeth Clark-Lewis, "Within the first two decades of the twentieth century, household work lost its importance as an occupation for white women. By contrast, the number of African-American female household workers *increased* by 43 percent. . . . African-American women were forced into a 'servant caste.'" Elizabeth Clark-Lewis, "'This Work Had a End': African-American Domestic Workers in Washington, D.C., 1910–1940," *"To Toil the Livelong Day": America's Women at Work, 1780–1980*, ed. Carol Groneman and Mary Beth Norton (Ithaca: Cornell UP, 1987) 197–98.

57. This long list of titles includes films as varied as *The Seeress* (American Mutoscope & Biograph, 1904), a short tableau in which an older Black woman sits with a young white woman at a table and reads her fortune using a deck of cards; *The Stolen Pig* (Vitagraph, 1907), a comedy about "Mammy" and "Rastus" stealing a pig and disguising it as their baby; *Mammy's Ghost or between the Lines of Battle* (Vitagraph, 1911), in which a Black female domestic helps a father (a Confederate officer) and son chase a Union soldier out of their home by making him believe there is a ghost in the attic; and *Old Mammy's Charge* (Majestic, 1913), a drama in which a Black female domestic raises the orphaned daughter of a white southern couple in the North following the Civil War.

58. The final emblematic shot of "Mandy" is not unlike the early film *Laughing Ben* (American Mutoscope & Biograph, 1901), in which an elderly Black man in close-up (shot as an "old plantation" type at the Pan-American Exposition in Buffalo, New York) repeatedly spreads a toothless grin.

59. Michael Rogin notes that actress Hattie McDaniel, "before she was turned into the most famous motion picture mammy of all time," wrote and performed a song called "Dentist Chair Blues," which uses a trip to the dentist as an extended metaphor for describing a sexual encounter. See Rogin 111.

60. Clark-Lewis notes that live-in maids often could not attend Sunday "day services" because of their job obligations, so they frequently attended church services at night. Clark-Lewis 209.

61. Snead, "Spectatorship and Capture" 5: "We seem to find the color black repeatedly overdetermined, marked redundantly, almost as if to force the viewer to register the image's difference from white images. Marking makes it visually clear that black skin is a 'natural' condition turned into a 'man-made' sign."

62. Knight 32.

CHAPTER 2

1. As explained in chapter 1, I use the term "preclassical cinema" to describe filmmaking practices film historians have designated as "early" (from the beginnings of motion picture production to around 1907) and "transitional" (from around 1907 to the midteens), before the "classical" paradigm achieved dominance.

2. An exceptional discussion of the intersection of class, ethnic, and racial politics in the development of preclassical film culture is Alison Griffiths and James Latham, "Film and Ethnic Identity in Harlem, 1896–1915," *American Movie Audiences: From the Turn of the Century to the Early Sound Era*, ed. Melvyn Stokes and Richard Maltby (London: BFI, 1999) 46–63.

3. See, for example, Noel Ignatiev, *How the Irish Became White* (New York: Routledge, 1995); David R. Roediger, *The Wages of Whiteness: Race and the Making of the American Working Class* (London: Verso, 1991); Ruth Frankenberg, *White Women, Race Matters: The Social Construction of Whiteness* (Minneapolis: U of Minnesota P, 1993); and Toni Morrison, *Playing in the Dark: Whiteness and the Literary Imagination* (1992; New York: Vintage, 1993). For more specific discussion of constructions of "whiteness" and the cinema, see Richard Dyer, *White* (New York: Routledge, 1997); and Daniel Bernardi, "The Voice of Whiteness: D. W. Griffith's Biograph Films (1908–1913)," *The Birth of Whiteness: Race and the Emergence of U.S. Cinema*, ed. Daniel Bernardi (New Brunswick: Rutgers UP, 1996) 103–28.

4. According to Musser, "Lucy Daly's 'Pickaninnies' [from the "Passing Show"] were the first African Americans to appear before a motion picture camera." Charles Musser, *Edison Motion Pictures, 1890–1900: An Annotated Bibliography* (Gemona, Italy: Smithsonian Institution/Le Giornate del Cinema Muto, 1997) 133. For full descriptions of Edison's early Black dance films see Musser, *Edison* 133–34, 157–58. Information on Black vaudevillian James Grundy in Henry T. Sampson, *Blacks in Blackface: A Source Book on Early Black Musical Shows* (Metuchen: Scarecrow, 1980) 372; and Sampson, *The Ghost Walks: A Chronological History of Blacks in Show Business, 1865–1910* (Metuchen: Scarecrow, 1988).

5. *Cake Walk* is described in American Film Institute, *The American Film Institute Catalog of Motion Pictures Produced in the United States: Film Beginnings, 1893–1910*, comp. Elias Savada (Metuchen: Scarecrow, 1995) 144 (hereafter cited as *Film Beginnings*).

6. Musser, *Edison* 174; Sampson, *Ghost* 70–71.

7. *Edison Films* no. 62, July 1901, qtd. in Musser, *Edison* 574.

8. *A Hard Wash* was among the first films exhibited by the Biograph Company in the fall of 1896. For a discussion of *A Hard Wash*, and the joke about getting the baby truly clean, see Charles Musser, *The Emergence of Cinema: The American Screen to 1907* (Berkeley: U of California P, 1990) 148–49. For a description of *A Morning Bath*, see Musser, *Edison* 250. While stills indicate that these films look extremely similar (same action, plain light-colored back-

ground), it seems that the mothers are dressed slightly differently, and *A Hard Wash* features a washtub with handles on the sides.

9. Audience reaction to *A Hard Wash* appears in the *Kansas City Star* 2 Dec. 1896, rpt. in Kemp Niver, *Biograph Bulletins, 1896–1908* (Los Angeles: Artisan, 1971) 20. The appeal of baby films is indicated in the catalogue description of Biograph's *When Babies Quarrel*: "Two very small babies playing; one steals all blocks, and the other cries." This film, *Children Feeding Ducklings*, and *Babies Playing on a Hot Day* are listed in the Biograph bulletin as "Children's Pictures," indicating their appeal to young audiences. This listing also includes a baby-washing film entitled *The Baby's Bath*, which reportedly shows "a fond mother giving her little girl baby her morning bath." This film, like the others listed, does not indicate the baby's race, suggesting to me that they treat white subjects. American Mutoscope & Biograph *Catalogue*, Spring 1902, rpt. in Niver, *Biograph Bulletins* 71.

10. The only exception I have seen is *Mammy's Child* (alt. title *Mammy's Chile*; Powers [or Crystal?], 1913), in which a white child actress wears blackface and a messy, woolly-haired wig in her portrayal of a pickaninny. An important exception to this general practice is the casting of white actresses (not always children) in the role of Topsy in various versions of *Uncle Tom's Cabin*.

11. *Lubin's Films* Jan. 1903: 36, in Charles Musser, Reese V. Jenkins, and Thomas E. Jeffery, eds., *A Guide to Motion Picture Catalogues by American Producers and Distributors, 1894–1908: A Microfilm Edition* (Frederick: U Publications of America, 1985); Musser, *Emergence* 331.

12. "Authentic" Black dance films (without much of a framing narrative) proliferated during the early years of film production, tapering off after 1904. Black baby-washing and watermelon-eating films decline after 1903.

13. This was a natural move for early filmmakers, not only because many early film entrepreneurs showed their films alongside live performance in vaudeville theaters but also because of other theatrical ties. For example, the prominent early film producer-exhibitor William Selig had a background in minstrel shows: "About 1894, this young man, who often indulged his fancy for parlor magic, took to the road, billing himself as 'Selig, Conjurer.' From this his act developed and expanded into a minstrel show attraction that also provided him with the appellation of 'Colonel.'" Kalton C. Lahue, ed., *Motion Picture Pioneer: The Selig Polyscope Company* (South Brunswick: Barnes, 1973) 11.

14. For instance, Sampson includes in this chapter descriptions of *Darktown Duel* (Vitagraph, 1912), *Laughing Ben* (American Mutoscope & Biograph, 1902), and *Ten Pickaninnies* (Edison, 1908) with a notation that they feature Black performers, as opposed to whites in blackface. Henry T. Sampson, *Blacks in Black and White: A Source Book on Black Films*, 2nd ed. (Metuchen: Scarecrow, 1995) 23–129.

15. "Edison Film: The Watermelon Patch," no. 268, 24 Oct. 1905, rpt. in Musser, Jenkins, and Jeffery, *Catalogues*.

16. When Fletcher recalls the kinds of roles Blacks would play in these films (under the direction of Edwin Porter), he does not describe them as

stereotypical: "There were no 'types,' just colored men, women and children." In addition to finding the Black performers, Fletcher doled out their pay: "At the end of each day, [William] Gilroy [Porter's assistant] would hand me the money to pay off. I am not quite sure, but I think it was three dollars a day for each of the people. Bailey and I got eight dollars each." Tom Fletcher, *100 Years of the Negro in Show Business: The Tom Fletcher Story* (New York: Burdge, 1954) 121–22, cited in Eileen Landay, *Black Film Stars* (New York: Drake, 1973) 13–14.

17. See Alison McMahan's discussion of the recently rediscovered *A Fool and His Money* (Solax, 1912) in *Alice Guy Blaché: Lost Visionary of the Cinema* (New York: Continuum, 2002). Lubin's stock company included seasoned vaudeville performers John (Junk) Edwards and Mattie Edwards, who appeared in *Coon Town Suffragettes* (1914), *Mandy's Chicken Dinner* (1914), *In Zululand* (1915), and other comedies. Sampson notes that although the Edwardses found steady film work, most Black performers had difficulty gaining film acting experience because they were limited to roles as extras, and because "most film producers employed black actors on an ad hoc basis with very few appearing in more than one film." Sampson, *Blacks in Black and White* 26–28.

18. For instance, Tom Gunning has pointed out to me that Black actors were not employed at the Biograph studio.

19. For instance, *Chicken Thieves* (Edison, June 1897) features actual Blacks in the title roles, whereas *Who Said Chicken?* (American Mutoscope & Biograph, 1900) uses a white actor in blackface.

20. Linda Williams, *Playing the Race Card: Melodramas of Black and White from Uncle Tom to O. J. Simpson* (Princeton: Princeton UP, 2001).

21. Although Black performers were frequently praised for their special abilities in comedy films, a review of Lubin's *Coon Town Suffragettes* (1914) notes with surprise that the film is "well acted, considering that the cast is made up of genuine colored people." *Moving Picture World* 21 Feb. 1914, qtd. in Sampson, *Blacks in Black and White* 52–53.

22. Sampson, *Blacks in Black and White* 26, 54–55. Sampson includes stills from the film illustrating the different modes of representation used for depicting the development of this Black female character.

23. *Biograph Bulletin* 143, 12 June 1907, rpt. in Niver, *Biograph Bulletins* 358.

24. This observation is based on my viewing of the film and others in the Paper Print Collection at the Library of Congress, Motion Picture, Broadcasting and Recorded Sound Division. An earlier light-skinned figure, a little boy, is featured in the dancing sequence in Edison's *The Watermelon Patch* (1905), discussed later in the chapter (see fig. 18).

25. See Thomas Cripps, *Slow Fade to Black: The Negro in American Film, 1900–1942* (Oxford: Oxford UP, 1977) 22; James R. Nesteby, *Black Images in American Films, 1896–1954: The Interplay between Civil Rights and Film Culture* (Washington: UP of America, 1982) 17; Peter Noble, *The Negro in Film* (London: Skelton Robinson, 1948) 28, 255. Although critics have noted that

Blacks are absent from the melting pot finale, it is notable that the film's Jewish characters are not included in the final shot either.

26. Susan Courtney, "Hollywood's Fantasy of Miscegenation," diss., U of California, Berkeley, 1997, 52.

27. *Biograph Bulletin* 94, Mar. 2, 1907, rpt. in Niver, *Biograph Bulletins* 290. The lack of textual references to light-skinned characters might suggest that a greater number of such characters may appear in (now lost) early films, but they are not identified as such in surviving publicity materials.

28. The use of "darkened down" makeup in this film reported in Phyllis R. Klotman, *Frame by Frame I: A Black Filmography* (1979; Bloomington: Indiana UP, 1997) 124–25. See also Noble 256.

29. *The Birth of a Nation* features this as well, when white characters disguised in blackface spy on Black renegades who are played by white actors (in blackface).

30. *Moving Picture World* 13 Apr. 1909, qtd. in Sampson, *Blacks in Black and White* 48.

31. *Moving Picture World* 7 Sept. 1912, qtd. in Sampson, *Blacks in Black and White* 72–73. The review also complains that "the photography is so-so."

32. Cripps 11. Daniel Leab, on the other hand, prefiguring most Black film scholars, suggests that there were no differences between preclassical and classical representations of Blackness: "By 1915, the story film of feature length was well-established. These changes in the American film industry, however, made little difference in the treatment of black characters." Daniel J. Leab, *From Sambo to Superspade: The Black Experience in Motion Pictures* (New York: Houghton, 1975) 11.

33. Musser, *Edison* 54–55: "Although Thomas Cripps in *Slow Fade to Black* sees these early films as relatively free of offensive stereotyping in their depiction of African Americans, the catalog descriptions help to show how racial prejudices were assumed and perpetuated. Cripps's assessment of entry no. 559, *Colored Troops Disembarking* ('black men with weapons in hand marched down a gangplank on their way to Cuba'), as affirming black dignity is contradicted by the catalog description which describes their behavior as 'laughable.' "

34. Films shot in Fort-de-France, Martinique, in September 1902 were taken when Edison cameramen were dispatched there to take "Genuine Pictures of the Ruined City of St. Pierre" after the eruption of Mount Pelee. A second group of Caribbean travelogues was shot during April 1903 "on the midwinter cruise of the S.S. 'Prinzessin Victoria Luise' of the Hamburg-American Line." This set of films *(Native Woman Washing a Negro Baby in Nassau, BI; Native Women Washing Clothes at St. Vincent, BWI; West Indian Girls in Native Dance; Native Women Coaling a Ship and Scrambling for Money [West Indies]; Native Women Coaling a Ship at St. Thomas, DWI; Wharf Scene and Natives Swimming at St. Thomas, DWI)* is extant at the Library of Congress, Motion Picture, Broadcasting and Recorded Sound Division.

35. For a detailed discussion of the production and reception of travelogue films, see Jennifer Peterson, "World Pictures: Travelogue Films and the Lure of the Exotic, 1890–1920," diss., U of Chicago, 1999.

36. Edison Manufacturing Co., *Catalogue*, Sept. 1902, qtd. in *Film Beginnings* 715.

37. E. Ann Kaplan, *Looking for the Other: Feminism, Film, and the Imperial Gaze* (New York: Routledge, 1997) 6.

38. For example, Tera Hunter describes the widespread association of African Americans and the spread of tuberculosis, which was attributed to poor hygiene. In a caricature Hunter cites from the *Atlanta Constitution*, a group of Blacks labeled "Your Washerwoman," "Your Butler," "Your Driver," "Your Cook," and so on, are gathered around the bedside of a Black TB patient in an ill-kept Black home. The item, published in 1914, was originally titled, "Can You Wonder It Spreads?" Tera Hunter, *To 'Joy My Freedom: Southern Black Women's Lives and Labors after the Civil War* (Cambridge: Harvard UP, 1997) 198.

39. Turn-of-the-century jokes about Black people and soap (Black desires to wash themselves white; contrast of dirty/Black/dark with clean/white/light) were reflected in numerous soap advertisements featuring Blacks, particularly Black babies and children. Marilyn Kern-Foxworth describes such advertisements in *Aunt Jemima, Uncle Ben, and Rastus: Blacks in Advertising, Yesterday, Today, and Tomorrow* (Westport: Greenwood, 1994) 31–33. One of the most popular turn-of-the-century American advertising campaigns featured the Gold Dust Twins, two African American children used for the marketing of Gold Dust washing powder. The Gold Dust Twins were created by Edward W. Kemble, a staff artist for the *Daily Graphic* (who in later years "literally created his own one-man Negro-stereotype industry, with dozens of racist illustrations for books and journals, including his 1896 'classic,' *Kemble's Coons*"). Richard J. Powell, *Black Art and Culture in the 20th Century* (London: Thames and Hudson, 1997) 25. The Gold Dust Twins were featured in various print ads, and in 1902 two Black children, David Henry Snipe and Thomas (last name unknown) were hired to portray them at a Chicago trade convention; they appeared as "live trademarks" in a large exhibit. Likenesses of "Goldie" and "Dustie" remained popular for decades (in magazines and on billboards, trade cards, and a variety of promotional items, including hand-held mirrors, thermometers, tin containers, calendars). Kern-Foxworth 46–48. In 1903, American Mutoscope & Biograph produced a promotional film, *The Gold Dust Twins* (extant at the Library of Congress, Motion Picture, Broadcasting and Recorded Sound Division), featuring the dark-skinned twins wearing only their trademark short (white) skirts, scouring a dishpan beneath the company's slogan: "Let the Gold Dust Twins Do Your Work."

40. Booker T. Washington, *Up from Slavery* in *Three Negro Classics* (1901; New York: Avon, 1965) 123. Washington did not originate this philosophy, but he perpetuated this important lesson he learned as a student at Hampton Institute.

41. Maguire & Baucus, *Edison Films,* 20 Jan. 1897, 4, qtd. in Musser, *Edison* 250.

42. American Mutoscope & Biograph Picture, *Catalogue,* Nov. 1902, qtd. in *Film Beginnings* 827.

43. This kind of representation would be echoed seven years later in footage shot at Tuskegee Institute, intended to show "people a thousand miles away just what the school is actually doing and what industrial education, as Booker T. Washington conceives it, means." In an article outlining plans to make the film, the producers announced that it would show students "at work in the fields, planting, plowing, milking, working in the dairy and building roads." "Moving Pictures of Tuskegee Institute," *Nickelodeon* 15 May 1910: 262 (thanks to Jennifer Peterson for this item). The film, *A Trip to Tuskegee* (financed by a group of Black businessmen from Boston), emphasized industrial over academic training per Washington's program of placing Black character building and economic uplift before social equality and intellectual pursuit. However, unlike the American Mutoscope & Biograph films shot at the Lincoln School, *A Trip to Tuskegee* was produced with both white and Black audiences in mind. In addition to being screened to white trustees and potential supporters (such as its exhibition at a meeting at Carnegie Hall), it was shown across the country in Black churches. See Lester Walton, "Moving Pictures of Tuskegee," *New York Age* 10 Jan. 1910: 6, cited in Griffiths and Latham 56. Though the dates of these articles may cause some confusion, the *Nickelodeon* piece reports on a meeting held several months earlier, in January 1910; the film seems to have been completed and exhibited by the time this planning meeting was reported.

44. Tom Gunning, " 'The Whole World within Reach': Travel Images without Borders," *Travel Culture: Essays on What Makes Us Go,* ed. Carol Traynor Williams (Westport: Praeger, 1998) 35.

45. George M. Fredrickson, *The Black Image in the White Mind: The Debate on Afro-American Character and Destiny, 1817–1914* (1971; Hanover: Wesleyan UP, 1987) 251.

46. *Biograph Bulletin* 39, 27 Dec. 1904, rpt. in Niver, *Biograph Bulletins* 143. The similarly violent punishment of black thieves in *A Nigger in the Woodpile* (American Mutoscope & Biograph, 1904) is described in the introduction and chapter 1.

47. For more on the complex cultural meanings of lynching and its representations (particularly in modern "realist" discourses as expressed in forms like literary realism, journalism, and photography), see Jacqueline Goldsby, *A Spectacular Secret: The Cultural Logic of Lynching in American Life and Literature* (Chicago: University of Chicago P, forthcoming).

48. *Biograph Bulletin* 39, 27 Dec. 1904, rpt. in Niver, *Biograph Bulletins* 142.

49. F. Z. Maguire & Co., *Catalogue* [Mar. 1898], 15–16, qtd. in Musser, Jenkins, and Jeffery, *Catalogues* 307.

50. These include films like *Up-to-Date Cakewalk* (Edison, 1898–99), *Bally-Hoo Cake Walk* (American Mutoscope & Biograph, 1901), and *Comedy Cake Walk* (American Mutoscope & Biograph, 1903).

51. "Edison Film: The Watermelon Patch."

52. Charles Musser notes that the idea of covering the Black characters with soot is one of its many racial "jokes": "This joke played with the 'childish' belief that black skin is black because it is covered with soot." Charles Musser, *Before the Nickelodeon: Edwin S. Porter and the Edison Manufacturing Company* (Berkeley: U of California P, 1991) 313. Also, in addition to the other jokes I describe later as being motivated by the spatial relation between the Blacks inside the cabin and the whites on the outside, Musser observes a cinematically "fascinating" juxtaposition, which perhaps reveals Porter's "unconscious racism": "the contrast between the exterior scenes in which the handful of rednecks dwarf the tiny shack and the interior scenes in which the shack comfortably holds twenty 'darkies'—reducing them to the size of pygmies" (313).

53. Constance Balides discusses films such as *What Happened on Twenty-third Street, New York City* (Edison, 1901), in which a woman's skirt is blown up by air from a vent in the sidewalk; *A Windy Day on the Roof* (American Mutoscope & Biograph, 1904), in which a man looks up a woman's skirt when it is lifted by the wind while she hangs laundry; and *The Gay Shoe Clerk* (Edison, 1903), in which a female shopper exposes her ankle (in close-up) to a male shoe salesman. See Constance Balides, "Scenarios of Exposure in the Practice of Everyday Life: Women in the Cinema of Attractions," *Screen* 34.1 (1993): 19–37.

54. Modern Black labor problems seem to have international relevance. In the Italian-produced film *Wanted: A Colored Servant* (Italia, 1908), a clerk is sent out to hire a Black servant, but when he places an advertisement, far too many applicants arrive for the job. Sampson describes the film's conclusion: "Pandemonium reigns supreme at the home of the 'proprietor,' and when the clerk returns he is promptly evicted and the waiting tribe of Africans set upon him." See Sampson, *Blacks in Black and White* 125; production company information from *Film Beginnings* 1156.

55. Such films include Griffith's *His Trust* and *His Trust Fulfilled* (Biograph, 1911), as well as *The Confederate Spy* (Kalem, 1910), *A Slave's Devotion* (Broncho, 1913), and *For His Master's Sake* (aka *For Massa's Sake*, Pathé, 1911), in which Uncle Joe sells himself and his family back into slavery to help pay off the gambling debts of his former master's son.

56. John Hope Franklin and Alfred A. Moss Jr., *From Slavery to Freedom: A History of African Americans*, 6th ed. (New York: McGraw, 1988) 279.

57. Typically, Black characters seem to be merely positioned as props or victims of jokes and gags, as in *Dixie Duo Down South* (1910) (cited with no production company data in Sampson, *Blacks in Black and White* 57), in which two white girls terrorize numerous Black characters with their mischievous behavior). In many other films, however, the Black figure plays a more am-

biguous role. We see this not only in *A Bucket of Cream Ale* but also in two of Edison's "Happy Hooligan" comedies. *In Hooligan at the Sea Shore* (1900), Hooligan tricks a stylish young "dude" into wearing his tattered rags. After a "colored servant girl" mistakes the dude for a tramp, she becomes involved in the film's raucous concluding water fight. In *Hooligan in Central Park* (1900), a "colored nurse" supervising two children secures the help of a policeman after Hooligan takes over a park bench by accosting the women sitting there. Both films described in Musser, *Edison* 626–27.

58. Miriam Hansen, *Babel and Babylon: Spectatorship in American Silent Film* (Cambridge: Harvard UP, 1991) 39; Judith Mayne, "Uncovering the Female Body," *Before Hollywood: Turn-of-the-Century Film from American Archives,* ed. Charles Musser and Jay Leyda (New York: American Federation of the Arts, 1987) 63–67.

59. Lynn Kirby, *Parallel Tracks: The Railroad and Silent Cinema* (Durham: Duke UP, 1997) 99.

60. Lauren Rabinovitz, *For the Love of Pleasure: Women, Movies, and Culture in Turn-of-the-Century Chicago* (New Brunswick: Rutgers UP, 1998) 85–87.

61. Hansen 39.

62. *Biograph Bulletin* 55, 27 Nov. 1905: 12, rpt. in Niver, *Biograph Bulletins* 202.

63. Eileen Bowser, "Racial/Racist Jokes in American Silent Slapstick Comedy," *Griffithania* 53 (1995): 41. Bowser provides a long list of films (produced between 1903 and 1924) in which white men mistake Black women for white women in their lustful pursuits.

64. Susan Courtney, "What Happened in the Tunnel and Other American Scenes," unpublished manuscript, 1999.

65. The dangers of collusion between Black and white women are also demonstrated in Lubin's comedy *Coon Town Suffragettes* (1914), in which Black women (led by washlady Mandy Jackson) ape white feminist thought and activities (e.g., temperance, gender equality) by raiding a gin mill and forcing their lazy husbands to work. These aggressive Black women subdue (stereotypically) not only their ineffectual husbands but the "coon town" police as well. The film uses Black women (the ridiculous notion of any sort of Black feminism) to mock white women's political organization. But it also suggests that alliances between white and Black women could result in a dangerous empowerment of those lowest on the social ladder. See descriptions in Sampson, *Blacks in Black and White* 52, and *Moving Picture World* 21 Feb. 1914.

66. I would also argue that the representation of Black women as willing participants in these interracial switches further masks any possibility of white male desire for Black women. In this way, these films help to deflect and disavow claims that white men, not Black men, used interracial rape as a tool of political terrorism, as claimed by activists like Ida B. Wells and artists like Oscar Micheaux (in the film *Within Our Gates* [1920], discussed in chapter 7),

who also sought to set the record straight about the practice of sexual violence, particularly in the South. By illustrating that Black women are the ones who instigate and/or knowingly participate in interracial kisses, and by characterizing them as inherently "unattractive" (fat, dark-skinned), these films insist that white men would never actively pursue Black women. Rather, any romantic or sexual interactions between Black women and white men would have to be initiated by the Black female.

67. Some significant deviations from the foregoing discussion of interracial kiss films can be seen in *Under the Old Apple Tree* (American Mutoscope & Biograph, 1907). The film is set in the front yard of a rural white home, marking the space more an extension of the intimate space of family residence than a public area. Still, tensions between public and private are evident in the way the film stages a constantly shifting set of interrupted interactions between lovers, and potential lovers, on a bench beneath the apple tree. In this film, when the elderly white suitor mistakenly makes a pass at his Black maid, several characters laugh, but his white love interest (the Widow Jones) does not. Unlike those films set in urban contexts and/or on trains, this film takes place in a space where the breach of traditional social and racial hierarchies is, at least superficially, less likely and less acceptable. See description in *Biograph Bulletin* 112, 4 Nov. 1907, rpt. in Niver, *Biograph Bulletins* 314.

68. Susan Courtney has argued that the surprising appearance of a Black baby in a white household functions as the logical (and more explicit) extension of the miscegenation threat posed in interracial kissing films: "We don't see interracial sexual contact as such, but its potential outcome." Courtney, "Hollywood's Fantasy," 38. See, for example, *How Charlie Lost the Heiress* (American Mutoscope & Biograph, 1903).

69. This plot is repeated in other films, including the Harold Lloyd comedy *Bashful* (1917), described in Bowser "Racial/Racist Jokes" 41.

70. According to Bowser, there are films in which Blacks are "whitened" (usually with flour). One such film is *Hallow-e'en in Coon-Town* (American Mutoscope, 1897).

71. Interesting twists on this theme occur when Blacks are the ones who blacken white characters out of vengeance (e.g., *The Colored Man's Revenge* [Pathé, 1907]). At least one film illustrates that blackening can occur not just on the outside but also on the inside. In *In Humanity's Cause* (1913), a white solider receives a transfusion from a Black man and becomes depraved as a result. Here we have a literalization of "mixed blood" so horrible that it requires that both the recipient and the donor die at the end of the film. Significantly, this is a dramatic film, which, unlike the comedies I have been describing under this category, contains a narrative, moral, and political point grounded in ideological structures rather than a humoristic effect.

72. Eric Lott, *Love and Theft: Blackface Minstrelsy and the American Working Class* (New York: Oxford UP, 1995) 124.

73. Clyde Taylor, "The Re-birth of the Aesthetic in Cinema," *The Birth of Whiteness: Race and the Emergence of U.S. Cinema*, ed. Daniel Bernardi (New

Brunswick: Rutgers UP, 1996) 26–27. In terms of the film's operations as a "farce comedy," Jeffery Alan Triggs notes that according to George Bernard Shaw, "the public's interest in farce was akin to its interest in 'the public flogging of a criminal,' and that farce appealed to 'the deliberate indulgence of that horrible, derisive joy in humiliation and suffering which is the beastliest element in human nature.'" This would seem to describe the appeal of the near lynching in *A Close Call,* in which the public "humiliation" of being mistaken for a Negro is posited as the film's primary comic element. Jeffery Alan Triggs, "Roughing It: The Role of Farce in the Little Rascals Comedies," *New Orleans Review* 16.3 (1989): 31.

74. For example, the film *Chicken Thieves* (Edison, 1897), featuring Black actors, is described as follows: "A capital picture, depicting an occupation commonly attributed to and sometimes proven against the *colored* race. . . . A *darkey* thief appears 'round the corner, carrying a tattered sack. . . . two foul are handed to him by a *black* confederate" (F. Z. Maguire & Co., *Catalogue* [Mar. 1898], 15–16, qtd. in Musser, Jenkins, and Jeffery, *Catalogues* 307). Ten years later, the comedy *The Wooing and Wedding of a Coon* (Selig, 1907), which features white actors in blackface, is advertised with a similar variety of black labels: "In *The Wooing and Wedding of a Coon* we present a comedy subject replete with humor. . . . The opening shows a *colored* nursemaid. . . . But the *dusky* belle is coy. . . . her father and mother, typical old *darkies* of before the war time" *(Selig Supplement* no. 70, Nov. 1907, rpt. in Musser, *Catalogues).* Other markers of "Blackness" that appear frequently in preclassical film discourse designate foreign Blacks (native, West Indian, Zulu [typically fictional]) and Black character types (Rastus, Sambo, Mammy) played by Blacks and whites.

75. *Moving Picture World* 7 Feb. 1913, qtd. in Sampson, *Blacks in Black and White* 91.

76. *Moving Picture World* 11 Jan. 1913, qtd. in Leab 17.

CHAPTER 3

1. "Negroes Laughing at Themselves," *Chicago Broad Ax*, 28 Sept. 1918: 4.

2. "Negroes Laughing" 4.

3. Black northern and urban migration increased dramatically around 1916, when World War I interrupted the flow of European immigrant labor to U.S. urban industrial centers, sending labor agents south to recruit Black workers. The promise of higher-paying jobs and liberation from repressive racial arrangements lured many southern Blacks across the Mason-Dixon Line. According to figures cited by Carole Marks, approximately 454,000 African Americans moved northward between 1910 and 1920. See Carole Marks, *Farewell—We're Good and Gone: The Great Black Migration* (Bloomington: Indiana UP, 1989) 2.

4. Manthia Diawara, "Black Spectatorship: Problems of Identification and Resistance," *Black American Cinema*, ed. Manthia Diawara (New York: Rout-

ledge, 1993) 211–20; James Snead, "Spectatorship and Capture in King Kong: The Guilty Look," in James Snead, *White Screens, Black Images: Hollywood from the Dark Side*, ed. Colin MacCabe and Cornel West (New York: Routledge, 1994) 1–27; bell hooks, "The Oppositional Gaze," *Black Looks: Race and Representation* (Boston: South End, 1992) 115–31. See also Miriam Thaggert, "Divided Images: Black Female Spectatorship and John Stahl's *Imitation of Life*," *African American Review* 32 (1998): 481–91.

5. Yuri Tsivian, *Early Cinema in Russia and Its Cultural Reception*, trans. Alan Bodger (1991; Chicago: U of Chicago P, 1998) 1–2.

6. For a discussion of *Native Son* as a migration narrative, see Lawrence R. Rodgers, *Canaan Bound: The African-American Great Migration Novel* (Urbana: U of Illinois P, 1997) 102; for a discussion of how *The Bluest Eye*, among other migration narratives, illustrates the politics of negotiating new urban rules, see Farah Jasmine Griffin, *"Who Set You Flowin'?": The African American Migration Narrative* (New York: Oxford UP, 1995) 102. Richard Wright describes his narrative approach in "How Bigger Was Born," introduction to *Native Son* (1940; New York: Harper Perennial, 1987) xxxii: "I wanted the reader to feel that Bigger's story was happening *now*, like a play upon the stage or a movie unfolding upon the screen. Action follows action, as in a prize fight. . . . I told of Bigger's life in close-up, slow-motion. . . . I had long had the feeling that this was the best way to 'enclose' the reader's mind in a new world, to blot out all reality except that which I was giving him."

7. Examples include Black spectatorship of live theater in Paul Lawrence Dunbar, *Sport of the Gods* (1903); of the spectacle of lynching in James Weldon Johnson, *The Autobiography of an Ex-Colored Man* (1912); of minstrel performance in Nella Larsen, *Quicksand* (1928); and of movies in Gwendolyn Brooks, *Maud Martha* (1953).

8. Toni Morrison, *The Bluest Eye* (New York: Holt, 1970) 97 (hereafter cited as *BE*).

9. On the effects of manipulative fantasies of cinematic romantic "love" on working-class women viewers, see Siegfried Kracauer, "The Little Shopgirls Go to the Movies," *The Mass Ornament: Weimar Essays*, ed. and trans. Thomas Y. Levin (Cambridge: Harvard UP, 1995).

10. Pauline's escapist fantasy world in the movies echoes the fall of her own daughter, Pecola, into a delusional state triggered by her desire to have blue eyes so that she will be noticed and valued in a world that renders Black girls invisible.

11. Richard Wright, *Native Son* (1940; New York: Harper Perennial, 1987) 30 (hereafter cited as *NS*).

12. Bigger and Jack "fell silent abruptly" when the film reached its climax, in which the leading lady's millionaire husband rushes into the nightclub where she is sitting with her boyfriend. " 'What do you reckon he wants?' Bigger asked, as though he himself was outraged at the sight of the frenzied intruder. 'Damn if I know,' Jack muttered preoccupiedly" (*NS* 34).

13. Snead 23.

14. In an extreme example, Chicago-born dancer and actress Jeni LeGon (who appeared in numerous Hollywood and race films during the 1930s and 1940s) regularly patronized the Regal's mixed programs as a child. But unlike Bigger Thomas, she was interested in the live dance acts, not the films. She watched the specialty dance performances during each of their segments, then during the motion picture portions of the program she went into the lobby to practice and refine the dance steps she had observed. Interview by Yvonne Welbon and the author, 1 Mar. 2000.

15. Jacqueline Bobo, *Black Women as Cultural Readers* (New York: Columbia UP, 1995) 3. Bobo's observations about Black spectatorship are unique because her findings are based on empirical methods of research. She observes the responses of focus groups of Black women with whom she organized screenings and discussions, and interviews. Although Bobo is able to carefully track these spectators' variable perspectives in relation to the films they viewed, she does not fully account for how the specific circumstances of the viewing situation (movie theater versus arranged screening; within a "general audience" versus a small group of Black women) might affect spectatorial responses. And, although Bobo insists that spectatorship is a negotiated practice, she is most interested in its "oppositional" rather than its "complicit" moments. When she reads Black women's spectatorial practices as stemming from an "oppositional impulse that has fueled Black women's history of resistance," she suggests, much like Diawara and hooks, that Black spectatorship can only be reconciled politically if Black viewers disavow false, incongruous film images. Bobo, 92.

16. Michele Wallace, "Race, Gender and Psychoanalysis in Forties Film: *Lost Boundaries, Home of the Brave,* and *The Quiet One*," *Black American Cinema*, ed. Manthia Diawara (New York: Routledge, 1993) 264. Wallace's reference to the "bisexual" possibilities of spectatorship points to significant revisions of Laura Mulvey's rigid formulation of how spectator positioning and cinematic visual pleasure are structured by gender. According to Judith Mayne, these "recent explorations of alternative models of spectatorship have moved away from Lacan, and toward Freud, and in particular toward the postulation of bisexuality, of the vacillation between masculine and feminine positions as a key component in sexual identity. . . . In cinematic terms, this would suggest that cinematic identification is never masculine or feminine, but rather a movement between the two." Judith Mayne, *Cinema and Spectatorship* (London: Routledge, 1993) 71. Explorations of spectatorial transvestism, bisexuality, or sexual ambiguity include Mulvey's "Afterthoughts on 'Visual Pleasure and Narrative Cinema' Inspired by *Duel in the Sun*," *Framework* 15–17 (1981): 12–15; Miriam Hansen on female spectatorship of the films of Rudolph Valentino in *Babel and Babylon: Spectatorship in American Silent Film* (Cambridge: Harvard UP, 1991), especially chs. 11 and 12; and David Rodowick, "The Difficulty of Difference," *Wide Angle* 6.3 (1984): 16–23.

17. Turning away from the usual emphasis on dominant Hollywood cinema and the ways it speaks primarily to white audiences, Reid looks at "black-

oriented" films produced with significant Black creative control. Reid suggests that African American comedies, family films, and action films allow for a range of reading strategies on the part of an interracial audience. His Bakhtinian notion of "polyphonic" spectatorship proposes that viewers can read the problems and possibilities of different genres and modes of production (i.e., racism in studio-distributed comedies, sexism and homophobia in Black "independent" action films). Mark Reid, *Redefining Black Film* (Berkeley: U of California P, 1993) 41–42.

18. Hansen 7. See also Elizabeth Alexander's discussion of how moments of collective Black looking, particularly at public displays of violence against Black bodies (e.g., the whipping of slaves, the mutilated body of Emmett Till, the police beating of Rodney King), produce a sense of shared racial history, memory, and identity. Elizabeth Alexander, "Can You Be BLACK and Look at This? Reading the Rodney King Video(s)," *Public Culture* 7 (1994): 77–94.

19. My formulation of reconstructive spectatorship owes much to the work of Hazel V. Carby (*Reconstructing Womanhood: The Emergence of the Afro-American Woman Novelist* [Oxford: Oxford UP, 1987]); and Henry Louis Gates Jr. ("The Trope of a New Negro and the Reconstruction of the Image of the Black," *Representations* 24 [1988]: 129–55), who, in different ways, have addressed the challenges African Americans faced when they attempted to enter into public discourses at the turn of the twentieth century. Both critics describe the problems and contradictions inherent in African Americans' efforts to "establish a public presence" (Carby 6) and to put forth a new "public face of the race" (Gates 132). What is significant about both accounts is that they demonstrate that Black efforts to refute racist dominant discourses were designed not only to change the Black image in the white mind but also to reformulate the Race's image of itself. While Carby and Gates describe how African Americans staged their reconstructive interventions in the realm of literary production, I am interested in how African Americans continued the reconstructive process in their activities as audiences and consumers, particularly with reference to mass culture, at this historical moment.

20. James R. Grossman, *Land of Hope: Chicago, Black Southerners, and the Great Migration* (Chicago: U of Chicago P, 1989) 4.

21. The class structure in the Black Belt was not organized solely by levels of income or occupation, since only a small percentage of the population consisted of Black professionals or Blacks with accumulated wealth. Rather, class stratification was based on factors such as educational level, stability of income, length of residence in the city, membership in particular organizations and churches, and leisure habits. Grossman 128–32, 153. In her study of Black women's clubs in turn-of-the-century Chicago, Anne Meis Knupfer examines class difference in the African American community by using a "Weberian stratification model" which "fleshes out social class positioning to include the concepts of privilege, status, and prestige, particularly in terms of group legitimacy." Anne Meis Knupfer, *Toward a Tenderer Humanity and a Nobler Womanhood: African American Women's Clubs in Turn-of-the-Century Chicago*

(New York: New York UP, 1996) 4. Factors like skin color and hair texture also played a major role in the stratification of classes within the African American community, as many members of the Black "elite" were not immediately recognizable as "Black" in appearance.

22. Grossman 145–47. Such "uplift" strategies were common in industrial centers/migrant destinations across the North.

23. Betsey Lane, "War Declared on Aprons and Caps in Street Cars," *Chicago Defender* 25 May 1918: 12. The public spaces Lane cites are significant here, revealing views about gender and class that were held by many members of Chicago's Black elite. Lane explicitly describes what is inappropriate dress and behavior for female shoppers and theatergoers with a clear understanding that women consumers in these venues are as much a part of the spectacle of urban consumption as the items/shows being sold. Lane's article—placed on the women's page—is addressed primarily to women, both to instruct working-class women and to provide a guide for middle-class women who can uplift by their example. For more on the politics of respectability (and the policing of Black female public behavior and sexuality), see Hazel Carby, "Policing the Black Woman's Body in an Urban Context," *Critical Inquiry* 18 (1992): 738–55. For a discussion of race uplift-inflected discourses on "appropriate behavior" in Black movie theaters during this period, see Pearl Bowser and Louise Spence, *Writing Himself into History: Oscar Micheaux, His Silent Films, and His Audiences* (New Brunswick: Rutgers UP, 2000) 83–84.

24. Grossman 99; Chicago Commission on Race Relations, *The Negro in Chicago: A Study of Race Relations and a Race Riot* (Chicago: U of Chicago P, 1922) 301–3 (hereafter cited as *NC*). The significance of the streetcar as a stage for Black urban performance is also illustrated in *Daughters of the Dust*, in a scene in which Viola Peazant, who has established herself in the urban North, instructs her migrating young female relatives in proper streetcar deportment.

25. "Negroes Laughing" 4.

26. The following year, William Foster (Chicago's pioneering Black filmmaker and entertainment columnist) similarly mobilized the metaphor of being recorded by a moving picture camera in an effort to prescribe race uplift through respectable public behavior: "Let every one so live and conduct himself as if he were to be caught on a 'close-up' or a 'long shot' he will be so acting and living that he will help the race he represents." Juli Jones Jr. (nom de plume for William Foster), *Half-Century Magazine* June 1919, qtd. in Bowser and Spence 109.

27. See *NC* 97–103. LeRoi Jones (Amiri Baraka) notes the uncomfortable and dangerous racial arrangements that limited Black enjoyment of leisure activities—specifically moviegoing—in the repressive South when he writes that some migrants, "like my father, left [the South] very suddenly after unfortunate altercations with white ushers in movies." LeRoi Jones, *Blues People: Negro Music in White America* (New York: Morrow, 1963) 96.

28. See Lizabeth Cohen, *Making a New Deal: Industrial Workers in Chicago, 1919–1939* (Cambridge: Cambridge UP, 1990); Kathy Peiss, *Cheap*

*Amusements: Working Women and Leisure in Turn-of-the-Century New York* (Philadelphia: Temple UP, 1986); Roy Rosenzweig, *Eight Hours for What We Will: Workers and Leisure in an Industrial City, 1870–1920* (Cambridge: Cambridge UP, 1983).

29. On the major role of jazz and blues musical accompaniment in Black Belt theaters, see Mary Carbine's extraordinary study, " 'The Finest outside the Loop': Motion Picture Exhibition in Chicago's Black Metropolis, 1905–1928," *Camera Obscura* 23 (1990): 9–41.

30. The notion of flânerie, moving through urban space with a wandering gaze, was developed in Walter Benjamin's study of nineteenth-century Parisian arcades, inspired by the writings of Charles Baudelaire. Many scholars have extrapolated from Benjamin's use of the flâneur as the quintessential figure of distracted modern subjectivity. As Vanessa R. Schwartz has observed, the term "flânerie" is referenced so frequently in work on film spectatorship that it "has begun to be used as a shorthand for describing the new, mobilized gaze of the precinematic spectator." Vanessa R. Schwartz, "Cinema Spectatorship before the Apparatus: The Public Taste for Reality in Fin-de-Siècle Paris," *Viewing Positions: Ways of Seeing Film,* ed. Linda Williams (New Brunswick: Rutgers UP, 1994) 88. Key works informing my understanding of flânerie include Susan Buck-Morss, *The Dialectics of Seeing: Walter Benjamin and the Arcades Project* (Cambridge: MIT P, 1989); and Miriam Hansen, "Benjamin, Cinema and Experience: 'The Blue Flower in the Land of Technology,' " *New German Critique* 40 (1987): 179–224. For descriptions of the flâneur in relation to the surrealist practice of arbitrary spectatorship, see Tsivian 40 ("boredom" quotation); and Giuliana Bruno, *Streetwalking on a Ruined Map: Cultural Theory and the City Films of Elvira Notari* (Princeton: Princeton UP, 1993) 56.

31. Though numerous scholars have reflected on the flâneur's legacy as a privileged bourgeois and male subject, few have explored the question of his racial identity, or the possibilities and limits of flânerie for nonwhite subjects. The path toward such an investigation may begin in works by scholars who describe the existence, activities, and social meaning of the (white) female counterpart of the flâneur, the flâneuse (discussed briefly in the next chapter). See Janet Wolff, "The Invisible Flâneuse: Women and the Literature of Modernity," *Theory, Culture and Society* 2.7 (1985): 37–46; Susan Buck-Morss, "The Flaneur, the Sandwichman and the Whore: The Politics of Loitering," *New German Critique* 39 (1986): 99–140; Anne Friedberg, "Les Flâneuses du Mal(l): Cinema and the Postmodern Condition," *Viewing Positions: Ways of Seeing Film,* ed. Linda Williams (New Brunswick: Rutgers UP, 1994) 59–83; and Bruno 49–53. See also Houston Baker's discussion of Booker T. Washington's conservative rejection of the notion of Black flânerie (and the insurgent mobility it might evoke) in *Turning South Again: Re-thinking Modernism/Re-reading Booker T.* (Durham: Duke UP, 2001) 60–63.

32. Bruno 56.

33. This arrested trajectory recalls bell hooks's observation that many Black women "stop looking" at films altogether, an act of "turning away [as]

one way to protest, to reject negation" (hooks 121). This act is at once defiant and defeatist. It demonstrates Black women's refusal to accept their cinematic negation (much like the "oppositional gaze"), but it also replicates the Black woman's absence from and marginalization within the screen and the social space of the cinema—the Black woman does not assert her physical presence as a challenge to these practices.

34. Chris Looby, "Bigger Thomas Goes to the Movies," Mass Culture Workshop, University of Chicago, 21 Oct. 1994). Prior to going to the Regal, Bigger considers a few ways in which he might kill time before the robbery, including physical activities like running or having sex with his girlfriend, Bessie, and consuming other forms of mass culture, such as listening to swing music or reading a detective magazine. Bigger's selection of the movies and his masturbatory prelude to the film screening recall Barthes: "One goes to the movies as a response to idleness, leisure, free time. . . . Vacancy, inoccupation, lethargy; it is not in front of the film that one dreams—it is without knowing it, even before one becomes a spectator." Roland Barthes, "Leaving the Movie Theater," *The Rustle of Language* (New York: Hill, 1986) 345, qtd. in Bruno 47.

35. Gates 133.

36. *NC* 303–4; Grossman 154.

37. *NC* 232–34. This act was amended several times (in 1903 and 1911) to add greater specificity to the definition of "public accommodations."

38. *NC* 318.

39. Kristin Thompson, "The Formulation of the Classical Narrative," in David Bordwell, Janet Staiger, and Kristin Thompson, *The Classical Hollywood Cinema: Film Style and Mode of Production to 1960* (New York: Columbia UP, 1985) 174. For more on the relationships between industrial shifts in the production, distribution, and exhibition of films and the transition to the set of film-viewer relations that came to be associated with classical narrative style and modes of representation and address, see Ben Brewster, "A Scene at the 'Movies,'" *Early Cinema: Space, Frame, Narrative*, ed. Thomas Elsaesser (London: BFI, 1990) 318–25; Charles Musser, "The Nickelodeon Era Begins: Establishing the Framework for Hollywood's Mode of Representation," also in *Early Cinema: Space, Frame, Narrative* 256–73; and Tom Gunning's account of the transition from the "cinema of attractions" to a "cinema of narrative integration" in, among other places, *D. W. Griffith and the Origins of American Narrative Film: The Early Years at Biograph* (Urbana: U of Illinois P, 1991).

40. Hansen 79.

41. "By 1917, the [classical] system was complete in its basic narrative and stylistic premises" (Thompson 157). Classical styles did not completely replace older ones at this time, but the classical paradigm became the predominant stylistic option.

42. Lillian Gish reports that Griffith saw film as "the universal language that had been predicted in the Bible, which was to make all men brothers because they would understand each other. This could end wars and bring about

the millennium." Quoted from *Dorothy and Lillian Gish* (New York: Scribner's, 1973) in Hansen 77.

43. Noel Burch, "A Primitive Mode of Representation," *Early Cinema: Space, Frame, Narrative*, ed. Thomas Elsaesser (London: BFI, 1990) 220–21; Tom Gunning, "The Cinema of Attractions: Early Film, Its Spectator and the Avant-Garde," also in *Early Cinema: Space, Frame, Narrative* 57.

44. White anxieties about Black spectatorial empowerment and interracial viewing are evidenced by efforts by local and state authorities across the nation to suppress screenings of the Johnson-Jeffries fight film (1910), in which outspoken African American boxer Jack Johnson defeated the Great White Hope, Jim Jeffries. Hansen notes that a cartoon inspired by the Johnson-Jeffries fight appeared in *Moving Picture World* 7.8 (20 Aug. 1910: 403), illustrating "a mixed audience of middle-class blacks having a good time and middle-class whites obviously resenting just that; the caption: 'There's a reason'" (i.e., for segregation). See Hansen 311. For a fuller discussion of the contested circulation of Johnson films, see Dan Streible, "Race and the Reception of Jack Johnson Fight Films," *The Birth of Whiteness: Race and the Emergence of U.S. Cinema*, ed. Daniel Bernardi (New Brunswick: Rutgers UP, 1996) 170–200.

45. These stars are repeatedly mentioned in the *Chicago Defender* entertainment pages, in articles titled simply by the actors' names. Bara's appearances in films showing in two Black Belt theaters during the same week *(Romeo and Juliet* and *Carmen)* are mentioned in items on "The States" and "The Star," 30 Dec. 1916. Other *Defender* articles make special mention of the films of Clara Kimball Young, Annette Kellerman, Tom Mix, and Sessue Hayakawa.

46. Wallace 264.

47. "Movie Gleanings," *Chicago Defender* 9 Sept. 1916.

48. Noble Johnson made his first film appearance in Lubin's *The Eagle's Nest* in 1909. Dubbed "The Ebony Francis Bushman" by the Black press, the handsome and imposing Johnson (6'2", 225 pounds) went on to appear in more than fifty Hollywood films over the course of his career. His credits include D. W. Griffith's *Intolerance* (1916, as a chariot driver); the Universal serials *The Red Ace* (1917–18) and *The Bull's Eye* (1918); as well as *The Four Horsemen of the Apocalypse* (1921); *The Ten Commandments* (1923, as the bronze man); *Topsy and Eva* (1927, as Uncle Tom); *Moby Dick* (1930, as Queequeg); *King Kong* (1933, as the jungle chief); and *She Wore a Yellow Ribbon* (1949). Flyers and typescripts in the George P. Johnson Negro Film Collection, Department of Special Collections, Charles E. Young Research Library, University of California at Los Angeles; Henry T. Sampson, *Blacks in Black and White: A Source Book on Black Films*, 2nd ed. (Metuchen: Scarecrow, 1995) 529–33; Thomas Cripps, *Slow Fade to Black: The Negro in American Film, 1900–1942* (Oxford: Oxford UP, 1977) 130; Ephraim Katz, *The Film Encyclopedia*, 2nd ed. (New York: Harper, 1994) 704.

CHAPTER 4

1. Thomas Cripps, *Slow Fade to Black: The Negro in American Film, 1900–1942* (New York: Oxford UP, 1977) 11. Gregory Waller opens his chapter on Black moviegoing in Lexington, Kentucky, with a similar observation, but with a different set of explanations, made by an "unnamed showman" in a 1907 issue of *Moving Picture World:* "Strange thing that moving pictures do not appeal to the masses of negroes. . . . [T]he average negro wants to see a show with an abundance of noise, something like a plantation minstrel, with lots of singing and dancing and horseplay. He doesn't seem to grasp the idea of moving pictures." This observation lends support for Rick Altman's suggestion that early film exhibition did not always include musical accompaniment ("The Silence of the Silents," *Musical Quarterly* 80 [1997]: 648–718). Still, this white showman's sense that Blacks cannot "grasp" silent moving pictures (as opposed to musical minstrel performance) does not account for the ways in which live performances between films and frequent scenes of "dancing and horseplay" in early films (i.e., dance films, slapstick comedies) might have bridged these different types of shows for early viewers, Black or otherwise. The showman goes on to point out that "the persons in the pictures are white," and "when a negro goes to a show it pleases him to see black faces in the performance. But no pictures are made with Senegambian faces." In addition to the questions Waller raises regarding the intent and implications of these comments, I would add that the showman's observations seem quite erroneous, since Black audiences routinely consumed media featuring no Black subjects (as discussed in chapter 3), and given the fact that many films produced prior to 1907 feature "black faces"—not just whites in blackface, but also actual Black subjects and actors (as discussed in chapters 1 and 2). *Moving Picture World* 1, no. 14 (8 June 1907): 216–17, qtd. in Gregory Waller, *Main Street Amusements: Movies and Commercial Entertainment in a Southern City, 1896–1930* (Washington: Smithsonian Institution P, 1995) 161.

2. Everett writes: "The earliest news of, and commentary on, the cinema in the black press that I have located dates back to 1909 editions of both the *Baltimore Afro-American Ledger,* and *The New York Age.* . . . [I]t appears that racial segregation governing the public sphere . . . militated against the widespread access of African American audiences to the new medium at its founding." Anna Everett, *Returning the Gaze: A Genealogy of Black Film Criticism, 1909–1949* (Durham: Duke UP, 2001) 51–52.

3. Julie Ann Lindstrom, " 'Getting a Hold Deeper in the Life of the City': Chicago Nickelodeons, 1905–1914," diss., Northwestern U, 1998, 254–56. Lindstrom notes that the intersection of Thirty-first and State Streets, the heart of Chicago's African American community and a major transportation transfer point, "had one of the biggest clusters of nickelodeons on the south side." Although many of the theaters in this area "were not exclusively

African-American in their patronage," several advertised in Chicago's leading Black newspaper, the *Defender*.

4. *Washington Bee* 9 July 1910: 4, qtd. in Dan Streible, "The Harlem Theatre: Black Film Exhibition in Austin, Texas, 1920–1973," *Black American Cinema*, ed. Manthia Diawara (New York: Routledge, 1993) 222.

5. Barbara Stones, *America Goes to the Movies: 100 Years of Motion Picture Exhibition* (North Hollywood: National Association of Theatre Owners, 1993) 20; Gregory Waller cites entertainment writer Juli Jones (pseudonym used by theatrical agent and pioneer Black filmmaker William Foster), who estimated that "there were 112 'colored' theaters in the United States in 1909, with those outside major cities being mostly 'five and ten cent theaters, vaudeville and moving pictures.'" *Indianapolis Freeman* 13 Mar. 1909: 5, qtd. in Waller 162. Four years later, Foster reported that there were 214 theaters owned by Blacks serving a Black clientele. *Moving Picture World* 25 Oct. 1913: 363, qtd. in Eileen Bowser, *The Transformation of Cinema: 1907–1915* (Berkeley: U of California P, 1990) 10.

6. Streible, "Harlem Theatre" 221–36; Waller, esp. 161–79; Robert C. Allen and Douglas Gomery, *Film History: Theory and Practice* (New York: Knopf, 1985) 205–7; Matthew Bernstein and Dana White's major research project, "Segregated Cinema in a Southern City: Atlanta 1895–1996," has generated many illuminating articles and papers, including "Theater Location and Community Building: A Geography of Racial Entrepreneurship and Urban Development in Black Atlanta, 1914–1936," Orphans of the Storm II: Documenting the 20th Century, A Symposium on Film Preservation, University of South Carolina, 30 Mar. 2001; Alison Griffiths and James Latham, "Film and Ethnic Identity in Harlem, 1896–1915," *American Movie Audiences: From the Turn of the Century to the Early Sound Era*, ed. Melvyn Stokes and Richard Maltby (London: BFI, 1999) 46–63; Mary Carbine, "'The Finest outside the Loop': Motion Picture Exhibition in Chicago's Black Metropolis, 1905–1928," *Camera Obscura* 23 (1990): 9–41. For a comparative discussion of film exhibition to Black audiences in specific locations across the country from the silent period through the 1980s, see Douglas Gomery, *Shared Pleasures: A History of Movie Presentation in the United States* (Madison: U of Wisconsin P, 1992) 155–70.

7. Waller 165.

8. I discuss the perceived dangers of the nickel movie theater, particularly its reputation as "a recruiting station for vice," in more detail in the next chapter.

9. Lauren Rabinovitz, *For the Love of Pleasure: Women, Movies and Culture in Turn-of-the-Century Chicago* (New Brunswick: Rutgers UP, 1998) 50.

10. Rabinovitz 48.

11. Historians disagree as to whether or not Edison's kinetoscope was actually featured at the fair. See Rabinovitz 192–93n1; and Charles Musser, *Before the Nickelodeon: Edwin S. Porter and the Edison Manufacturing Company* (Berkeley: U of California P, 1991) 498–99n15.

12. Robert W. Rydell, *All the World's a Fair: Visions of Empire at American International Expositions, 1876–1916* (Chicago: U of Chicago P, 1984) 67. Rydell's chapter 2 explores quite broadly the racial dynamics of the World's Columbian Exposition.

13. Ida B. Wells and Frederick Douglass, "The Reason Why the Colored American Is Not in the World's Columbian Exposition," *Selected Works of Ida B. Wells-Barnett,* ed. Trudier Harris (New York: Oxford UP, 1991) 46–137. Wells and Douglass collaborated on this project after having taken different sides on the issue of Black participation in the fair, echoing a larger rift within the Black community. Wells objected to the lack of formal Black input and called for a boycott of the exposition. Douglass, who participated in the fair as the delegate from Haiti (he was U.S. minister to Haiti at the time), thought it best to take advantage of any opportunity for Black involvement. Douglass's stirring speech, "The Race Problem in America," delivered at the fair, convinced Wells that Black participation was crucial on this international stage. Robert W. Rydell, "A Cultural Frankenstein? The Chicago World's Columbian Exposition of 1893," *Grand Illusions: Chicago's World's Fair of 1893* (Chicago: Chicago Historical Society, 1993) 145–48; Ida B. Wells, *Crusade for Justice: The Autobiography of Ida B. Wells,* ed. Alfreda M. Duster (Chicago: U of Chicago P, 1970) 118–19.

14. Wells 115–22.

15. St. Clair Drake and Horace R. Cayton, *Black Metropolis: A Study of Negro Life in a Northern City* (1945; Chicago: U of Chicago P, 1993) 51. Binga's attendance at the fair is noted in Ernest R. Rather, comp. and ed., *Chicago Negro Almanac and Reference Book* (Chicago: Chicago Negro Almanac, 1972) 51; Anderson and Abbott are described in James R. Grossman, *Land of Hope: Chicago, Black Southerners, and the Great Migration* (Chicago: U of Chicago P, 1989) 130.

16. Wells 116, 118–19; Allan H. Spear, *Black Chicago: The Making of a Negro Ghetto, 1890–1920* (Chicago: U of Chicago P, 1967) 52.

17. Rydell, *All the World's a Fair* 53.

18. Drake and Cayton 47, 49.

19. Drake and Cayton 48. They describe the *Conservator* as the mouthpiece of the "small Negro business and professional class," 47. For further discussion of the *Conservator,* see Ralph Nelson Davis, "The Negro Newspaper in Chicago," M.A. thesis, U of Chicago, 1939.

20. Spear 11. Census reports from Spear 12.

21. Drake and Cayton 53.

22. Spear 29; Drake and Cayton 49.

23. Spear explores these differences in Black leadership at length in chapters 2 and 3, 51–89.

24. In addition to opposing the "Colored American Day" at the World's Fair, many elite Black leaders opposed other instances of what they saw as self-segregation, including a kindergarten for Negro children, and even the establishment of Provident Hospital, a facility open to Black patients, doctors, and

nursing students, who were routinely turned away by other Chicago hospitals. Spear 52–53. Dr. Daniel Hale Williams cofounded Provident Hospital (first located at Twenty-ninth and Dearborn and later at Thirty-sixth and Dearborn), a model of how members of this elite group secured resources from Black and white (Philip Armour, Marshall Field, George Pullman) sources, creating interracial institutions to address Black community needs.

25. Spear 71.

26. Spear 72–82.

27. African Americans lived in other areas of Chicago as well, such as Morgan Park, Hyde Park, and Evanston. Still, compared with cities like Cleveland, Philadelphia, and Boston, the rigidly segregated Black Belt in Chicago formed quite early: "Only Chicago had a sharply defined black belt before 1900." Kenneth L. Kusmer, "The Black Urban Experience in American History," *The State of Afro-American History: Past, Present and Future,* ed. Darlene Clark Hine (Baton Rouge: Louisiana State UP, 1986) 109.

28. Spear 91.

29. Spear 94–95.

30. Spear 107–8. Other exclusive clubs included the Manasseh Society for interracial couples. Spear notes that eventually some of the services lodges provided, such as insurance, were taken over by commercial enterprises.

31. For example, the Appomattox Club, which had a clubhouse at 3441 S. Wabash, hosted an anniversary party for Mr. and Mrs. John T. Morton. The front-page *Defender* write-up of the event described the party's decor ("cut flowers, fern and palm") and listed those in attendance, along with the gifts they brought (e.g., "Mr. & Mrs. B. F. Moseley, silver bread tray"; "Mrs. M. C. Cowan, china asparagus dish"). "Mr. and Mrs. John T. Morton," *Defender* 4 June 1910.

32. Grossman 131.

33. *Defender* 18 May 1912. A contact address for the Chautauqua is listed at 3125 S. State.

34. "The Negro Fellowship League," *Chicago Defender* 11 June 1910: 1.

35. "Stereopticon Exhibition, Free," *Chicago Defender* 17 Feb. 1912. Charles Musser points out that among white institutions, these kinds of illustrated lectures were embraced by two cultural groups—those with refined, genteel sensibilities who sponsored "middle-brow cultural events," and church-based groups seeking to provide alternative cultural events to corrupting amusements. In many ways, the uplift project of Black settlements like the Negro Fellowship League represents an amalgam of these groups. Charles Musser, *The Emergence of Cinema: The American Screen to 1907* (Berkeley: U of California P, 1990) 41–42.

36. *Rhea's New Citizen's Directory of Chicago, Ill. and Suburban Towns* (Chicago: McCleland, 1908) n.p.

37. Spear reports that "notices of activities at the Chateau de la Plaisance appeared weekly in the *Broad Ax* from 1907 through 1910." Spear 117. Appearances by Mrs. Washington, Williams, and the Leland Giants mentioned in the "personals" column, *Chicago Defender,* 31 July 1909.

38. Spear 117.

39. *Rhea's Directory* n.p.

40. "Amusement Notes," *Broad Ax* 13 Oct. 1900: 4.

41. On occasion, both the *Defender* and the *Broad Ax* ran generic stories about the film industry. One of the *Defender's* earliest surviving mentions of moving pictures is a front-page item describing Thomas Edison's development and demonstration of a "talking pictures" process ("Talking Pictures," *Chicago Defender* 1 Oct. 1910: 1). In 1915, the *Broad Ax* announced the production of *The White Terror,* an educational drama coproduced by the Universal Film Company and the National Tuberculosis Association about the dangers of TB ("The White Terror, a Movie with Punch and Purpose," *Broad Ax* 12 June 1915: 1). Later that year, the *Broad Ax* ran a small item noting the exponential growth of the film production industry, now "rated as the fifth largest industry of the United States," and describing a new projector that can run three mounted reels of film successively ("Three Reels," *Broad Ax* 28 Aug. 1915). Items like these are most likely prewritten by press agents.

42. Sylvester Russell, "Negro Yiddish Theaters and Other Notes," *Defender* 9 Apr. 1910: 6.

43. Russell, "Negro Yiddish" 6. Even in his discussion of Jewish theaters, Russell is more interested in the qualities of Jewish live performance than the films that are shown: "The Yiddish actors are splendid performers and very good-looking people with enviable masses of black, curly hair. They are always good singers and nimble dancers and nearer like the colored people than any other race of white actors."

44. Moya Luckett, "Cities and Spectators: A Historical Analysis of Film Audiences in Chicago, 1910–1915," diss., U of Wisconsin, Madison, 1995, 4.

45. Minnie Adams, "Musical and Dramatic," *Defender* 17 Feb. 1912.

46. Minnie Adams, "Musical and Dramatic," *Defender* 16 Mar. 1912.

47. Minnie Adams, "Musical and Dramatic," *Defender* 27 Jan. 1912, and "Musical and Dramatic," *Defender* 13 Apr. 1912. Adams's review of "East Lynee" (probably the popular melodrama *East Lynne*) describes one scene in the film—"the depicting of a train disaster was gruesome, but wonderful"— and is the most detailed of her film reviews I could locate. Adams's writings focused on the Grand and Monogram Theaters, both of which advertised that they regularly screened moving pictures. Her later reviews of the Pekin Theatre emphasize live performance as well.

This version of *East Lynne* is not the Fox version starring Theda Bara (1916); it may be one of two earlier productions, one by Selig Polyscope or another by Vitagraph, both originally released in June 1908. American Film Institute, *The American Film Institute Catalog of Motion Pictures Produced in the United States: Film Beginnings, 1893–1910,* comp. Elias Savada (Metuchen: Scarecrow, 1995) 295.

48. Everett 44.

49. Foster's productions are celebrated in "The States Theater," *Defender* 9 Aug. 1913 (describing *The Railroad Porter*) and "The States," *Defender* 18 Oct.

1913 *(The Fall Guy)*; upcoming screenings of *Quo Vadis* at the Lux Theater are announced in "The Lux," *Defender* 1 Nov. 1913; the reopening of the Star Theater by Black proprietor W. H. Riley is described in "New Star Theater," *Defender* 22 Nov. 1913, and "The Star," *Defender* 6 Dec. 1913.

50. Everett 41–44.

51. Everett cites Bragg's insightful discussion of screen acting technique and technical aspects of production (e.g., makeup, lighting, literary adaptation) in "On and off the Stroll," *Defender* 1 Aug. 1914, qtd. in Everett 45–46.

52. Of course, many of the businesses praised in the *Defender*'s social and theatrical notes also bought advertising in the newspaper, offering another distinction between the *Defender*'s role in promoting Black participation in mass culture and that of a political newspaper like the *Broad Ax*, which featured little advertising from places of public amusement and rarely promoted leisure activities in its copy.

53. "31st and State Streets," *Defender* 12 Feb. 1910: 1.

54. Shane White and Graham White, *Stylin': African American Expressive Culture from Its Beginnings to the Zoot Suit* (Ithaca: Cornell UP, 1998) 228.

55. J. Hockley Smiley, "State Street 'The Great White Way,'" *Defender* 11 May 1912.

56. Smiley. The (uncredited) writer of the "31st and State Streets" article assures readers that "despite the crowd that gathers there each night, Lieutenant Hanley of the Stanton avenue station, will tell you that there is never any trouble."

57. Drake and Cayton 47. See also Daniel Q. Kelly, "'Ballum Rancum': Entertainment in Chicago's Demimonde, 1889–1919," *Ragtime Ephemeralist* 3 (2002): 184–99. Kelly points out that there were two distinct "red light" districts that have been routinely mistakenly conflated. One "Levee," known as Custom House Place, was centered around the Dearborn train station and thrived between 1890 and 1910 until reformers shut it down. This area featured a section known as "Coon Hollow" due to the "large colored population, permanent and floating, which thrived there." C. R. Wooldridge, *Hands Up! In the World of Crime* (Chicago: Thompson and Thompson, 1901) 313, qtd. in Kelly 190. The second "'new' larger Levee," which spread from the corner of Twenty-second Street and Armour Avenue, was closer to the large South Side Black Belt described in this chapter.

58. Drake and Cayton 55–56.

59. Hazel V. Carby, "Policing the Black Woman's Body in an Urban Context," *Critical Inquiry* 18 (1992): 751–52.

60. Carby 738–55.

61. Smiley.

62. Vice Commission of Chicago, *The Social Evil in Chicago: A Study of Existing Conditions* (Chicago: Vice Commission of the City of Chicago, 1911) 38. The commission, a predominantly white male group of clergy, educators, physicians, judges, and business leaders, was appointed by Chicago mayor

Fred A. Busse in 1910 to study existing vice conditions and make recommendations for its suppression.

63. *Social Evil* 38.

64. *Social Evil* 38–39.

65. *Social Evil* 39.

66. "31st and State Street."

67. According to sociologist William Henry Jones, the barbershop plays a larger recreational role for Blacks than for whites and is unique because it creates an informal recreational environment within a commercial space. William Henry Jones, *Recreation and Amusement among Negroes in Washington, D.C.: A Sociological Analysis of the Negro in an Urban Environment* (Washington: Howard UP, 1927) 88. In addition to locations within the Black Belt, African American men enjoyed other places of amusement, such as the Railroad Men's Headquarters, also known as the Budweiser Cafe, located south of the Black Belt at 5050 South State, offering the "finest liquors and cigars, good music." *Defender* 3 Sept. 1910.

68. "31st and State Street."

69. Smiley n.p.

70. White and White 233. White and White cite evidence from the late 1910s and 1920s indicating Black middle-class concerns about this kind of public behavior displayed by recent migrants, but such masculinist displays were clearly a long-standing tradition on the Stroll.

71. "Take Your Time," music written by Joe Jordan, words by Harrison Stewart, with substitute verses written by Lester Walton and performed by Ernest Hogan for the production "Rufus Rastus." Published by the Pekin Publishing Company, 1907. Many thanks to Terry Parrish for calling my attention to this item from his collection.

72. *Defender* 17 June 1911.

73. "Illa Vincent the Great," *Defender* 29 Apr. 1911: 1.

74. Anne Meis Knupfer, *Toward a Tenderer Humanity and a Nobler Womanhood: African American Women's Clubs in Turn-of-the-Century Chicago* (New York: New York UP, 1996) 124.

75. Knupfer describes homes and settlements established by women like Ida B. Wells (Negro Fellowship League), Elizabeth Lindsay Davis (Phyllis Wheatley Club/Home), and many others, in an effort to meet the needs of a rapidly growing Black urban population. See Knupfer 65–107.

76. *Social Evil* 39.

77. Knupfer 69.

78. Knupfer 104. James Grossman points out that although the YMCA was celebrated by many Black Chicagoans when it was founded in 1911, others criticized it as "elitist," noting its high membership fees. Although the YMCA offered "glee clubs, baseball leagues, and other leisure activities designed to compete with the temptations of State Street," Grossman observes that it was not particularly successful in attracting recent migrant laborers: "Implicitly

through its wholesome recreational programs and explicitly through meetings that often accompanied such programs, the Wabash YMCA provided a podium for white industrialists and black middle-class leaders who wished to address a small minority of newcomers who could be enticed through its doors." Grossman 141–42.

79. Smiley.

80. "Booker T. Washington," *Broad Ax* 20 Jan. 1900: 1.

81. Grossman 4.

82. Emmett J. Scott, comp., "Additional Letters of Negro Migrants of 1916–1918," *Journal of Negro History* 4 (1919): 428. I quote the letters as they appear in Scott's compilation, assuming that they have been transcribed (spellings, punctuation, emphases, etc.) as closely as possible from the original handwritten sources.

83. Scott, "Additional Letters" 430.

84. Scott, "Additional Letters" 432.

85. Emmett J. Scott, comp., "Letters of Negro Migrants of 1916–1918," *Journal of Negro History* 4 (1919): 336. Actually, a number of hopeful migrants write that they would be happy to locate in a small town up North, rather than a big city like Chicago, because they are "not choice about locating in the city." Thus while many potential migrants were attracted to the social and economic advantages of northern living, they had reservations about the quality of life in a large metropolis. Scott, "Letters" 430–34.

86. Grossman 191–95.

87. Spear 156. As a central if contested service and cultural institution in the Black Belt, the Wabash Avenue YMCA served as a key site for the collection and analysis of data pertaining to African American culture and experience, both informal and formal. The site served as the headquarters of the Association for the Study of Negro Life and History, founded in 1915 by Carter G. Woodson.

88. Grossman 194.

89. W. E. B. Du Bois, *The Souls of Black Folk* in *Three Negro Classics* (1903; New York: Avon, 1965) 307–8.

90. E. Franklin Frazier, "Recreation and Amusement among American Negroes: A Research Memorandum," 15 July 1940, 3–8.

91. Chicago Commission on Race Relations, *The Negro in Chicago: A Study of Race Relations and a Race Riot* (Chicago: U of Chicago P, 1922) 99–100.

92. John Collier, "Leisure Time, the Last Problem of Conservation," *Playground* 6.3 (1912): 94.

93. Collier 101. Collier's notions about leisure time as a potentially "great creative agent" echoes Du Bois's sense that the best use of leisure time involves the development of culture. Collier writes, "Let us hope that we may, as ancient Athens did, use leisure time to create great ideals, great loyalties, great power" (94). Clearly, though, this is not taking place in Collier's view, in large measure

due to the base content of amusements designed for profit rather than moral or cultural uplift. Thus, whereas Du Bois nine years earlier made the prophetic observation that the "problem of the twentieth century is the problem of the color-line," Collier's lack of attention to racial difference in urban environments leads him to identify a different, central problem of "modernity"—that of conserving leisure time: "The 20th century problem is the conservation, which means the utilization of the leisure time of the people, for only in this way shall we get an educated people, and only through an educated people can we hope to secure economic justice, responsible political freedom, or the conservation of the resources of the earth." Collier 94.

94. Scott, "Additional Letters" 440.

95. *Negro in Chicago* 97–103.

96. *Negro in Chicago* 99.

97. "The Dreamland Cafe, William Bottoms, Proprietor, 3520 S. State Street," *Broad Ax* 7 Sept. 1918: 12.

98. Although the *Broad Ax* did include "personal and social items" about Black Chicago (i.e., the activities of fraternal organizations), it did not cover commercial amusements.

99. *Negro in Chicago* 102.

100. *Negro in Chicago* 102.

101. *Negro in Chicago* 98.

102. "No 'Movies' for Race; Mob Puts Shows to Bad" and "'Stroll' Moves Southward," *Defender* 23 May 1914: 1.

103. "The Douglas," *Defender* 10 Feb. 1917.

104. Scott, "Additional Letters" 458.

105. Grossman 91.

106. Donna L. Franklin, *Ensuring Inequality: The Structural Transformation of the African-American Family* (Oxford: Oxford UP, 1997) 74.

107. *Negro in Chicago* 95, 96. Here the Thomases prefigure the social isolation experienced by migrant Pauline Breedlove in Toni Morrison's novel *The Bluest Eye* (discussed in chapter 3), as well as her turn to commercial leisure. Toni Morrison, *The Bluest Eye* (New York: Holt, 1970) 93–98.

108. *Negro in Chicago* 99.

109. *Negro in Chicago* 232.

110. *Negro in Chicago* 310.

111. *Negro in Chicago* 97.

112. Spear 48.

113. Spear 207.

114. "Theater's Dastardly Conduct," *Defender* 9 Mar. 1912: 1.

115. "Particular Points in Playdom," *Defender* 16 Mar. 1912.

116. Spear 207.

117. Farah Jasmine Griffin, "*Who Set You Flowin'?*": The African-American Migration Narrative* (New York: Oxford UP, 1995) 4–5.

118. Drake and Cayton 73–75. See also Grossman 152, 164.

119. "Mr. George A. Wilson," *Defender* 4 June 1910: 1; and Frank S. Heffron, "Colonial Theater Refuses Colored Gentlemen—Fined," *Defender* 11 June 1910: 1.

120. "Colonial Theater Refuses" 1.

121. "Mrs. Monroe L. Manning Refuse [sic] Jim Crow Seat at Globe Theatre," *Defender* 19 Nov. 1910: 1. Monroe L. Manning is listed as a railroad porter in the 1908 *Rhea's Directory* n.p.

122. *Negro in Chicago* 101.

123. Knupfer 69–71.

CHAPTER 5

1. Mary Carbine, " 'The Finest outside the Loop': Motion Picture Exhibition in Chicago's Black Metropolis, 1905–1928," *Camera Obscura* 23 (1990): 9.

2. According to Henry Sampson, Edward Lee opened the first Black-owned movie theater in the United States at Thirteenth and Walnut Streets in Louisville, Kentucky, sometime before 1913. Other early Black theater owners mentioned by Sampson include Robert Church, Sherman H. Dudley, and E. C. Brown. Henry T. Sampson, *Blacks in Black and White: A Source Book on Black Films,* 2nd ed. (Metuchen: Scarecrow, 1995) 7, 13.

3. Allan H. Spear, *Black Chicago: The Making of a Negro Ghetto, 1890–1920* (Chicago: U of Chicago P, 1967) 76. Ida B. Wells details the negative reaction to Motts's conversion of the Pekin in *Crusade for Justice: The Autobiography of Ida B. Wells,* ed. Alfreda M. Duster (Chicago: U of Chicago P, 1970) 289–95.

4. Wells 293. See also the discussion of the Pekin controversy in Anne Meis Knupfer, *Toward a Tenderer Humanity and a Nobler Womanhood: African American Women's Clubs in Turn-of-the-Century Chicago* (New York: New York UP, 1996) 125–26.

5. Dan Streible, "Race and the Reception of Jack Johnson Fight Films," *The Birth of Whiteness: Race and the Emergence of U.S. Cinema,* ed. Daniel Bernardi (New Brunswick: Rutgers UP, 1996) 179. In a footnote, Streible explains that the Pekin name was franchised nationally and "became a signifier of African American popular culture" 196n27.

6. Mark H. Haller, "Policy Gambling, Entertainment, and the Emergence of Black Politics: Chicago from 1900 to 1940," *Journal of Social History* 24 (1991): 719–39.

7. Haller 723.

8. Wells 293.

9. Lauren Rabinovitz, *For the Love of Pleasure: Women, Movies and Culture in Turn-of-the-Century Chicago* (New Brunswick: Rutgers UP, 1998) 120.

10. Sylvester Russell, "Musical and Dramatic," *Defender* 12 Feb. 1910. Russell refers here to the original, "old" Grand Theater (see my discussion of the two Grand Theaters later in this chapter). It is not clear that the "old" Grand featured motion pictures, so the performance Russell describes may not

have occurred at a moving picture exhibition house, making his logic here even more suspect and revealing.

11. Knupfer 103.

12. Chateau de Plaisance advertisement, *Defender* 19 Feb. 1910. This ad ran in many issues during early 1910.

13. Vice Commission of Chicago, *The Social Evil in Chicago: A Study of Existing Conditions* (Chicago: Vice Commission of the City of Chicago, 1911) 247–48.

14. Ralph Nelson Davis, "The Negro Newspaper in Chicago," M.A. thesis, U of Chicago, 1939, 60–61. Davis reports that in 1915, "the race problem headline items constituted 61 per cent of the total items." However, two years later, in 1917, "there was an increase in the news selection of happenings on crime, suicide, disaster, and accidents (the type of material frequently and continuously treated by the sensational American Press as big news). The 1917 headline display of sensational news comprised 32 per cent of the total items. With the increase in the sensational items, there was a corresponding percentage decrease in the race problem items," a drop from 61 percent in 1915 to 37 percent in 1917. Davis 78.

15. Carbine 19.

16. "Two Years," *Defender* 23 June 1917.

17. Owners of the States Theater hosted benefits for the Old Folks and Phyllis Wheatley Homes, as well as a legal fund-raiser for Joe Campbell (the African American prisoner at Joliet discussed in chapter 1), organized by theatrical writer Tony Langston along with Ida B. Wells. "Many Benefits," *Defender* 13 May 1916. The States held a benefit organized to raise money for medical expenses for popular Black entertainers, the Griffin sisters. "Griffin Benefit," *Defender* 27 July 1918: 6. A benefit to "purchase Christmas remembrances for our boys at the training camps" was held at the Pickford Theater on December 14, 1917. *Defender* 29 Dec. 1917.

18. Information about the Pekin and other Black Belt theaters discussed throughout this chapter (addresses, number of seats, dates of operation, ownership, etc.) is gleaned from several sources, including Carbine's appendix, "Motion Picture Theaters, 1909–1928" 41; Sampson, Appendix C, "Theaters Catering to Black Patronage, 1910–1950," in *Blacks in Black and White* 634–49; Joseph R. DuciBella, ed., *Theaters of Chicago* (Washington: Theatre Historical Society of America, 1973), and a version of *Theaters of Chicago* (with theaters listed by street) at the Theatre Historical Society in Elmhurst, Illinois; the on-line South Side Jazz Club Project (Jazz Clubs c. 1915–1940s, based on the research of Leon H. Lewis), Chicago Jazz Archive, Regenstein Library, University of Chicago (www.lib.uchicago.edu/e/su/cja/jazzmaps/ctlframe.htm); and reviews, articles and ads in the *Chicago Defender*, 1909–19. An excellent illustration of the locations of Black Belt entertainments and businesses is included in a map by Paul Eduard Miller and Richard M. Jones, "Chicago Jazz Spots, 1914–1928." The map includes many of the theaters discussed in this chapter and features details of the bustling intersections of Thirty-first and State

Streets and Thirty-fifth and State Streets. See Paul Eduard Miller, ed., *Esquire's 1946 Jazz Book* (1946; Cambridge: Da Capo, 1979).

19. William Howland Kenney, *Chicago Jazz: A Cultural History, 1904–1930* (New York: Oxford UP, 1993) 5.

20. Many thanks to Deborah Gillaspie for bringing the "Pekin Rag" and its cover image to my attention. See Tim Samuelson, "From Ragtime to Real Estate: Joe Jordan's Career as a Chicago Real Estate Developer," *Ragtime Ephemeralist* 3 (2002): 201. Like the other Black entrepreneurs described in this chapter, Jordan combined entertainment and business interests by entering the music publication business (the Pekin Publishing Company) and by building a retail and apartment building at the northeast corner of State and Thirty-sixth Streets.

21. Spear 76; Wells 289; Arna Bontemps and Jack Conroy, *Anyplace but Here* (1945; Columbia: U of Missouri P, 1966) 119.

22. Bontemps and Conroy 119. Samuelson cites a City of Chicago building permit (no. 24420) dated February 1, 1906. Samuelson 202n2. Dates regarding the Pekin's evolution (as café, saloon, gambling house, music hall, theater), as well as Motts's ownership, are conflicting. Did Motts already own the venue when Jordan's "Pekin Rag" was published in 1904? Did the Douglass Center benefit take place in 1905 (as suggested by the 5 May 1905 *Chicago Broad Ax* article cited by Meis Knupfer) or in 1906 (shortly after the devastating earthquake in San Francisco on April 18, 1906, as Wells remembers it)? It seems clear that the Pekin was noted as a "temple of music" prior to Motts's addition of a brick auditorium and the highly publicized inaugural stage productions in 1906. But its status as a "theater," and, moreover, one that sought to inspire race pride, begins in 1906.

23. Kenney 11.

24. Kenney 6.

25. Russell, "Musical and Dramatic," *Defender* 23 Apr. 1910.

26. Kenney reports that Motts "paid some of his customers $5 per day to help the Second Ward Aldermen register black voters and see that they voted on election days." Kenney 6.

27. "The Colored Press Association of Chicago Organized and News Bureau Established," *Defender* 17 Feb. 1912; Knupfer 87.

28. Henry Brown, "Chicago's Night Life of Former Years: Crimson! Alluring! Tragic!" *Abbott's Monthly* July 1930: 6.

29. "Pekin Theatre Still Closed," *Defender* 3 Feb. 1912; "Musical and Dramatic—Particular Paragraphs about the Profession," *Defender* 17 Feb. 1912. Motts's funeral was a huge event, attracting around four thousand people. Spear 77.

30. Minnie Adams, "Musical and Dramatic," *Defender* 9 Mar. 1912.

31. "Tallaboo at the Pekin," *Defender* 22 Nov. 1913.

32. White owners of the Pekin include George Holt, Frank Kaight, Thomas Chamales, William Adams, and Walter K. Tyler. Kenney 7.

33. "The Old Pekin Theater Has Come to Life Again as an Attractive Dance Hall," *Broad Ax* 9 Mar. 1918.

34. The Pekin was the site of a 1920 shootout between two West Side racketeers (Samuel J. "Nails" Morton and his colleague Hirshie Miller) and two plainclothes police detectives that resulted in the deaths of the officers. At that time the Pekin was owned by Daniel M. Jackson, a Black policy boss who regulated South Side gambling and entertainment activities via his connections with the Second Ward Republican machine. Jackson rose to power and prominence by marrying Robert Motts's sister, Lucy Motts. In a final, ironic move, Jackson sold the Pekin for $35,000 in 1924 to the city of Chicago, which converted it to a police station in 1925. It housed the Third District Police Station until it was demolished around 1950. Maurice Fischer, "Inside Chicago: Story of a South Side Dive That Became Police Station," *Chicago Daily News* 2 July 1948; Haller 725.

35. Sylvester Russell, "Musical and Dramatic" column, *Defender* 23 Apr. 1910.

36. Sylvester Russell, "The New Grand Theatre to Open Monday," *Defender* 18 Mar. 1911. Although newspaper items announce that the new Grand seated 800, Mary Carbine's source indicates that it seated 716, and the Theatre Historical Society gleaned from city records that the Grand had 500 seats. Carbine 41; DuciBella 12.

37. Russell, "The New Grand Theater Opens Its Doors," *Defender* 25 Mar. 1911.

38. Minnie Adams, "Musical and Dramatic" column, *Defender* 6 Apr. 1912.

39. "Famed Jazz House Demolished," *Chicago Daily News* [n.d.] 1950, clipping from the Theatre Historical Society of America; "Taps for the Grand Theater," *Chicago Sun-Times* 7 May 1959. The Grand was torn down "to make way for an Illinois Institute of Technology redevelopment project."

40. Russell, "The New Grand Theater Opens Its Doors," and advertisement, *Defender* 25 Mar. 1911.

41. *Defender* critic Tony Langston launched a campaign against the Ebony Film Corporation, which distributed a set of racially offensive comedies (*Aladdin Jones, Money Talks in Darktown,* and *Two Knights of Vaudeville*). Langston secured promises from the managers of most of the Black Belt theaters that they would not book Ebony product, not only because these films were offensive but because they were "crap" and "punk," that is, old films that were unsuccessful in their first run. Mr. Klein, manager of the Monogram, wrote to Langston regarding the questionable films: "We ran most of that stuff over a year ago and it was a mess. It was 'first run' then. It must be junk now." Tony Langston, "Ebony Films," *Defender* 1 July 1916; Langston [title not legible], *Defender* 8 July 1916. I presume Mr. Klein of the Monograms and Mr. Johnson of the Grand are white because Langston does not make a point to identify them as members of the Race.

42. "New Monogram Theater" advertisement, *Defender* 22 Dec. 1917.

43. Sylvester Russell, "Musical and Dramatic" column, *Defender* 4 Mar. 1910.

44. Charles A. Sengstock Jr., *Jazz Music in Chicago's Early South-Side Theaters* (Northbrook: Canterbury P of Northbrook, 2000) 40.

45. Dunham recalls, "The Grand and the Monogram theaters had ceased to compete with each other because of the inpouring torrent from the South. They were so pressed for space that each generously encouraged patronage of the other. The fact that both houses were run by the same management may also have had something to do with this magnanimity." My research does not indicate that both theaters were run by the same management. Katherine Dunham, *A Touch of Innocence: Memoirs of Childhood* (1959; Chicago: U of Chicago P, 1994) 58–59.

46. Dunham 59.

47. Dunham 59–60.

48. Ethel Waters with Charles Samuels, *His Eye Is on the Sparrow* (New York: Bantam, 1951) 94.

49. The States' seating capacity is listed as 686 in Carbine and as 675 in DuciBella.

50. *The Battle Cry of Peace* is advertised in the *Defender* 15 Jan. 1916; *Damaged Goods* in *Defender* 8 Jan. 1916; *The Common Law* in *Defender* 18 Nov. 1916; *Joan the Woman* in *Defender* 30 June 1917; *Cleopatra* in *Defender* 13 July 1918; *Intolerance* ads in the *Defender* 3 Nov. 1917; 10 Nov. 1917; 24 Nov. 1917; 22 Dec. 1917; and 29 Dec. 1917.

51. *The Railroad Porter* described in the *Defender* 9 Aug. 1913; *The Trooper of Troop K* (also billed as *The Trooper of Company K*) in *Defender* 28 Oct. 1916; *A Man's Duty* in *Defender* 27 Sept. 1919; *The Homesteader* screenings at the States listed in the *Defender* 5 Apr. 1919: 9; and 12 Apr. 1919: 9.

52. Jane Gaines, "Fire and Desire: Race, Melodrama, and Oscar Micheaux," *Black American Cinema*, ed. Manthia Diawara (New York: Routledge, 1993) 55.

53. "States Theatre Displays Vile Race Pictures," *Defender* 30 May 1914.

54. "Insulting Film Plays Have Been Canceled," *Defender* 16 Mar. 1918: 6.

55. Miss Helen Greene mentioned in Tony Langston, "Musical and Dramatic" column, *Defender* 16 Jan. 1915; various States bands described in Langston, "Musical and Dramatic" column, *Defender* 9 Jan. 1915; Langston, "Screen Houses," *Defender* 22 Dec. 1917; States Theatre ad, *Defender* 1 Mar. 1919: 13.

56. Tony Langston, "Two Years," *Defender* 23 June 1917.

57. Langston, "Two Years."

58. The continued closing of the States, Owl, and Lincoln noted in "Special Announcement," *Defender* 19 Oct. 1918: 6; improvements to the States described in "States Theater," *Defender* 9 Nov. 1918: 6.

59. Advertisement, *Defender* 22 Dec. 1917.

60. Tony Langston, "Theatrical Review," *Defender* 1 Jan. 1916.

61. Tony Langston, "New Owl Theater," *Defender* 27 Jan. 1917.

62. Tony Langston, "The New Owl," *Defender* 3 Feb. 1917.

63. Langston, "New Owl Theater."

64. Langston, "The New Owl."

65. Tony Langston, "Theatrical Review," *Defender* 22 Dec. 1917.

66. "Changed Hands," *Defender* 2 Feb. 1918: 4; see *Defender* notices for Hammond chain screenings of *Why America Will Win* (9 Nov. 1918) and *Vigilantes* (7 Dec. 1918).

67. DuciBella indicates Newhouse & Burnham as designers of the Phoenix; Hammond and Pail [Paul?] are named as proprietors and O. C. Hammond as manager in *Defender* 17 June 1911; Tony Langston, "Theatrical Review," *Defender* 16 Jan. 1915.

68. "The Phoenix Fares Well with New Pictures," 1 July 1911.

69. Sylvester Russell, "The Phoenix Theatre Shows Good Pictures," *Defender* 1 July 1911; and Russell, "Musical and Dramatic," *Defender* 22 July 1911.

70. Everett 40.

71. Sengstock 23. The erection of the Vendome announced in an advertisement in the *Defender* 22 Dec. 1917. The Vendome's seating differs in Carbine (1,265), DuciBella (1,500), and *Defender* 9 Nov. 1918 (1,300).

72. The Vendome, along with other buildings and lots along the Stroll, was acquired by the expanding campus of the Illinois Institute of Technology (formerly the Armour Institute of Technology, discussed in the introduction). Although the institute demolished many structures, it used the Vendome for storage during the 1940s before tearing it down. A memorandum regarding potential renovations describes the Vendome's physical specifications: "This building is approximately 75 feet wide by 120 feet deep with a 30 foot domed ceiling. . . . On either side of the main entrance 2 stores are partitioned off making rooms about 15' × 15'. The balcony is about 30 feet by 75 feet (the width of the building). Above the balcony is a projection room 8 feet by 10 feet." W. J. Parduhn, Superintendent of Buildings and Grounds, memorandum to Morgan Fitch, President of Senior Class, 20 May 1942, Henry T. Heald Papers, RG 6.2.3, Box 2, Folder 7, University Archives, Paul V. Galvin Library, Illinois Institute of Technology, Chicago, Illinois.

73. The Vendome showed big features such as William Fox's *Why I Would Not Marry*, "The Colossal 1919 Morality Drama" about the "unseen dangers confronting girls through marriage." The film was booked at the States, Owl, and Vendome Theaters, and the successive screenings were advertised together. Screenings of *The Homesteader* advertised in *Defender* 1 Mar. 1919: 11.

74. "Pickford Sold," *Defender* 26 Oct. 1918; seating from DuciBella; Lux mentioned in "Musical and Dramatic," *Defender* 1 Nov. 1913.

75. "Screen Houses"; "The Pickford," *Defender* 1 June 1918.

76. Tony Langston, "The Hammonds," *Defender* 9 Nov. 1918: 6.

77. Everett 55.

78. Tony Langston, "Among the Movies—The Washington," *Defender* 5 July 1918; Roosevelt ad regarding showing of *The Homesteader* in *Defender* 1 Nov. 1919; Tony Langston, "Theatrical Review—Among the Movies—The Airdome," *Defender* 3 June 1916.

79. "Atlas Theater Opens," *Defender* 3 Oct. 1914.

80. "New Star Theater," *Defender* 22 Nov. 1913.

81. *History of Chicago and Souvenir of the Liquor Interest: The Nation's Choice for the Great Columbian Exposition* (Chicago: Belgravia, 1891) n.p.

82. Spear 77; Kenney 10; William M. Tuttle Jr., *Race Riot: Chicago in the Red Summer of 1919* (1970; Urbana: U of Illinois P, 1996) 165.

83. Items about and ads for Jones's establishments appeared often in the Black press. For example, the *Broad Ax*, 28 Aug. 1915, carried an ad for "Teenan Jones' Place, 3445 S. State Street. The finest and most UP-TO-DATE BUFFET and CAFE on the South Side. First-Class Entertainers." Mention of the Caroline Girls in *Defender* 14 Oct. 1916.

84. "Henry (Teenan) Jones, owner of Elite Cafe No. 2," in *Broad Ax* 7 Dec. 1918: 2.

85. Spear 77.

86. Kenney 10.

87. "Bill Foster" is listed as the manager of the Star in *Defender* 13 Oct. 1917; 20 Oct. 1917; 3 Nov. 1917; 22 Dec. 1917; Sampson 172. Prior to Jones's purchase, the Star was managed briefly by Black real estate giant and bank founder Jesse Binga, *Defender* 1 July 1916.

88. Spear 77.

89. Other race film companies in Chicago during this period include the Micheaux Book and Film Company, with offices downtown (538 S. Dearborn) and later on the Stroll (3457 S. State Street); the Delight Film Corporation, just north of the Black Belt (2139 S. Wabash); the white-owned Fife Production Company (4001 Cottage Grove) and Ebony Film Corporation (Transportation Building, 608 S. Dearborn); as well as the Democracy Photoplay Company, the Pyramid Pictures Corporation, and the Railroad Men's Amusement Association. Information on these companies from notes and correspondence in the George P. Johnson Negro Film Collection, Department of Special Collections, U of California at Los Angeles, as well as Sampson (on Micheaux 151, Foster 172, Peter P. Jones 183, Royal Gardens Motion Picture Company 188, Ebony Film Corporation 200), *Simms' Blue Book and National Negro Business and Professional Directory* (1923, Cleveland: Gordon, 1977); and Arnie Bernstein, *Hollywood on Lake Michigan: 100 Years of Chicago and the Movies* (Chicago: Lake Claremont P, 1998) 46–60. Actor Samuel T. Jacks of the Royal Gardens Motion Picture Company appeared in several films produced by the Ebony Film Corporation (discussed in chapter 6) and in Oscar Micheaux's *Within Our Gates* (1920) as Rev. Wilson Jacobs (discussed in chapter 7).

CHAPTER 6

1. William Foster, *Indianapolis Freeman* 20 Dec. 1913, qtd. in Henry T. Sampson, *Blacks in Black and White: A Source Book on Black Films*, 2nd ed. (Metuchen: Scarecrow, 1995) 174.

2. Hunter C. Haynes, *Indianapolis Freeman* 14 Mar. 1914, qtd. in Sampson, *Blacks in Black and White* 178.

3. Oscar Micheaux, *Pittsburgh Courier* 13 Dec. 1924, qtd. in Sampson, *Blacks in Black and White* 168.

4. [Tony Langston], "Ebony Film Cancelled," *Chicago Defender* 12 May 1917: 4.

5. Hunter C. Haynes began making films after establishing a diverse entrepreneurial career. He built a successful razor strop manufacturing company in Chicago, then moved his business to New York. After dabbling in the "brokerage and loan business," then the "transfer and truckage business," Haynes became a producer for the white-owned Afro-American Film Company, making comedies starring well-known Black stage performers. Haynes established his own film production company in August 1914. Sampson, *Blacks in Black and White* 176–79. *Uncle Remus' First Visit to New York* is not extant.

6. Abbie Mitchell was a well-known and accomplished performer of the vaudeville and legitimate stage. She was one of the female stars of the Bert Williams and George Walker "In Dahomey" company during its record-breaking run in London in 1903, and one of the leading performers with the prestigious Lafayette Players Stock Company in New York. Tom Brown was also a veteran vaudeville star known throughout the United States and Europe; he, too, joined the Lafayette Players during his long and diverse career. Other notable cast members of *Uncle Remus' First Visit to New York* included Billy Harper, Wesley Jones, and Allie Gilliam. Sampson, *Blacks in Black and White* 179. See also Henry T. Sampson, *Blacks in Blackface: A Source Book on Early Black Musical Shows* (Metuchen: Scarecrow, 1980), for biographical information on Mitchell (404–5) and Brown (344–46).

7. Sampson, *Blacks in Black and White* 275.

8. The "Rastus" name and stereotype are used in a number of early film comedies starring white comedians in blackface, such as *How Rastus Got His Turkey* (Pathé-Freres, 1910); *Rastus in Zululand* (Lubin, 1910); *Rastus Knew It Wasn't* (Lubin, 1914); *Rastus' Riotous Ride* (Pathé, 1914); and *Rastus' Rabid Rabbit Hunt* (Electric, 1915—animation). See descriptions in Sampson, *Blacks in Black and White* 73, 99–102.

9. Early mainstream, white-cast films that take up this common theme include *Reuben Buys a Gold Brick* (Lubin, 1902); *Rube and Mandy at Coney Island* (Edison, 1903); *Rube in the Subway* (or *Reuben in the Subway*, American Mutoscope & Biograph, 1905); and *Rube Brown in Town* (American Mutoscope & Biograph, 1907).

10. *Indianapolis Freeman* 26 Nov. 1914, qtd. in Sampson, *Blacks in Black and White* 276.

11. Sampson, *Blacks in Black and White* 276.

12. Foster's other films include *The Fall Guy* (1913); *The Grafter and the Girl* (1913); *The Butler* (1913); *Mother* (1914); *The Barber* (1916); *Birth Mark* (191?); *Brother* (191?); *Fool and Fire* (191?); and *A Woman's Worst Enemy* (191?).

13. Sampson, *Blacks in Black and White* 172, 174. The *Defender* reported in 1913 that *The Railroad Porter* was "known from coast to coast" (from "The States Theater" article cited previously), but specific data about exhibition outside of Chicago are scant.

14. Mark A. Reid, *Redefining Black Film* (Berkeley: U of California P, 1993) 8.

15. Description of Foster's *The Railroad Porter* (aka *The Pullman Porter*, 1913) from the *New York Age* 25 Sept. 1913. For Reid, the inclusion of markers like "fashionably dressed" and "café" society indicate that Foster's comedies represented "respectable" Black characters, in contrast with the markers of Blackness featured in white-produced comedies (e.g., poverty, servitude).

16. In her biography of pioneer Black filmmaker Oscar Micheaux, who worked as a Pullman porter, Betti VanEpps-Taylor describes the benefits of the job, which offered "a chance to see the world, the status of professional costume consisting of a neat uniform versus laborer's denims, urbanity and sophistication, as opposed to rural simplicity, and means to mingle with a variety of sophisticated, wealthy, influential people." Although Micheaux describes the many negative aspects of the job (racism, low pay) in his novel *The Conquest* (1913), he used his experiences on the railroad to learn about business opportunities (including homesteading) and to observe Black life in many sections of the country, activities that played a major role in his development as an artist and entrepreneur. Betti Carol VanEpps-Taylor, *Oscar Micheaux . . . Dakota Homesteader, Author, Pioneer Film Maker: A Biography* (Rapid City: Dakota West, 1999) 22–27. See also Jack Santino, *Miles of Smiles, Years of Struggle: Stories of Black Pullman Porters* (Urbana: U of Illinois P, 1989).

17. See "The States Theater," *Defender* 9 Aug. 1913.

18. "The States Theater."

19. "The States Theater."

20. "The States," *Defender* 18 Oct. 1913.

21. "Foster's R.R. Porter," *Defender* 22 Nov. 1913. According to the article, the Majestic audience so enjoyed Foster's film that they exhibited the kind of "inappropriate" spectatorial behavior frequently attributed to Black Belt audiences: "When it was screened patrons jumped up and shouted, some laughed so loud that ushers had to silence them."

22. *Moving Picture World* 10 Aug. 1918: 770. Ebony comedies produced (or at least announced as future releases in the trade press) in 1917 and 1918 include *A Black Sherlock Holmes, Do the Dead Talk, The Hypocrites, The Janitor, Good Luck in Old Clothes, A Black & Tan Mixup, A Busted Romance, Are Working Girls Safe, Devil for a Day, Mercy, The Mummy Mumbled, The Porters, When You Hit—Hit Hard, Wrong All Around, When Cupid Went Wild, Some Baby, Spooks, A Milk Fed Hero, The Bully, Ghosts,* and *He Ran for Mayor.* Trade press articles and advertisements include *Moving Picture World* 8 Dec. 1917: 1483; 15 Dec. 1917: 1648; 4 May 1918: 665, 717, 729, 745; 18 May 1918: 1009, 1012, 1037; 8 June 1918: 1450, 1474; 22 June 1918: 1766; *Exhibitor's Herald* 22 Dec. 1917: 30; 6 Apr. 1918: 12; 13 Apr. 1918: 20, 30; 20 Apr.

1918: 36; 27 Apr. 1918: 8, 27; 4 May 1918: 8; 18 May 1918: 12, 36; 1 June 1918: 34; 8 June 1918: 9, 29; 15 June 1918: 8, 24, 34; *Motography* 20 Apr. 1918: 780; 8 June 1918: 1110.

23. According to Sampson, twenty-six of the Black actors working for Ebony were members of the George M. Lewis Stock Company. Sampson, *Blacks in Black and White* 201.

24. For further discussion of these Historical/Ebony films, see Gerald Butters, *Black Manhood on the Silent Screen* (Lawrence: UP of Kansas, 2002) 182–85.

25. Sampson's discussion of Pollard describes him as a Black filmmaker who sought to provide positive Black representations, to assist the Black-owned Lincoln Motion Picture Company with securing a distribution deal with General Film, and to eliminate the use of offensive Black "dialect" in intertitles to represent Black speech. Sampson, *Blacks in Black and White* 201–4. In contrast, Thomas Cripps describes Pollard in the following negative light: "The worst exploiters of blacks were not the honest hustlers like [William] Foster but rather men like Luther J. Pollard, the black boss of Ebony Pictures, who espoused race pride in their publicity sheets throughout the war years but then ground out the traditional black stereotypes." Thomas Cripps, *Slow Fade to Black: The Negro in American Film, 1900–1942* (Oxford: Oxford UP, 1977) 80.

26. L. J. Pollard, letter to George P. Johnson, 12 June 1918, George P. Johnson Negro Film Collection, Department of Special Collections, U of California at Los Angeles (hereafter referred to as GPJC).

27. The following discussion of the Ebony films *The Comeback of Barnacle Bill, A Reckless Rover,* and *Spying the Spy* is based on prints viewed at the Library of Congress, Motion Picture, Broadcasting and Recorded Sound Division.

28. Although the credits are unclear in the Library of Congress print of this film, the part of the Chinese laundry owner appears to be played by Black actor Sam T. Jacks, who appears in other Ebony films and as the Reverend Wilson Jacobs in Oscar Micheaux's *Within Our Gates* (1920, discussed in the next chapter). Jacks also served as an officer of the Chicago-based Royal Gardens Motion Picture Company.

29. [Tony Langston], "Ebony Films," *Defender* 1 July 1916.

30. [Langston], "Ebony Films."

31. Lincoln's achievement was frequently framed in terms of its departure from offensive comic Black stereotypes. For example, J. Dooley, manager of the Atlas Theater in Chicago's Black Belt, praised Lincoln's first film, *The Realization of a Negro's Ambition,* as follows: "The Lincoln Company has done something in getting away from the cheap and low stuff called 'comedy' by other producers." "Realization," *Defender* 14 Oct. 1916: 4.

32. "Lincoln Motion Picture Corporation," typescript c. May 1917, GPJC.

33. See my discussion in chapter 3 of Noble Johnson's appeal to Black audiences in his "mainstream" and race film appearances.

34. Ebony Film Corporation, *Financial Statement,* May 1918; Lincoln Motion Picture Company, *Articles of Incorporation,* 20 Jan. 1917, both in GPJC.

35. No prints of Lincoln films survive, except for fragments of its 1920 release, *By Right of Birth* (in GPJC). My descriptions of Lincoln films are taken from Sampson, *Blacks in Black and White;* Cripps; Reid; and materials (synopses, advertisements, reviews, and stills) contained in the GPJC.

36. "Photo-Play," *Defender* 26 Aug. 1916: 4.

37. Jones and Paul cited in advertisement, "Some of the Many Testimonials of the Drawing Power, the Merit and Demand for LINCOLN PRODUCTIONS," GPJC.

38. Noble Johnson was born in Colorado Springs, Colorado, on April 18, 1881. At the age of fifteen, Johnson quit school to travel with his father, Perry J. Johnson, a nationally known racehorse owner and trainer. Noble Johnson befriended a number of ranchers, and at age seventeen decided to be a cowboy. Johnson worked for various cattle and mining companies and stables, living in cities such as Denver, San Francisco, Portland, and Seattle. Johnson's work experiences, particularly with horses, helped him to develop skills he would use as a stunt man and actor, especially in "western" films. Documents in the GPJC, and Sampson, *Blacks in Black and White* 529.

39. John Hope Franklin and Alfred A. Moss Jr., *From Slavery to Freedom: A History of Negro Americans,* 6th ed. (New York: McGraw, 1988) 293.

40. George P. Johnson, *Collector of Negro Film History,* Oral History Program, University of California at Los Angeles, 1970, 53.

41. *California Eagle,* 14 Oct. 1916.

42. M. W. Dogan, letter to D. Ireland Thomas (New Orleans–based distributor of Lincoln films), 24 Feb. 1917, GPJC.

43. Tony Langston, letter to George P. Johnson, 30 Oct. 1916, GPJC.

44. A. B. McAfee, letter to the Lincoln Motion Picture Company, 9 Aug. 1918, GPJC.

45. Johnson 55. Perhaps Washington Theater manager Chester Paul is related to George Paul, who managed Chicago's States and Owl Theaters during this period, just as several members of the Hammond family managed Black Belt theaters.

46. George P. Johnson kept copies of dozens of letters he wrote to and received from newspapers, distributors, exhibitors, and other race film companies across the country on behalf of Lincoln. Johnson's records constitute one of the most detailed accounts of the scope and the major figures of the race film industry, particularly during the silent era. GPJC.

47. "Information Blank (Theatres)," GPJC. Noble Johnson continued to act in Universal films while serving as leading actor, writer, and president at Lincoln.

48. "The Secret of Getting Rich!" c. 1917 and "Three Strong Reasons Why You Should Buy Lincoln Motion Picture Co. Shares," c. 1921, GPJC.

49. "Lincoln Motion Picture Corporation," typescript c. May 1917, GPJC.

50. At the bottom of a letter received from Ebony officer L. J. Pollard, George P. Johnson wrote the following note to his brother, Noble: "Some plan to consolidate the Lincoln & Ebony might be put over. White men with money are backing Ebony. Pictures are being released now purely on General Film's prestige. . . . A consolidation of both with Gen. Offices in Chicago studio in Chicago and Los Angeles and Gen. Film releasing, comedies, dramas, book novelizations, news events, etc. A consolidation backed by Press, Defender, etc. and others might enable $1,000,000 Corp and results."

Although the content and tone of Ebony films seem incompatible with the Lincoln aesthetic, an alliance could have generated the capital Lincoln needed to stabilize and expand its operations. L. J. Pollard, letter to George P. Johnson, 12 June 1918, GPJC.

51. Minutes from a Lincoln board meeting indicate that Noble Johnson resigned from Lincoln because the company was not proving profitable. However, George P. Johnson writes elsewhere that Noble was forced to quit Lincoln because owners of theaters catering to Black audiences (particularly Black Belt theaters in Chicago) complained about Johnson's appearance as leading man in Lincoln films, which were drawing Black viewers away from theaters playing Universal films in which he played smaller roles. Minutes of the Lincoln Motion Picture Company board meeting, 3 Sept. 1918, and other documents, GPJC.

52. Films representing Black troops during the Spanish-American War include Edison's *Colored Troops Disembarking* and *Steamer Mascotte Arriving at Tampa* (both 1898). Later "newsreel" representations of pre–World War I Black military service include *Colored Troops at Chillicothe* (Finley Film Company, 191?).

53. Franklin and Moss 294.

54. Franklin and Moss 294–97; Herbert Aptheker, "The Afro-American in World War I," *Afro-American History: The Modern Era* (New York: Citadel, 1971) 159–72.

55. *The Messenger,* a newspaper published in New York by A. Philip Randolph and Chandler Owen, was one of the very few Black publications that refused to support the war. Randolph and Owen were sentenced to jail for publishing the article "Pro-Germanism among Negroes." Franklin and Moss 308. Aptheker mentions incidents in Columbia, Tennessee, and Birmingham, Alabama, in which Blacks were arrested "upon the charge of rebellion and treason." Aptheker notes that examples of opposition like these are difficult to trace because they were so deeply buried by the censorship and propaganda machines that kept only "acceptable" responses to the war in public view. Aptheker 163.

56. Emmett J. Scott was appointed special assistant to the secretary of war in order to handle racial issues. Du Bois, a former adversary of Washington and his "Tuskegee Machine," expressed his (unexpected) support of the war in his editorial in the July 1918 issue of the *Crisis,* entitled "Close Ranks." Franklin and Moss 295, 308.

57. Quoted in Franklin and Moss 300.

58. Franklin and Moss 304–5.

59. George P. Johnson, letter to Charles S. Hart, Director, Division of Films, Committee on Public Information, 12 Aug. 1918, GPJC. Subsequent references to Johnson's plan are also taken from this letter, as well as various other documents in GPJC.

60. George P. Johnson, letter to Charles S. Hart, 19 Sept. 1918, rpt. in Richard Wood, ed., *Film and Propaganda in America: A Documentary History*, 5 vols. (New York: Greenwood, 1990). Vol. 1, 212.

61. Leslie Midkiff DeBauche, *Reel Patriotism: The Movies and World War I* (Madison: U of Wisconsin P, 1987) xvi.

62. Frank R. Wilson, letter to Lincoln Motion Picture Company, 31 Oct. 1918, GPJC.

63. A letter dated Aug. 28, 1918, from the French Pictorial Service, 220 West Forty-second Street, New York City, to George P. Johnson (c/o Tony Kingston [Langston], 3129 So. State St., Chicago, Ill., Lincoln booking agent and *Defender* theatrical critic) indicates: "We are sending you by Parcels Post, Special Delivery—1 Reel depicting Colored Troops at the front in France." Two months later, in a letter dated October 28, 1928, the service wrote: "We hope your initial showing in Chicago will be very successful, and as soon as we have more pictures of Negro troops we will promptly take the matter up with you." Box 15, folder "French Pictorial Service," GPJC. Johnson indicates in his oral history that after the Chicago premiere the footage was "shown by our representatives throughout the United States." Johnson 49.

64. Johnson reports in his oral history: "I got a permit from the War Department to go down there. I took the cameraman along, Harry Gant, a white fellow, and we went down there for two days. That whole regiment turned out, and they paraded and jumped and did everything for us there. . . . They were very famous and that picture just went like hotcakes all over the United States. Tuskegee and everybody, they all liked that fine." Johnson 129.

65. On Foster's plans to record the Eighth Regiment's send-off, see *Defender* 27 Apr. 1918. Advertising for Micheaux's *Homesteader* premiere indicates that the film was to be screened with footage of the "return of the 'victorious' Eighth, the 'Black Devils' who sent the Kaiser into oblivion." The compilers of the most authoritative Oscar Micheaux filmography to date suggest that Micheaux may have shot this footage, though he is not named specifically as filmmaker: "WE SENT OUT CAMERA MAN AND DIRECTOR TO GRANT, where bright, clear pictures of each company and their officers were taken, SO YOU CAN SEE AND RECOGNIZE THEM. See, therefore, the REAL pictures of your heroes, which are shown only in their own armory this week." *Defender* 22 Feb. 1919, cited in "An Oscar Micheaux Filmography: From the Silents through His Transition to Sound, 1919–1931," compiled by Charles Musser, Corey K. Creekmur, Pearl Bowser, J. Ronald Green, Charlene Regester, and Louise Spence in Pearl Bowser, Jane Gaines, and Charles Musser, eds., *Oscar Micheaux and His Circle: African-American Filmmak-*

*ing and Race Cinema of the Silent Era* (Bloomington: Indiana UP, 2001) 233.

66. Rather than acquire footage from white producers, Black filmmakers documented Black soldiers in films such as *Negro Soldiers Fighting for Uncle Sam* (Peter P. Jones Photoplay Co., 1916); *Doing Their Bit* (Toussaint Film Co., series 1918–); and *Heroic Negro Soldiers of the World War* (Frederick Douglass Film Co., 1919). Other nonfiction films regarding Black World War I soldiers include *Colored Americans* (dist. by Mutual Film Corp., 1918); *Our Boys at Camp Upton* (1918); *Ninety Second Division on Parade* (Turpin Film Co., 1919); *Our Colored Fighters* (Downing Film Co., 1919); *From Harlem to the Rhine* ([probably] U.S. War Dept., 1920); and *Our Colored Soldier Boys in Action Over There* (U.S. Government Official War Film, 1921). Titles gleaned from Sampson, *Blacks in Black and White,* and Craig W. Campbell, *Reel America and World War I: A Comprehensive Filmography and History of Motion Pictures in the United States, 1914–1920* (Jefferson: McFarland, 1985).

67. Sampson, *Blacks in Black and White* 250.

68. Franklin and Moss 311.

69. Enlarged reprint from the *Monitor* (Omaha, NB), 28 Aug. 1919, GPJC.

70. Black-controlled film companies in operation during and just after Lincoln's reign include the Frederick Douglass Film Company, the Booker T. Film Company in Los Angeles, the Maurice Film Company in Detroit, Monumental Pictures Corporation in Washington, D.C., and Colored Feature Photoplay, Incorporated, in New Jersey/New York City. For discussion of these and subsequent Black-owned film companies, see Sampson, *Blacks in Black and White* 179–98.

CHAPTER 7

1. Micheaux's relationship with George P. Johnson is described in Henry T. Sampson, *Blacks in Black and White: A Source Book on Black Films,* 2nd ed. (Metuchen: Scarecrow, 1995) 149–50; Thomas Cripps, *Slow Fade to Black: The Negro in American Film, 1900–1942* (Oxford: Oxford UP, 1977) 184; Betti Carol VanEpps-Taylor, *Oscar Micheaux . . . Dakota Homesteader, Author, Pioneer Film Maker: A Biography* (Rapid City: Dakota West, 1999) 96–97; and numerous documents in the George P. Johnson Negro Film Collection, Department of Special Collections, U of California at Los Angeles (hereafter referred to as GPJC). Micheaux turned to writing novels after the failure of his homesteading activities. The novels he published before he began filmmaking—*The Conquest* (1913), *The Forged Note* (1915), and *The Homesteader* (1917)—reveal a great deal about his biography, as well as his perspectives on western homesteading and interracial relationships.

2. Pearl Bowser and Louise Spence, "Identity and Betrayal: *The Symbol of the Unconquered* and Oscar Micheaux's 'Biographical Legend,'" *The Birth of Whiteness: Race and the Emergence of U.S. Cinema,* ed. Daniel Bernardi (New Brunswick: Rutgers UP, 1996) 67.

3. Of the Micheaux films I discuss here, only versions of *Within Our Gates* (1920) and *The Symbol of the Unconquered* (1920) are extant. As yet, no prints of *The Homesteader* (1919) or *The Brute* (1920) have resurfaced. For descriptions of these films, I rely on advertisements and reviews, as well as summaries in Bowser and Spence, "Identity," and their exemplary book-length study, *Writing Himself into History: Oscar Micheaux, His Silent Films, and His Audiences* (New Brunswick: Rutgers UP, 2000); Sampson; Cripps; and Bernard L. Peterson Jr., *Early Black American Playwrights and Dramatic Writers: A Biographical Directory and Catalog of Plays, Films, and Broadcasting Scripts* (New York: Greenwood, 1990). Release dates and exhibition venues are also gleaned from "An Oscar Micheaux Filmography: From the Silents through His Transition to Sound, 1919–1931," compiled by Charles Musser, Corey K. Creekmur, Pearl Bowser, J. Ronald Green, Charlene Regester, and Louise Spence in Pearl Bowser, Jane Gaines, and Charles Musser, eds., *Oscar Micheaux and His Circle: African-American Filmmaking and Race Cinema of the Silent Era* (Bloomington: Indiana UP, 2001) 228–77.

4. Micheaux's obsession with this tale—which closely parallels his own life experiences—resulted in two sound versions of this story, *The Exile* (1931) and his last production, *The Betrayal* (1948). For an extended discussion of the relationships between Micheaux's biography and his novels and films, see VanEpps-Taylor. Shooting at Ebony Studios noted in "An Oscar Micheaux Filmography" 231.

5. On the popularity of *The Homesteader* upon its release in Chicago, despite objections raised by ministers, see Bowser and Spence *Writing Himself* 13. Micheaux's repeated castigations of ministers in many of his novels and his films are thinly veiled criticisms of his father-in-law, the prominent Chicago minister Elder N. J. McCracken, whom Micheaux blamed for the dissolution of his marriage. See VanEpps-Taylor 63–71. The compilers of the "Oscar Micheaux Filmography" note that the Chicago Censor Board "ordered substantial cuts, including the complete elimination of the characters Orlean and Ethel," prompting Micheaux to advertise the film (in the *Defender* 1 Mar. 1919: 11) as "Passed by the Censor Board Despite the Protests of Three Chicago Ministers Who Claimed That It Was Based upon the Supposed Hypocritical Actions of a Prominent Colored Preacher of This City." "An Oscar Micheaux Filmography" 233.

6. Oscar Micheaux, letter to exhibitors, Mar. 1919, GPJC.

7. See Micheaux's treatise on the West as the space for the Race's best chances for the future in "Where the Negro Fails," *Defender* 19 Mar. 1910; Micheaux's unsuccessful attempt to visit his wife at her father's home in Chicago made front-page headlines: "MR. OSCAR MICHEAUX IN CITY, Seemed to Be in Family Mix-Up Yet Would Not Speak; Seen with Dr. Daily at Father-in-Law's Door, but Neither He nor the Doctor Were Admitted," *Defender* 29 Apr. 1911.

8. "Photoplay" section, *Master Musician* Oct. 1919: 15.

9. Advertisement, *Monitor* 29 July 1920: 3.

10. Although the currently circulating print of *Symbol* (restored by the Museum of Modern Art and Turner Classic Movies, with a score composed and performed by Max Roach) lists the film's white antagonist as "August Barr" and played by Louis Déan, the compilers of "An Oscar Micheaux Filmography" cite sources naming this character "Tom Cutschawl," played by Edward E. King. "An Oscar Micheaux Filmography" 238–39.

11. Bowser and Spence, "Identity" 61.

12. John Hope Franklin and Alfred A. Moss Jr., *From Slavery to Freedom: A History of Negro Americans,* 6th ed. (New York: McGraw, 1988) 311–12.

13. " 'Symbol of the Unconquered,' Oscar Micheaux Great Picture to Show the KuKlux in Europe," *Chicago Star* 1 Oct. 1921: 1. Antilynching activist Ida B. Wells used similar tactics by embarking on lecture tours in Europe to expose the atrocities white Americans perpetrated against African Americans. See *Crusade for Justice: The Autobiography of Ida B. Wells,* ed. Alfreda M. Duster (Chicago: U of Chicago P, 1970).

14. According to Bernard L. Peterson, "The film was considered too sensational because of its erotic love scenes, racial violence, and realistic scenes of low life in black drinking and gambling joints, and failed to gain the censor's approval in Chicago." Peterson 135.

15. *New York Age* 18 Sept. 1920, qtd. in Bowser and Spence, *Writing Himself* 177.

16. See Bowser and Spence, *Writing Himself* 130, for a discussion of *The Brute*'s detailed illustration of a "well-appointed parlor" (perhaps that of gambling boss Bull Magee).

17. Charlene Regester outlines how the Black press shifted from offering almost uniform praise for early Black filmmaking to voicing more detailed criticism of its Black images and production values in "The African-American Press and Race Movies, 1909–1929," in *Oscar Micheaux and His Circle* 34–49. See also Anna Everett's discussion of Walton's response to *The Brute* in *Returning the Gaze: A Genealogy of Black Film Criticism, 1909–1949* (Durham: Duke UP, 2001) 161–62.

18. In later films, Micheaux would continue to use a North/South contrast to explain character motivations (*The Notorious Elinor Lee,* 1940) or to clear up misunderstandings that threaten narrative closure (*Lying Lips,* 1939). Other Micheaux films that feature other migration narratives include *The Exile* (1931; sound remake of *The Homesteader,* about a man who moves from Chicago to homestead in South Dakota); *Birthright* (1924; a Harvard graduate tries to start a school for Negro children in the Deep South; remade with sound in 1939); *The Spider's Web* (1926; a Harlem woman travels to a small town in Mississippi and back again; remade with sound as *The Girl from Chicago,* 1932); *Swing* (1938; a couple travels from Birmingham to Harlem).

19. On miscegenation and the "mulatto" figure in American literature, see Werner Sollors, *Neither Black nor White yet Both: Thematic Explorations of Interracial Literature* (New York: Oxford UP, 1997); and James Kinney, *Amalgamation! Race, Sex, and Rhetoric in the Nineteenth-Century American*

*Novel* (Westport: Greenwood, 1985). On the African American migration narrative, see Farah Jasmine Griffin, *"Who Set You Flowin'?": The African American Migration Narrative* (New York: Oxford UP, 1995); and Lawrence R. Rodgers, *Canaan Bound: The African-American Great Migration Novel* (Urbana: U of Illinois P, 1997).

20. Like Sylvia, all three characters diverge from the one-way pattern of many migration narratives (the move from South to North) by making several journeys between South and North. The Ex-Colored Man and Helga Crane also migrate to Europe and back. Frances Ellen Watkins Harper, *Iola LeRoy* (1892; Oxford: Oxford UP, 1988); James Weldon Johnson, *The Autobiography of an Ex-Colored Man* (1912) in *Three Negro Classics* (New York: Avon, 1965) 391–511; Nella Larsen, *Quicksand* (1928; New Brunswick: Rutgers UP, 1986).

21. Although Iola grew up comfortably in the South believing that she was white, her return there after the revelation of her Black heritage is fraught with traumatic events, not the least of which is being remanded into slavery. The Ex-Colored Man witnesses a lynching in the South that impels him to renounce his Black heritage and pass for white. Helga Crane feels alienated in the repressive, upwardly mobile atmosphere of a southern Black college at the start of the novel. When she returns to the South at the novel's conclusion—with hopes of "uplifting" a poor, rural Black population—she again feels woefully out of place, but this time she becomes too physically and psychologically drained to escape.

22. The end of the scene in which Conrad sees Sylvia with Armand Gridlestone is missing from the restored print of the film. Perhaps there was more footage (and more explanatory intertitles) in original prints of the film that would have included a more detailed account of what happened between Armand, Sylvia, Conrad, and Alma at this point in the narrative. Still, the Library of Congress's explanatory note that Conrad leaves the room without hearing Sylvia's explanation suggests that Micheaux did not yet reveal Sylvia's "secrets" to the viewer.

23. Toni Cade Bambara quotation from the documentary film *Midnight Ramble: Oscar Micheaux and the Race Film*, dir. Bestor Cram and Pearl Bowser, The American Experience, 1994. For a discussion of *Within Our Gates* as a response to *The Birth of a Nation* (particularly in its representations of rape and lynching), see Jane Gaines, "Fire and Desire: Race, Melodrama, and Oscar Micheaux," *Black American Cinema*, ed. Manthia Diawara (New York: Routledge, 1993) 49–70.

24. Representations of urban criminals are common in the scenes of urban encounter in migration narratives. I should note, however, that the casting of a dark-skinned actor in the role of the thief, who is apprehended by the light-skinned Dr. Vivian, reveals Micheaux's frequent (but by no means universal) mobilization of color-based typing and hierarchies in his films.

25. J. Ronald Green, *Straight Lick: The Cinema of Oscar Micheaux* (Bloomington: Indiana UP, 2000) 29.

26. Carby notes that Harper presents Iola's attraction to Dr. Latimer not in "base" physical, sexual terms but rather as "spiritual." I would argue that Micheaux's awkward treatment of Vivian's marriage proposal (as discussed later) functions to similarly circumvent sticky questions of Black sexuality. Like Harper, Micheaux "initially utilize[s] romantic convention and then discard[s] the romance." Hazel Carby, *Reconstructing Womanhood: The Emergence of the Afro-American Woman Novelist* (Oxford: Oxford UP, 1987) 79–80.

27. Michele Wallace, "Oscar Micheaux's *Within Our Gates:* The Possibilities for Alternative Visions," *Oscar Micheaux and His Circle* 58–59.

28. Green 29.

29. In addition to its many other contradictions, Vivian's patriotic speech does not address the problem of advocating America's imperialist military actions against people of color abroad in light of its racist practices and policies at home.

30. Bowser and Spence, *Writing Himself* 109.

31. Anna Julia Cooper, *A Voice from the South* (1892; Oxford: Oxford UP, 1988) 31.

32. Gaines, "Fire and Desire" 52.

33. Gaines, "Fire and Desire" 50; Bowser and Spence, *Writing Himself* 15–16.

34. Before arranging for a second run of the film in Omaha, Johnson asks Micheaux to "kindly eliminate from the second reel all the objectionable lynching scenes such as has caused trouble in other communities." Letter, George P. Johnson to Oscar Micheaux, 4 Oct. 1920, GPJC. Bowser and Spence wonder "if the film was, at one point, arranged in chronological order," or "maybe there had been other lynchings in the second reel." Bowser and Spence, *Writing Himself* 146.

35. Jane Gaines, "*Within Our Gates:* From Race Melodrama to Opportunity Narrative," *Oscar Micheaux and His Circle* 75; Bowser and Spence, *Writing Himself* 134.

36. Creekmur's insightful analysis of the politics of adaptation in Micheaux's work describes *Within Our Gates*'s relation (at the levels of content and form) to Charles Chesnutt's *The Marrow of Tradition* (1901). Corey Creekmur, "Telling White Lies: Oscar Micheaux and Charles W. Chesnutt," *Oscar Micheaux and His Circle* 147–58.

37. Creekmur 156.

38. Griffith quoted in Michael Rogin, "'The Sword Became a Flashing Vision': D. W. Griffith's *The Birth of a Nation*," *Representations* 9 (1985): 157.

39. Gaines, *Within Our Gates* 80.

## CONCLUSION

1. The photographs, drawn mostly from the files of the Farm Security Administration, depict Black subjects in a range of contexts: southern share-

croppers and northern factory workers; children crowded around rural shacks and in Chicago kitchenette apartments. David Bradley reports that Wright was asked to write the text for the book of photographs while enjoying the phenomenal success of *Native Son* in mid-1940. The editors at Viking expected that the text would "take up a mere twenty pages. But Wright became fascinated with telling a story which was very much his own story. Twenty pages quickly became more than fifty." Wright "went through as many as six revisions of each section" and "delivered the manuscript in mid-July 1941 and then withdrew it for still more revisions before allowing it at last to leave his hands." David Bradley, "Preface," *12 Million Black Voices*, text by Richard Wright, photo direction by Edwin Rosskam (1941; New York: Thunder's Mouth, 1988) xiv.

2. Wright 90–139.

3. Wright 93.

4. Houston A. Baker Jr., *Modernism and the Harlem Renaissance* (Chicago: U of Chicago P, 1987) 9–13.

5. Race filmmakers have been criticized for failing to leave behind structures (e.g., studios, production companies, distribution networks) upon which subsequent generations could build a vital Black film industry. Further, critics like James Nesteby argue that early Black filmmakers failed to establish representational or aesthetic models from which subsequent Black cinemas could draw: "The first [silent] generation's efforts . . . were rarely built upon by the second [sound] generation. An aesthetics of black film did not develop." Nesteby goes on to argue that when a third wave of Black filmmaking emerged in the late 1960s, it had nothing to inherit from the race film era: "The independent Afro-American films of the first two generations had lost the opportunity to write an even more significant chapter in the history of film culture and the black image in films." James R. Nesteby, *Black Images in American Films, 1896–1954: The Interplay between Civil Rights and Film Culture* (Washington: University P of America, 1982) 93, 95.

6. William M. Tuttle Jr., *Race Riot: Chicago in the Red Summer of 1919* (1970; Urbana: U of Illinois P, 1996) 12.

7. Tuttle 14, 23.

8. Tuttle points out that McKay's poem was published in the *Liberator* in July 1919, earlier than is generally believed (208). See my discussion in chapter 7 of *Within Our Gates* as a response to the riots.

9. St. Clair Drake and Horace R. Cayton summarize the lesson that the riots taught white Chicagoans who had come to see the Negro as a "problem": "The Negro had come to Chicago to stay!" St. Clair Drake and Horace R. Cayton, *Black Metropolis: A Study of Negro Life in a Northern City* (1945; Chicago: U of Chicago P, 1993) 70.

10. Henry Sampson notes that "the golden years of black film production occurred in the early 1920s with 1921 being the peak year for the number of films released." Henry T. Sampson, *Blacks in Black and White: A Source Book on Black Films*, 2nd ed. (Metuchen: Scarecrow, 1995) 7. Sampson notes that

race film production began to slump shortly thereafter, even before the prohibitive costs of sound, because the number of Black-owned theaters declined dramatically in the mid-1920s as white businessmen sought to profit from the lucrative African American market. These white owners and managers, Sampson claims, would not charge special, higher admission prices for Black-produced films as Black owners and managers had done. Without this subsidy, Black filmmakers could no longer generate the same level of income they needed from this limited market to sustain themselves. Sampson 9.

11. For more on race films, Black audiences, and Hollywood's racial politics during the 1920s through 1940s, see (among other sources mentioned throughout the book) Sampson, *Blacks in Black and White;* Thomas Cripps, *Slow Fade to Black: The Negro in American Film, 1900–1942* (Oxford: Oxford UP, 1977); G. William Jones, *Black Cinema Treasures Lost and Found* (Denton: U of North Texas P, 1991); and Arthur Knight, *Disintegrating the Musical: Black Performance and American Musical Film* (Durham: Duke UP, 2002).

12. For an excellent survey, see Paula Massood, *Black City Cinema: African American Urban Experiences in Film* (Philadelphia: Temple UP, 2003).

13. Massood 61.

14. Writings on contemporary African American cinema abound. Among other readings, the following list contains some particularly useful accounts of the cycles I describe. On "Blaxploitation," see Ed Guerrero, *Framing Blackness: The African American Image in Film* (Philadelphia: Temple UP, 1993) ch. 3; and Mark Reid, *Redefining Black Cinema* (Berkeley: U of California P, 1993) ch. 4. On the L.A. Rebellion, see Ntongela Masilela, "The Los Angeles School of Black Filmmakers," *Black American Cinema,* ed. Manthia Diawara (New York: Routledge, 1993) 107–17, as well as Nathan Grant, "Innocence and Ambiguity in the Films of Charles Burnett" (135–55), and Mike Murashige, "Haile Gerima and the Political Economy of Cinematic Resistance" (183–203), both in *Representing Blackness: Issues in Film and Video,* ed. Valerie Smith (New Brunswick: Rutgers UP, 1997). On Spike Lee, see Lee, *Spike Lee's Gotta Have It: Inside Guerilla Filmmaking* (New York: Simon, 1987); Wahneema Lubiano, "But Compared to What? Reading Realism, Representation, and Essentialism in *School Daze, Do the Right Thing,* and the Spike Lee Discourse," *Black American Literature Forum* 25 (1991): 253–82; and S. Craig Watkins, *Representing: Hip Hop Culture and the Production of Black Cinema* (Chicago: U of Chicago P, 1998) chs. 4 and 5. On the "boys in the hood" cycle, see Watkins, chs. 6 and 7; Jacquie Jones, "The New Ghetto Aesthetic," *Wide Angle* 13.3&4 (1991): 32–43; and Paula Massood, "Mapping the Hood: The Genealogy of City Space in *Boyz N the Hood* and *Menace II Society,*" *Cinema Journal* 35.2 (1996): 85–97.

15. These include studies by Gregory Waller, *Main Street Amusements: Movies and Commercial Entertainment in a Southern City, 1896–1930* (Washington: Smithsonian Institution P, 1995) ch. 7, on exhibition to Black audiences in Lexington, Kentucky; Dan Streible, "The Harlem Theater: Black Film Exhibition in Austin, Texas, 1920–1973," *Black American Cinema,* ed.

Manthia Diawara (New York: Routledge, 1993) 221–36; and Matthew Bernstein and Dana White's extensive research on film exhibition in Atlanta, including its segregated Black theaters. Matthew Bernstein and Dana White, "'The Avenue' and 'the Street': Race Film Exhibition and the Norman Company Films in 1920s Atlanta," Society for Cinema Studies conference, San Diego, CA, 6 Apr. 1998; and Matthew Bernstein, "Run/Zone/Clearance across the Color Line: Distributing Films in Segregated Atlanta," Society for Cinema Studies, Chicago, 11 Mar. 2000.

# Bibliography

The bibliography does not include periodical sources (such as the *Chicago Broad Ax*, the *Chicago Daily News*, the *Chicago Defender*, and *Moving Picture World*) for the articles, advertisements, and theater listings that are cited in the notes.

## ARCHIVES AND SPECIAL COLLECTIONS

Black Film Center/Archive. Indiana University. Bloomington, IN.
British Film Institute. London, UK.
Chicago Historical Society. Chicago, IL.
Chicago Jazz Archive. University of Chicago. Chicago, IL.
Chicago Public Library. Chicago, IL.
Department of Buildings. City of Chicago. Chicago, IL.
George Eastman House. Rochester, NY.
George P. Johnson Negro Film Collection. Department of Special Collections. University of California at Los Angeles. Los Angeles, CA.
Illinois Institute of Technology. Chicago, IL.
Margaret Herrick Library, Academy of Motion Picture Arts and Sciences. Los Angeles, CA.
Motion Picture, Broadcasting and Recorded Sound Division. Library of Congress. Washington, DC.
Office of the Recorder of Deeds. Cook County, IL. Chicago, IL.
Theatre Historical Society of America. Elmhurst, IL.

## BOOKS AND ARTICLES

Adero, Malaika. *Up South: Stories, Studies and Letters of This Century's Black Migrations.* New York: New Press, 1993.
Alexander, Elizabeth. "Can You Be BLACK and Look at This? Reading the Rodney King Video(s)." *Public Culture* 7 (1994): 77–94.

Allen, Robert C., and Douglas Gomery. *Film History: Theory and Practice.* New York: Knopf, 1985.

Altman, Rick. "The Silence of the Silents." *Musical Quarterly* 80 (1997): 648–718.

American Film Institute. *The American Film Institute Catalog of Motion Pictures Produced in the United States: Film Beginnings, 1893–1910.* Comp. Elias Savada. Metuchen: Scarecrow, 1995.

Aptheker, Herbert. *Afro-American History: The Modern Era.* New York: Citadel, 1971.

Asbury, Herbert. *Gem of the Prairie: An Informal History of the Chicago Underworld.* New York: Knopf, 1940.

Baker, Houston A., Jr. *Modernism and the Harlem Renaissance.* Chicago: University of Chicago Press, 1987.

———. *Turning South Again: Re-thinking Modernism/Re-reading Booker T.* Durham: Duke University Press, 2001.

Baker, Ray Stannard. *Following the Color Line: American Negro Citizenship in the Progressive Era.* 1908. New York: Harper, 1964.

Baldwin, Brooke. "The Cakewalk: A Study in Stereotype and Reality." *Journal of Social History* 15 (1981): 205–18.

Baldwin, James. *The Devil Finds Work.* New York: Dial, 1976.

Balides, Constance. "Scenarios of Exposure in the Practice of Everyday Life: Women in the Cinema of Attractions." *Screen* 34.1 (1993): 19–37.

Baudry, Jean-Louis. "Ideological Effects of the Basic Cinematographic Apparatus." *Narrative, Apparatus, Ideology: A Film Theory Reader.* Ed. Philip Rosen. New York: Columbia University Press, 1986. 286–98.

Bernardi, Daniel. "The Voice of Whiteness: D. W. Griffith's Biograph Films (1908–1913)." *The Birth of Whiteness: Race and the Emergence of U.S. Cinema.* Ed. Daniel Bernardi. New Brunswick: Rutgers University Press, 1996. 103–28.

Bernstein, Arnie. *Hollywood on Lake Michigan: 100 Years of Chicago and the Movies.* Chicago: Lake Claremont Press, 1998.

Bernstein, Matthew. "Run/Zone/Clearance across the Color Line: Distributing Films in Segregated Atlanta." Society for Cinema Studies. Chicago, 2000.

Bernstein, Matthew, and Dana White. "'The Avenue' and 'The Street': Race Film Exhibition and the Norman Company Films in 1920s Atlanta." Society for Cinema Studies. San Diego, 1998.

Bertellini, Giorgio. "Italian Imageries, Historical Feature Films and the Fabrication of Italy's Spectators in Early 1900s New York." *American Movie Audiences: From the Turn of the Century to the Early Sound Era.* Eds. Melvyn Stokes and Richard Maltby, 1999. 29–45.

Best, Stephen M. "The Subject of Property: Race, Prosthesis, and Possession in American Culture, 1865–1920." Diss. University of Pennsylvania, 1997.

Bhabha, Homi. *The Location of Culture.* London: Routledge, 1994.

Bobo, Jacqueline. *Black Women as Cultural Readers.* New York: Columbia University Press, 1995.

Bogle, Donald. *Toms, Coons, Mulattoes, Mammies, and Bucks: An Interpretive History of Blacks in American Films.* New York: Continuum, 1990.

Bontemps, Arna, and Jack Conroy. *Anyplace but Here.* 1945 *(They Seek a City).* Columbia: University of Missouri Press, 1966.

Borchert, James. *Alley Life in Washington: Family, Community, Religion and Folklife in the City, 1850–1970.* Urbana: University of Illinois Press, 1980.

Bordwell, David, Janet Staiger, and Kristin Thompson. *The Classical Hollywood Cinema: Film Style and Mode of Production to 1960.* New York: Columbia University Press, 1985.

Bowser, Eileen. "Racial/Racist Jokes in American Silent Slapstick Comedy." *Griffithania* 53 (1995): 35–42.

———. *The Transformation of Cinema: 1907–1915.* Berkeley: University of California Press, 1990.

Bowser, Pearl, Jane Gaines, and Charles Musser, eds. *Oscar Micheaux and His Circle: African-American Filmmaking and the Race Cinema of the Silent Era.* Bloomington: Indiana University Press, 2001.

Bowser, Pearl, and Louise Spence. "Identity and Betrayal: *The Symbol of the Unconquered* and Oscar Micheaux's 'Biographical Legend.'" *The Birth of Whiteness: Race and the Emergence of U.S. Cinema.* Ed. Daniel Bernardi. New Brunswick: Rutgers University Press, 1996. 56–80.

———. *Writing Himself into History: Oscar Micheaux, His Silent Films, and His Audiences.* New Brunswick: Rutgers University Press, 2000.

Brewster, Ben. "A Scene at the 'Movies.'" *Early Cinema: Space, Frame, Narrative.* Ed. Thomas Elsaesser. London: BFI, 1990. 318–25.

Brooks, Gwendolyn. *Maud Martha.* 1953. Chicago: Third World Press, 1993.

Brown, Henry. "Chicago's Night Life of Former Years: Crimson! Alluring! Tragic!" *Abbott's Monthly.* July 1930: 4–6+.

Bruno, Giuliana. *Streetwalking on a Ruined Map: Cultural Theory and the City Films of Elvira Notari.* Princeton: Princeton University Press, 1993.

Buck-Morss, Susan. *The Dialectics of Seeing: Walter Benjamin and the Arcades Project.* Cambridge: MIT Press, 1989.

———. "The Flaneur, the Sandwichman and the Whore: The Politics of Loitering." *New German Critique* 39 (1986): 99–140.

Burch, Noel. "A Primitive Mode of Representation?" *Early Cinema: Space, Frame, Narrative.* Ed. Thomas Elsaesser. London: BFI, 1990. 220–27.

Butler, Cheryl. "The Color Purple Controversy: Black Women's Spectatorship." *Wide Angle* 13.3&4 (1991): 62–69.

Butters, Gerald. *Black Manhood on the Silent Screen.* Lawrence: University Press of Kansas, 2002.

Campbell, Craig W. *Reel America and World War I: A Comprehensive Filmography and History of Motion Pictures in the United States, 1914–1920.* Jefferson: McFarland, 1985.

Carbine, Mary. "'The Finest outside the Loop': Motion Picture Exhibition in Chicago's Black Metropolis, 1905–1928." *Camera Obscura* 23 (1990): 9–41.

Carby, Hazel. "Policing the Black Woman's Body in an Urban Context." *Critical Inquiry* 18 (1992): 738–55.

——. *Reconstructing Womanhood: The Emergence of the Afro-American Woman Novelist.* New York: Oxford University Press, 1987.

Chicago Commission on Race Relations [Charles S. Johnson]. *The Negro in Chicago: A Study of Race Relations and a Race Riot.* Chicago: University of Chicago Press, 1922.

Chicago Urban League. *Annual Reports.* 1916–23.

Childs, John Brown. "Concepts of Culture in Afro-American Political Thought." *Social Text* 4 (1981): 28–43.

Clark-Lewis, Elizabeth. " 'This Work Had a End': African-American Domestic Workers in Washington, D.C., 1910–1940." *"To Toil the Livelong Day": America's Women at Work, 1780–1980.* Ed. Carol Groneman and Mary Beth Norton. Ithaca: Cornell University Press, 1987. 196–212.

Clover, Carol J. *Men, Women, and Chainsaws: Gender in the Modern Horror Film.* Princeton: Princeton University Press, 1992.

Cohen, Lizabeth. *Making a New Deal: Industrial Workers in Chicago, 1919–1939.* Cambridge: Cambridge University Press, 1990.

Collier, John. "Leisure Time, the Last Problem of Conservation." *Playground* 6.3 (1912): 93–106.

Cooper, Anna Julia. *A Voice from the South.* 1892. Oxford: Oxford University Press, 1988.

Courtney, Susan. "Hollywood's Fantasy of Miscegenation." Diss. University of California, Berkeley, 1997.

Crary, Jonathan. "Modernizing Vision." *Viewing Positions: Ways of Seeing Film.* Ed. Linda Williams. New Brunswick: Rutgers University Press, 1994. 23–35.

Cripps, Thomas. "The Making of the Birth of a Race: The Emerging Politics of Identity in Silent Movies." *The Birth of Whiteness: Race and the Emergence of U.S. Cinema.* Ed. Daniel Bernardi. New Brunswick: Rutgers University Press, 1996. 38–55.

——. "Oscar Micheaux: The Story Continues." *Black American Cinema.* Ed. Manthia Diawara. New York: Routledge, 1993. 71–79.

——. *Slow Fade to Black: The Negro in American Film, 1900–1942.* Oxford: Oxford University Press, 1977.

Dash, Julie. *Daughters of the Dust: The Making of an African American Woman's Film.* New York: New Press, 1992.

Davis, Ralph Nelson. "The Negro Newspaper in Chicago." M.A. thesis. University of Chicago, 1939.

Dawson, Michael. "A Black Counterpublic?: Economic Earthquakes, Racial Agenda(s), and Black Politics." *Public Culture* 7 (1994): 195–223.

DeBauche, Leslie Midkiff. *Reel Patriotism: The Movies and World War I.* Madison: University of Wisconsin Press, 1997.

Dent, Gina, and Michele Wallace, eds. *Black Popular Culture.* Seattle: Bay Press, 1992.

Diawara, Manthia. "Black American Cinema: The New Realism." *Black American Cinema*. Ed. Manthia Diawara. New York: Routledge, 1993. 3–25.

———. "Black Spectatorship: Problems of Identification and Resistance." *Black American Cinema*. Ed. Manthia Diawara. New York: Routledge, 1993. 211–20.

Doane, Mary Ann. *The Desire to Desire: The Woman's Film of the 1940s*. Bloomington: Indiana University Press, 1987.

Doane, Mary Ann, Patricia Mellencamp, and Linda Williams, eds. *Re-Vision: Essays in Feminist Film Criticism*. Los Angeles: American Film Institute, 1984.

Drake, St. Clair, and Horace R. Cayton. *Black Metropolis: A Study of Negro Life in a Northern City*. 1945. Chicago: University of Chicago Press, 1993.

Du Bois, W. E. B. "Close Ranks." *Crisis* 16 (July 1918): 111.

———. *Dusk of Dawn: An Essay toward an Autobiography of a Race Concept. Writings*. 1903. Ed. Nathan Huggins. New York: New American Library, 1986.

———. *The Souls of Black Folk. Three Negro Classics*. 1903. New York: Avon, 1965. 207–389.

DuciBella, Joseph R. *Theaters of Chicago*. Washington: Theatre Historical Society of America, 1973.

Dunbar, Paul Lawrence. *Sport of the Gods*. 1903. New York: Penguin, 1999.

Duncan, Otis Dudley, and Beverly Duncan. *The Negro Population of Chicago: A Study of Residential Succession*. Chicago: University of Chicago Press, 1957.

Dunham, Katherine. *A Touch of Innocence: Memoirs of Childhood*. 1959. Chicago: University of Chicago Press, 1994.

Dyer, Richard. *White*. New York: Routledge, 1997.

Ellison, Ralph. "The Shadow and the Act." *Shadow and Act*. 1964. New York: Vintage, 1995. 273–81.

Erens, Patricia. *Issues in Feminist Film Criticism*. Bloomington: Indiana University Press, 1990.

Everett, Anna. "Lester Walton's Écriture Noir: Black Spectatorial Transcodings of 'Cinematic Excess.'" *Cinema Journal* 39.3 (2000): 30–50.

———. *Returning the Gaze: A Genealogy of Black Film Criticism, 1909–1949*. Durham: Duke University Press, 2001.

Fanon, Frantz. *Black Skin, White Masks*. New York: Grove, 1967.

Fletcher, Marvin. *The Black Soldier and Officer in the United States Army, 1891–1917*. Columbia: University of Missouri Press, 1974.

Fletcher, Tom. *100 Years of the Negro in Show Business: The Tom Fletcher Story*. New York: Burdge, 1954.

Frankenberg, Ruth. *White Women, Race Matters: The Social Construction of Whiteness*. Minneapolis: University of Minnesota Press, 1993.

Franklin, Donna L. *Ensuring Inequality: The Structural Transformation of the African-American Family*. Oxford: Oxford University Press, 1997.

Franklin, John Hope, and Alfred A. Moss Jr. *From Slavery to Freedom: A History of Negro Americans*. 6th ed. New York: McGraw, 1988.

Frazier, Edward Franklin. "Recreation and Amusement among American Negroes." *Carnegie-Myrdal Study: The Negro in America. Research Memoranda for Use in Preparation of Dr. Gunnar Myrdal's* An American Dilemma. 1940. Milkwood, NY: Kraus-Thompson Organization, 1973. Microfilm.

Fredrickson, George M. *The Black Image in the White Mind: The Debate on Afro-American Character and Destiny, 1817–1914*. 1971. Hanover: Wesleyan University Press, 1987.

Friedberg, Anne. "Les Flâneuses du Mal(l): Cinema and the Postmodern Condition." *Viewing Positions: Ways of Seeing Film*. Ed. Linda Williams. New Brunswick: Rutgers University Press, 1994. 59–83.

———. *Window Shopping: Cinema and the Postmodern*. Berkeley: University of California Press, 1993.

Gaines, Jane. *Fire and Desire: Mixed Race Movies in the Silent Era*. Chicago: University of Chicago Press, 2001.

———. "Fire and Desire: Race, Melodrama, and Oscar Micheaux." *Black American Cinema*. Ed. Manthia Diawara. New York: Routledge, 1993. 49–70.

Gates, Henry Louis, Jr. "New Negroes, Migration, and Cultural Exchange." *Jacob Lawrence: The Migration Series*. Ed. Elizabeth Hutton Turner. Washington: Rappahannock, 1993. 17–21.

———. "The Trope of a New Negro and the Reconstruction of the Image of the Black." *Representations* 24 (1988): 129–55.

Goldsby, Jacqueline. *A Spectacular Secret: The Cultural Logic of Lynching in American Life and Literature*. Chicago: University of Chicago Press, forthcoming.

Gomery, Douglas. *Shared Pleasures: A History of Movie Presentation in the United States*. Madison: University of Wisconsin Press, 1992.

Goodwin, E. Marvin. *Black Migration in America from 1915–1960*. Lewiston: Mellen, 1990.

Green, J. Ronald. *Straight Lick: The Cinema of Oscar Micheaux*. Bloomington: Indiana University Press, 2000.

———. " 'Twoness' in the Style of Oscar Micheaux." *Black American Cinema*. Ed. Manthia Diawara. New York: Routledge, 1993. 26–48.

Griffin, Farah Jasmine. *"Who Set You Flowin'?": The African-American Migration Narrative*. New York: Oxford University Press, 1995.

Griffiths, Alison, and James Latham. "Film and Ethnic Identity in Harlem, 1896–1915." *American Movie Audiences: From the Turn of the Century to the Early Sound Era*. Ed. Melvyn Stokes and Richard Maltby. London: BFI, 1999. 46–63.

Grossman, James R. *Land of Hope: Chicago, Black Southerners, and the Great Migration*. Chicago: University of Chicago Press, 1989.

Guerrero, Ed. *Framing Blackness: The African American Image in Film*. Philadelphia: Temple University Press, 1993.

Gunning, Tom. "The Cinema of Attractions: Early Film, Its Spectator and the Avant-Garde." *Early Cinema: Space, Frame, Narrative*. Ed. Thomas Elsaesser. London: BFI, 1990. 56–62.

———. "Crazy Machines in the Garden of Forking Paths: Mischief Gags and the Origins of American Film Comedy." *Classical Hollywood Comedy*. Ed. Kristine Brunovska Karnick and Henry Jenkins. New York: Routledge, 1995. 87–105.

———. *D. W. Griffith and the Origins of American Narrative Film: The Early Years at Biograph*. Urbana: University of Illinois Press, 1991.

———. "Non-Continuity, Continuity, Discontinuity: A Theory of Genres in Early Films." *Early Cinema: Space, Frame, Narrative*. Ed. Thomas Elsaesser. London: BFI, 1990. 86–94.

———. "'The Whole World within Reach': Travel Images without Borders." *Travel Culture: Essays on What Makes Us Go*. Ed. Carol Traynor Williams. Westport: Praeger, 1998. 25–37.

Gutman, Herbert G. *Work, Culture, and Society in Industrializing America*. New York: Knopf, 1976.

Habermas, Jürgen. *The Structural Transformation of the Public Sphere: An Inquiry into a Category of Bourgeois Society*. 1962. Ed. Thomas Burger. Cambridge: MIT Press, 1989.

Hall, Stuart. "Cultural Identity and Cinematic Representation." *Framework* 36 (1989): 68–81.

Haller, Mark H. "Policy Gambling, Entertainment, and the Emergence of Black Politics: Chicago from 1900 to 1940." *Journal of Social History* 24 (1991): 719–39.

Halley, Lois Kate. "A Study of Motion Pictures in Chicago as a Medium of Communication." M.A. thesis University of Chicago, 1924.

Hansen, Miriam. *Babel and Babylon: Spectatorship in American Silent Film*. Cambridge: Harvard University Press, 1991.

———. "Benjamin, Cinema and Experience: 'The Blue Flower in the Land of Technology'" *New German Critique* 40 (1987): 179–224.

———. "The Mass Production of the Senses: Classical Cinema as Vernacular Modernism." *Modernism/Modernity* 6 (1999): 59–77.

Harper, Frances Ellen Watkins. *Iola Leroy*. 1892. Oxford: Oxford University Press, 1988.

Harrison, Alferdteen, ed. *Black Exodus: The Great Migration from the American South*. Jackson: University Press of Mississippi, 1991.

*History of Chicago and Souvenir of the Liquor Interest: The Nation's Choice for the Great Columbian Exposition*. Chicago: Belgravia, 1891.

hooks, bell. *Black Looks: Race and Representation*. Boston: South End, 1992.

Hunter, Tera. *To 'Joy My Freedom: Southern Black Women's Lives and Labors after the Civil War*. Cambridge: Harvard University Press, 1997.

Ignatiev, Noel. *How the Irish Became White.* New York: Routledge, 1995.

*Intercollegian Wonder Book, or, the Negro in Chicago 1779–1927.* Chicago: Washington Intercollegiate Club of Chicago, 1927.

Jacobs, Lewis. *The Rise of the American Film.* New York: Teachers College Press, 1939.

Jerome, V. J. *The Negro in Hollywood Films.* New York: Masses and Mainstream, 1950.

Johnson, George P. *Collector of Negro Film History.* Oral History Program, University of California at Los Angeles, 1970.

Johnson, James Weldon. *The Autobiography of an Ex-Colored Man. Three Negro Classics.* 1912. New York: Avon, 1965. 391–511.

Johnston, Claire, ed. *Notes on Women's Cinema.* London: Society for Education in Film and Television, 1972.

Jones, G. William. *Black Cinema Treasures Lost and Found.* Denton: University of North Texas Press, 1991.

Jones, Jacquie. "The New Ghetto Aesthetic." *Wide Angle* 13.3&4 (1991): 32–43.

Jones, LeRoi. *Blues People: Negro Music in White America.* New York: Morrow, 1963.

Jones, William Henry. *Recreation and Amusement among Negroes in Washington, D.C.: A Sociological Analysis of the Negro in an Urban Environment.* Washington: Howard University Press, 1927.

Kaplan, E. Ann. *Looking for the Other: Feminism, Film, and the Imperial Gaze.* New York: Routledge, 1997.

Kasson, John F. *Amusing the Million: Coney Island at the Turn of the Century.* New York: Hill and Wang, 1978.

———. *Rudeness and Civility: Manners in Nineteenth-Century Urban America.* New York: Hill and Wang, 1990.

Keller, Alexandra. "Disseminations of Modernity: Representation and Consumer Desire in Early Mail-Order Catalogs." *Cinema and the Invention of Modern Life.* Ed. Leo Charney and Vanessa R. Schwartz. Berkeley: University of California Press, 1995. 156–82.

Kelly, Daniel Q. "'Ballum Rancum': Entertainment in Chicago's Demimonde, 1889–1919." *Ragtime Ephemeralist* 3 (2002): 184–99.

Kenney, William Howland. *Chicago Jazz: A Cultural History, 1904–1930.* New York: Oxford University Press, 1993.

Kern-Foxworth, Marilyn. *Aunt Jemima, Uncle Ben, and Rastus: Blacks in Advertising, Yesterday, Today, and Tomorrow.* Westport: Greenwood, 1994.

Kinney, James. *Amalgamation! Race, Sex, and Rhetoric in the Nineteenth-Century American Novel.* Westport: Greenwood, 1985.

Kirby, Lynn. *Parallel Tracks: The Railroad and Silent Cinema.* Durham: Duke University Press, 1997.

Kisch, John, and Edward Mapp. *A Separate Cinema: Fifty Years of Black Cast Posters.* New York: Noonday, 1992.

Kletzing, Henry F., and William H. Crogman. *Progress of a Race, or the Re-*

*markable Advancement of the Afro-American.* New York: Negro University Press, 1897.

Klotman, Phyllis R. *Frame by Frame I: A Black Filmography.* 1979. Bloomington: Indiana University Press, 1997.

Knight, Arthur. *Disintegrating the Musical: Black Performance and American Musical Film.* Durham: Duke University Press, 2002.

Knupfer, Anne Meis. *Toward a Tenderer Humanity and a Nobler Womanhood: African American Women's Clubs in Turn-of-the-Century Chicago.* New York: New York University Press, 1996.

Koszarski, Richard. *An Evening's Entertainment: The Age of the Silent Feature Picture, 1915–1928.* Berkeley: University of California Press, 1990.

Kracauer, Siegfried. "The Little Shopgirls Go to the Movies." *The Mass Ornament: Weimar Essays.* Ed. and trans. Thomas Y. Levin. Cambridge: Harvard University Press, 1995. 291–304.

Kusmer, Kenneth L. "The Black Urban Experience in American History." *The State of Afro-American History: Past, Present and Future.* Ed. Darlene Clark Hine. Baton Rouge: Louisiana State University Press, 1986. 91–122.

Lahue, Kalton C., ed. *Motion Picture Pioneer: The Selig Polyscope Company.* South Brunswick: Barnes, 1973.

Lamott, Ann. *Traveling Mercies: Some Thoughts on Faith.* New York: Pantheon, 1999.

Landay, Eileen. *Black Film Stars.* New York: Drake, 1973.

Larsen, Nella. *Quicksand.* 1928. New Brunswick: Rutgers University Press, 1986.

Leab, Daniel J. *From Sambo to Superspade: The Black Experience in Motion Pictures.* Boston: Houghton, 1975.

Lee, Spike. *Spike Lee's Gotta Have It: Inside Guerilla Filmmaking.* New York: Simon, 1987.

Lindstrom, Julie Ann. "'Getting a Hold Deeper in the Life of the City': Chicago Nickelodeons, 1905–1914." Diss. Northwestern University, 1998.

Lofgren, Charles A. *The Plessy Case: A Legal-Historical Interpretation.* Oxford: Oxford University Press, 1987.

Logan, Rayford. *The Negro in American Life and Thought: The Nadir, 1877–1901.* New York: Dial, 1954.

Logsdon, Joseph A. "The Reverend Archibald J. Carey and the Negro in Chicago Politics." M.A. thesis University of Chicago, 1961.

Looby, Chris. "Bigger Thomas Goes to the Movies." Mass Culture Workshop. University of Chicago, 1994.

Lott, Eric. *Love and Theft: Blackface Minstrelsy and the American Working Class.* New York: Oxford University Press, 1995.

Lubiano, Wahneema. "But Compared to What? Reading Realism, Representation, and Essentialism in *School Daze, Do the Right Thing,* and the Spike Lee Discourse." *Black American Literature Forum* 25 (1991): 253–82.

Luckett, Moya. "Cities and Spectators: A Historical Analysis of Film Audiences in Chicago, 1910–1915." Diss. University of Wisconsin, Madison, 1995.

MacGregor, Morris J., and Bernard J. Nalty. *Blacks in the United States Armed Forces: Basic Documents.* Vols. 3 and 4. Wilmington: Scholarly Resources, 1977.

Mahar, Karen Ward. "Women, Filmmaking, and the Gendering of the American Film Industry, 1896–1928." Diss. University of Southern California, 1995.

Mapp, Edward. *Blacks in American Films: Yesterday and Today.* Metuchen: Scarecrow, 1971.

Marks, Carole. *Farewell—We're Good and Gone: The Great Black Migration.* Bloomington: Indiana University Press, 1989.

Masilela, Ntongela. "The Los Angeles School of Black Filmmakers." *Black American Cinema.* Ed. Manthia Diawara. New York: Routledge, 1993. 107–17.

Massood, Paula. *Black City Cinema: African American Urban Experiences in Film.* Philadelphia: Temple University Press, 2003.

———. "Mapping the Hood: The Genealogy of City Space in *Boyz N the Hood* and *Menace II Society.*" *Cinema Journal* 35.2 (1996): 85–97.

May, Lary. *Screening Out the Past: The Birth of Mass Culture and the Motion Picture Industry.* Chicago: University of Chicago Press, 1980.

Mayne, Judith. *Cinema and Spectatorship.* London: Routledge, 1993.

———. "Immigrants and Spectators." *Wide Angle* 5.2 (1982): 32–41.

———. "Uncovering the Female Body." *Before Hollywood: Turn-of-the-Century Film from American Archives.* Ed. Charles Musser and Jay Leyda. New York: American Federation of the Arts, 1987. 63–67.

McMahan, Alison. *Alice Guy Blaché: Lost Visionary of the Cinema.* New York: Continuum, 2002.

Meier, August. *Negro Thought in America, 1880–1915.* Ann Arbor: University of Michigan Press, 1963.

Micheaux, Oscar. *The Conquest.* 1913. College Park: McGrath, 1969.

———. *The Homesteader.* 1917. College Park: McGrath, 1969.

*Midnight Ramble: Oscar Micheaux and the Story of Race Movies. The American Experience.* Dir. Pearl Bowser and Bestor Cram. 1994.

Miller, Monica. "Figuring the Black Dandy: Negro Art, Black Bodies, and African-Diasporic Ambitions." Diss. Harvard University, 2000.

Miller, Paul Eduard, ed. *Esquire's 1946 Jazz Book.* 1946. Cambridge: Da Capo, 1979.

Morrison, Toni. *The Bluest Eye.* New York: Holt, 1970.

———. *Playing in the Dark: Whiteness and the Literary Imagination.* 1992. New York: Vintage, 1993.

Mould, David H. *American Newsfilm 1914–1919: The Underexposed War.* New York: Garland, 1983.

Mulvey, Laura. "Afterthoughts on 'Visual Pleasure and Narrative Cinema' Inspired by *Duel in the Sun.*" *Framework* 15–17 (1981): 12–15.

———. "Visual Pleasure and Narrative Cinema." *Narrative, Apparatus, Ideol-*

*ogy: A Film Theory Reader.* Ed. Philip Rosen. New York: Columbia University Press, 1986. 198–209.

Murray, James P. *To Find an Image: Black Films from Uncle Tom to Super Fly.* Indianapolis: Bobbs-Merrill, 1973.

Musser, Charles. *Before the Nickelodeon: Edwin S. Porter and the Edison Manufacturing Company.* Berkeley: University of California Press, 1991.

———. *Edison Motion Pictures, 1890–1900: An Annotated Bibliography.* Gemona, Italy: Le Giornate del Cinema Muto/Smithsonian Institution Press, 1997.

———. *The Emergence of Cinema: The American Screen to 1907.* Berkeley: University of California Press, 1990.

———. "The Nickelodeon Era Begins: Establishing the Framework for Hollywood's Mode of Representation." *Early Cinema: Space, Frame, Narrative.* Ed. Thomas Elsaesser. London: BFI, 1990. 256–73.

Musser, Charles, Reese V. Jenkins, and Thomas E. Jeffery, eds. *A Guide to Motion Picture Catalogues by American Producers and Distributors, 1894–1908: A Microfilm Edition.* Frederick: University Publications of America, 1985. Microfilm.

Negt, Oskar, and Alexander Kluge. *Public Sphere and Experience.* 1972. Trans. Peter Labanyi, Jamie Owen Daniel, and Assenka Oksiloff. Minneapolis: University of Minnesota Press, 1993.

Nesteby, James R. *Black Images in American Films, 1896–1954: The Interplay between Civil Rights and Film Culture.* Washington: University Press of America, 1982.

Nielson, David Gordon. *Black Ethos: Northern Urban Negro Life and Thought, 1890–1930.* Westport: Greenwood, 1977.

Niver, Kemp. *Biograph Bulletins 1896–1908.* Los Angeles: Artisan, 1971.

Noble, Peter. *The Negro in Film.* London: Skelton Robinson, 1948.

Null, Gary. *Black Hollywood: The Negro in Motion Pictures.* Secaucus: Citadel, 1975.

Patterson, Lindsay. *Black Films and Film-Makers.* New York: Dodd, Mead, 1975.

Peiss, Kathy. *Cheap Amusements: Working Women and Leisure in Turn-of-the-Century New York.* Philadelphia: Temple University Press, 1986.

Peterson, Bernard L., Jr. *Early Black American Playwrights and Dramatic Writers: A Biographical Directory and Catalog of Plays, Films, and Broadcasting Scripts.* New York: Greenwood, 1990.

Peterson, Jennifer. "World Pictures: Travelogue Films and the Lure of the Exotic, 1890–1920." Diss. University of Chicago, 1999.

Philpot, Thomas Lee. *The Slum and the Ghetto: Neighborhood Deterioration and Middle-Class Reform, Chicago, 1880–1930.* New York: Oxford University Press, 1978.

Pines, Jim. *Blacks in Films: A Survey of Racial Themes and Images in the American Film.* London: Studio Vista, 1975.

Powell, Richard J. *Black Art and Culture in the 20th Century.* London: Thames and Hudson, 1997.

Pribram, E. Deidre. *Female Spectators: Looking at Film and Television.* London: Verso, 1988.

Rabinovitz, Lauren. *For the Love of Pleasure: Women, Movies, and Culture in Turn-of-the-Century Chicago.* New Brunswick: Rutgers University Press, 1998.

Rather, Ernest R. *Chicago Negro Almanac and Reference Book.* Chicago: Chicago Negro Almanac, 1972.

Reckless, Walter C. *Vice in Chicago.* Chicago: University of Chicago Press, 1933.

Redkey, Edwin S. *Black Exodus: Black Nationalist and Back-to-Africa Movements, 1890–1910.* New Haven: Yale University Press, 1969.

Reid, Mark. *Redefining Black Film.* Berkeley: University of California Press, 1993.

*Rhea's New Citizen's Directory of Chicago, Ill. and Suburban Towns.* Chicago: McCleland, 1908.

Rhines, Jesse. *Black Film/White Money.* New Brunswick: Rutgers University Press, 1996.

Richings, G. F. *Evidences of Progress among Colored People.* Philadelphia: Ferguson, 1902.

Rodgers, Lawrence R. *Canaan Bound: The African-American Great Migration Novel.* Urbana: University of Illinois Press, 1997.

Rodowick, David. "The Difficulty of Difference." *Wide Angle* 6.3 (1984): 16–23.

Roediger, David R. *The Wages of Whiteness: Race and the Making of the American Working Class.* London: Verso, 1991.

Rogin, Michael. *Blackface, White Noise: Jewish Immigrants in the Hollywood Melting Pot.* Berkeley: University of California Press, 1996.

———. "'The Sword Became a Flashing Vision': D. W. Griffith's *The Birth of a Nation,*" *Representations* 9 (1985): 150–95.

Rose Bibliography, American Studies Program, George Washington University. *Analytical Guide and Indexes to* The Crisis *1910–1960.* 3 vols. Westport: Greenwood, 1975.

Rosen, Philip, ed. *Narrative, Apparatus, Ideology: A Film Theory Reader.* New York: Columbia University Press, 1986.

Rosenzweig, Roy. *Eight Hours for What We Will: Workers and Leisure in an Industrial City, 1870–1920.* Cambridge: Cambridge University Press, 1983.

Ross, Karen. *Black and White Media: Black Images in Popular Film and Television.* Cambridge: Polity, 1996.

Rydell, Robert W. *All the World's a Fair: Visions of Empire at American International Expositions, 1876–1916.* Chicago: University of Chicago Press, 1984.

———. "A Cultural Frankenstein? The Chicago World's Columbian Exposition of 1893." *Grand Illusions: Chicago's World's Fair of 1893.* Chicago: Chicago Historical Society, 1993. 141–70.

Sampson, Henry. *Blacks in Black and White: A Source Book on Black Films.* 2nd ed. Metuchen: Scarecrow, 1995.

———. *Blacks in Blackface: A Source Book on Early Black Musical Shows.* Metuchen: Scarecrow, 1980.

———. *The Ghost Walks: A Chronological History of Blacks in Show Business, 1865–1910.* Metuchen: Scarecrow, 1988.

Samuelson, Timothy. *Black Metropolis Historic District.* Chicago: Department of Planning and Development, 1994.

———. "From Ragtime to Real Estate: Joe Jordan's Career as a Chicago Real Estate Developer." *Ragtime Ephemeralist* 3 (2002): 201–9.

Santino, Jake. *Miles of Smiles, Years of Struggle: Stories of Black Pullman Porters.* Urbana: University of Illinois Press, 1989.

Schwartz, Vanessa. "Cinema Spectatorship before the Apparatus: The Public Taste for Reality in Fin-de-Siècle Paris." *Viewing Positions: Ways of Seeing Film.* Ed. Linda Williams. New Brunswick: Rutgers University Press, 1994. 87–113.

Scott, Emmett J. "Additional Letters of Negro Migrants of 1916–1918." *Journal of Negro History* 4 (1919): 412–65.

———. "Letters of Negro Migrants of 1916–1918." *Journal of Negro History* 4 (1919): 290–340.

Scott, Estelle Hill. *Occupational Changes among Negroes in Chicago.* Chicago: Works Projects Administration, Illinois, 1939.

Sengstock, Charles A., Jr. *Jazz Music in Chicago's Early South-Side Theaters.* Northbrook: Canterbury Press of Northbrook, 2000.

Shohat, Ella, and Robert Stam. *Unthinking Eurocentrism: Multiculturalism and the Media.* London: Routledge, 1994.

*Simms' Blue Book and National Negro Business and Professional Directory.* 1923. Cleveland: Gordon, 1977.

Singer, Ben. *Melodrama and Modernity: Early Sensational Cinema and Its Contexts.* New York: Columbia University Press, 2001.

Smith, Valerie, ed. *Representing Blackness: Issues in Film and Video.* New Brunswick: Rutgers University Press, 1997.

Snead, James. *White Screens, Black Images: Hollywood from the Dark Side.* Ed. Colin MacCabe and Cornel West. New York: Routledge, 1994.

Sollors, Werner. *Neither Black nor White yet Both: Thematic Explorations of Interracial Literature.* New York: Oxford University Press, 1997.

Spear, Allan H. *Black Chicago: The Making of a Negro Ghetto, 1890–1920.* Chicago: University of Chicago Press, 1967.

Spillers, Hortense J. "Mama's Baby, Papa's Maybe: An American Grammar Book." *diacritics* 17.2 (1987): 65–81.

Staiger, Janet. *Bad Women: Regulating Sexuality in Early American Cinema.* Minneapolis: University of Minnesota Press, 1995.

———. "Class, Ethnicity, and Gender: Explaining the Development of Early American Film Narrative." *Iris* 11 (1990): 13–25.

Stead, William T. *If Christ Came to Chicago.* London: Review of Reviews, 1894.

Steward, T. G. *The Colored Regulars in the United States Army*. 1904. New York: Arno, 1969.

Stewart, Jacqueline. "Negroes Laughing at Themselves? Black Spectatorship and the Performance of Urban Modernity." *Critical Inquiry* 29 (2003): 650–77.

———. "What Happened in the Transition? Reading Race, Gender and Labor between the Shots." *American Cinema's Transitional Era: Audiences, Institutions, Practices*. Ed. Charlie Keil and Shelley Stamp. Berkeley: University of California Press, 2004. 103–30.

Stokes, Melvyn, and Richard Maltby, eds. *American Movie Audiences: From the Turn of the Century to the Early Sound Era*. London: BFI, 1999.

Stones, Barbara. *America Goes to the Movies: 100 Years of Motion Picture Exhibition*. North Hollywood: National Association of Theatre Owners, 1993.

Streible, Dan. "The Harlem Theatre: Black Film Exhibition in Austin, Texas: 1920–1973." *Black American Cinema*. Ed. Manthia Diawara. New York: Routledge, 1993. 221–36.

———. "Race and the Reception of Jack Johnson Fight Films." *The Birth of Whiteness: Race and the Emergence of U.S. Cinema*. Ed. Daniel Bernardi. New Brunswick: Rutgers University Press, 1996. 170–200.

Studlar, Gaylyn. "Masochism and the Perverse Pleasures of the Cinema." *Quarterly Review of Film Studies* 9 (1984): 267–82.

Taylor, Clyde. "The Re-birth of the Aesthetic in Cinema." *The Birth of Whiteness: Race and the Emergence of U.S. Cinema*. Ed. Daniel Bernardi. New Brunswick: Rutgers University Press, 1996. 15–37.

Thaggert, Miriam. "Divided Images: Black Female Spectatorship and John Stahl's *Imitation of Life*." *African American Review* 32 (1998): 481–91.

Thissen, Judith. "Jewish Immigrant Audiences in New York City, 1905–1914." *American Movie Audiences: From the Turn of the Century to the Early Sound Era*. Ed. Melvyn Stokes and Richard Maltby. London: BFI, 1999. 15–28.

Travis, Dempsey. *An Autobiography of Black Jazz*. Chicago: Urban Research Institute, 1983.

Triggs, Jeffery Alan. "Roughing It: The Role of Farce in the Little Rascals Comedies." *New Orleans Review* 16.3 (1989): 31–38.

Trotter, Joe William, Jr., ed. *The Great Migration in Historical Perspective: New Dimensions of Race, Class and Gender*. Bloomington: Indiana University Press, 1991.

Tsivian, Yuri. *Early Cinema in Russia and Its Cultural Reception*. 1991. Trans. Alan Bodger. Chicago: University of Chicago Press, 1998.

Turner, Patricia A. *Ceramic Uncles & Celluloid Mammies: Black Images and Their Influence on Culture*. New York: Anchor, 1994.

Tuttle, William M., Jr. *Race Riot: Chicago in the Red Summer of 1919*. 1970. Urbana: University of Illinois Press, 1996.

VanEpps-Taylor, Betti Carol. *Oscar Micheaux . . . Dakota Homesteader, Author, Pioneer Film Maker: A Biography*. Rapid City: Dakota West, 1999.

Vice Commission of Chicago. *The Social Evil in Chicago: A Study of Existing Conditions*. Chicago: Vice Commission of the City of Chicago, 1911.

Wallace, Michele. "Race, Gender and Psychoanalysis in Forties Film: Lost Boundaries, Home of the Brave, and the Quiet One." *Black American Cinema*. Ed. Manthia Diawara. New York: Routledge, 1993. 257–71.

———. "*Uncle Tom's Cabin*: Before and after the Jim Crow Era." *TDR: The Drama Review* 44.1 (2000): 137–56.

Waller, Gregory. *Main Street Amusements: Movies and Commercial Entertainment in a Southern City, 1896–1930*. Washington: Smithsonian Institution Press, 1995.

Warren, Kenneth W. *Black and White Strangers: Race and American Literary Realism*. Chicago: University of Chicago Press, 1993.

Washington, Booker T. *A New Negro for a New Century: An Accurate and Up-to-Date Record of the Upward Struggles of the Negro Race*. Chicago: American Publishing House, 1900.

———. *Up from Slavery. Three Negro Classics*. 1901. New York: Avon, 1965. 23–205.

Waters, Ethel, with Charles Samuels. *His Eye Is on the Sparrow*. New York: Bantam, 1951.

Watkins, S. Craig. *Representing: Hip Hop Culture and the Production of Black Cinema*. Chicago: University of Chicago Press, 1998.

Weiss, Nancy J. *The National Urban League, 1910–1940*. New York: Oxford University Press, 1974.

Wells, Ida B. *Crusade for Justice: The Autobiography of Ida B. Wells*. Ed. Alfreda M. Duster. Chicago: University of Chicago Press, 1970.

Wells, Ida B., and Frederick Douglass. "The Reason Why the Colored American Is Not in the World's Columbian Exposition." *Selected Works of Ida B. Wells-Barnett*. Ed. Trudier Harris. New York: Oxford University Press, 1991. 46–137.

White, Shane, and Graham White. *Stylin': African American Expressive Culture from Its Beginnings to the Zoot Suit*. Ithaca: Cornell University Press, 1998.

Williams, Linda. "Introduction." *Viewing Positions: Ways of Seeing Film*. New Brunswick: Rutgers University Press, 1994. 1–20.

———. *Playing the Race Card: Melodramas of Black and White from Uncle Tom to O. J. Simpson*. Princeton: Princeton University Press, 2001.

Willis-Thomas, Deborah. *Black Photographers, 1840–1940: An Illustrated Bio-Bibliography*. New York: Garland, 1985.

Wolff, Janet. "The Invisible Flâneuse: Women and the Literature of Modernity." *Theory, Culture and Society* 2.7 (1985): 37–46.

Wood, Richard, ed. *Film and Propaganda in America: A Documentary History*. Vol. 1. New York: Greenwood, 1990.

Wright, Richard. *Native Son*. 1940. New York: Harper Perennial, 1987.

———. *12 Million Black Voices*. Photo direction by Edward Rosskam. 1941. New York: Thunder's Mouth, 1988.

# Index

kiss films, 81–84, 271nn63,65,66, 272n67; "nigger in a woodpile" connotation of, 14–15, 256n24; in plantation films, 62–63, 80, 270n55; as representational dilemma, 52–53; sexualized Black woman of, 47–48, 263n59; tragic mulatto, consequences of, 228–29, 306nn20,21; uplift marriage of, 230–32, 307n26; in urban entertainment settings, 60–62, 267n27; as Vice Commission concern, 134–35
*Intolerance* (film), 174, *175*
*Iola LeRoy, or Shadows Uplifted* (Harper), 228–29, 232, 306nn20,21, 307n26

Jacks, Samuel T., 186, 197, *199*, 227, 299n28
Jackson, A. L., 143
Jackson, Daniel M., 293n34
Jackson, Robert R., 126
*James Grundy/Buck and Wing Dance* (film), 54
*James Grundy/Cake Walk* (film), 54
Jeffries, Jim, 280n44
Jelks, John Earl, *xviii*
Jewish theaters, 127–28, 285n43
*Joan the Woman* (film), 174
Johnson, Elijah, 159
Johnson, George P., 197; on Noble Johnson's resignation, 301n51; Lincoln Company, promotion/production strategies of, 209–10, 300n46, 301n50; war films proposal of, 212–14, 302nn59,63,64
Johnson, Jack, 159, 280n44
Johnson, James Weldon, 228–29
Johnson, John "Mushmouth," 158, 183
Johnson, Kathryn M., 261n37
Johnson, Noble, 209, 300n47; Hollywood film roles of, 111–12, 280n48; Lincoln Company of, 203, 210, 301n51; production stills of, *112, 206, 208*; western themes of, 204, 207–8, 300n38
Johnson, Ralph, *240*
Jones, Elsie, 54
Jones, Henry "Teenan," 158, 159, 183, *184*, 185, 195, 204, 296n83
Jones, John G., 123

Jones, Juli. *See* Foster, William
Jones, LeRoi (Amiri Baraka), 277n27
Jones, Peter P., 10, 210
Jones, Theodore W., 123–24
Jones, William Henry, 287n67
Jordan, Joe, 136, 163–64, 287n71, 292n20
Jordan's Century First-Class Billiard and Pool Room (Chicago), 126–27
Josephs, Nathan, 176, 177
Junior, Yvonne, 197, 198
Juvenile Protective Association (Chicago), 128

Kaight, Frank, 292n32
Kaplan, E. Ann, 68
Kellerman, Annette, 280n45
Kelly, Daniel Q., 286n57
Kemble, Edward W., 268n39
Kenna, Michael "Hinky Dink," 159
Kenney, William Howland, 163, 183, 292n26
Kern-Foxworth, Marilyn, 268n39
Keystone Hotel (Chicago), 135
*Killer of Sheep* (film), 248
King, Edward E., 305n10
King, W. H., 209
*King Kong* (film), 99
Kirby, Lynn, 82
*A Kiss in the Dark* (film), 81, 82, 83
Kleine, George, 213
Kletzing, Henry F., 260–61n35
Kluge, Alexander, 12, 255–56n20
Knight, Arthur, 49
Knupfer, Anne Meis, 139–40, 160, 260–61n35, 276–77n21, 287n75
Ku Klux Klan, 216, 223–25, 305n13

Ladies' Whist Club (Chicago), 125
Lafayette Theatre (New York), 216
Lakeside Club (Hyde Park), 183
Lamott, Anne, 14–15
Lane, Betsey, 102, 277n23
Langston, Tony, 129, 209; on Black-cast comedy, 190, 202; on Ebony films, 293n41; film industry columns of, 130–31; on Owl Theater, 177; on States Theater, 176; on *Trooper* film, 207
Larsen, Nella, 229

| | |
|---:|:---|
| Compositor: | Sheridan Books, Inc. |
| Indexer: | Patricia Deminna |
| Text: | 10/13 Aldus |
| Display: | Aldus |
| Printer/Binder: | Sheridan Books, Inc. |